WHO REALLY
OWNS IRELAND?

Matt Cooper is a radio and TV broadcaster, newspaper columnist and bestselling author. Matt presents and edits the daily news, current affairs and sports programme *The Last Word* on Today FM. He writes a weekly newspaper column for the *Irish Daily Mail* that is published each Saturday and 'The Last Post' column on the back page of the *Business Post* each Sunday. He was editor of the *Sunday Tribune* for over six years and their National Journalist of the Year. This is his sixth book.

WHO REALLY OWNS IRELAND?

How we became tenants in our own land –
and what we can do about it

MATT COOPER

GILL BOOKS

Gill Books
Hume Avenue
Park West
Dublin 12
www.gillbooks.ie

Gill Books is an imprint of M.H. Gill and Co.

978 07171 96012

Designed by Bartek Janczak
Structural edit by Rachel Pierce
Edited by Adam Brophy
Proofread by Sally Vince
Printed and bound in Great Britain by Clays Ltd, Elcograf S.p.A.
This book is typeset in 11 on 16pt, Minion Pro

The paper used in this book comes from the wood pulp of
sustainably managed forests.

A CIP catalogue record for this book is available from the
British Library.

5 4 3 2 1

To my family

CONTENTS

WHO OWNS IRELAND?

Land and property ownership have had a deep impact on Irish history and, arguably, its psyche. This was emphasised by the schooling many of us experienced growing up, with its focus on how British rule led to a denial of many rights to the Irish, particularly those of the Catholic faith, and especially to own our land. The landlord–tenant relationship was central to what we learnt about the Great Famine of the mid-nineteenth century, the belief that essentially foreign landlords – even if born on this island because they professed to British nationality – had kept or sold the food that the general population needed. They were able to do so because they had confiscated the land and allowed only minimal holdings to the native population, for which they charged excessive rent. We had become tenants in our own land.

The late nineteenth-century rise in nationalism – and the early twentieth-century revolution that led to our independence from British rule – can be traced in large part to the formation of the Irish National Land League, Conradh na Talún, and what became known as the Land War, with the Catholic Church to the forefront of organising a political movement. The term 'rack-rent' became synonymous with excessive charges to tenants and evictions of those unable to pay; it became a hated feature of what was seen as British-enforced law on behalf of landlords. Land League co-founder Michael Davitt's slogan of 'The land of Ireland for the people of Ireland' went into folklore. Resistance to evictions was organised, leading sometimes to violence. The twenty-first-century distaste in Ireland for evictions has its roots here.

The aspirations of the 1916 rebellion, as set out in the Proclamation of Independence, declare 'the right of the people of Ireland to the ownership of Ireland' and add in the same sentence 'to the unfettered control of Irish destinies, to be sovereign and indefeasible. The long usurpation of that right by a foreign people and government has not extinguished the right …'. The Proclamation continues to assert the right to control but nowhere does it adequately offer a definition as to how the ownership of Ireland's land should be shared by the citizens of this newly declared state. The Proclamation went on to guarantee 'religious and civil liberty, equal rights and equal opportunities to all its citizens, and declares its resolve to pursue the happiness and prosperity of the whole nation and of all its parts'.

. Greatly influenced by deference to the Catholic Church, our political leaders did not embrace the Marxist or communist beliefs of shared ownership of land and the means of production and the sharing of the proceeds more equitably, which were taking hold in other parts of the world. The Catholic Church was opposed to godless communism – and any assault on private property rights – and that was effectively that as far as Ireland was concerned. As our new political classes emerged, the commitment to private property became entrenched. The 1937 Constitution of Ireland confirmed this, declaring that the State would vindicate the property rights of every citizen. This means that any individual or corporate entity has a right to own, transfer and inherit property and bequeath it upon death. The State has guaranteed to pass no law to abolish these rights. However, there is one caveat: Article 43 acknowledges that these rights ought to be regulated by the principles of social justice. This means that the State may pass laws limiting the right to private property in the interests of the common good.

This is all part of being a republic, a form of government in which a state is ruled by elected representatives of the citizen body. The government sets laws and rules, subject to change. It doesn't mean that the people own everything in common or on a shared basis. We don't live in some kind of socialist state. Ireland belongs to all of us as citizens, but some own the land and the property that sits on it, and others don't, and wealth flows accordingly.

The State does control certain lands on our behalf. It owns and maintains commonly used pieces of land, such as the streets and roads and our public parks, and its commercial state bodies also acquire chunks to allow them to fulfil their mandates. However, the remainder of the country is owned by individuals, families, trusts, partnerships, companies, farmers, financial institutions, religious entities, sporting organisations, charities, co-ops, community groups, and others. Land (and the properties on it) is bought and sold, for profit or loss, or it is kept for generations. It is mortgaged or debt-free, bringing the banks and others who hold liens over property as security for loans into the equation and giving them power over borrowers. It produces income, or it does not. It is kept in good nick, or it is left derelict. It is owned by natives and foreigners. Increasingly, again, by foreigners, although that is very much part of an international trend.

Who owns the land and the properties that stand on it controls, in effect, much of our country. That impacts how everyone lives. The owners, subject to certain State-enforced restrictions, decide what gets put on the land and who gets to use it, if we can buy it from them or merely rent it, or even use it at all. The rights conferred upon private property mean that much of the space of the country is not available for access to us without the permission of the owners.

Land and property owners control the number of houses and apartments that the rest of us compete to buy or rent, the office spaces and factories where we go to work, the shops where we purchase our essential items and material luxuries, the restaurants and pubs where we eat, drink and meet, the green spaces and indoor arenas on which we play or watch others compete for our enjoyment, the venues where we enjoy cultural events, the farms on which our food is grown and livestock reared for slaughter or export, or where our power is generated.

Outside of the small patches of land that some of us own – usually nothing more than our homes on which many of us still owe mortgages – we are tenants on the rest of the island, paying the bills for the use of other people's space. This matters because it excludes many – and provides great benefit to those who have been able to gain that control.

In Ireland, property is arguably the most valuable or important of what are called the asset classes. By mid-2022 the Central Bank of Ireland reported that the net wealth of Irish households had exceeded €1 trillion, with property ownership accounting for €649 billion of that. Property is the chief dividing line between rich and poor in this State. That gap is widening.

There has been an extraordinary transfer of ownership of land and property in Ireland since what has become known as The Great Recession which resulted from the global banking crisis of 2008 and lasted, roughly, to the end of 2012. One of the conditions of the humiliating rescue of the national finances by the Troika – the European Commission, European Central Bank and International Monetary Fund – in late 2010 was the enforced sale of many State-controlled assets. This included, by virtue of the State taking responsibility for the liabilities of most of the banks, land and property. It contributed to the rescue of the State's finances but created a whole new set of difficult dynamics that are not always fully understood.

As 2023 progressed, the issues around not having enough affordable housing for our rising population became the dominant political theme. Many of the complaints seemed contradictory. Rents for many were too high relative to income, despite laws to restrict rental increases in designated areas, yet simultaneously some landlords complained that they couldn't get a sufficient return from their investments and sought to sell. A temporary ban on evictions ended in March 2023 amid considerable rancour; some tenants given notice by their landlords found there was nowhere for them to go, yet the government insisted that this would be better for the system in the medium to long term. Home builders said they couldn't get planning permission to build on land they owned, yet tens of thousands of granted permissions had not been acted upon. Those who complained about there not being enough new housing were often at the forefront of objections that either delayed or denied construction. The system upon which everyone depended was mired in controversy because of internal shortcomings and possible illegality.

Those who wanted to buy from the limited stock often failed to get large enough mortgages. Many of those who had mortgages struggled as interest rates went up. Generational divides intensified. Meanwhile, environmental concerns about where people should live – the old rural/urban divide – returned, as did debate about the type and suitability of our housing stock.

The Russian invasion of Ukraine provided a shock to an international economic system still recovering from the unprecedented Covid shutdown; as 2023 progressed, it was clear that further change in the valuations and holding of land and property was upon us. Consumer price inflation – which is different from asset price inflation – had taken hold and even if the increase in prices had moderated somewhat, they were still rising. Central banks were making borrowing money more expensive by increasing interest rates, so investors returned to 'safer' assets, such as government bonds, believing that the risk involved in purchasing property was not worth it. This applied to both commercial and residential property, despite the demand remaining for the latter while falling for the former. Indeed, any transactions taking place for properties other than for use as homes seemed to be at lower prices.

If the foreign private capital upon which we had become so reliant was going to be harder to source, would Irish capital, either public or private, step in? It seemed not, so this increased the pressure on the government to use its now regular and growing annual budget surpluses on more housing; it seemed reluctant because of the fear that the booming corporation taxes could not be maintained. But could it persuade those who held so much money in Irish savings to invest instead, or would they too eschew the risk?

So many questions and so much debate as to what might constitute the correct answers. In attempting to find those answers, what we uncover is a deep and far-reaching story with wide ramifications.

This is the story about where we live, all of us, the common ground we share, the collective. But it is not straightforward. It is the story of how public and private interests intersect and sometimes collide. It is where national and international capital competes and seeks profit but sometimes suffers financial loss. It is about how power and money influence and control the present and the future of Ireland … sometimes for good and sometimes for bad.

It is about our society, our politics, our economy, our environment. It is about those who have and those who don't. It is about tangible and intangible gains and losses. It is about what we see every day … and what goes on in those parts of the country we don't see unless it is put in front of our eyes. It is both urban and rural, it is about preservation, regeneration and creation. It is about dereliction and shiny new trophy buildings.

It is about idealism and pragmatism. It is about compromise. It is about a changing Ireland and how that is happening at a pace we can scarcely control.

It is about housing, both rented and owned, workplaces, shopping centres, pubs and restaurants, hotels, churches, theatres, student accommodation, sports facilities, windfarms and forests: all the things that we may take for granted but that we need to be provided and managed for us.

It is a story that affects every single one of us living on this island, which is why it is an important story to tell.

PART 1

OWNING THE PAST

To go forward, we must first go back. While Ireland in 2023 is in overall financial good health – for the most part, because nothing is ever perfect – that was far from the case a decade and a half ago and for a number of years afterwards. It was the response to that economic crisis that has left us where we are today. That is where the roots of the present-day situation lie.

ONE

THE MICROCOSM: O'CONNELL STREET, DUBLIN CITY

Easter Sunday, 27 March 2016 was a landmark date for this nation. A solemn commemoration took place on O'Connell Street, in front of a grandstand facing the General Post Office. President Michael D. Higgins oversaw proceedings, alongside his two living predecessors Mary McAleese and Mary Robinson, Taoiseach Enda Kenny and a host of political leaders past and present as well as various dignitaries and guests. The main street of our capital city was packed to capacity to watch nearly 3,000 members of the defence forces and emergency services parade to pay a centenary tribute to the rebels of the Easter Rising of 1916 whose actions set in train the creation of this 26-county State.

To many, the GPO is Ireland's most iconic building, providing the backdrop to many of our most important national celebrations, including the annual St Patrick's Day parade. It is certainly one of the most visually imposing and impressive of our buildings, one for the ages. More than two centuries old, the neo-Classical building was seized by the self-proclaimed provisional government of the new republic as part of the Rising, partly for tactical but also for symbolic reasons. Its interior was destroyed by fire during the siege by British soldiers but the shell remained standing, as did its centrepiece, the boldly projecting portico of six fluted Ionic columns supporting an entablature and cornice. Thankfully, the new State decided in 1924 to rebuild rather than level the site and start anew. Inside the GPO, customers can enjoy the Art Deco beauty of the reconstructed main hall. They can also enter the specially created visitor centre – opened in 2016 – which gives locals and tourists the opportunity to understand the history of the Easter Rising. However, the offices behind, which have housed the staff of An Post for decades, are no longer fit for purpose and the company has moved to the tallest new office building in the country, the Exo in the north docklands, leaving the future of the building uncertain.

Parts of O'Connell Street, one of Europe's widest streets, have been put to good use in the twenty-first century. It is no longer a street dominated by cars as access is now restricted to public transport and emergency services. The footpaths have been doubled in width to 11 metres and a granite-paved, tree-lined central median installed in an excellent example of the good common use of public space. The Spire has extended towards the sky since the turn of the millennium, a monument that essentially stands for nothing and therefore offends few, other than those who don't like its aesthetic. Since 2017 tram lines allow the Luas to run one-way up towards the north side of the city, with the return journey on the parallel Marlborough Street.

In the 1950s, the street was truly Dublin's main central boulevard, its cinemas hosting major premieres with visiting stars, the Gresham Hotel being the premier five-star destination of choice for movie-stars and millionaires visiting Ireland. Over the decades, however, the grandeur faded and the condition of O'Connell Street has long been a national talking point and, to some, an embarrassment. All along the street there is vacancy and dereliction, and some of the shops that remain open are cheap and tatty. It has gained a reputation, more than partly deserved, as dangerous; drug-dealing takes place openly and assaults are unfortunately too common, even during daylight hours. Many Irish people avoid it entirely unless passing through it to get to Croke Park for Gaelic games or concerts. Tourist numbers suggest a 5:1 ratio in favour of visiting the south side of the River Liffey in preference to the north side.

If they are not warned off and visit, they often high-tail it back to the other side of the city quickly, although Temple Bar also has more than its share of increased social misbehaviour. O'Connell Street is not a place where people live either: the potential for apartment living above the shops, of creating a vibrant living environment in the darker hours of evening time, has been largely ignored.

The heart of Dublin city needs investment to restore it to its former glory, to restore the prestige of the days when this was known as Sackville Street, and to make us all proud of it as the central area of the capital city of our nation. That requires money, imagination and ambition but, despite dereliction, change is too often opposed and nothing happens.

At the northern end of O'Connell Street, there's a major site, behind hoardings, that has been derelict since 1979, redevelopment having been stalled both by economic circumstances and objections. The glaring void is 5.5 acres, largely vacant since the Carlton Cinema closed in October 1994. The beautiful Art Deco façade of that building remains but all behind it has been demolished. Two businessmen, Richard Quirke (a former Garda who owns a slot machines 'emporium' on the street) and Paul Clinton (an architect who is now a successful publican) formed the Carlton Group in the 1990s, unsuccessfully proposing a national conference centre financed by an up-market casino. The next idea of a 'Millennium Mall' was delayed by legal rows with Treasury Holdings, a company controlled by Johnny Ronan and Richard Barrett, which also wanted the licence for a conference centre on the site. Dublin City Council (DCC) successfully issued a compulsory purchase order (CPO) on the site in 2001, the city manager justifying this on the basis of it being 'the most important site in the entire city'.

There was a suggestion that the Abbey Theatre be relocated there. This was dismissed by the government on the now almost hilarious grounds that legal disputes about the ownership of the site would delay any construction for too long. Later, the Green Party's Eamon Ryan suggested that RTÉ should sell its Donnybrook campus – for use as housing – and build a new broadcasting complex on O'Connell Street, for television, radio and concert performances, as a cultural anchor for the city centre. Instead, the council sold the site to developer Joe O'Reilly and his company Chartered Land.

Chartered was best known as the builder of the Dundrum Town Centre in south Dublin – which was marketed for a time as Europe's biggest such venue – and part-owner of the Ilac shopping centre on Henry Street (off O'Connell Street) in the city and the Pavilions shopping centre in Swords to the north of Dublin. It seemed a good choice given O'Reilly's track record in developing centres to which large numbers of shoppers went, at least if that was what was deemed best for the area that shopping was to take precedence over cultural use. In 2010 Chartered was granted planning permission for a €900 million redevelopment, to include shops, restaurants and a car park, 800,000 square feet in size. British department store John Lewis was lined up as the anchor tenant. The permission from An Bord Pleanála (ABP), which gave Chartered seven years to complete the development instead of the usual five, came too late to be acted upon: in expanding its empire Chartered had racked up enormous debts – running into billions of euro – and was not in a position to finance the development. And with the country in an economic downturn, few saw the potential for a new shopping centre.

A new entity called the National Asset Management Agency (NAMA) took control of Chartered's loans on behalf of the State, but after a few years of partnership, during which no further progress was made with developing the site, NAMA sold the site. Hammerson, a British retail property developer, acquired it as part of a bigger purchase of Chartered's debts, gaining control of all of its shopping centres at what seemed a knock-down price.[1]

1   Chartered prospered again from 2015 onwards, using money from the Abu Dhabi investment fund to build the most expensive apartment block in the country on the site of the old Berkeley Court hotel on Lansdowne Road, taking back control of Killeen Castle in county Meath and investing in a number of other developments.

This purchase created political sensitivities for some, not least because of the British identity of the new owners. Part of the site includes Moore Lane and, more importantly, Moore Street, the location to which the 1916 rebels fled and were captured after the GPO went on fire. Chartered's original plans included the demolition of some buildings. Republican activists and historians had engaged in an earlier campaign to save as much of Moore Street as possible from redevelopment. Numbers 14–17 were declared a national monument in 2007, but campaigners wanted more buildings on the street – which has shops and street stalls but is badly run down – included for protection. They headed for the courts and in 2016 High Court judge Max Barrett declared nearly all of the buildings on the east side of Moore Street, as well as the laneways leading to it, to be part of the 1916 Rising battlefield and therefore protected as part of the official register. The State appealed his decision and it was overturned by the Court of Appeal in 2018. However, a compromise was offered. The State took ownership and possession of numbers 14–17 and proposed their redevelopment as a Rising Commemorative Centre, at an estimated cost of at least €16.25 million. In early 2023, the work had not yet started.

Hammerson decided on new plans, including the demolition of some buildings and other structures on Moore Street and Moore Lane. However, it promised to preserve the 'scars of the 1916 battlefield' by highlighting in chalk the bullet-holes in the walls at Nos 10–11 and 12–13 and protecting them behind glass viewing screens. This wasn't good enough for the likes of Gerry Adams, the former leader of Sinn Féin who denies a personal past IRA involvement. 'Moore Street holds a special place in the history of Ireland,' Adams wrote in one submission to the planning authorities. 'No 16 Moore Street was where five of the seven signatories of the proclamation held their last meeting before the surrender,' he said, claiming the plans were in breach of the Venice Charter and other international guidance on the conservation and restoration of historic buildings. But there was no threat to number 16; it was other buildings further up the street that had been nominated for demolition.

An air of dereliction was palpable as I walked Moore Street on a sunny Saturday afternoon in September 2022. There was nothing to suggest to any visitor the history of the street, other than a small plaque high on the wall of one of the shuttered houses. Behind the buildings on Moore Street were surface car parks or empty spaces and an underground car park on Moore Lane. Anything, surely, would be better than this ugly, wasteful mess.

Hammerson had downscaled its plans for the site. Its first suggestion was for an enclosed shopping complex running west from O'Connell Street to Moore Street, and north of Henry Street to Parnell Street. Prompted by Covid – and by the acceleration in the trend in retail towards online ordering – it changed that in mid-2021, cutting the proposed size of the now €500 million scheme by 15 per cent and the number of shops dramatically, increasing office space and suggesting two hotels with 210 rooms in total, the restoration of the now derelict Conway's pub, and 94 apartments that would be available for rent rather than being sold. At its tallest, the scheme would be seven storeys over the ground. The plans also included a new east–west pedestrian street between O'Connell Street and Moore Street, the restoration of the cinema façade, two new civic squares and an underground station for the State's latest proposal of a new Metrolink rail line. Three protected structures, 42 O'Connell Street – the last remaining, and vacant, Georgian house on the street – O'Connell Hall at the back of No 42 and Conway's pub, would also be restored.

Mary Lou McDonald, now Sinn Féin party leader and local constituency TD, lodged a formal appeal against the public plaza. She claimed, 'Moore Street, famed for its street market traditions and 1916 Rising connections, is Dublin's historic core and as such provides the city's uniqueness in terms of a tourist offering and a sustainable, socially just and economically vibrant regeneration opportunity for the north inner city'. She insisted that the planning application failed 'to protect and preserve this area of unique historical, architectural, social, cultural and economic importance'. DCC planning officers disagreed, however, seeing the opportunity for the regeneration of a clearly neglected site. It said that the proposed developments 'will complement the development of the adjacent National Monument as a commemorative centre for the 1916 Rising'.

Hammerson had its own financial issues by this stage, leading to speculation that it would not be able to proceed with the redevelopment, even with all the necessary permissions in place. It was trying to fill retail space at the Ilac centre and noted the difficulties other landlords were having in keeping retail tenants in place on Henry Street, traditionally Ireland's busiest shopping street. It also noted the change of use being implemented at Clery's department store.

If the O'Connell Street area is to be revitalised, then the revamp at Clery's, due to reopen in late 2023, might kick-start things. Nearer the southern end of O'Connell Street, and on its eastern side, the landmark shopping store closed permanently after a highly controversial and opportunistic property transaction in 2015. Clery's had first opened in 1853, and became one of Europe's oldest purpose-built department stores. It was totally destroyed at the time of the Easter Rising but was rebuilt beautifully, with a colonnaded façade, wide marble internal staircase and many columns, tearooms and the famous Clery's clock under which many Dubliners arranged to meet in the days before mobile phones.

But as a department store, it had struggled for years in a changing retail environment, partly because it was regarded as old-fashioned and dated, but also because of a move by consumers to newer shops and centres on Henry Street or across the river. Its woes were exacerbated by the economic crash of 2008. Watching the twentieth-century ambitions of Arnott's new owners on nearby Henry Street for a major redevelopment of the shopping complex (which ultimately never happened), Clery's management had embarked on its own ill-fated property buying frenzy in the O'Connell Street area, again using borrowed money. When it all went wrong, Bank of Ireland seized the property by putting receivers in charge, ending the 70-year ownership by the Guiney family, originally from Kerry.

In September 2012 Gordon Brothers, a more than century-old Boston-based investment group, bought the business from receivers for just €12 million. It borrowed €10 million from Bank of Ireland which, in turn, is believed to have written off another €10 million of the money it was owed by the previous owners. Gordon provided the usual PR rhetoric: it was 'committed' to 'revitalising' Clery's fortunes, to facilitating a 'fresh start' and was 'acutely conscious of and respectful towards [Clery's] heritage and tradition'.

In what would prove subsequently to be a highly significant move, it split the business into two parts: a property company that owned the building and remaining land; and an operating entity for the ongoing retail business. Then it sold both businesses in 2015 for €29 million, repaying Bank of Ireland the borrowed money but receiving a massive return on what was essentially an investment of just €2 million in equity, all for less than three years of involvement.

The bigger story was in the behaviour of the buyer, which was the Natrium consortium led by Irishwoman Deirdre Foley of D2 Private (who got her money from Quadrant Real Estate, a US company backed by Australian pension fund money) in partnership with a London company called Cheyne Capital Management. Immediately, Natrium sold Clery's operating business to specialist insolvency practitioners in the UK for just €1 and they, in turn, applied to the High Court, with no warning to staff, to have Irish liquidators appointed. Trading ceased immediately. The operating business had lost €2 million in the 12 months to February 2014, and Natrium didn't want to either manage the business or shoulder further losses. However, the property business, which leased the Clery's store to the operations company, had turned a profit of nearly €5 million for the same period, which showed that, combined, the business was profitable. But it wasn't profitable enough for Natrium; what was of real interest to it was the potential of revamping the store for different use.

The workers were disposed of with haste and for as little money as possible. The 130 employees of the store – and about 330 people working for concession-holders – lost their jobs with no notice and little compensation, nothing other than statutory redundancy, the minimum required by the State and, in this case, €2.5 million in total. Gordon Brothers wrote to Natrium on completion of the deal, expressing 'serious concerns' about what had happened, as the seller had apparently thought it had sold the business as a going concern. It subsequently agreed to pay €785,000 to partially reimburse concessionaires who had been turfed out unceremoniously.

Natrium unveiled a plan for a redevelopment that would create a 'minimum' of 1,700 jobs and turn Clery's into a 'major new mixed-used destination'. It got planning permission from DCC within 18 months. But the workers, via trade union SIPTU, appealed to ABP. In March 2017 SIPTU withdrew the appeal after it received compensation, believed to be about €1 million, to distribute to the workers.

In 2018, Natrium sold everything for €63 million, an extraordinary twist from which it is believed D2 Private took €8 million, with Cheyne doing even better. In an incredibly self-serving exit statement, Foley said that the purchaser's 'aspirations for this site vindicate our vision when we bought in 2015. We helped lay the groundwork for the redevelopment. Natrium saw the potential for this wonderful property on an iconic street which had been neglected for 40 years.'

The buyers were a consortium led by Press Up Group, a company that had aggressively grown in the hospitality business since the crash and which also dabbled in property development. It was run by Matt Ryan and, more pertinently perhaps, by Paddy McKillen junior, the son of property investor Paddy senior who had managed to navigate the Celtic Tiger crash with his wealth intact. They bought the business with

Europa Capital, a division of New York-based real estate firm Rockefeller Group, and Core Capital, described as 'a family office for private investors'. The latter had been established in 2007 by Derek McGrath and offered what it called 'a cradle to grave investment function, from site acquisition to investment sale'.

The new development changed the nature of Clery's. The basement, ground and first floors are to be used now for retail and Clery's Quarter, as it is now known, has two major international retail chains arriving as anchor tenants. Premium fashion group Flannels, part of Mike Ashley's Fraser Group, signed a deal to occupy half of its retail space and Swedish fashion chain H&M is taking the remaining 2,787 square metres for its largest Dublin city centre store. Talk of an Apple store proved to be unfounded. There are also restaurants and bars but overhead there are three floors of offices, over 90,000 square feet, a panoramic rooftop restaurant and a 176-bedroom four-star hotel.

Every distance in Ireland is measured from the GPO on O'Connell Street. It is the designated base-point. How we measure our use of our land, our ambition for it and our pride in it can be compared to our partial approach to making O'Connell Street a stand-out location, a worthy landmark for both citizens and visitors alike, something that gives us more pride. It may be overly ambitious to say that it could be an Irish version of the Champs-Élysées in Paris, but it could at least be better if an effort was made and decisions taken to act were actually implemented, which is something that can be said about the way we do a lot of things in Ireland.

TWO

HOW WE LANDED HERE

Everything that affects the ownership of land and property in Ireland in the 2020s goes back to the early twenty-first-century government under Fianna Fáil's leadership and to the subsequent actions taken by the Fine Gael–Labour coalition to try and recover control of our own destiny.

Early twenty-first-century Ireland saw property ownership as the passport to personal and national wealth. It was our equivalent of an American-style late nineteenth-century gold rush. Money was available cheaply from the banks as we enjoyed the dubious benefits of our membership of the new single currency, the euro, leading people to borrow to buy property either to live in or to rent to someone else. Eager developers sought to be the suppliers. Rising property prices gave those who had bought early a false impression of their true standing, as the assumed worth of their properties was in many cases far larger than their debts. The so-called wealth effect came into play as many borrowed money for consumption or other investment (often in holiday homes or rental properties) on the basis of the assumed, but temporary, values of their homes. Older people were encouraged to 'release equity' by borrowing again on the value of homes where their mortgages had been paid down or off. Pension plans were based on property investments: people were advised to buy a house or apartment, cover the costs of a mortgage with rental income and then sell it later at a higher price to fund their retirement years.

By 2006 the widespread assumption remained that property prices would only go up, giving rise to a state of collective economic euphoria. Those who cautioned that this could not continue indefinitely were accused of being begrudgers, pessimists and, worse, traitors. Some experts promised a wondrous thing called a 'soft landing': if, for some reason, house prices stopped rising, they would not fall downwards, or if they did, it would only be by a fraction of the previous rise. What was called the Celtic Tiger era – so dubbed because the Irish economy was roaring ahead aggressively – was in reality a Celtic bubble. And it burst.

There were many reasons but, firstly, the banks ran out of the money needed to fuel the machine. Then, more pertinently, as the values of assets backing their loans fell from excessive levels, the banks became insolvent. These financial institutions – both Irish and international operating in Ireland – had lent recklessly to the developers and builders who were building houses and apartments everywhere. To make sure that the builders sold the homes to cover the repayments to the banks, the banks had provided individuals, couples and families with the loans to buy those properties, spectacularly misjudging their future repayment capacity. They advanced 100 per cent loans so that people didn't need savings to put in equity, as had been the traditional way of securing a mortgage. They offered up to 40 years to repay the loans to those who were on low incomes: sometimes people were allowed to borrow a sum as much as six, eight or even ten times their annual income. It was a carousel, but a dangerous one; the speed kept picking up until it suddenly stalled and threw off many.

Property values had to readjust to reflect the reality of economic capacity rather than wishful thinking. This was an international problem, but it impacted Ireland disproportionately. Our property spurt in the first part of the century had been faster than almost anyone else's and we had further to fall. Within four years the value of houses and commercial property in Ireland would drop by 60 per cent.

What made things worse for Ireland was the introduction, with the support of Fine Gael and Sinn Féin from the opposition benches, of the infamous bank guarantee of September 2008, whereby the State promised to make good on the bank debts without realising their extent and the State's inability to cover them. The Irish-owned banks had to be rescued with a €64 billion State investment that could scarcely be afforded. The National Asset Management Agency (NAMA) was set up to take control of many of the loans that developers and investors couldn't repay. The idea was that by getting their 'bad' loans off their books, they could return to going about their normal business. NAMA bought the largest loans from five banks and building societies – AIB, Bank of Ireland, EBS, Permanent TSB and Irish Nationwide – for €30.5 billion, on loans that amounted to €72.3 billion. The amounts involved were deemed to be the up-to-date market value of the loans, based on the assumed value of the underlying assets at the time of transfer. The valuation was a tacit acknowledgement that the chances of recouping the remaining money – over €40 billion – were slim to non-existent. There was a stated determination to get borrowers to repay every cent they owed the banks, but the reality was that it wasn't possible. The best that could be done was to ensure they repaid the amount that equalled what NAMA had paid the banks for the loans, especially as the State had borrowed that money to create NAMA.

We learnt a lot about the true financial state of those who had been living it up as Ireland's wealthiest. Three developers had debts of more than €2 billion each and 12 others had more than €1 billion each with the Irish banks. Of the total amount transferred to NAMA, over €61 billion was with just 190 borrowers. Many of the companies were owned by individuals and their families. Some had given personal guarantees, making them liable to personal bankruptcy. The reality was that bankruptcy would not bring about the recovery of the money. That didn't stop NAMA from insisting on the receivership or liquidation of some of the biggest developers in the country, so-called no-hopers, who were subjected to 'enforcement action'. As companies floundered, some of the most prominent developers from the boom (most of whom featured in my 2009 book *Who Really Runs Ireland?*) headed for personal bankruptcy: Bernard McNamara, Liam Carroll, Paddy Kelly, John Fleming, Derek Quinlan, Seán Dunne, Jim Mansfield and Ray Grehan among them.

NAMA had ended up with a motley collection of unfinished housing estates and commercial office blocks in Ireland and abroad. All sorts of unexpected issues arose. For example, NAMA became Ireland's biggest golf course operator, with more than 30 premium courses under its control. It became the biggest hotel operator, with loans for 83 Irish hotels, eight of which were five-star properties and 33 four-star at a time when potential customers were curtailing their holidaying and spending.

NAMA had turned out to be only a very partial solution to our crisis. Even after the big transfers, the banks were still laden with loans on which customers could not make repayments. Many of these were commercial loans under €20 million in size, which was the NAMA threshold for transfer. Home loans were as significant for some lenders. Banks like Permanent TSB, for example, had not lent to developers but to home-owners on very generous terms and now faced extinction as borrowers were unable to make repayments.

Meanwhile, Anglo Irish Bank, an Irish stock market-quoted bank that under the stewardship of the now reviled Seán Fitzpatrick had been the bubble's totem, was discovered to have bad loans of €22.5 billion. It was taken into State ownership and subsequently renamed the Irish Banking Resolution Corporation as if that would make us forget it. The plan was to work out that mess separately to NAMA.

It turned out that the Irish banks had not been the sole offenders when it came to reckless lending. Foreign-owned banks Ulster Bank, ACC (Rabobank), Bank of Scotland (Ireland) and National Irish Bank were just as bad, if not worse. Overall, their bad loans altogether were another NAMA in scale, and these banks sought to sell the underlying properties into a moribund market. The government was unable to control their decisions and actions.

The government had enough of its own problems. Tax revenues evaporated and it was unable to find anyone 'in the markets' to lend to it to cover day-to-day bills such as pensions, unemployment benefits and State employee pay. In late 2010 it all came to a head, in humiliating fashion. The International Monetary Fund teamed up with the European Central Bank and European Commission – the three institutions becoming known to us as the Troika – to provide emergency rescue funds on terms that demanded swingeing cuts in public spending and tax increases on the incomes of those who had kept their jobs. Construction activity almost entirely stopped, adding to unemployment and reducing tax revenues further. The country went into a form of collective grieving, experiencing the five stages of grief: denial, anger, bargaining, depression and acceptance.

THE OUTSIDER VIEW

In March 2011 the overriding emotion was anger and an angry public swept Fianna Fáil (and the Greens) from power in a general election. This brought the Fine Gael and Labour parties into a coalition government, one of the most important in the history of the State. It also meant that outsiders were brought in to offer advice.

John Moran was one such: he had never served in the public sector but was invited in to bring fresh thinking to officialdom. Moran was a qualified lawyer who had started his career with the Shannon-based aircraft leasing giant GPA before moving to New York from McCann Fitzgerald, an Irish firm of solicitors, to a career merging law with investment banking. He had become a senior figure at Zurich Bank at a young age before taking time out to live in France and own and manage juice bars. Moran had joined the Central Bank of Ireland initially as head of wholesale banking supervision in 2010, the year before Michael Noonan took office as Minister for Finance, and only then moved to the

Department of Finance, where he served as secretary general between 2012 and 2014. Noonan's wife had been one of his schoolteachers.

More than a decade on from then, Moran is clear on what had to be done: 'We had to put a floor under the asset prices or they would've continued in free fall.' Hardly any commercial property traded in Ireland in 2011, the exception being the €100 million purchase by Google of a major office development called Montevetro, located a stone's throw from NAMA's offices in the National Treasury Management Agency (NTMA) on North Wall Quay. If nothing was trading it implied that nothing had value (even if that clearly wasn't true), theoretically wiping out all the money the State had put into NAMA. 'Mechanisms were put in place to try and encourage foreign capital into Ireland because we had none in this country and that seems to have been forgotten,' said Moran. 'We could not get Irish institutions to invest money in Ireland, could not convince Irish pension funds to buy Irish government bonds. It was hard to persuade people that the Irish State would not default, that the euro wasn't going to break up and we'd have to return to the punt.'

Subsequently, the government and its advisors were accused of selling too quickly, and of allowing the transfer of great swathes of Irish assets to foreign opportunists. Moran believes little criticism was voiced at the time, and that hindsight is easy to offer. 'Imagine if I had walked into the Minister's office in 2012 with this great new plan that we'd worked up in the Department of Finance to sit out the property recession because we thought our properties were undervalued. Remember we had just gotten into this crisis because of property speculation and developers, and we can't borrow money on the public markets, but we're going to become property speculators because I think that property prices will go up in the future and therefore we'll recoup a lot more money [than by selling now]? The concept that we would bet the country again, a second time, on real estate values simply doesn't make sense.'

The government did not have the luxury of being able to wait for property values to recover. The purchase and sale of all kinds of property came to a near halt, making NAMA's job of recovering its investment and the chances of the banks sorting out the remainder of their loans much more difficult to achieve. If the banks were reluctant to provide loans, then somebody else was going to have to provide money to grease the machine of property transactions. Even the wealthy Irish who had retained their wealth were fearful of risking any of it in Irish investments. However, as Moran went on tour around the USA and Europe, he began to pick up positive signals: 'There was more confidence in Ireland's future from people outside Ireland, whether it was buying Bank of Ireland, Irish Life (the insurance company) or government bonds.' Noonan introduced a raft of what subsequently became highly controversial tax measures specifically designed to attract international investment to Ireland.

The cavalry was about to arrive.

PART 2

OWNING THE LAND

Over the last decade, Ireland has had the most extraordinary transfer of ownership of assets. Sales at prices lower than what the assets had been bought for meant the crystallisation of losses for previous owners and, by extension, the State picking up much of the tab on our behalf. A subsequent surge in values made some assets even more expensive than they ever were in the days of the Celtic Tiger madness and provided their new owners with enormous profits.

THREE

THE AMERICANS RIDE IN

Former US President Bill Clinton was the star salesman at the 'Invest in Ireland' conference that took place in New York in February 2012. He told the investors present, who he described as having 'money in the banks', that there was somewhere to spend all of that cash. 'Now is the time to invest in Ireland, where property is a steal and you've got the best-educated workforce and everybody is all dressed up with no place to go,' the former US President declared, with the full support of the Irish government.

At an Ireland Funds event in Florida the following month, Hilary Weston, an Irishwoman whose family owned the Brown Thomas department store in Dublin, introduced Wilbur Ross as 'a white knight, riding to Ireland's rescue'. He was usually called other things: 'Mr Distress', 'the king of bankruptcy', 'the king of the turnaround' and 'a vulture'. His reputation had been made by taking control of failed companies in the steel, coal, textiles and car parts industries and restoring them to financial viability, taking big profits from doing so before turning his attention to Ireland. Ross told his largely wealthy audience: 'We're not used to being rock stars. We're not U2.'

Ross was celebrated as a key figure in a group that took control of Bank of Ireland in 2011. The government had provided €4.5 billion in rescue capital for the bank but did not want to spend more by taking it into State ownership, as it had done with all the other Irish banks. Ross's associates included the Canadian insurer Fairfax Financial Holdings, the Boston-based Fidelity Investments and two Californian investment firms, Capital Group and Kennedy Wilson. These came together to buy 34.9 per cent of Bank of Ireland's shares. Ross took 9 per cent of the overall total and said publicly that he expected to triple his money within three years, having secured the shares at a 40 per cent discount to their apparent 'book value'. And he made his money as he had hoped.

'There was plenty of blame to go around for all sorts of things that were done wrong, but right now should be a period of healing, a period of rehabilitation, a period of getting on with it,' Ross said in one interview. In another, a year later, he added: 'Ireland is a high-tech economy, with non-cyclical exports, good infrastructure, a young workforce and Irish people understand they have to get through this tough period. I have great confidence it will be the first of the peripheral economies to recover.'

He was conscious of not being seen as a vulture, given that vultures 'eat dead flesh off a carcass'. He defended his profit-making motive – 'you can make good gains and yet do good' – and held himself out as some kind of altruist: 'We're helping a whole country of very deserving people to do better, like in the cowboy movies – the troopers are coming.'

Ross's arrival – and that of the other new Bank of Ireland shareholders – was partly facilitated by the work of two Irishmen, Nick Corcoran and Nigel McDermott of Cardinal Capital. It also had contact with Bill McMorrow, the controlling 22 per cent shareholder in the investment firm Kennedy Wilson. McMorrow arrived in Dublin in late November 2010 with a reputation for investing which others feared, particularly in Japan in 1994 when that country was still undergoing the after-effects of a property crash a few years earlier. McMorrow has distant Irish roots – from Manorhamilton in County Leitrim – but he enlisted Bobby Shriver, nephew of US president John F. Kennedy (and partner, with U2 lead singer Bono, in the (Product)Red brand to promote Third World businesses) to make introductions in Ireland. He had dozens of meetings where he heard little other than negativity, but McMorrow is one of those investors who deliberately goes against conventional wisdom, and believes in buying when everyone else is selling.

Kennedy Wilson first bought Bank of Ireland Real Estate Investment Management, a subsidiary of the main bank, which managed about €1.6 billion of commercial property, mainly in Europe. This provided an introduction to Bank of Ireland boss Richie Boucher, who was trying to raise equity capital from private sector sources to avoid nationalisation. McMorrow liked his story, particularly that the bank would be the only non-State-controlled one in the country if it got fresh investment – and that it would have far less competition to contend with than in the previous decade as foreign banks exited the market. McMorrow contacted Prem Watsa, the Indian-born, Toronto-based billionaire who controlled Fairfax. When they met, McMorrow discovered that Watsa had been talking to Ross already about the Irish bank. They formed an investment group with Cardinal Capital.

It was only the start of an Irish spending spree by McMorrow that initially reached €600 million. Kennedy Wilson teamed up with Deutsche Bank to buy about 150 loans from the Irish operations of the UK Lloyds Bank, taking in about 100 properties from 25 borrowers, mainly offices and shops. These loans had an original value of €360 million but were purchased for just €61 million. Kennedy Wilson bought the debt to the Shelbourne Hotel on St Stephen's Green for an estimated €110 million (after the previous owners, led by Bernard McNamara and Jerry O'Reilly, spent €265 million on it) and took control of the hotel operations.[2] It paid €30 million for the 138-bedroom, four-star Portmarnock hotel and golf resort on 178 acres. The previous owners, Capel Developments, had paid €70 million for it in 2005.[3] It bought the major apartment development at the Irish Army's former Clancy Barracks at Islandbridge on the River Liffey near Heuston Station and, in time, added hundreds more apartments there.

Over the next decade, it would spend, sometimes in partnership

2   In 2022 it revalued the hotel at €234 million.
3   In 2019 Kennedy Wilson sold it to Canadian hoteliers Northland Properties for over €50 million.

with others, an estimated €1.8 billion buying Irish properties and €1.5 billion developing them; it recouped over €770 million through the sale of a small number of assets acquired. It bought over 1,800 apartments in Ireland, built as many and sold 136, leaving it with 3,520 homes in Dublin and Cork, the second largest landlord in Ireland. It purchased 1.8 million square feet of office or retail space, built one million more, and sold 800,000 square feet. Ireland would become its second-largest market by revenue after the US and account for about 15 per cent of the group's global total. It took joint control, with Axa, of Vantage, a 442-apartment complex in Leopardstown. It would become the most visible developer of new apartments along the Stillorgan dual-carriageway into Dublin. It bought the 265-apartment Grange complex and adjacent land from NAMA for €153 million and then extended the complex to 663 homes. It bought the Leisureplex site after buying the Stillorgan shopping centre across the road and obtained permission for 232 apartments in five blocks of four to eight storeys.

Blackstone also arrived early. Founded in 1985 by a group of top US investment bankers led by Stephen Schwarzman, Blackstone was one of the world's largest private equity investment firms, with more than $80 billion of assets under management. In 2010, Schwarzman said he would 'wait until there's really blood in the streets' before investing in Europe. 'As we look at the current situation in Europe, we're basically waiting to see how beaten-up people's psyches get, and where they're willing to sell assets,' he said.

By 2012 Blackstone was in Ireland, buying a quarter of the key telecoms infrastructure company Eircom, bidding unsuccessfully for ownership of Bord Gáis and buying a batch of office buildings from NAMA. It got the Burlington Hotel in Dublin 4, the second largest in the country with 501 bedrooms and extensive conference and banqueting facilities on a 3.8-acre site, for just €67 million. Only five years earlier Bernard McNamara had paid €288 million for it, with plans to demolish it and the adjacent Irish headquarters of Axa Insurance and to construct an office and retail complex – with some expensive luxury apartments too – which he reckoned could be worth over €1 billion. He never got the chance, going bankrupt with debts of over €1.5 billion. Blackstone put about another €20 million into an overdue refurbishment. Less than four years later it sold the hotel for €180 million to German investor Deka Immobilien. It also made tens of millions of euro in profits on various properties purchased from NAMA and sold again in the same time frame. It did make charitable donations – useful, but small compared to the size of the profits made – to Irish universities, however, and plaques thanking Blackstone can be seen at UCC – where one of its Irish directors, Gerry Murphy, had taken his degree – and at Trinity College Dublin.

Between 2012 and 2015 American money poured into Ireland in a bewildering array of deals, far too many to mention here. Property investors could see technology and financial services companies expanding but lacking the additional modern office space they needed. With demand exceeding supply, rents went up. Hotels could be bought for a fraction of their construction cost. The rate of return implied on many investment properties in Ireland was a multiple of that on offer in countries such as Luxembourg or Germany. The foreigners had the field largely to themselves as the downturn had wiped out a large amount of Irish wealth and very few Irish investors were capable of assembling the money to buy, plus the Irish banks didn't have the capacity to offer loans, even with interest rates very low.

The Americans mostly didn't buy individual assets, other than large, obvious, stand-out ones, because that would have taken too much time. They preferred instead to acquire entire loan books from the departing foreign banks, taking their chances on what they would find within the portfolios – having done as much investigation as was practicable beforehand – and then selling or keeping whatever took their fancy. They controlled the debt secured against large amounts of commercial and residential property, personal loans, mortgages and businesses. This gave them economic control of the assets, rather than physical posses-sion, and immense power, with the ability to seize the assets if the loan was not repaid or restructured on their terms.

NAMA initially sold its loans slowly, but the foreign-owned banks rushed to sell. The list of private equity, hedge funds and investment banks buying grew quickly. Goldman Sachs (the Wall Street invest-ment bank known as the Vampire Squid for its ability to suck money out of deals) ended up as one of Ireland's largest hotel operators and owners, its portfolio expanding to include the Crowne Plaza hotels in Dublin and Dundalk, plus a number of Holiday Inns. It took control of shopping centres, such as the Laurence Shopping Centre in Drogheda from local builder Gerry Maguire, and medical facilities, such as the Whitfield Clinic in Waterford. It purchased 3,500 home mortgages from US multinational General Electric (GE).

Pimco, founded by legendary investment figure and avid stamp-col-lector Bill Gross and with an estimated $2 trillion in assets under its control, took control of many of the loans connected to Liam Carroll, a former billionaire builder who went bankrupt. It collected over €5 mil-lion a year in rent from offices it let to three government departments, Justice, Agriculture and Social Protection, to the HSE and even to An Garda Síochána.

About 1,000 professionals found themselves owing money to CarVal, a part of Cargill, the largest privately held company in the US. Anglo-Irish Bank's private client division had been the go-to bank for wealthy and aspirant individuals who wanted to speculate on property during the boom. It extended about €600 million to the professional classes, who not only bought investment properties but sometimes formed amateur property syndicates to go into development themselves – to sneers from those who did this full-time. Doctors, dentists, accoun-tants, sports stars, lawyers and television personalities were among those now in hock to Anglo and, by extension, to the State. Their ownership of some of Ireland had been brief. CarVal bought these loans for just

30 per cent of their original value and hired Australian firm Pepper Asset Servicing to manage what became known as the 'dentists and doctors book'. Pepper itself bought €600 million worth of loans from Danske Bank that covered loans on some 270 properties in receivership. It spent about €250 million in buying another €600 million in residential home loans from GE Capital Woodchester Home Loans.

Apollo was founded in 1990 by Leon Black, a former Drexel Burnham Lambert banker who assembled a notably expensive art collection and who by 2022 was embroiled in personal scandal – linked to his friendship with the late Jeffrey Epstein – that brought him out of the business pages and onto the news pages. The private equity group had a total of $105 billion in assets under management at the end of June 2012 when it came to Ireland. That year it paid stg£149 million to buy a portfolio of distressed commercial property loans in Ireland from Lloyds Banking Group for just one-tenth of their original value. Apollo hired local advisors, such as Brian Goggin, the former chief executive of Bank of Ireland, to work for it. Lloyds, which had purchased Halifax Bank of Scotland in 2009 and got Bank of Scotland (Ireland) as part of the deal, was one of the foreign banks with the biggest losses to face in Ireland. It had stg£16.1 billion worth of loans in Ireland, but 85.5 per cent of those loans were regarded as impaired (not making full payments) or unlikely to be repaid in full. Lloyds also sold a stg£1.6 billion portfolio of mortgages to Goldman Sachs and CarVal.

Cerberus, a New York distressed debt and asset specialist with $25 billion under management and chaired by former US vice-presidential candidate Dan Quayle, was another eager buyer. As was Oaktree, a global asset management firm with $77.1 billion under management, primarily on behalf of pension funds, foundations, endowments and sovereign wealth funds, and often worked through its affiliate, Mars Capital. There was Davidson Kempner, Canyon Capital and Ellis Short, Sunderland football club's American owner at the time, who brought in Kildare Partners to Ireland. KKR & Co. Inc., one of the world's most talked about private equity groups, hired former AIB chief executive Michael Buckley as an advisor and took luxury offices on St Stephen's Green.

Starwood Capital, based in Connecticut and headed by Barry Sternlicht, already had $22 billion of assets under management, including the Louvre Hotel Group, the Etoile in Paris and Baccarat Hotel, before it arrived in Ireland. When Starwood bought NAMA's €810 million Project Aspen portfolio of debts owed by developers David Courtney and Jerry O'Reilly it got around 30 office and retail properties, including the Garda station on Harcourt Terrace in Dublin (vacant until 2023 and then demolished), several Superquinn supermarkets and the Merrion Gates development in Sandymount. It paid just €200 million but NAMA remained as a minority partner in the deal to take some share in any upside on disposals.

Some foreign banks began to re-engage with the Irish market, or at least those who had not been burnt during the collapse; while all of the buying funds had their own money, they topped it up with debt and found that Bank of America, Nomura (Japan), Deutsche Bank (Germany) and Royal Bank of Canada were among those willing to support their purchases.

All of these transactions were manna to the professional classes in Ireland, with enormous fees being paid to solicitors, accountants and tax consultants, and even estate agents. Some firms set up dedicated units simply to service US funds. Their local knowledge came in handy as they exploited tax laws set up two decades previously to make Ireland an attractive location for international debt securitisation, to bolster investments in the IFSC. However, these companies – known as Section 110 companies – could also hold a wide range of financial assets, commodities, plants and machinery and offset the loans used for purchase against tax. Now these companies were used to hold loans bought from NAMA, IBRC (Irish Bank Resolution Corporation) and foreign banks and to minimise the tax on annual income or eventual profits paid to the State. It was tax avoidance – which is legal – but it was against the spirit of the original intention of the legislation. 'While they may be in a position to make a handsome profit, the strategies they employ may not be consistent with the long-term economic and social interests of the state,' then opposition TD Michael McGrath, who became Minister for Public Expenditure in June 2020 and then Minister for Finance in December 2022, told the Dáil in 2015.

McGrath's complaints arose from the consequences of the government ordering the liquidation of IBRC in February 2013, a measure it was thought would speed up the sale of loans, although there was no great expectation for the accelerated pace of what would actually happen. This surprising and controversial decision, the legislation for which was rushed through the Dáil in hours despite objections from the board of IBRC, resulted in the appointment of KPMG – through its partners Kieran Wallace and Eamonn Richardson – to oversee the work of selling about €18 billion in remaining loans.

Borrowers from the bank were given the opportunity to buy their loans as part of the process, at a discount, if they could find some other bank or partner to provide the funds. This write-down was effectively a subsidy, but the argument was that it was warranted if it saved jobs. However, this contrasted with the rules NAMA applied to borrowers, as set by legislation: it was not allowed to sell loans back to indebted developers at a discount. It also contrasted with the position being applied to home mortgage-owners: there were no debt relief or write-downs there, maybe only a restructuring of the terms upon which the full mortgage would be repaid if the new purchasers of the debt offered such deals. While some IBRC borrowers were able to cut deals with the liquidators to avoid their debts being sold onwards, the biggest deals were with American buyers.

Lone Star was far and away the biggest buyer of IBRC loans, added to other deals it was doing with banks. By early 2014 it was reckoned to have spent about €5 billion in Ireland, buying loans that at one stage had a face value of €13 billion. It acquired Irish loan portfolios with mortgages secured against as many as 15,350 residential properties, including buy-to-lets and personal dwellings. It purchased Start Mortgages, a subprime mortgage business, from Investec bank. It had around 70 loans secured by underlying collateral of more than 400 properties, including hotels, nightclubs, shopping centres and offices, mainly in Dublin and, to a lesser extent, in the regions. It had bought over 600 acres of Dublin development land with the potential for up to 7,000 homes.

This gave Lone Star's creator, John Grayken, an idea.

Grayken may well be Ireland's wealthiest citizen. Born an American, this Texan gave up his citizenship and became Irish in 1999, just four years after he established Lone Star in Dallas. He bought Japanese golf courses, bad corporate loans in Germany, distressed debt in Canada, and even a Korean bank. England appears to be the home of this American-born Irishman; he lives in a Surrey mansion previously occupied by Prince Andrew's ex-wife Sarah Ferguson. He has raised $45 billion from banks and investors through 12 funds, all of which specialise in the purchase of so-called distressed assets.

In January 2014 Grayken went to Davos, to the World Economic Forum, where he met Michael Noonan, then the Irish Minister for Finance. Grayken pitched his idea of buying the remainder of NAMA in its entirety. Noonan thought about it, not for too long, and declined. Politically it would have been a hard sell, to allow one buyer to have the lot, no matter what price it was prepared to pay. A buyer would look to make whatever profit it could and that would be eagerly tracked and reported by the media and especially by opposition politicians. But Noonan was aware that Blackstone had a similar interest in NAMA. It made him think that there must be more value in the agency's assets than he and his officials had thought and that this was the time to sell as much as possible. Noonan was conscious that international investors might move on to the next distressed market in Europe before too long.

In July 2014 a public announcement was made: NAMA would sell almost €10 billion in loans and assets over the next two-and-a-half years, a figure just shy of the €15 billion it had sold since its creation five years earlier. NAMA needed to match demand from investors to the supply of loans without driving prices down. It would find, to its delight, that the investors would keep buying and that even more Americans, and Europeans too, would join the posse. Prices would keep going up which, when they rose higher than anyone could have expected, would lead to its own unexpected consequences.

FOUR

TROPHY ASSETS

It wasn't just big commercial assets in urban locations – with the potential for income and capital gain if bought cheaply – that attracted foreign investment. Some wealthy investors liked the look of rural Ireland, particularly old country mansions and estates that could be kept for personal enjoyment and hobby pursuits, or that could be redeveloped to offer leisure and recreational facilities to the monied classes. They may not have been titled, but they were the new lords of the manors and while they may not have been cheap, they liked to take the opportunity to buy cheaply before sometimes spending indulgently.

HOG'S HEAD

Waterville in South Kerry was once known as the small town that played host many summers to the famous Hollywood movie star Charlie Chaplin who took holidays at the Butler's Arms Hotel, as did Walt Disney in 1946. In October 2018 the newly opened Lodge at Hog's Head Golf Club had a rare day when it welcomed locals and others who came from elsewhere in Ireland. The course hosted a special golf day for former Kerry GAA players and others to honour the 80th birthday of its most famous local, Mick O'Dwyer, manager of eight All-Ireland winning sides. It was a rare occasion for it to be thrown open to locals and visitors from around Ireland (myself included, as host of a fundraiser for the local GAA club it was sponsoring), albeit by invitation only.

The entrance to the new hotel is not easily found, its name displayed on a low wall that's easily missed. This establishment – with just 48 bedrooms – is not looking for walk-in business. Once residents and members gain admittance, they enter a world of luxury. This may be the finest of the many five-star hotels in Kerry. If ever the cliché 'no expense was spared' is true, then this is it, and this is something built in the years after the excesses of the Celtic Tiger era. The hotel, full of timber beams imported from the US and local stone, is entirely modern in its interior, as are the various individual four-bedroom lodges – fully served by the hotel – that share the space overlooking Lough Currane. This is the site of an old Great Southern Hotel that was demolished to make way for the modern new structure, with a spa, sauna, jacuzzi and swimming pool, as well as the lodges.

Similarly, there are no signs to advertise the golf club although it is clearly visible from the main road. The avenue to the brand-new luxurious clubhouse is secured by an electric gate. Those wanting to gain admission are admitted only after identifying themselves at a speakerphone. The clubhouse facilities are of a standard that might be expected in a five-star hotel. It is estimated by locals that up to €80 million was spent on the whole project. But it is open for only seven months in the year, closing at the end of October and reopening the following April.

The town already has an impressive golf course of considerable renown, funded by American money. Waterville GC was constructed in the 1960s by a Kerry-born, American-based millionaire called John A. Mulcahy, who wanted to build an Irish equivalent of the famous US Winged Foot club and clubhouse in Mamaroneck, New York State. His friends Claude Harmon (father of the famous commentator Butch, who also coached Tiger Woods for a decade) and Judge Joseph F. Gagliardi helped an Irish golf course architect, Eddie Hackett, shape a links that came to be ranked among the world's very best. When John A. Mulcahy died, his ashes were buried on the famous short 17th hole at Waterville, otherwise known as Mulcahy's Peak. Ownership then passed to a group of Irish Americans from Connecticut, all of whom were also members of Winged Foot. They included one of Wall Street's most legendary figures, John Meriwether, the founder of Long-Term Capital Management, a hedge fund whose collapse almost brought down the global financial system in 1998. He is also a prominent figure in the Michael Lewis book *Liar's Poker*.

Tony Alvarez and Byran Marsal, principals of the New York-based international management consulting firm that bears their names, made their fortunes by leading the restructuring of accountancy firm Arthur Anderson, brought down by its part in the Enron scandal, and Lehman Brothers when it imploded in 2008, the first majority casualty of the crash that brought about the Great Recession. Their fees for the Lehman work came in at over $600 million. Their consulting firm has over 3,000 employees in 45 cities in 18 countries and has an annual turnover of more than $1 billion. They are estimated to enjoy a personal wealth of well over $3 billion.

The duo were members at the very private and expensive Old Head of Kinsale course in County Cork. Its owner, John O'Connor, told Marsal of land available at Waterville because the owners – a local builder and a London investor – were under pressure from Bank of Ireland for the repayment of loans advanced to develop it. Marsal viewed it and in early 2014 bought the former Waterville Lake Hotel (built by Mulcahy and once used as a short-lived Club Med venue) and the Skellig Bay Golf Club for a knockdown €1.8 million. There had been ambitious plans for the venue, but they paled into insignificance compared to what the new American owners had in mind. They envisaged a retreat for American golfers, who could fly into Cork or Shannon and then be transported by helicopter or luxury vans, depending on what they were prepared to pay, to play the courses in Waterville, with perhaps trips to the likes of the even better courses at Ballybunion or Tralee or the Old Head in Kinsale, while enjoying the facilities at Hog's Head as their base. Elite members and friends could have an even better deal: a seat on a private Gulfstream jet – Hog's Head Air, with the distinctive hog logo, complete with pot belly and golf club on the wing – that can bring up to 22 golfers into Kerry Airport before travelling on by helicopter to Waterville. Access to the Irish public is limited, usually just to friends of members. While it is possible to ask to book a round of golf midweek, the advertised prices of €275 per person tends to keep the riff-raff, and the Irish, away. Few locals tended to complain because the resort created jobs and brought money to the area.

PARKNASILLA RESORT AND SPA

Sneem in south County Kerry is about a 40-minute drive from Waterville. It has its own five-star hotel, Parknasilla Resort and Spa, but this one is very much focused on the Irish market. Its golf course, constructed using equipment from the political Healy-Rae family, unusually is just 12 holes in length instead of the normal 18 because the original developer ran out of money and land to finish it. Bernard McNamara bought it in the mid-2000s for €40 million. Worse, he spent at least €30 million on enlarging and upgrading the resort and building 62 self-catering lodges and villas on the grounds. It was one of the first major provincial hotels to be sold by NAMA, for a mere €10 million, in 2012 to Jacqui Safra, a Swiss-Lebanese businessman and banker who became known as the financier of Woody Allen's movies during the 1990s.

Safra knew the estate well, having previously purchased and staffed a home on Garnish Island (which shouldn't be confused with the publicly open venue in Bantry Bay). He also bought a private 140-acre woodland and garden island, Rossdohan Island, in Kenmare Bay near the resort, which had been previously developed by a family from Dublin, the Walkers, for an additional €2 million and has restored it with rare trees and specimen plants. Although it can be accessed or viewed from a boat, there is also a bridge under which a tidal creek runs and the eastern side of the island has jade-coloured waters and a seal colony. The new ownership of Parknasilla meant that this could all be protected and enjoyed, as well as bringing money into the area.[4]

BALLYFIN

As with Hog's Head, the Ballyfin project was a personal one, although without a golf club on the grounds of this nineteenth-century neoclassical manor estate in County Laois. Fred Krehbiel bought and renovated the 35,000-plus square foot home (which had been rebuilt in the 1820s) and 600-acre estate that was falling into disrepair, but died less than a decade later, aged 80, in July 2021. It had been run by the Roman Catholic Patrician Brothers order as a boarding school for more than 70 years.

Krehbiel was the former chief executive of Molex, an Illinois-headquartered electronic components company that had expanded into Europe through an Irish manufacturing base in Millstreet, County Cork in 1971. Krehbiel retired as chief executive in 2001 but remained as chairman of the family-dominated company until it was sold to Koch Industries for $7.2 billion; it was reported that Fred got $600 million of this. He came to Ireland because his wife, Kay, was an Irishwoman who had emigrated to the US as a nurse in her twenties.

It has been estimated that Krehbiel spent at least €50 million on refurbishing and refurnishing the house – which raises questions as to how much interest the inheritors of his estate will retain in this Irish venture. Ballyfin has only 21 bedrooms to generate revenue, which is why one night can cost €2,000 per couple. It is stuffed with the most expensive antique paintings and furniture: in the gold drawing room

---

4   In 2023, Safra hit the international headlines when he sold a book known as the Codex Sassoon at Sotheby's in New York for $38.1 million. Sold by the dealers as 'arguably the most influential book in human history' and the 'foundational cornerstone to civilisations and communities around the globe', it is the oldest known complete Hebrew Bible, dating to the ninth or tenth century, and includes all 24 books, minus about eight leaves, and the first ten chapters of Genesis. It is regarded as the foundation for Judaism and other Abrahamic faiths, including Christianity.

there is a large glass chandelier that was previously owned by Napoleon Bonaparte's sister, Princess Maria Annunciate Caroline Murat, the former queen of Naples. In the modern era, its guests have included Hollywood star George Clooney and his wife Amal, while Kanye West and Kim Kardashian honeymooned there.

CASTLEMARTIN

John Malone is believed to own more than 2.2 million acres of land in the US, more than any other individual, about 3,437 square miles, which represents a holding more than one-tenth of the size of the island of Ireland in control of one person. Malone has described his weakness for land as a 'virus' he caught from Ted Turner, the man who set up CNN and who was also married for a time to actor Jane Fonda. Malone's main home is on the edge of the Rocky Mountains in Colorado, but he owns forests in New Hampshire and Maine, more than 500,000 acres of ranch land in New Mexico and cattle farms in Wyoming. Malone is the chairman and largest voting shareholder of the Liberty group of media companies, giving him influence in the US on a par with that of Rupert Murdoch.

Malone bought Castlemartin, the Irish estate of bankrupted billionaire Tony O'Reilly, in 2014, as described in my 2015 biography of O'Reilly, *The Maximalist*. Malone added a massive Gothic-style mansion on 400 acres to his holdings after his wife reportedly took a shine to Wicklow's Humewood Castle, a Victorian-built estate that he bought for €8 million in 2012. In 2014, he also bought the 840-acre Ballylinch Stud at Thomastown, County Kilkenny, once part of the Mount Juliet estate, bringing his Irish holdings to over 2,200 acres.

Malone's acquisitions go beyond those for personal enjoyment. The bulk of his purchases in Ireland have been of hotels, although his main company, Liberty, owns Virgin Media in Ireland, including TV stations and a broadband network. Deciding he wanted to benefit from local knowledge, he formed the John Malone Partnership with two Irishmen, Paul Higgins and John Lally. Early acquisitions included the Beacon,

Morgan and Spencer hotels in Dublin, which had been developed by Paul Fitzpatrick and sold for €150 million. They also bought the Trinity Capital hotel on Pearse Street in Dublin for €35 million, the Clarion at the IFSC for €35 million and the Westin, a five-star property on Westmoreland Street, for €65 million. Outside Dublin, the Strand Hotel in Limerick, overlooking the River Shannon and close to Thomond Park, the home of Munster rugby, was bought for more than €20 million.

The Malone Partnership was the second post-crash buyer of what was known as the Four Seasons Hotel – in Ballsbridge, Dublin 4, near the British embassy – but which was renamed The Intercontinental. It had been bought by London and Regional Properties, founded by British billionaires Ian and Richard Livingstone, for a bargain €15 million, a quarter of what the hotel had cost to develop originally, but which also amounted to not much more than €76,000 per room. The cheap price was attributed to losses arising from an annual ground rent of €700,000 to the RDS and an expensive long-term management agreement with Four Seasons to manage it. They more than trebled their money by selling to Malone's consortium. But the rich American seemed to believe that he was still getting value for money.

DOONBEG

Donald Trump was one of the earlier investors in post-crash Ireland, but while he was one of the smaller ones, he arguably made the most noise about it, facilitated by eager locals and a supine government. Trump always attracted a crowd, even before he became a presidential candidate in the USA. He was reality television's idea of a businessman, courtesy of his role in the hit show *The Apprentice*, and someone who had featured in celebrity media coverage for decades as his marriages waxed and waned. However, the deference shown to him at Shannon Airport in February 2014, when he arrived to visit his new golf resort acquisition at Doonbeg in County Clare, symbolised how desperate indigent Ireland had become.

A military salute was not supplied but otherwise, Trump was received in a similar manner to many heads of State touching down at this airport in previous years, long in advance of his residence at the Oval Office. The billionaire Trump arrived in his private aircraft – a Boeing 757 jet with a list price of $75 million and with his name emblazoned in gold upon its carriage – to be met by a welcoming party led by Michael Noonan along with three women strumming harps and singing traditional Irish tunes. The céad míle fáilte was totally unnecessary; Trump was a man who always provided a great welcome for himself.

Noonan subsequently defended the ludicrousness of the red-carpet treatment: 'I've no connection with Donald Trump but I can assure you if it was the IDA that was bringing a factory into Clare and I was invited to go down there and there was 300 jobs in it, I'd be there,' he told RTÉ Radio One. 'This man says he's going to spend at least double the purchase price for investment down there.'

Actually, Trump paid little more than half the mooted purchase price, €8.7 million instead of the reported €15 million. 'Doonbeg is an already terrific property that we will make even better. It will soon be an unparalleled resort destination with the highest standards of luxury,' he boasted. 'I must tell you that so far the Irish government has been terrific. They want this to be great.'

The locals had decided that they would indulge Trump if he would keep the golf course and hotel at Doonbeg open. Up to 300 jobs depended on him. Otherwise, the wild gusts of wind on the west coast of Ireland could propel a considerable amount of tumbleweed across the resort and the manicured course would return to its original wild state and the local pubs and shops would empty. Doonbeg is remote and small. The population – 262 in the 2016 census – sustains little other than tourism. Even then, the beauty of the stark and bare countryside – and the views of the Atlantic – doesn't have attractions like the Cliffs of Moher to recommend it to tourists.

The hotel at Doonbeg – called a lodge – was built with 218 suites, an expansive spa and several restaurants at a cost not far short of €30 million when it opened in 2002. It made heavy losses during the Celtic Tiger boom years, losing €10 million across 2006 and 2007, and even more during the Great Recession before going into receivership with debts of €80 million in January 2014. The receivers brought in Trump, who already had two Scottish courses in Aberdeen and Turnberry. Trump wasn't some kind of hotel or golf course visionary, however, despite his bombast. It was known that his Scottish ventures were loss-making, but it wasn't until well into his time as US president that the *New York Times* got copies of 15 years of his tax returns and discovered that Trump had reported $315.6 million worth of losses at his golf courses around the world since 2000. He didn't buy the company that ran Doonbeg – which was liquidated – but he got its assets debt-free: the golf course, the hotel and seven unsold suites. He promised a new function room for weddings and conferences and other non-golf events, and a swimming pool. He claimed he was encouraged by one of Ireland's most famous businessmen: 'We were applying for [permission to add] a ballroom. Mr O'Leary from Ryanair, who I have great respect for, called me. Michael told me: "No one will ever use any other ballroom." We spoke and he told me I had bought one of his favourite places in Doonbeg.'[5]

Of all things, Trump's first move was to build a wall. If he subsequently wanted one along the Mexican border to keep immigrants out of the US, in Ireland he sought a 2.8-kilometre-long, 4.5-metre-high coastal wall on the public beach adjoining the golf course to keep water, not people, out. The planning application contained a reference to the erosion effects of climate change on the coastline, which some mocked because Trump was already a well-known global warming denier. Trump said problems had been caused because the famous golfer and course designer Greg Norman 'had not been allowed to use the right land', implying that Trump expected concessions to be made in return

5   The ballroom remains unbuilt at the time of writing.

for his investment, especially as he assumed all the politicians would be compliant to his wishes.

But environmentalists fought him and the planning authorities took their side. Trump was forced to compromise. What was built was a more modest barrier involving steel piles driven into the ground, with a protective barrier of limestone boulders at the base, as part of a €5 million investment in improving the course. Trump was more successful in joining others to block the construction of a wind farm in the area.

The property now trades under the Trump International Golf Links and Hotel Ireland banner. Trump visited as US President in 2019 and again in May 2023. He had promised to invest €45 million in total, including the original purchase price, but not surprisingly is believed to have come up somewhat short. While he is widely unpopular in Ireland, that does not apply at Doonbeg, where the locals are happy that his popularity with some Americans and Russians has brought added custom to the property.

Trump now claims the estate to be worth far more than when he bought it, although it has accumulated large losses under his management: in a 2023 disclosure of income and assets, required in the US, he attributed it a value of between €22.7 million and €45.5 million. He told reporters during a May 2023 visit that 'It's called Doonbeg on the Ocean. It's not a new name, but we're adding the word "ocean". Because I said to myself, "It's on the ocean, if it's on the ocean, we call it Doonbeg on the Ocean, we have the ocean, and nobody else does, so that's what we're calling it". He said the name Trump would also remain on the property; an attraction to some, a repellent to others. Environmental campaigners remained wary of him: Friends of the Irish Environment (FIE) brought legal proceedings against sand trap fencing allegedly constructed at Doonbeg during 2022.

The need for buyers of hotels was common across the country. Just as Ireland was building 90,000 new houses in the mid-part of the century's first decade, it was also building hotels all over the country in both urban and rural areas. There were some budget hotels and some family ones in rural areas, but there was also a rush to luxury. If golf courses were not included in 'the estate', there were likely to be luxury spas offering expensive treatments to the newly flush-with-cash Irish as well as to the overseas tourists. Banks were eager to supply loans to finance acquisition and construction, partly because the apparent financial returns were skewed by the provision of capital allowance tax incentives. In 2006 there were 51 hotels opened, the highest number in one year. Local authorities eagerly granted permissions, almost irrespective of the location, looking for money from development levies and ongoing rates. Locals were happy about the jobs. AIB was joined by Bank of Scotland (Ireland) and Ulster Bank in pumping out money to developers. But the reality was that too many hotels had been built for tax breaks in locations where they could not run businesses efficiently without those concessions.

In 2008, hotel construction stopped as suddenly as house building. The capital values attributed to existing hotel properties collapsed. As Irish people couldn't afford their weekend breaks and foreigners came in smaller numbers, many operators couldn't generate the revenue they needed to cover day-to-day running costs, let alone the interest bills on money borrowed for either the purchase or construction of the hotels. NAMA, by default, ended up as the country's biggest hotel operator and looked to sell as many as it could as quickly as possible, to whoever would buy, just as the foreign-owned banks were doing the same.

By 2012 more than 100 hotels nationwide – out of a total then of about 900 – had either gone into receivership or closed and there was a particular fear that 2013 would see many more fail. It was reckoned that the value of hotels in the sector had fallen by about 60 per cent from the peak. There was a desperation to sell rather than allow corporate versions of the housing ghost estates to blot the landscape and carefully manicured gardens and estates return to the wild. It meant that almost any buyer would be facilitated, if they had money, with few or no questions asked as to the source of that money.

CASTLEMARTYR RESORT

Two of Cork's major hotels went into Chinese ownership. As well as visiting Ballyfin, Kanye West and Kim Kardashian also spent part of their honeymoon at the Castlemartyr Resort, a 220-acre resort about 20 miles east of Cork city, a hotel and golf club that has also hosted Bill Clinton and Bruce Springsteen. When the resort opened at the tail end of the Celtic Tiger boom it was marketed as Ireland's first six-star hotel. It was a seventeenth-century manor house – previously operated as a boarding school by the Carmelite nuns – renovated and extended by Barry Supple, with a golf course and clubhouse added in a €70 million project. The original house was converted into 11 luxury suites and a 60-seater fine-dining restaurant. The chapel was deconsecrated and turned into a cocktail bar. The building was extended to give a total of 109 luxury bedrooms and suites, and connected to a glass-fronted contemporary wing that includes a spa, fitness centre, a 20-metre swimming pool, a ballroom and conference facilities. Supple was one of the first casualties of the property downturn and his business went into liquidation in 2012. A Chinese businessman, Zhenxin Zhang, became the majority shareholder, buying it from NAMA for €14 million, less than a fifth of the Supple investment.

FOTA ISLAND RESORT

Fota Island Resort was another trophy golf resort to come under Chinese ownership. It had been developed by the Fleming Group in 2006 after Cork builder John Fleming purchased the original Fota golf course in 2004 from the Killeen Group, owned by the Mahony family, the Toyota car distributors. Using 500 acres on the island just outside Cork city, shared with Fota Wildlife Park, Fleming added two more golf courses to the original course which had hosted the Irish Open in both 2001 and 2002. The group also built the 131-bedroom five-star hotel complete with a state-of-the-art leisure centre and spa and 54 holiday lodges, with planning for another 160. It all cost more than €90 million. Fleming was bankrupted during the crash and NAMA sold the resort to Chinese investors, the Beijing-based Kang family, for just €20 million. The Kangs also bought the Kingsley Hotel on the Carrigrohane Straight in Cork City, opposite the County Hall, even though it was built on a floodplain and had seriously flooded in November 2009 when the opening of the ESB dam at Inniscarra contributed to a near-disastrous flood of Cork city centre. Reinstatement of the building took nearly five years.

NUREMORE HOTEL

A Chinese national, Kai Dai, took control of the Nuremore Hotel in County Monaghan. A landmark venue in Carrickmacross, the Nuremore Hotel was the centre of much of the area's social life. Kai Dai was one of Ireland's biggest cash-for-visa brokers; he is believed to have raised around €50 million through a scheme described later in this book. His LinkedIn profile claims the Huawen Foundation has been operating in Ireland since 2014, founded under Central Bank of Ireland regulation to facilitate inward investment from China to Ireland. It says that his main company, Kylin Prime Group, has been a Swiss resident since 2017. His website describes him as a 'serial entrepreneur' and while it boasts a University of Cambridge qualification, is sketchy on his origins.

However, the Nuremore Hotel, controlled by his Huawen Foundation, shut suddenly early in 2023 and was quickly vandalised. In late March 2023, a provisional liquidator was placed over Huawen after a court heard that Kai Dai was a 'shadowy figure' who might 'engage in manoeuvres' to place the Nuremore Hotel 'outside the reach of creditors'. The petition was taken by Yan Wang, a Chinese investor who had subscribed for €1 million in loan notes through Dai's company. The provisional liquidator provided a report to the High Court that showed over €85 million had gone into and out of the company's bank accounts over ten years, but that only €39 was left in them. The report found that recipients of over €66 million in transfers appeared to be five companies connected to Dai either through directorship or shareholding, as well as €1.7 million to Dai himself. The financial statements disclosed that some of the payments were made for 'professional consultancy fees'. The liquidation of the company was confirmed.

MORRISON HOTEL

In 2012, when Elena Baturina bought the Morrison Hotel in Dublin, few in NAMA seemed too worried about the sources of her wealth as long as she supplied the €22 million asking price. Coming up with the cash wasn't considered a problem: her wealth was estimated at €1 billion, even after the collapse of the financial markets in previous years. But the source of her wealth had long been an issue for conversation among envious and suspicious Russians. Her husband was Yuri Luzhkov, mayor of Moscow from 1992 until 2010 when he was sacked by Vladimir Putin amid accusations of corruption. Luzhkov responded that these accusations were politically motivated. Baturina fled Russia in 2010 with their two daughters; Luzhkov cited fears for his family's safety as the reason for their departure.

As mayor of Moscow, Luzhkov controlled the budgets for the modernisation of the Russian capital after its dour Soviet period. There was a construction boom as skyscrapers were built, enormous new ring roads were put in place and historical buildings were bulldozed. Luzhkov was dogged by allegations of corruption over city construction contracts and he acted in autocratic fashion: he described gay pride parades as 'satanic', banned opposition rallies, pushed to have a statue of the founder of Russia's secret police restored, and planned to honour Stalin during Moscow's Victory Day parade.

His wife, who graduated from the Moscow Management Institute, apparently built her fortune from a plastics factory making buckets. She parlayed that into Inteco, Moscow's biggest construction and real estate empire. In 1995 the concession for the building of the Luzhniki, Moscow's largest stadium, just happened to be granted to Inteco. In 2004 Inteco got the licence to build Grand Park, a luxury complex of apartments on the outskirts of Moscow. Baturina denied her marriage to Luzhkov boosted her business career. She sold the business in 2011 and does not seem to have been back to Russia since, living in London and Vienna. Her husband died in Germany in 2019.

The Morrison was the first hotel asset sold by NAMA. Conceived by the famous Irish clothes designer John Rocha, the stylish and modern building with 145 bedrooms was built by the late publican Hugh O'Regan in 1999. When it opened it charged what was then a headline-grabbing €200 per night for a room. However, O'Regan over-expanded his business empire and became highly indebted. Weighed down by those debts and the loss of private assets, O'Regan died tragically in November 2012.

Baturina got the property at what turned out to be a bargain price, just over €159,000 per bedroom. She invested about €10 million in a revamp. She would be able to sell it a decade later for €65 million to a UK venture capital company, Zetland, after taking many multi-million-euro dividend payments over the decade. No questions were asked on the way in, and none on the way out. These were the very definitions of transactional relationships; it was the level to which the impact of the crash had reduced our expectations as to what we would do with much of what stood on our land. We simply traded it and if sometimes we got good new owners, then maybe we were lucky. But sometimes we weren't.

FIVE

A LITTLE LOCAL MONEY IN THE MIX

Ireland has an almost schizophrenic relationship with some of its most famous billionaires. There can be a degree of fawning, a bowing down to great wealth, access to government arriving easily and praise from the aspirational and somewhat less wealthy readily forthcoming. Others are more suspicious about the sources of the wealth and the means of accumulating it, and, in what is often a major topic for discussion, the payment of taxes upon it. Many of our billionaires live part-time in Ireland but reside in other tax-friendly jurisdictions where they can legally limit the proportion of their annual incomes and wealth that is taxed.

That said, the purchase and sale of property and land in Ireland is taxed with stamp duties and capital acquisition and gains taxes, irrespective of where ownership of the property is held. However, there are ways and means of getting around that, with the use of specially established vehicles to hold ownership of assets and of loans rather than equity to exercise control. The billionaires are able to afford the best financial and legal advice to accomplish that.

Even after the Great Recession, the assumption remained that certain Irish individuals continued to be billionaires, despite making investments that had fallen in ascribed value. Many of these men – it is almost always men – had property in their portfolios, but not a reckless proportion of it. The richer these men were, the less likely they were to have offered personal guarantees about the repayment of debt, keeping their liabilities limited to the companies they owned. Debts on a property would not have to be covered by the sale of other assets. This meant that when the time came, and property assets were available cheaply, they either had the cash or the backing of banks to allow them to pounce and make a killing.

Five prominent Irish billionaires stick out as among the most prominent opportunists in the aftermath of the crash: JP McManus, John Magnier, Michael O'Leary, Denis O'Brien and Larry Goodman. They were assumed billionaires who signed sizeable cheques to buy property or businesses based on property in the era when almost everything was available for sale.

JP MCMANUS

McManus, a Swiss resident, built Ireland's biggest and most expensive house during the boom, although it was his wife Noreen who lived more of the year at Martinstown Stud in Kilmallock, County Limerick. Built in a faux-Palladian style, and designed by the Swiss architect Andre Durr, it is estimated to have cost about €100 million to put the house and gardens in place.

But it was an old castle nearby to which McManus turned in the aftermath of the crash: Adare Manor. Since the twelfth century, there has been a succession of large castles on the site on which the current Adare Manor stands. In the mid-nineteenth century, the second Earl of Dunraven decided to rework the existing classic Georgian mansion in the style of a Tudor Revival manor and that is the base of what stands over the River Maigue today. While many in the area starved during the Famine, a fortunate few got work building this enormous residence. More than a century later, in the late 1980s, Tom Kane, an American former Wall Street executive and fighter pilot from the Vietnam era, bought it and converted it into a 62-bedroom hotel with a golf course attached. Kane struggled financially to cover its operating costs, despite help from McManus's close associate Dermot Desmond, a multi-millionaire, and another American, Ken Langone, the founder of the Home Depot chain of DIY stores.

McManus paid about €30 million in 2015 to take possession of the 842-acre estate. He is believed to have spent anywhere up to another €100 million subsequently, over a period of 18 months, to conduct a major restoration and reconstruction with over 800 builders and trades-people involved. A new wing in replica grey limestone with 42 additional bedrooms was added, linked to the original building by a colonnade. He also added two three-bedroom garden cottages, eight lodges and a new golf course with a clubhouse.

It was the main hotel where the bulk of the work was done, down to repairing or replacing every single roof tile, cleaning, polishing or replac-ing every individual carving and employing specialist conservationists to renew each nineteenth-century leaded window. Air-conditioning was installed throughout and new curtains and carpets were specially commissioned, with the curtains in the lobby area at least 30 feet in height. All of the previous furniture and fittings were sold and replaced with antiques sourced in the UK and US. The bedrooms were supplied with king- or super-king-sized beds that require two staff to make up because of their size and the weight of the 300-thread count Garnier Thiebaut French sheets. A new ballroom was constructed to take up to 350 people, with a high gold-leaf ceiling and gold-topped columns. There is a gym, swimming pool and a 28-seat cinema. The formal Oak Leaf restaurant won a Michelin star in 2020. Afternoon tea and break-fast are served in the Gallery, the second longest room in Ireland after Trinity College's Long Room. Its vast vaulted room holds wood carvings, antique tapestries, three massive fireplaces and stained-glass windows. There are over 60 chefs employed in the hotel and nearly 600 staff at peak times. Activities on offer include trout fishing, falconry, archery and clay pigeon shooting. And golf, of course.

The golf course was revamped dramatically by famous designer Tom Fazio to bring it up to the required championship standards. About 4,000 trees were removed as part of the permit approval process, all replaced by new trees in other parts of the estate. There were 220,000 tonnes of sand brought into the 170 acres which make up the golf course, laid to a depth of 12 inches on the greens and 9 inches on the fairways. Behind every green, there is space to take grandstands, a conduit to lay fibre on the entire course and a road network to allow for movement for television trucks and everything else needed for a major event. This is where golf's Ryder Cup will be held in 2027 … and the State has committed €50 million towards the staging costs. However, long-standing local members have been shocked by sharp increases in annual membership fees, reaching €15,000 per head in 2023. Non-members must also book into the expensive hotel if they want to play a round. The most basic package starts at €1,250 for a night but suites can cost five times that.

The political deference to McManus has always been a subject of some interest, especially as the source of much of his wealth is shrouded in mystery. McManus has not paid income tax or capital gains tax in Ireland since 1995, according to a letter provided by the Revenue Commissioners to a court case in the USA in 2017. However, the McManus Charitable Foundation is estimated to have raised more than €100 million for local causes. Some of the funding of the charity appears to come from pre-tax income from property interests in the UK; the transfer of the money reduces the tax paid there. Cystic fibrosis and mental health care have benefited from the beneficence, as have cancer clinics and youth services. Nobody knows, however, how his largesse to charities compares with the amount of tax he has avoided in Ireland legally by basing his place of residence in Switzerland.

JOHN MAGNIER

McManus' closest friend and business associate, John Magnier, who is also a Swiss resident, is probably Ireland's largest owner of agricultural land. At the start of this century, Coolmore Stud was known to cover about 7,000 acres of prime farmland, extending from Fethard in south Tipperary across the Golden Vale into north Cork and the Castlehyde Stud in Fermoy. Within the last two decades, its ownership of farmland in the area is understood to have increased substantially.

Coolmore Stud is a remarkable enterprise, a genuine Irish world leader albeit in a rarefied and exclusive industry: thoroughbred horse breeding. It has been valued at over €4 billion in the racing press. Formed in the early 1970s by Magnier (born in 1948), his father-in-law Vincent O'Brien (deceased but regarded as the greatest racehorse trainer of the twentieth century) and English multi-millionaire Robert Sangster (also now deceased), the trio had the idea of having a centre where retired successful racehorses were sent to stud, 'covering' mares to produce foals that had the potential to be the next generation of successful racehorses. They would either own the mares themselves, or sell the offspring to others, or they would provide the service to other mare owners.

When I visited nearly two decades ago I found a centre developed like a five-star hotel for horses. It is beautiful, full of sculptured grazing paddocks, carefully clipped hedges that act as shelter belts from the elements as well as keeping expensive horses apart at those times when they are not wanted together, well-kept private roads and modern stables. In the busy months, there can be as many as 900 mares present to be 'covered'. Conventional farming also takes place, both beef production and tillage farming. There are about 1,000 people employed in Ireland.

Coolmore itself – and other offshoots in Australia and Kentucky in the US – is now owned by Linley Investments, an Isle of Man-based company set up by Magnier. Supporters of the enterprise highlight that it is not dependent on foreign ownership or the grants available to foreign enterprises located here. It no longer enjoys tax exemptions on income that it once enjoyed, to some controversy. Profits from Coolmore have financed expansion into other areas of business and speculation, almost always in conjunction with McManus. Magnier, who spent a brief period as a Senator appointed when Charles Haughey was Taoiseach, is a tax resident abroad now, with homes valued in the tens of millions of euro each in Geneva, Marbella and Barbados, where he is co-owner with McManus of the Sandy Lane Hotel, as well as in Tipperary. He is a prominent art collector, with a portfolio believed to be valued in the hundreds of millions of euro, primarily eighteenth-century British paintings, twentieth-century Irish art, equestrian art and modern art.

Coolmore is believed to have approached many farmers in the area when they were nearing retirement age or facing financial difficulties with offers for private treaty sales. It has also been active in securing land at auction, concentrating on buying old country houses and estates. It is known that two of Magnier's children bought Bengurragh House and 110 acres, of which 22 acres were advertised as suitable for development, on the outskirts of Cahir, County Tipperary in 2018 for €720,000. Annesgift House, another eighteenth-century historic house is owned by another adult child. Coolmore has also taken possession of and redeveloped the landmark Cashel Palace Hotel, which closed in 2014. The 1730s Palladian building was built originally by Church of Ireland Archbishop of Cashel Theophilus Bolton as his private residence. It has been revamped into a very expensive high-end hotel. Meanwhile, in nearby Fethard the ancient almshouse has been redeveloped into a museum. The plaque on the wall notes that the building was saved 'by the people of Fethard with help from South Tipperary County Council, Tipperary Leader, the Heritage Council of Ireland, Fáilte Ireland and, of course, John Magnier, Principal of Coolmore Stud'.

MICHAEL O'LEARY

Ryanair chief executive Michael O'Leary, believed to be a billionaire because of his 4 per cent shareholding in the airline and extensive property interests at home and abroad, may have become well-known for his successful National Hunt horse-racing ventures but he has also expanded his basic farming interests dramatically. Starting from his Gigginstown House farm in Mullingar, he has expanded and assembled agricultural lands around County Westmeath estimated at 2,200 acres in size. His farms are broken into different units in the midlands, with Fennor Farm, in County Westmeath, acting as home to the Gigginstown Angus herd. Locals say that his agents are active in buying whatever land becomes available and in asking farmers if they are interested in selling. O'Leary has remained a tax resident in Ireland, unlike many of Ireland's other richest people.

DENIS O'BRIEN

O'Leary became chief executive at Ryanair after a stint as personal assistant to Tony Ryan, the founder of both the airline and aircraft leasing firm GPA. O'Leary's predecessor in that role was Denis O'Brien. He is one of those who pays his personal tax outside of Ireland, in Malta. He was previously resident in Portugal at the time of selling mobile phone company Esat Telecom in 2000 for a personal windfall of €250 million, which he parlayed into a much bigger fortune with the creation of the Digicel company in the Caribbean.[6]

His original winning of the Esat licence has become shrouded in controversy and was the subject of a public tribunal of inquiry. The findings, always disputed publicly by O'Brien but not challenged legally, were that Minister for Communications Michael Lowry had 'secured the winning' of the mobile phone licence competition for O'Brien's Esat Digifone and that O'Brien had made two payments to Lowry, in 1998 and 1999, totalling about £500,000, and had supported a loan of stg£420,000 given to Lowry in 1999.

Controversy would continue to follow O'Brien. He became embroiled in a battle for control of Independent News and Media,

---

6   He lost control of Digicel in 2023 after surrendering the majority of its equity
     to debt-holders in a restructuring. It was estimated, however, that he had taken
     about $2 billion from the business prior to that.

Ireland's biggest media company and lost an estimated €500 million by buying overpriced shares even as the financially-troubled company benefited from a major debt write-down from its bankers to save it. But even though nursing such an enormous loss – and having sizeable debts as well as assets – O'Brien was looking to buy, and property was among his desires.

O'Brien had been a regular investor in Irish property since the 1990s. He owned several buildings in the Grand Canal Basin area of Dublin, including the Malthouse, and had traded in property at the IFSC. He was always prepared to wait before embarking on the development of assets – and had the financial resources to be patient. He purchased Canada House, at the junction of St Stephen's Green and Earlsfort Terrace in Dublin 2, in 2001 for around €22 million. In 2005 Dublin City Council granted permission for the building to be demolished and replaced with a nine-storey building that would have included three floors of luxury apartments. That development never took place. O'Brien reapplied for the construction of a seven-storey building of over 7,500 square metres. In the meantime, the site became vacant and derelict and known as a location for homeless people and addicts to congregate.

O'Brien was among the first to spot the potential recovery in the demand for office space and engaged Bernard McNamara, returning from bankruptcy in the UK, to conduct the reconstruction of Canada House at an estimated cost of about €30 million. Even after carrying the costs of years of vacancy, he was reckoned to have turned a major profit on the development, as it was purchased for over €85 million by the global French investment fund CNP Assurance. It installed the world's largest aircraft leasing company, AerCap, as its tenant.

One of O'Brien's first purchases after the crash was Ballynahinch Castle, a hotel in Galway, for which he paid €6.5 million in 2013 and then refurbished. He also took control of facilities company Siteserv at a cost of €45 million, buying its debt from IBRC at a hefty discount, leading to a commission of inquiry (which eventually found that he did nothing wrong in securing control of the company, even if others faced further legal issues). Less commented upon, because the seller of the debt was Ulster Bank and not the State, O'Brien also did the same at the Beacon Private Hospital in Sandyford, Dublin, buying the €207.5 million debt and – in a loan-to-own move – ousting the American operators, the University of Pittsburgh Medical Centre (UPMC), by calling for immediate repayment of its debts. To its fury, UPMC was left to sell its equity ownership for a nominal amount.

Subsequently, O'Brien moved the tax residency of a company that owned the debt of the hospital in 2016. Up until then, O'Brien had used Ragazza, a section 110 company, to house the hospital's debt. The section 110 vehicle earned €6.7 million in interest payments from the loans in 2015 but paid just €250 tax. It had been able to write off all but €1,000 as expenses. In 2016, the government shut that loophole, so O'Brien moved the tax residency of the company to Luxembourg, removing two of his Irish executives as directors and appointing two Luxembourg-based financial advisors instead, so it could be said that the company was managed and controlled from there.

LARRY GOODMAN

Luxembourg has also featured prominently in the tax arrangements employed by Larry Goodman. Although the so-called Beef Baron, who controls a large chunk of the agricultural industry in Ireland and beyond, remains personally tax resident in Ireland, his business has placed many of its assets in Luxembourg to benefit from its tax treatments, adding greatly to his wealth and reducing what is paid in tax in Ireland.

Goodman was one of the most high-profile and controversial figures in twentieth-century Irish business. His trading methods and political lobbying made him the centre of a special tribunal of inquiry. He was something of a reckless gambler in the late 1980s, speculatively and misguidedly investing in two major UK stock market-quoted food companies. Things really went badly wrong for him when Iraq reneged on payment for delivery of £180 million worth of beef. The government had to introduce special legislation to allow for a mechanism to protect his company from collapse. He was allowed to keep part of the business but had to sell his other assets, including a portfolio of commercial property. In the years that followed, and after he regained ownership of his beef business, Goodman bought back every piece of property he had been forced to sell. After the crash, he moved to expand that portfolio again.

The most prominent of his purchases was the old Bank of Ireland headquarters on Baggot Street in Dublin 2. It had been purchased in 2006 for €212 million by a consortium of wealthy developers led by Derek Quinlan and Paddy Shovlin, both later bankrupted, and hotelier brothers Anthony and Patrick Fitzpatrick. Their redevelopment plans were disrupted, first by a planning refusal, then by DCC's designation of the complex as a protected structure, and finally by their own financial destruction. Goodman was able to buy the property in 2013 for a reported €40 million. He got a modernist office complex over three blocks that had been constructed in two phases between 1968 and 1978. The Record of Protected Structures focuses on protecting the city's Georgian and Victorian architecture and only includes buildings of the late twentieth century if they are considered 'exceptional'. The façades of the building and plaza were added to the record in 2010 because it was judged to be 'Dublin's finest example of the restrained and elegant Miesian style' by DCC's conservation department. Goodman invested an estimated €100 million in refurbishing both the exterior and interiors and renamed the 219,000 square foot property as Miesian Plaza. He let most of the space to the Department of Health: the building became one of Ireland's most recognised during the Covid crisis as the location for daily press briefings. It's likely many people watching believed the epicentre of the Covid response to be located at a building owned by the State, but, like so much else, it was in private hands with our State as the tenant.

SIX

THE RETURN OF THE COMERS

The five men listed in the previous chapter weren't the only assumed billionaires to invest in property in Ireland in the aftermath of the Great Recession. There were two brothers, not particularly well-known, who spent even more in purchasing property from 2011 onwards. They now own land in Ireland that has an attributed value on the accounts of their companies of over €1.1 billion, bought for a fraction of that.

Luke and Brian Comer, born in 1957 and 1960, were two of eight children who grew up in Glenamaddy, County Galway. They trained as plasterers and set up their own business as young men, working for some of the most successful developers of the era, including Ken Rohan. They left for London in 1984 when work in Ireland was in short supply during yet another recession. They gathered cash and after Brian nearly died in a car crash in 1992, which left him in a coma for four weeks, they began a well-timed acquisition spree in the fast-growing British economy, largely funded by Bank of Ireland, that included building apartment blocks for rent, office and business parks, health clubs and retail units. In 2005 they headed for Germany and spent about €350 million on a portfolio that included the landmark Berlin office tower Die Pyramide. Some of the money was borrowed from Anglo-Irish Bank. They did so well that the brothers became tax residents in Monaco, although Brian had a home in Hertfordshire in the south of England with its own private nine-hole golf course. Luke's sons, Luke junior and Barry, stayed in Ireland to manage the business here.

They did not escape the crash completely unscathed. Three companies behind Royal Connaught Park, an upmarket residential development in Hertfordshire, went into administration with total debts of stg£167 million. The Comers bought the companies back for stg£71.6 million, leaving Bank of Ireland and others to write off the balance. The rest of the business was unaffected and the Comers were able to avoid entry to NAMA or personal bankruptcy. Instead, a large number of banks and alternative lenders continued to lend them money to assist in a major foray in Ireland.

One of their first purchases was one of the ugliest remaining monuments to the crash, which can still be seen at Sandyford, on the south side of Dublin city, near the M50 motorway. The Sentinel, as the building is known, was to be the centrepiece of the Rockbrook development by Corkman John Fleming, one of the first bankruptcy victims of the crash. It sat on an 11.3-acre site, much of which has been developed since, that Fleming purchased for €245 million in 2006. Five years later the 14-storey shell of the unfinished Sentinel was sold to the Comers for just €850,000.

The Comers also took advantage of the financial demise of another set of brothers from Glenamaddy, Ray and Danny Grehan of Glenkerrin Properties. In 2005, with financial support from AIB and National Irish Bank, the Grehans spent €171.5 million for little more than two acres in Ballsbridge, Dublin 4, on the site of the old University College Dublin (UCD) Veterinary College. They received planning permission for a €600 million, 430,000 square foot development of offices, shops, a leisure centre, restaurants and 87 luxury apartments, buildings ranging from seven to nine storeys in height. But the Grehans were bankrupt by the time permission was obtained. The Comers won a tender to buy the cleared site for €22 million, which they built out as luxury apartments for rent and offices to make a considerable profit.

Probably the cleverest of all their purchases was the unfinished 190,000 square foot, six-storey Beckett Building on East Wall Road, which had been built by Liam Carroll. Receivers sold it to the Comers for just €5 million in 2013. The Comers spent about €30 million fitting it out and then agreed on a 15-year lease with Facebook (now Meta). Only a few years later it sold the building to the South Korean Kookmin Bank for €101 million.

A typically speculative purchase was of 850 acres of mountainous land in Mayo close to existing wind farms, the only potential use for the land. They bought the 63 vacant and unfinished houses of the Glendale estate in Tullow, County Carlow, at a price of just €10,000 each in 2012. They paid €8 million for Milner's Square in Santry in north Dublin, 130 apartments already completed – at an average purchase price of €61,500 – with the potential to add the same number again. The following year they paid €75 million for a portfolio of 640 rental apartments and over 18,000 square metres of retail space in Dublin and Cork. Island Key, near the IFSC, and Orchard Gardens in Cork City each had around 150 apartments, while the much larger Tallaght Cross East development came with most of the commercial space and the 48-bed vacant Glashaus hotel. They also bought Auburn Park, a development of 45 high-end apartments and duplexes near Castleknock in west Dublin that was launched in 2007, for about €6.75 million, or an average of €150,000 per apartment. At launch, the Auburn Park properties were priced from €475,000 for a one-bed apartment up to €750,000 for a three-bed duplex. The 14-storey Falcon's View tower in Blanchardstown in west Dublin was bought for €11.3 million.

The brothers have worked to a maxim: if it cost more to build than the asking price, the risk is minimal. They have been very active in their native Galway: taking control of the Bun na Coille housing estate in Moycullen after developer McInerney had gone bust with only a portion of the planned houses built; finishing Bun na Leaca, a gated estate of 14 townhouses in Galway city; the Silver Seas block of 18 apartments on Cappagh Road; and a block called Howley Square in Oranmore. They also bought a 30-acre site in Roscairn. In Galway city centre they spent about €13 million buying a two-acre site, the Odeon, on the eastern side of Eyre Square, although it was years before they sought to exploit its potential, rebuilding it as One Galway Central. This acquisition was a joint venture with Padraic McHale from Ballinrobe in County Mayo; the McHale family had made its fortune in farm machinery. The Comers entered another joint venture with a local family, the Burkes, to take ownership of the Nox Hotel on the Headford Road.

In 2014 they purchased a 220-acre site between Dublin Airport and the M50 that they have called Metro Park, as it contains the planned location for a future metro station. The Comers unsuccessfully lobbied Fingal County Council in 2016 to remove the prohibition on residential development in the noisiest zone immediately around the airport and to specifically designate an area outside the proposed metro station as suitable to build homes. However, the Comers have continued to talk up their plans, having hired the famous London-based architects Foster & Partners – who designed landmark buildings such as Apple's HQ in California, Berlin's renovated Reichstag, and The Gherkin in London – to create a masterplan for a development that could potentially cost €2 billion. The plan is for about 15.5 million square feet of space with towers of 30 storeys at their highest. Although the government has announced, again in 2022, plans to proceed with the Metro, the economics of what the Comers have proposed would need to be confirmed. In 2017 they put a value on this land of €22.5 million. By 2022 the estimated value, with the Comers having done nothing with the land other than suggest plans, had increased to €53 million, according to registered accounts detailed in the *Business Post*.

The Comers paid about €8 million for the Palmerstown House estate and golf course with 690 acres on the Dublin–Kildare border that had been owned by the late Jim Mansfield. Luke owns Brookfield Stud at Dunboyne in Meath but also bought Castletown Demesne, a Georgian mansion on nearly 450 acres in County Kildare, for €10 million in early 2015. He subsequently announced a plan for house-building for about

140 acres, with the remaining land devoted to a stud farm. Between the various stud farms, it's estimated that he owns about 8,000 acres in Ireland.

The brothers also bought the old Kilternan golf and country club for €6.6 million, on land straddling the Dublin–Wicklow border. It had been the site for an eco-resort planned by the late Hugh O'Regan, who had spent €171 million borrowed from Irish Nationwide on it. While some of the land has been put to use – for activities such as movie productions and grazing horses – redevelopment has been painfully slow, although they now claim a value on the land of €49.2 million. And that is one of the criticisms that has been directed at the Comers. They have said that 'when prices are lower than building costs you won't start building', which seems reasonable, but it meant that dereliction had become an issue for them to address.

One of their more controversial purchases – again with the McHale family – was of the derelict Corrib Great Southern Hotel on the eastern outskirts of Galway City in 2013 for €3.8 million. The hotel had been purchased in 2007 by Gerry Barrett, who had planned a residential development on the seven-acre site. Permission was granted to demolish the building in 2010 but was never acted upon. The old hotel was vandalised and became the site of anti-social behaviour, including arson attacks, but in 2015 a Comer company told Galway City Council of an 'inability to source funding' for the demolition. It would not be until 2022 that clearance of the site began. The group was also criticised for delaying the completion of 80 vacant homes it had purchased at Ballysadare, four miles south of Sligo town.

And then there is the Sentinel, one of their first purchases. More than a decade after they had purchased it, the shell remained standing, unfinished, an ugly testament to the economic crash, a lingering blight on the landscape. There had been multiple planning applications from the Comers for new use and promises that it would be finished, and more were forthcoming in 2023 with talk again of building 102 apartments now that new planning permission had been obtained. But, at the time of writing, it remains unlovely and unloved, a visual insult to all of us. There can be no more excuses, though, as early in 2023 the Comers purchased the adjacent Rockfield residential development site from I-RES, for an undisclosed amount, and indicated a commitment to building 428 apartments there. However, there was no cost to the Comers in doing nothing with the Sentinel for over a decade, in wasting what could have been something of use at a time of need. Indeed, there may well be a reward for them as the economics of the previous decade have contributed, without them having to do anything, to an increase in the value of this piece of dereliction. What they bought for €850,000 they now value at €4.5 million before any work has even started on it.

PART 3

OWNING THE CONSEQUENCES

In early 2020 IDA Ireland introduced a Special Recognition Award to 'recognise the contribution of our clients to Ireland'. The first was presented by Taoiseach Leo Varadkar and IDA Ireland to Apple and was accepted by Tim Cook, the company's CEO, at a special 'Looking to the Future' event in the National Concert Hall in January of that year. Presentation of the second award was delayed until 2022 because of Covid when Varadkar, now Tánaiste, travelled with IDA executives to California to present it to Alphabet (the parent company of Google) CEO Sundar Pichai at a 'Building the Future Together' event. There are a couple of ways of looking at this type of gesture: one is that it is the ultimate in sucking up to entities on which we have become dependent; another is that it is a very pragmatic and appropriate way of maintaining mutually beneficial relationships that we want to protect. But does it mean that Ireland is, in a way, 'owned' by its multinational residents, that they hold an inequitable and unsuitable amount of power?

SEVEN

TAKE A BITE OF THE APPLE
... OR NOT

One of the big issues at the intersection of twenty-first-century global politics and economics is the balance of power in the relationship between gigantic multinational corporations and governments of various sizes.

Many believe that the burden of paying taxes falls too heavily on ordinary individuals, while corporate entities are charged at lesser rates and then do everything possible to reduce their payments further. It is seemingly human nature to want to pay as little tax as possible, to regard it as a burden, as something that is a necessary contribution but that others should pay. Most individuals, unless wealthy enough to move their domicile or afford the services of advisors who know where they can avail of loopholes in the laws, pay whatever they are levied wherever they live. Corporations, however, or at least the really big international ones, can deliberately minimise their tax payments in a way that is characterised as avoidance, which is legal, rather than evasion, which is not.

The European Commission (EC) tried to go to war with the corporate giants in the mid-2010s, the shape-shifters who shuffled sales revenues and profits around the globe in a complex web that few were able or had the resources to track. The international tax system was complicated but some individual countries were reluctant to participate in reform: they benefited more than others from their part in the complexity, setting their own rates as a claim of sovereignty, doing deals to facilitate the movement of international capital, taking part of the riches in return.

In 2016 the EC took action and Ireland found itself in the unusual position of being offered the opportunity to pick up a very useful €14.3 billion cash bonus that it decided it didn't want. The EC found, after investigation and a legal process, that Apple – one of the world's richest companies – had underpaid its corporate taxes over a number of years because of a special sweetheart deal with the Irish State going back to the twentieth century. This, the EC said, was contrary to EU laws and it ordered the Irish government to get the revenue commissioners to collect the money it said was owed.

Apple appeared to serve as a test case, a quasi-proxy for the multinational sector as a whole. If the EC was to enforce the tax demand successfully, it could then go after many other companies, with a precedent set. It was almost ironic that a country that proudly declared its military neutrality picked one side so firmly in what is effectively an economic war – and, in doing so, picked the side of which it is not part. Ireland aligned itself firmly with Apple, even though we are a member state of the European Union that the Commission represents.

Cue an enormous domestic political row, with opposition politicians on the left demanding that the State take the money – more than a year's entire corporation tax take at the time – and spend it. The allegation was that not doing so would constitute, among other things, national supplication to the power of the American corporate sector. It was argued too that Apple had enough cash to clear the entire existing national debt of our government, that it wouldn't miss this chump change. That wasn't how Apple would have seen it. Apple is ruthless in its chase for profit and has reviewed its commitment to Ireland, where it employs more than 6,000 people, on occasion because of our rising operating costs. It is believed that the influence of Cork woman Cathy Kearney, the vice president in charge of European operations, has been central to keeping the company rooted in Ireland in the twenty-first century.

The government's dilemma was multi-fold: it worried about the potential loss of Apple as an employer and also, ironically, as a major tax-payer, but was also conscious that other American firms might look askance at a perceived loss of Ireland's reliability as a stable and safe environment in which to do business. Should Apple decide to head for the exit door, then others might follow.

Apple didn't threaten that publicly. 'We now find ourselves in the unusual position of being ordered to retroactively pay additional taxes to a government that says we don't owe them any more than we've already paid,' said Tim Cook, successor to the late Steve Jobs as chief executive, when he went on RTÉ Radio One in the aftermath of the decision. He used a marriage analogy to reassure everyone of mutual commitment, with no prospect of a divorce initiated by Apple. But that didn't make the arrangement one of equals. Apple held all of the power, as it had the runaway money. It was bound by the domestic laws, not just in relation to tax but employment, but its ability to leave at a low cost relative to its enormous reserves meant that the Irish government was constrained in its ability to exercise its own sovereign rights and take this money.

Therefore, when Apple legally appealed the EC decision, the Irish government supported the American multinational, denying any special state aid was given to Apple contrary to EU laws. The government decision was recommended by IDA Ireland and supported by Fianna Fáil, then in opposition, and not just because it had been in government when Apple had arrived in Cork in 1980 for its first manufacturing facility outside of the US.

It was a pragmatic calculation. Foreign multinational companies employed 250,000 people in Ireland at the time (and many more since). They may have paid less corporation tax than many would have liked, but they still stumped up an enormous amount, which continued to grow dramatically every year after that. By 2023 the annual corporation tax was running at over €24 billion and was the basis for projected government surpluses in coming years that would be essential to the financing of all sorts of spending. They contributed payroll taxes and PAYE from the many (mostly) highly paid workers they employed. They also formed trading relationships with many Irish companies, supporting hundreds of thousands of jobs. A broken Ireland had recovered after the Great Recession because of their presence – and more and more of them came to contribute jobs and taxes as the IDA successfully mounted a campaign to bring more of them here. To have taken this particular money from Apple would have been short-sighted, as a subsequent boom in corporate tax revenues and employment numbers proved.

Maybe we were too hard on ourselves, too sensitive to the criticism from abroad, and offered by some politicians at home, that we had become a 'tax haven', too concerned that it does us reputational damage. A tax haven is a pejorative term, but such an entity is often prized more for its secrecy than its attractive tax rates. Whatever else it is, Ireland is transparent in what it offers. It might better be described as a 'facilitator' for international tax planning. The publicity has never stopped new multinationals from locating in this country; indeed, it may have attracted many. The EC admitted that the Apple case 'does not call into question Ireland's general tax system or its corporate tax rate'.

It didn't mean that Apple got everything that it wanted, however, because some things were beyond the power of the government to gift, no matter how much it wanted to help. Apple gave up on one major Irish expansion, at Athenry in County Galway, essentially because of delays caused by the opposition of just three people, only two of whom were subsequently found to be exercising their legal rights appropriately.

In February 2015, Apple announced that it wanted to build a single-storey, hyper-scale data centre extending to almost 265,000 square feet at Derrydonnell, a rural woodland area owned by the State forestry company Coillte, about three miles outside Athenry. The area was bordered by Athenry Golf Club, some small farms and Lisheenkyle primary school. Apple was attracted by the site's size – having the potential for a further seven units in future years – its location near motorways, screening by trees from view and proximity to US-Ireland submarine cables. It wanted the facility to be operational by 2017. It had been assisted by the IDA and Coillte in finding this location, one of 25 it examined over nearly a year. The data centre was budgeted at €850 million and would have been the biggest ever investment made by a multinational west of the River Shannon, employing 150 people when open and 300 during the construction phase.

Apple made its planning application quickly – and in it included a two-kilometre public walkway and a new woodland area. There were 20 observations and objections in total, which included concerns about potential flooding and the impact on bats, badgers and pedigree sheep. One local resident described himself as an avid astronomer and worried that light from the data centre might affect the enjoyment of his hobby. Apple received approval from Galway County Council in September 2015, with 20 conditions attached relating to access and the environment. Eight people appealed this decision to An Bord Pleanála (ABP), which held its own series of public hearings before in turn giving approval in August 2016. Possibly the most significant objection came from resident Allan Daly, an American-born engineer married to a local woman. He raised concerns about power usage, focusing in particular on Apple's ability to power the centre entirely from renewable energy and to adhere to an environmental impact study. ABP found in Apple's favour.

Three objectors, including Daly and solicitor Sinead Fitzpatrick, now sought a judicial review. Apple successfully applied to have the hearing fast-tracked to the Commercial Court and final submissions were made by parties in March 2017, but adjournment after adjournment followed. In the meantime, Apple was building a similar data centre in Northern Denmark – announced on the same day as the Galway investment – which would soon become operational. Its frustrations were growing and weren't helped when Brian McDonagh was identified as one of the objectors.

McDonagh was one of three brothers who had borrowed €22 million in 2007 to buy land in County Wicklow for the construction of a data centre. ABP refused permission and McDonagh fought a legal action that he finally won in 2013, by which stage Ulster Bank was looking for repayment of his debt. Some of the anti-Athenry location campaigners suggested that Apple build at his site instead. Indeed, McDonagh had actually approached Apple on this basis. Mr Justice Paul McDermott decided that McDonagh did not have the legal standing to take the case as he did not live close to the site and had not participated in the planning process. The Judge also admonished McDonagh for not disclosing at an early stage that he was a director and shareholder of Ecologic Data Centre, the Wicklow location, and that he had previously pitched his site to Apple. He accused him of a 'lack of candour in these proceedings'. McDonagh's excuse was that he took the legal action to see if ABP had made a 'mistake' in disallowing his original application but allowing Apple's.

The case taken by Daly and Fitzpatrick went to the Supreme Court where judgment in Apple's favour was delivered in April 2019. But by then Apple had abandoned the project and opted instead for a second data centre in Denmark. Cook said that while his company remained committed to Ireland, 'I would hope that the process can just work faster because businesses need a level of certainty over time. That doesn't mean that every call should be what we want or what any company wants, but the speed of it is key.'

IDA boss Martin Shanahan was measured in his response. 'We need a much higher degree of predictability in relation to our planning processes. Not predictability about outcomes, but definitive timelines that are appropriate for the pace at which the commercial world works,' he said. In June 2021 hopes rose that Apple might be coming back to its original plan. It submitted a fresh application to Galway County Council, seeking a five-year extension to the planning permission it was first awarded in 2016. However, this seems to have been a measure to protect value for the site in the event it might be able to sell it to someone else to develop.

We continue to chase new multinational investment and early 2023 saw much success in the regions, particularly in Limerick, Galway and Cork, where housing for potential employees was more affordable. We do whatever we have to do to facilitate the technology companies, the pharmaceutical giants and financial companies that have put down roots in Ireland. There may be little point in debating the ethics and morality of these actions and in refusing the business if other countries then exploit the opportunity we'd provide to them by refusing the foreign investment. The reality is that our government – indeed almost any government – does not have the strength to act alone against multi-national companies unless all governments act together. This is not an Irish problem, but an international one.

We are not breaking the rules, but the rules themselves are the problem. We have to be pragmatic until the rules change for everyone. There's no point in cutting off the nose to spite the face, which is why we delayed for so long in the international campaign to set a minimum corporation tax rate of 15 per cent, higher than our existing 12.5 per cent rate, one of the lowest internationally. Our low tax rate could be seen as a clever way of giving state aid without breaking the rules. All other EU countries have their own ways to try to take advantage, but they're not necessarily as good at it as we are. But once we were bought, we had to show that we would stay bought.

EIGHT

INTEL INSIDE (BUT NOT IN ONE MAN'S LAND)

If foreign multinational companies were to manufacture in Ireland, particularly in high-value industries such as pharmaceuticals and technology, they would need land. But not everyone was agreeable to the potential use of the land identified, as the State was to discover when it tried to help Intel.

Thomas Reid owns Hedsor House farm, a 72-acre holding adjacent to the giant manufacturing complex owned by Intel, the computer semi-conductor fabricator, at Leixlip in County Kildare. The old stone house in which he resides dates back to the eighteenth century. Reid lives a near-spartan existence, his luxury being a VHS recorder attached to his television on which he watches re-runs of the 1980s American TV show *Dallas*. He spends his day tending to the livestock on his farm and when indoors listens to the radio or reads newspapers, many of which he keeps and which have accumulated in large piles, alongside firewood and used food packaging.

Reid allowed documentary filmmaker Feargal Ward access to his home and land to make a feature-length documentary, *The Lonely Battle of Thomas Reid*, that premiered in 2017. It portrayed a David fighting a Goliath, or rather two Goliaths: Ireland's Industrial Development Authority (IDA) and Intel, the giant US microprocessor manufacturer. The IDA wanted Reid's land for Intel; Reid wanted to stop Intel's expansion in the area.

Reid's grandfather purchased the land and house in the early twentieth century. To Reid, the land is priceless, no matter what money might be offered to him to sell it, probably enough that would make him a millionaire many times over. He doesn't want to live anywhere else. He has refused to even engage in any conversation about money. 'I told people, once you mention money, they have you, so that's what I didn't do,' he said.

The American company pitched up in Ireland in 1989, its arrival being heralded at the time, correctly, as a major inward investment for the State. Here was one of the world's most innovative and valuable companies choosing Ireland as a base outside of the US, promising enormous investment and many highly skilled jobs in manufacturing and research and development. It took possession of a former stud farm over 360 acres. It liked Ireland so much that it built additional manufacturing facilities, first in 1998, and then a massive refit in 2011. The 2014 announcement of a €3.63 billion spend on a three-year upgrade was described as the largest single corporate investment in the history of the State.

In 2017 it received planning permission for a further facility and again in 2021, as its investment in Ireland reached $22 billion. The number of Intel jobs hovered around 5,000 and on many occasions about 1,500 construction workers were on site. Leixlip boomed. Leave the M4 at junction 6 and a continuing house-building boom in the town is obvious; some locals now complain many children of long-standing residents can't afford to buy in the immediate area if they don't have income from Intel.

Intel never approached Reid about buying his land. In December 2011, IDA executives paid Reid a visit, even though his land, just 500m to the west of Intel's campus, was not zoned for development. He rebuffed suggestions that he sell, to the surprise of the IDA people; the body had purchased hundreds of tracts of land over the years all around the country, offering enough money to make any need to go to court to enforce a compulsory purchase order (CPO) redundant. The IDA had assembled sites at Cruiserath, Dublin, Carrigtwohill and Ringaskiddy in Cork, Athenry and Oranmore in Galway, Belview in Kilkenny and Mullagharlin in Louth, a portfolio at the time valued at more than €100 million. In November 2012 the IDA started legal moves for compulsory acquisition on the basis that Reid's land was of absolute strategic importance – but Reid fought back.

Reid lost his case in the High Court in 2013 when Mr Justice John Hedigan found the proposed CPO was provided for by law and was clearly intended to achieve the IDA's objective of encouraging industrial development. The judge also ruled that, in its dealings with Reid, the IDA had adopted every fair procedure possible. Reid appealed to the Supreme Court, where he claimed the IDA's efforts breached his property rights as well as his rights under the Constitution and the European Convention of Human Rights. He argued that if land was to be acquired for no specific immediate use, that could only be done with agreement from the owner. A CPO under the powers of the Industrial Development Act 1986, Section 16, must offer a specific purpose. The IDA submitted that it was sufficient to state simply 'industrial development' and that it was entitled to acquire Reid's lands under the cited section. In an affidavit, former IDA chief executive Barry O'Leary said its 'property solutions' were a 'pivotal component' in winning investment and jobs, 'a key element in the decision-making process undertaken by prospective investors'.

The Supreme Court decided that the IDA had exceeded its power, and that Section 16 did not confer any power on the IDA to acquire lands not required for immediate use but which might be utilised at some future time.

Documentary-maker Feargal Ward said: 'I came to recognise that *Reid* v *The IDA* was not some NIMBY farmer railing against all things modern and obstructing much-needed jobs in the area – this was actually a heroic lone individual attempting to protect the constitutional rights of all citizens on this island in a landmark legal action … What this lonely farmer was vehemently protesting against was the right of a private corporation to remove you from your house and lands because they wanted to – ultimately it was as simple and as alarmingly brutal as just this … His hope remains that farmers will farm his lands into the future, long after his neighbour's factory buildings are abandoned and overgrown with weeds.'

The law was changed as a result of the Supreme Court decision. In February 2018 the government introduced legislation to allow for greater legal certainty for CPOs on land required for industrial use, including in cases of foreign direct investment (FDI). The IDA now had the legal basis for future CPOs if a specific use was identified prior to purchase and the use of the land would be immediate. The IDA has powers now equivalent to the local authorities and An Bord Pleanála (ABP) was given a statutory role to review orders and to adjudicate in cases where they are resisted. No efforts have been made to date to purchase Reid's land; to do so would appear vengeful and almost certainly would result in a further legal dispute.

However, Reid had Intel in his sights. From 2012, he began legal actions each time Intel sought to expand – seven in all, even though none of these expansions infringed on his land. The most significant was a judicial review of an ABP approval in November 2019 for the doubling of manufacturing capacity that was to provide for 1,600 new jobs, an investment costing Intel €3.5 billion. In his judicial review application, Reid claimed the November 2019 decision permitting an extended and revised manufacturing facility was made contrary to EU Council directives, lacked sufficient reasons and was contrary to fair procedures and should be quashed.

Intel argued that the upgrading of the facility was essential in ensuring it remained a key location globally in the production of cutting-edge technology. The Supreme Court, after three days of hearings, agreed with Intel, although it took 18 months to reveal its decision. Construction continues, although there have been doubts about completion at times because of decisions at Intel head office about changing industry requirements and the 2022 tech sector slowdown. Ireland also missed out on a major additional Intel manufacturing complex, the American company opting for Magdeburg in Germany instead, where labour would be cheaper and the German government, with EU approval, was willing to offer enormous cash grants. Concerns about Ireland's ability to supply sufficient energy and water also impacted the decision of one of the country's largest and longest-supporting companies.

Reid, meanwhile, continues to live in his near-isolation, albeit in the shadow of the giant he appears to have come to despise for fear of the impact it might have on him and his chosen way of life. He has protected his personal domain, which makes him a hero to both those who champion the right to personal property and to those who distrust the profit motive of any multinational. But his campaign against Intel's use of other people's land, while unsuccessful, could have impacted enormously on the employment of thousands of people and their livelihoods, as well as on the State's receipt of large tax revenues. This tension and balance between personal rights and the funding of the common good surfaces regularly across the entire country.

NINE

HEADS IN THE CLOUDS: DATA CENTRES

Martin Shanahan, before departing as IDA chief executive late in 2022, warned that any moratorium on the construction of new data centres in the greater Dublin region would threaten Ireland's position as a European tech hub, that they were the essential pieces of infrastructure for the digital age. He believed a statement by Google that any ban on new data centres would send the 'wrong signal' about Ireland's ambitions as a digital economy and render any further investments in its infrastructure in the country 'impossible'.

British energy consultancy firm Baringa estimated that data centre operators invested €10 billion in Ireland over the past decade, while the computer services industry generated €134 billion in exports in 2020, representing 33 per cent of total exports. That produces enormous profits and, in turn, corporation tax receipts. Data centres are national utilities, providing the plumbing which allows the digital economy to operate. It's not just cloud-based IT solutions used by businesses that depend on them but also consumer demand for online services, from social media to e-shopping, to a whole host of entertainment platforms such as Netflix, YouTube and Spotify. It's not just the information and communications technology sector either, because our highly valuable financial services sector and pharmaceutical industry depend heavily on the infrastructure to operate.

We have 'hyperscalers' in Ireland, which are extremely large data centres, bigger than football pitches, and owned by the likes of Google, Amazon Web Services (AWS), Meta and Microsoft. The rest are 'co-location' or 'private' centres, meaning they are smaller sites, usually with multiple companies renting space in them. Geographical proximity to servers is important for the speed at which companies access their data. Location of data is also important for legal protection.

Ireland is regarded as highly suitable for data centres because of our location at the edge of Europe, high-grade fibre optic connectivity with the US and Europe, cheaper cooling systems because of the climate, and the low tax environment. Ireland has overtaken the four FLAP cities (Frankfurt, London, Amsterdam and Paris) as Europe's largest market for data centres; for example, the Dublin metropolitan area accounted for 25 per cent of the overall European industry market share by year-end 2018, compared to 24 per cent in London. More than 90 per cent of all data centres in Ireland are located in the greater Dublin region, with 65 of the facilities in operation close to the capital. Eight more are under construction near Dublin, and a further 37 are at various stages of the planning process but also hope to be located in Dublin.

However, data centres consume more energy in Ireland per year than all the country's rural dwellings combined, representing 14 per cent of all metered electricity consumption nationally. CSO figures show the electricity consumed by data centres increased by 144 per cent between 2015 and 2020. On a global average basis, data centres represent about 1 per cent of electricity demand. The growing volume of electricity demand is projected to outstrip supply and increase the risk of power cuts across Ireland.

EirGrid, the State body in charge of all this, failed to anticipate what was happening and did not secure enough new generation supply to match the power demand that would come from more than 70 data centres. In 2013, EirGrid didn't foresee the level of growth that would materialise; its 10-year capacity forecasts suggested data centre demand would only double by 2022 and would have 'a benign impact on the power system in general'. Energy demand increased five-fold in that period and could triple again by the end of the decade, especially as existing data centre sites have only been using about 30 per cent of their contracted power capacity. It is expected that this will increase sharply. As a result, data centres could constitute about 30 per cent of all electricity demand in the country by 2030.

CONFLICTING DESIRES

Not wanting data centres is a bit like having a mobile phone but not wanting phone masts. But lots of people don't, especially elected politicians at the local level. South Dublin County Council voted to remove data centres as a 'permissible use of land' in the south Dublin area until 2028, with 34 data centres within its council boundary deemed enough. This decision was challenged at the High Court by Irish-owned Echelon, which had received €855 million in contracts to complete four data centres. Similar suggestions were made in Fingal.

The Commission of Regulation of Utilities (CRU) ruled out a moratorium on new data centres, saying the location of future facilities and their ability to generate their own power supplies would need to be assessed on a case-by-case basis. However, the CRU issued a direction on new data centres in the greater Dublin area in November 2022 that led to EirGrid stopping the grant of licences to connect to the grid in the Dublin area until after 2028. 'EirGrid is now applying these criteria to all data centre applicants, many of which have decided not to progress their developments,' a spokesman said. As if that decision by the applicants was made of free choice.

However, it is also true that Dublin's grid infrastructure would be unable to transport power to more data centres than those already approved – regardless of the electricity supply available in the country. Yet developers prefer to locate data centres close to Dublin to avail of key high-speed fibre optic cables to move information. This network is not available in other parts of the country, other than Cork.

EirGrid and the CRU also mandated that any future developments must be built with on-site power generation to minimise their impact on the national grid, something that again is far easier said than done and essentially constituted an outsourcing of EirGrid's responsibility to the private sector.

An Taisce, a non-governmental body that describes itself as the National Trust for Ireland, contended that councils and the appeals board are granting permission for data centres on a case-by-case basis without adequately addressing the cumulative impacts of energy use. It claimed uninhibited development of data centres was diluting the benefits of renewable energy generation, even though it is very obvious that the majority of data centre operators and their clients are doing more than the State to develop clean energy sources. Government policy states that centres must align with the EU Climate Neutral Data Centre Pact, which recommends that all data centres have the ability to generate 1.3 times the energy they use.

It all prompted Leo Varadkar as Tánaiste to declare that Ireland would have to 'slow down the number of new data centres being connected, at least until we can ramp up the generation of renewable energy'. In the interim, 'we'll prioritise those that are linked to major jobs in Ireland, can use renewable energy and are in areas where the grid is strong'.

Instead of introducing a ban, the government published guidelines which included a preference for data centres that can demonstrate 'a clear pathway to decarbonise and ultimately provide net-zero data services', can make efficient use of the energy grid and can demonstrate the 'additionality of their renewable energy use in Ireland'.

Echelon, the Irish data centre developer led by Niall Molloy that is building TikTok's data centres, started judicial review proceedings against Dublin County Council (DCC). It told the High Court that the ban was unreasonable, irrational and breached various constitutional rights. Echelon, which is chaired by the former boss of HP Ireland

Martin Murphy, owns land in Clondalkin and Newcastle, County Dublin, and it claimed the ban was prejudicial to its businesses. This is arguably one of the country's most progressive companies: Echelon and the renewables division of utility SSE have plans for a €50 million power substation in Arklow, County Wicklow, and obtained planning permission for a €500 million, 100 megawatt-capacity data centre at the town's Avoca River industrial park. Echelon and SSE plan not just to plug the data centre into the substation but into the proposed second phase of the Arklow Bank offshore wind farm, providing them with a connection to the national grid.

US company EdgeConneX has built over 50 centres in more than 40 markets and boasts that the five largest businesses in the world by market capitalisation all trust it to provide critical data-centre capacity and facilities. In Dublin, it houses two purpose-built data centres and has bought enough land for five new data centres. It sought judicial review proceedings over the status of its land bank in Dublin. CyrusOne, which is building a new data centre campus near Clondalkin, also lodged a judicial review case against DCC. Seamus Dunne, who operates Interxion/Digital Realty's Irish data centre services, had a €300 million expansion to a data centre in Grange Castle nixed by EirGrid not providing supply, to the fury of some US clients. The company has facilities at Clonshaugh, Grange Castle and Park West business parks and had bought eight acres of land for expansion before the moratorium was introduced.

Vantage Data Centres, a US company that operates data centres in Europe, the Middle East and Africa, has permission for the construction of two data centres. However, DataPlex, an Irish data centre provider that was led by Eddie Kilbane, went into voluntary liquidation in August 2022 because it did not receive power contracts from EirGrid for two sites it had bought in Dublin, at Clonshaugh and Abbotstown. Kilbane had secured €100 million from the Dubai-based Damac Group, the private investment arm of Dubai billionaire Hussain Sajwani, and global infrastructure investor Chirisa Capital Management.

It wasn't as if other arms of the State were against the use of land for data centres. Irish wind farm developer Michael Murnane teamed up with JCD Group (owned by fellow Corkman John Cleary) to form Clonmont Developments, a joint venture with plans to build a 9,250 square metre centre – larger than the pitch at the Aviva – in Clonshaugh Business Park near Dublin Airport. It bought the property from NAMA.

There was a move to locate outside of the greater Dublin region. US operator T5 Data Centres formed a joint venture with JCD Group to develop on a 32.5-acre site in Little Island, County Cork. Meanwhile, Clare County Council aimed to attract Dublin-based firm Art Data Centres to Ennis town following the rezoning of a 126-acre site as an enterprise zone. An Taisce appealed ABP's approval of the €450 million centre and was joined by a coalition of local members of the Green Party, Friends of the Irish Environment and a group called Futureproof Clare. Among their complaints was that the centre would consume too much renewable energy that should be used elsewhere and that it would produce enormous carbon emissions, negating the effects of the savings being demanded of farmers, for example.

It all left the government with an enormous problem: the failure of EirGrid to provide the infrastructure to meet demand meant that carbon reduction targets for 2030 were in danger of being missed, potentially costing the State billions in EU-imposed fines, as well as doing irreparable damage to the environment that would cost future generations. However, those multinationals provide the tax revenues on which the government is dependent to finance the construction of the infrastructure that the multinationals need to make their taxable profits.

THE MULTINATIONALS SEEKING CYBERSPACE

Amazon became one of Ireland's biggest employers and corporation tax contributors as it used the country as a base for European expansion. It has taken large commercial office spaces in Dublin and its fleet of blue electric delivery vans has become increasingly prominent on Ireland's streets and roads, depositing parcels at houses all over the country, often to the horror of conventional retailers who feel they cannot compete with the scale of the offering from the US multinational, its discounted prices and speedy delivery. The vans are serviced from a gigantic new e-commerce warehouse at Baldonnell, highly visible on the road from Kildare to Dublin. Irish sales are small in the overall scheme of things for Amazon, but the company is about fulfilling 'the everything store' role as envisaged by its founder, Jeff Bezos, as its original purpose.

As Amazon developed computer technology to serve its customers it realised that it could sell that expertise to other businesses, and not just in retailing. Amazon, through its Amazon Web Services (AWS) division, has become one of the biggest pioneers of cloud computing, often known by the shorthand of 'the cloud'. This is the on-demand availability of computer system resources, such as data storage and computing power, without direct active management by the user. It is a form of outsourcing. The cloud is not, as some might be led to think, something 'up there' but is a series of connected data centres over multiple locations.

That is what AWS has used Ireland for outside of the US. It accounts for over one-third of all existing and planned data centre capacity in Ireland. It has data centres in operation or under development at 11 locations in Dublin, dotted loosely around the M50 from Clonshaugh to Mulhuddart to Blanchardstown to Tallaght, and further north near Drogheda and into Meath at Clonee. In its most recent planning application, it said that its operations in Ireland sustain 8,700 jobs, including 3,100 direct staff and another 3,900 working for contractors. It claims to have increased its economic output in Ireland by almost €7.5 billion over the decade to the end of 2022 and to have directly invested €4.4 billion over the same period.

It has received permission from various councils for almost every project it has proposed. EirGrid has agreed to provide it with connections wherever necessary on the basis that AWS has committed to take 100 per cent of the power it needs from renewable energy projects. It has signed purchase power agreements (PPAs) with three Irish wind farms in Galway, Donegal and Cork, although estimates suggest these will provide only one-fifth of its needs. It puts solar panels on the rooftops of new data centres, though this is likely to contribute only modestly to the facility's needs. 'Once all projects are operational, we will be the largest single corporate buyer of renewable energy in the country, and we won't stop here,' Amazon has promised.

ABP has been supportive. When it approved a data centre on an IDA business park on the outskirts of Drogheda, it said the new construction would not have a significant impact on climate or legally binding national emission targets for greenhouse gases. This has infuriated objectors such as An Taisce. It has been a particular focus for a lobby group called Not Here Not Anywhere (NHNA), which has claimed that the AWS expansion 'goes against the best interests of the country'. For one proposed Dublin development NHNA said the proposed use of diesel emergency generators would result in fossil fuels being used to power them on occasion. 'If the plant cannot be powered fully by renewable energy, it will lead to an increase in Ireland's greenhouse gas emissions between now and 2030, contravening the Climate Act, Climate Action Plan and National Planning Framework,' said the group's spokesperson, Angela Deegan. Greenpeace has produced an analysis that suggested 'if Amazon were to operate its existing and planned Irish data centres at full capacity 24/7, it could consume as much electricity annually as 1.5 million Irish households'.

Microsoft has 15 data centres in Ireland but in a proposed €900 million expansion at Grange Castle Business Park on Nangor Road, County Dublin, it suggested building its own large-scale standby gas power plant at a cost of €100 million. It said it needed 22 generators and 22 flue chimneys because its new data centres are 'located in what is noted as a constrained area in terms of electrical grid capacity'. It applied for special EPA licences to run diesel generators for prolonged periods in emergency scenarios, such as a power blackout, or an immediate request from the grid operator to reduce its electricity load. It is something of a catch-22 for the State: if it allows Microsoft and all the other data centre users the right to have their own capacity, it will remove demand from the overall grid but will also potentially add to carbon emissions. Microsoft has also signed a 15-year power purchase agreement with the US company GE to buy the entire supply from its Tullahennel wind farm in County Kerry.

One of the solutions proposed is that data centres and other high-energy businesses could be permitted to build direct power lines to solar and wind farms under new government plans. The 1999 Electricity Regulation Act states that solar and wind farms must connect to the national electricity grid to distribute their renewable energy. However, the renewable sector has complained that there can be long delays in getting these connections approved by EirGrid and ESB Networks, which manage and own the grid, respectively. Yet getting a connection request approved is obligatory before planning permission for a new data centre can be granted.

'I just get fed up with people saying, ah well, we shouldn't be using our electricity for this,' Eddie O'Connor, one of the pioneers in wind energy in Ireland and a former boss of Bord na Móna, told me during an interview for my podcast, 'Magnified'. 'This is precisely what you should be using your electricity for in a modern economy. We should be known as a country that does this. And I think it's extremely reactionary of people to say otherwise. These guys are going to build their data centres somewhere. If they put them anywhere else but Ireland, they'll have to use more electricity for air-conditioning and more fossil fuels. Locating them in Ireland is a good idea.' Meta, the company that owns social media giants Facebook and Instagram and that offers the WhatsApp communication service, has a giant data centre at Clonee in County Meath. It has been calculated that in 2021 it used the same amount of electricity, and emitted carbon at the same rate, as roughly 151,000 Irish homes. It uses as much water for its cooling systems as a

20,000-person town, such as Mullingar. Meta – which has a network of more than a dozen data centres globally – hasn't finished building in Clonee. Its campus there will span 150,000 square metres when completed, which is roughly the size of 20 football pitches. When Facebook first unveiled its data centre plans in Clonee, it said natural weather conditions in Ireland meant it would not need an expensive air-conditioning system to prevent the data centre hardware from overheating. It has also highlighted the potential to power the centre entirely with renewable wind energy.

But there is also more to the data centres than the energy they consume: it is about what information they hold and the use to which that is put, as well as the products and services they supply to their customers. So, what will Meta do with the data it harvests and holds? A Facebook whistleblower, Frances Haugen, revealed appalling practices at the company where the pursuit of profit was put ahead of the safety of users; users of Facebook can see unverified and dangerous content hosted regularly. It's not just Meta. The Irish Council for Civil Liberties has raised issues about 'digital self-determination' and whether we retained power and control over the data of our citizens or simply surrendered it, allowing the big tech giants running Ireland's largest data centres to monetise our personal data. There are potential security issues arising from every free app we have on our phones. As the saying goes, if you sign up for free, you become the product. Your data is used in ways you could never imagine, even if the companies say that everything is 'anonymised'. There are potential security implications of installing someone else's software on your devices, putting you at the mercy of the person who has provided that software to make sure there is nothing untoward happening.

The Data Protection Commission has come down hard on malpractices at Meta, issuing fines for hundreds of millions of euro, to the fury of Mark Zuckerberg's company, as well as banning the transfer of data to the US from the EU. The biggest fine of all came in May

2023, for a total of €1.2 billion, although it also emerged that our Data Protection Commissioner did not want to levy the fine and only did so after pressure from other EU member states to act in this way. Cracking down on Meta is unlikely to bring retribution from the US government (which has its own issues with the social media giant), but there might be greater problems in dealing with a Chinese social media giant that has also chosen Ireland as its European location.

TEN

CHINA: CORPORATE CHINA, CULTURAL CRISIS

When the rest of the western world had made up its mind about the apparent dangers of TikTok, the Chinese-owned and controlled social media app, Ireland was slower to act against it, compromised by our desire to protect the jobs and investment the Chinese company provided in Ireland. More than that, we were prepared to provide the location for its storage of data, not just from Irish people but from all across Europe.

TikTok is among the most-used social media platforms in the world, with one billion active monthly users and estimated annual revenues of $10 billion. It has been estimated that 21 per cent of the Irish population, according to a study conducted in 2022, uses the app every month. It is mainly younger people who subscribe, supplying or watching short-form videos, although the demographic is creeping upwards. As a result, there were enough users who had the app on their work phones that it became a concern that TikTok might be a Chinese Trojan Horse, a secret surveillance tool.

The fear was that the Chinese could harvest information from phones that had the app and that sensitive data relating both to private citizens and to government officials would be mined and transferred. The Chinese couldn't deny that this was possible but said they did not do that and would not do that. The sceptical were very wary, believing TikTok would do what the Chinese Communist Party (CCP) told it to do. The CCP owns 1 per cent of ByteDance, the TikTok parent company, and there is what's known as a 'Golden Share' arrangement: a nominal share, owned by the government, which could outvote all other shares in specified circumstances. It is a way for the Chinese government to control private businesses, even ones with investors from all over the world. China is an autocracy where respect for civil liberties, the rule of law and the basic rules of western engagement do not apply. The Chinese government, under its national security law, can request employees of any Chinese company to transfer data or information to China. In December 2022, TikTok admitted that its staff had used the app to spy on US-based journalists in an attempt to identify the source of internal leaks from other TikTok employees, having previously denied that this had happened.

While the American fears of Chinese surveillance and spying were long-standing, the European Commission only came to share those concerns in early 2023 and moved against TikTok. The European Parliament and several national governments, including cybersecurity hubs such as Germany, Estonia, the Netherlands and Britain, joined in instructing civil servants and politicians to remove the app. Even the BBC has warned its staff to get it off their phones.

Ireland has its concerns about what the Chinese do, too. When Minister Eamon Ryan led a delegation to China for St Patrick's Day in March 2023 they were issued with new computer devices for the week and single-use phones with new numbers, so-called burner phones. They were told not to bring any devices used for state business to China, as they would almost certainly be hacked, cloned or have software installed on them without their knowledge. The Irish Council for Civil Liberties (ICCL) called for the removal of security cameras made by Chinese company Hikvision from Leinster House over potential spying concerns. The Chinese Embassy labelled such concerns a 'conspiracy theory'.

When it came to TikTok, Taoiseach Leo Varadkar initially said the government was not advising workers to remove the app from official devices (until it later made the recommendation to do so). The reason for this more relaxed approach appeared to be that we had allowed TikTok to establish its European headquarters in Ireland, where it employed more than 3,000 people and had plans to add another 1,000 jobs.

Just as significantly, TikTok was building two major data centres in Ireland (and another in Norway) where it intended to store the personal data of over 150 million Europeans as part of its stated ambition to build a firewall between itself and possible Chinese government interference. TikTok said it would expect to complete the transfer of user data to these data centres by 2024. It said it expected to spend €1.2 billion annually on running the three data centres.

The company established what it called a Transparency and Accountability Centre in Dublin, which it claimed was designed to let 'experts and lawmakers to see first-hand how we're working to build a safe and secure platform for our growing and diverse community'. It promised to give sight of 'the code that drives our algorithm and to speak to our experts about how it operates'. It launched a campaign that it called Project Clover to highlight its apparent commitment to protecting data and its willingness to show exactly how and where it stores users' information, to create a 'secure enclave'. TikTok has described bans on its app as 'based on misplaced fears and seemingly driven by wider geopolitics'. But it's not just the western world that has worries. India banned the app entirely back in 2020, in a move that shut down its market of 1.4 billion to dozens of Chinese applications simultaneously. The Indian government called the app 'prejudicial to sovereignty and integrity of India, defence of India, security of state and public order' and said it was a 'sophisticated surveillance tool and that presents a serious national security threat'.

The Irish government outsourced control of TikTok to the Data Protection Commissioner (DPC). It started an investigation in November 2022 following an admission by TikTok that some EU citizens' data had been sent to China. It also investigated how TikTok handles the data of minors. Another cause for concern beyond surveillance emerges here: from the moment a user joins TikTok, the app's algorithm begins to populate a user's feed with viewing recommendations. There have been reports of self-harm, suicide and eating disorder videos being pushed on users. TikTok has said it takes all these concerns seriously and has teams to spot and remove dangerous content.

Ireland has many other good reasons to avoid upsetting the increasingly powerful, and always prickly, China. Economist Dan O'Brien has noted that in 2022 Ireland was the fourth biggest EU goods exporter to China in absolute terms, and the biggest on a per capita basis. 'By the later measure, exports were double those of Germany, the European country usually considered to be the most exposed to China,' he noted. The value of Irish microchip exports grew from €1.2 billion in 2015 to €10.7 billion in 2022, making microchips one of Ireland's largest exports. Of this, 77 per cent of the microchips produced in Ireland go to China, amounting to more than 63 per cent of our exports to the country. In 2023, the European Think-tank Network on China (ETNC) warned that our dependence on semiconductors in our trade relationship with China 'could threaten the country's economic security' because microchips had become a geopolitical pawn between China and the West.

Our agricultural sector previously lost major beef export contracts because of fears of meat infected by BSE and it took enormous effort to restore the trade, even though environmentalists cavilled at the idea of sending beef all the way to China, increasing emissions further after initial production.

The Chinese can be more demanding when it comes to trade and investment than other countries with which we do business, but the country continues to put money into Ireland. A Chinese flag flies alongside an Irish one outside of Bord na Móna's disused peat briquette factory in Littleton, County Tipperary. The plant is back in use because of Chinese investment, hosting Chinese-provided machines capable of recycling 24,000 tonnes of plastic annually. The Chinese company

Sabrina Integrated Services used to recycle plastic waste imported from Europe, but new environmental regulations imposed by Beijing closed down that trade. It now has a supply and management contract with Bord na Móna. The Irish company's waste subsidiary, AES, collects materials to fill the plant's capacity and there are expansion plans.

A Chinese company, Ganfeng Lithium, is prospecting for lithium, essential to the manufacture of mobile phones, in the Blackstairs mountains, along the Carlow–Wicklow border, under licence from the Department of the Environment. It is part of a consortium that has estimated that the Aclare deposit in east Carlow has 570,000 tonnes of the valuable element that could be extracted.

In 2023, Shein, the fast fashion retailer headquartered in Singapore, established its European base in Ireland, to the fury of many environmentalists. It has also faced US lawsuits about alleged copyright infringement.

Potentially even more significant was the arrival of contract medicines manufacturer WuXi Biologics in Dundalk. This Chinese company specialises in biologics, where drugs are made from living organisms instead of chemically synthesised molecules. It is used by 13 of the top 20 pharmaceutical companies globally; they use WuXi as a backup manufacturer or for additional capacity. WuXi has built 16 new factories globally but four of them in Dundalk, at a cost of about €1 billion, two for the manufacture of biologics and two for vaccines. Ireland gives the Chinese company access to talent in 'the only English-speaking country in the EU post-Brexit'. The low corporation tax compensates for the higher operating costs. It's not just the 600 jobs, many in highly skilled scientific and engineering roles, that were important to the government and the IDA. It was the first major foreign direct investment by a Chinese multinational in Ireland. All of the world's top ten global pharmaceutical companies have a sizeable presence but the arrival of a Chinese biological pharmaceuticals company was regarded as an important marker for the future, not just for new technology but for providing an alternative to a dependence on the US for investment. But at what price?

ELEVEN

CHINA: THE HARD IMPACT OF SOFT POWER

The Chinese government is often attributed with an interest in exercising soft power as much as hard power, of occupying and influencing cultural and intellectual space as much as gaining economic and political control. If the fear of losing commercial investment concentrates minds, then its willingness to provide finance for underfunded third-level education in Ireland has provided China with an opportunity to shape how we discuss or think about it.

Trinity College, in the heart of Dublin city centre, centuries old and hosting some of the country's most impressive classical buildings, is expensive to maintain because of its age. Its efforts to preserve its historic Old Library – home of the Book of Kells, one of the State's most treasured antiquities – are projected to cost about €103 million, for example.

The college hoped to get €30.8 million towards the cost of that project through the Immigrant Investor Programme (IIP), a scheme put in place by the government in 2012 to attract foreign money at one of the lowest ebbs of our economic fortunes. Run by the Department of Justice and administered through the Irish Naturalisation and Immigration Service (INIS), the IIP allows people 'of good character' from outside the European Economic Area to get residency status in Ireland. To do so, they must have a minimum net worth of €2 million and make a minimum of €1 million available for investment in Ireland over a three-year period. They do not get citizenship or a passport, just residency, an important distinction from a controversial previous programme that had seen some very wealthy foreigners essentially buy Irish passports, some of which were put to dubious use. There are strict rules regarding the source of funds and anti-money laundering safeguards that investors must satisfy before its officials approve them. An Interpol report is required on each individual. They must also have their own health insurance, and their residency rights do not entitle them to Irish welfare payments. IIP allows the families of investors to live in Ireland, too.

Most of the applicants pledge a minimum of €1 million to a business, donate €400,000 to charity, or can commit to giving a philanthropic 'endowment' donation of at least €500,000 to a project of public benefit, including to third-level institutions. Universities then apply to the INIS for finance through the endowment section of the IIP fund. Trinity has received tens of millions of euro from this source and said it regards it 'as appropriate to avail of a scheme that is run by the Department of Justice'.

In 2021, however, an internal government audit found the scheme open to widespread abuse and that governance needed to be 'significantly strengthened'. A report from the European Parliament said it was vulnerable to abuse by participants wishing to engage in tax avoidance. Notwithstanding that, roughly €1 billion was invested in Ireland through the IIP over a decade, the vast bulk coming from China and other Asian locations. Over 1,500 applicants received Irish visas. About a third of the money has gone to providing 3,500 social homes. Some has gone to our hospitals: international development group Bartra said it helped Tallaght Hospital raise €1.6 million in charitable donations for robotic surgery equipment and helped Beaumont Hospital to get €2 million towards a new operating theatre.

It was in the education sector where the loudest voices raised queries as to what was really being sold. Irish universities have depended on philanthropy for decades. The expansion of the NIHE Limerick into the

University of Limerick was made possible by hundreds of millions of euro contributed by the American benefactor Chuck Feeney. The same university's business centre was funded by JP McManus and named, apparently without any irony, after the city's most prominent twentieth-century socialist, Jim Kemmy. US investor Blackstone contributed millions to UCC and Trinity. There have been Irish donors, too – such as Lochlann Quinn, the late Peter Sutherland and Tony O'Reilly at UCD – who supplied millions of euro to fund modern buildings, with no strings attached other than naming rights. But the foreign money was dominant, especially when the State has underprovided for capital infrastructure developments and our third-level institutions use most of their money for day-to-day expenditure.

Trinity scaled back some of its capital investment programme because it was unable to secure the government funding it sought. Patrick Prendergast, whose ten-year term as provost concluded in 2021, committed Trinity to additional capital projects of more than €400 million from existing cash reserves, loans, philanthropy and government grants. Construction of its E3 Learning Foundry near the rear of the campus – a six-storey building to host the university's schools of engineering, natural sciences and computer science – started in early 2020 with a projected cost of €100 million. At Printing House Square, it built a very large new medical centre, sports facilities and a disability hub as a replacement for an existing office block (which had itself replaced the former Queen's Theatre). Its investments in student housing are detailed in another chapter (see Chapter 29).

However, Linda Doyle, Prendergast's successor, took a more realistic approach to expansion and reluctantly abandoned plans for Trinity East, a €1 billion 'innovation district' or campus expansion at Grand Canal Dock on a 5.5-acre site. It was to be strategically located alongside the offices of some of the world's biggest tech firms, but the government declined to supply the €150 million contribution requested. Instead, Doyle opted to refurbish existing buildings on the main campus, with a stronger focus on sustainability. The college did a land swap in the area with Denis O'Brien but continued to earmark American technology multinationals for funds to construct new buildings on the campus. Unfortunately, the tech slump of early 2023 diluted some of the ambitions in that regard.

UCD AND CHINA

At University College Dublin (UCD), while the bulk of corporate philanthropic investment has come from the United States, it too has sought Chinese capital investment, to the displeasure of many of its more aware staff. There are many political sensitivities associated with taking Chinese money: the country's aggression against Taiwan, its treatment of Uyghur Muslims, more than one million of whom may be in concentration camps, and its surveillance-heavy society being the most prominent. But there are academic issues too arising from the Chinese exercise of so-called soft power, which is the subtle use of propaganda to create a different impression of a country from its reality. China has a reputation for trying to influence the recipients of its largesse – as African nations, in particular, have discovered – and UCD has proven to be perhaps too willing to facilitate Chinese demands. The revelations late in 2022 that China had established units on Capel Street in Dublin that had the appearance of quasi-police stations raised legitimate fears about espionage and attempted control of Chinese students and citizens in Ireland.

The relationship between UCD and China goes back to 2006 and the opening of the first Confucius Institute at the Belfield Campus. Ostensibly, the idea was to promote Chinese language and culture in one of about 500 locations on the campuses of universities globally. On its website, the institute said its mission 'is to work with the Irish government, businesses and academia to develop stronger educational, cultural and commercial links between Ireland and China'. It was officially opened by Zeng Peiyan, then Vice Premier of the People's Republic of China, as a joint venture between UCD and Renmin University of China. In 2014, UCD's then President, Andrew Deeks, signed an agreement with Hanban, the world headquarters of Confucius Institutes, a body affiliated with the Chinese Ministry of Education, to build a new 2,000 square metre, three-storey building in 'temple-style', located, in the university's own words, 'at the heart of the UCD campus'. Confucius agreed to contribute €3 million, along with a matching contribution from the Irish government, with UCD pitching in €1.4 million. The institute would have 'exclusive free use' of the building for 50 years from 2016, and it was agreed that should UCD back out of hosting the institute it would be obliged to repay Hanban its contribution at a rate of €60,000 per year. UCD agreed to pay €500,000 a year towards the institute's running costs.

The building went over budget by nearly €5 million and in 2016 Deeks requested an extra €2.5 million from the Department of Education to complete its construction. Deeks argued that UCD had no option but 'to proceed in order to avoid a diplomatic incident', saying the Dublin building was the first Confucius centre to receive direct funding from Beijing and was 'receiving considerable scrutiny at the highest levels of the Chinese government'. Our government said no. It did this because of growing unease in some universities about the true intentions of the Chinese government. Cornell University in the US ended its exchange programmes with Renmin University, explaining that the Chinese university 'has actively suppressed speech, engaged in widespread surveillance and punishment of student activists, and even been complicit in forcibly detaining one of their own students'. Other universities in Canada and the US sent the institutes packing.

It was accepted in some quarters that the relationship with Chinese institutions could facilitate valuable intercultural engagement and exchange but as Professor Christopher Hughes, Emeritus Professor of International Relations at the London School of Economics and Political Science (LSE) and a highly regarded expert on Chinese policy, noted, it can be very difficult to distinguish 'the political mission from the cultural' in dealing with China. Hughes argued that 'a one-party state is able to use its growing economic capabilities to influence the work of universities in democratic societies'. He said, 'A university is understood to be one of the most important institutions shaping the values of democratic society. Its status as an independent source of critical knowledge is important not only for education but also for the healthy development of democracy itself.'

Many UCD academics, including the historian Diarmaid Ferriter and politics professor David Farrell, argued that it was inappropriate for an entity linked with an illiberal state to teach UCD students about China's own political system as part of an Irish degree programme. 'This is, after all, a state-funded Chinese entity under the control of the ministry of education of the People's Republic of China,' Farrell wrote in the *Irish Times*. He was particularly annoyed that the institute was permitted to teach a class on Chinese politics to UCD students and that the marks were part of the degree. The activities of the institute to promote culture or language should be 'ring-fenced' and kept separate from any academic teaching, he said. He also noted that 'the ruling party of China is a profoundly illiberal entity when it comes to the education sector. This has always been the case to varying degrees, but under current leader Xi Jinping the party has turbo-charged its control over intellectual inquiry.'

Critics of UCD's management charged that proposed changes to UCD's academic freedom policy to allow for 'divergent approaches' were a sop to China. The suggestion was dropped after a concerted campaign by academics. Yet in one of his last messages to staff before retiring as President at UCD in early 2022, Professor Andrew Deeks said he was 'disappointed by some of the misguided commentary' about the institute. He was 'particularly disturbed by implicit suggestions that the political loyalties of some colleagues can be inferred from their ethnicity'. The outraged academics responded that the debate was 'not about the

ethnicity of the staff' but the 'independence' governing teaching provided by the institute to undergraduate students.

A week after that controversy there was another when a UCD
statement about the Russian invasion of Ukraine was condemned by
academics as unduly weak – and linked to keeping China onside. 'In
talking to colleagues of mine who were in the room or rooms when that
statement was being talked about, the primary reservation on behalf of
the university was not to say something too strong for fear it could come
back and bite them in the arse on Confucius,' Professor Ben Tonra (a
political scientist) alleged. 'Were they to come out swinging on Ukraine,
then someone would ask "Why has UCD not come out swinging in
regard to China in regard to x or y", and in particular in relation to the
Confucius Institute.' Tonra said he was 'deeply sympathetic' to the need
for cash but that 'you cannot forget the core values on your way out the
door to raise money'. He said this was a result of a lack of State funding
leading universities to 'pursue everything and especially overseas students, overseas partnerships and research grants as income streams in
desperation to keep the lights on and pay the salaries'. The reality was
the relationship with China had become deep: UCD had already formed
joint colleges in Xi'an, Beijing and Guangzhou.

THE BATTLE OF CORE VALUES

It wasn't just in Dublin that there were concerns. NUI Galway got
its own Confucius Institute of Chinese Medicine centre in 2019, in a
partnership with Nanjing University. Maynooth University formed a
partnership with Fuzhou University to allow 300 students to enrol annually to study computer science, web development, electronic engineering
and robotics. University College Cork (UCC) got its own Confucius
Centre in 2006. In early 2021, however, UCC withdrew from forming
a 'joint college' to offer degrees in science, engineering, food science
and law with Minzu University, a Chinese university that specialises in
ethnic studies, after 50 of UCC's academics raised their concerns. Minzu

has a large proportion of its students from minority non-Han Chinese backgrounds and specialises in ethnic studies. It is overseen by a unit of the Chinese government charged with gathering intelligence on and influencing non-party individuals and organisations inside and outside China, at least according to US government bodies and the Central Intelligence Agency.

The National University of Ireland (NUI) had backed the proposal as 'operating very firmly within the NUI human rights guidelines' but UCC also commissioned a UK consultancy to investigate if the project would be contrary to UCC's 'core values'. The consultant pointed out that withdrawing on ethical grounds would make the continuance of existing relationships impossible and that Ireland 'walks a tightrope between its commercial ambitions and political views on China'. It also noted that the Irish government actively encourages third-level institutions to work in China 'as a way of increasing funding from external sources'. The British report also noted that Chinese scholars were often 'quite comfortable' with being under the control of the State. 'The fact that Chinese scholars can work comfortably under some State control is consistent with the Confucian values of Chinese culture.'

By late 2022 the Irish government had become very aware of the concern among its EU partners about the purchase of property throughout Europe by Chinese investors who, it was clear, could not operate without due deference to the power of the Chinese State and its one-party nominally communist government. There was an added concern regarding the possibility of a long-term project to undermine European education standards and introduce Chinese ones in their stead. The need for money to construct and refurbish buildings remained pressing, but the additional price that might be paid became more of an issue. In early 2023 the Irish government decided to end the IIP, a move for independence from giving too much in exchange for foreign investment.

PART 4

OWNING THE CAPITAL

The arrival of foreign money after the Great Recession did more than just pick up existing assets and land or help to provide the jobs that restored tax revenues. It contributed to a reshaping of our cities and towns, the very structure and look of them, raising major questions about the priorities of politicians, planners and profiteers and the use of the land and assets they purchased.

TWELVE

DUBLIN DOCKLANDS: THE LANDSCAPE SOUTH OF THE LIFFEY

The genesis of this book came from walks with my dog during the Covid-19 lockdowns, particularly when the 5-kilometre radius operated. We were joined often by my wife and one of our favourite routes was from the heart of Rathmines, where I live, as far as Portobello bridge and to turn right onto the city side of the Grand Canal – with more limited car traffic – to walk along the bank from there as far as the River Liffey and back.

After my first year in Dublin as a student coming from Cork – when I lived in a flat over a shop on Dame Street in the city centre – I stayed in three different rented flats and houses along the canal for the next five years. The Covid walks allowed me to witness the ongoing transformation of a large part of Dublin and got me wondering who was or would be in all of the new buildings, who was paying for it all, and to what use they were being put, whether as places to live, work, trade or play. My inquisitiveness led to many detours, to have a look at the many new buildings going up parallel to both sides of the canal and beyond.

At Portobello Bridge the ongoing development at Charlemont had caught the eye for years. An early project was a hotel by Dalata called the Clayton Hotel Charlemont, which started construction in 2016 and opened in November 2018 at a cost of €41.6 million. Dalata earned an almost immediate return when it sold the property to German property investor Deka Immobilien for €65 million, agreeing to rent it back at over €3 million annually. It was among a series of big investments in Ireland made by the German company, a subsidiary of Deka Group, which is owned by German Sparkasse, a network of publicly owned savings banks. Its property wing manages nearly €50 billion worth of property assets around the EU.

Alongside it is the Barge pub, part of the bankrupt Seán Quinn's former empire, which became a popular spot for outdoor drinking during Covid when 'takeaway' pints became the rage almost irrespective of the weather. In early 2023 it sold, for a reported €3.75 million, to McCafferty's, a pub chain run by a Donegal man Declan Boyle that already had pubs in Ireland, Britain, Spain and Dubai.

Behind that the decades-old council flats, many of which had fallen into near disrepair, were cleared for a regeneration that changed the local skyline and the social mix. The McGarrell Reilly Group, led by Sean Reilly, emerged from NAMA to develop 17,000 square feet of offices over two eight-storey blocks to be occupied by Amazon. There were also 184 private apartments and 75 social-housing apartments for DCC in a public–private partnership. In early 2023 an enormous additional site behind these new constructions, and nearer to the city centre, was cleared by Clancourt, a family firm headed by Charles Kenny, originally from Mayo, which has major developments nearby. On the same street is Charlemont Exchange, the former headquarters of ACC and subsequently Rabobank, bought by Marlet Property which added two floors to two of the blocks and one floor to the third. WeWork's name was prominently displayed on the expanded building fronting onto Charlemont Bridge and gave extra heft to an area that already had a Hilton hotel for a couple of decades.

Next, on the site of what was once a relatively modern building that housed the now defunct McConnell's ad agency, and alongside the Luas track, the Rohan Group demolished and rebuilt a site it picked up in 2015 from the debris of the Bernard McNamara empire implosion. It sold the new office development at 21 Charlemont to La Française Group – which manages about €64 billion in assets and is 92 per cent owned by Crédit Mutuel Nord Europe (CMNE), a banking and insurance group in Northern France and Belgium – for about €45 million, the French investor's first Irish purchase.

Walking down the canal I passed Harcourt Terrace where I had shared an apartment in an old Georgian house for about two years, directly opposite the now abandoned former Garda station. Shamefully, it was one of the few locations in the area unused, and for over a decade, although there were plans in 2023 to open an Educate Together primary school in what was a very attractive and solid red-brick building. In early 2023 the building was demolished. A bridge over the canal, built after I had left the area, accommodates the Luas track and a stop, just beside a landmark office development originally from the 1960s at Two Grand Parade. I was first in it as a young journalist in the late 1980s, covering press conferences by then owner, the cigarette manufacturer PJ Carroll. The building, a protected structure, was later the headquarters of Irish Nationwide Building Society. When it went bust, Amazon became a temporary tenant. Then the building, and an approximately one-acre site behind looking onto Dartmouth Square, was purchased by Hines Ireland in partnership with Hong Kong-based property investment firm Peterson Group. It has embarked upon a major six-storey extension, linked to the original building via a glazed atrium, giving an extra 15,000 square metres of floor space. Enabling works, at a cost of nearly €20 million, have been completed for the proposed station for the latest iteration of the Metro train line, to the frustration of many local residents.

Back on the northern side of the canal, several modern commercial buildings have been completed that front onto Adelaide Road. One is 55 Charlemont, a six-storey, 5,400 square metre standalone block developed by Paddy McKillen junior's Oakmount and let to Zendesk, a US provider of customer-service software. A slight diversion down Harcourt Terrace onto Adelaide Road (where the Department of Energy sits in an older but still modern block that looks onto the canal at the rear) also gives sight of an enormous new office block, the Cadenza, built at the corner of Earlsfort Terrace by Irish Life (a subsidiary of Canada Life). The building had been earmarked as a global HQ for the Irish tech company Intercom, which agreed to take the whole building on an 18-year lease. Intercom was founded in 2011 and has developed a software platform that brings messaging products for sales, marketing and customer support together. In 2018 it was valued at more than $1 billion, making it Ireland's first tech 'unicorn', but by 2023 it had become more circumspect about what capacity it needed. The giant US private equity investor KKR – which had offices on St Stephen's Green – agreed early in 2023 to take the top three floors of the Cadenza building, about 50,000 square feet of office space.

In sight of this new building is further development by Clancourt of its Park Place office scheme, which has three modern new buildings fronting onto Hatch Street, including one which is now the headquarters of IDA Ireland. Clancourt bought the site on Adelaide Road, again beside the Luas line, from Eir in 2015; it was previously an exchange building for Eir, hidden behind a plain concrete wall, and a tyre factory for Dunlop. Its development was delayed by legal wrangling about access with Johnny Ronan, who also owned property in the area. In 2023, it neared completion as two glass-fronted interconnecting headquarters office buildings at Four and Five Park Place, ten storeys in height.

Coming back to my usual canal walk, beyond Leeson Street Bridge the next striking modern development is owned by Irish Property Unit Trust (Iput), Ireland's largest commercial property fund. Having acquired the vacant Lad Lane apartment block, Fitzwilton House, Gardner House and Wilton Park House, the former home of IDA Ireland, Iput developed a €350 million, four-block office campus at Wilton Park, which has become LinkedIn's (owned by Microsoft) headquarters for Europe, the Middle East and Africa, employing thousands at a campus that is double the size of what was there previously. The project had attracted opposition from residents and An Taisce because of its scale and impact on the Georgian Wilton Park (which has become a livelier and more accessible public location since the redevelopment).

The site tells its own story of the fluctuations in valuations attached to land and property this century. Iput had previously owned Gardner House but sold it in 2006 for €83 million to a consortium involving the developer Gerry Conlon and businessmen Colum and Ciarán Butler, who have the Starbucks franchise for Ireland. The loans were acquired by Kennedy Wilson for about €45 million in 2015, which in turn sold it to Iput for €60 million.

Iput was founded in 1967 and is the biggest owner of office buildings in Dublin. Its shareholders include Irish pension funds and investment managers, as well as international institutional investors and charities. It owns more than 90 commercial properties, all but one in Dublin, and owns or partially owns about 40 offices in Dublin, including the new home of AIB on Molesworth Street. Its offices were valued at the time of writing at about €2.2 billion, some 70 per cent of its total assets. It also owns €400 million-plus worth of retail units – including seven on Grafton Street and three on Henry Street – and the same again in warehouses.

Across the canal are the Mespil Flats, one of the original 1960s build-to-rent developments in the country, owned by Irish Life until a highly controversial sale of the properties, with tenants in situ, in the early 1990s to a consortium that included the late RTÉ broadcaster Marian Finucane. Also on that stretch of road is the four-star Mespil Hotel, developed by the Kidney family as part of the Lee Hotel Group, open since 1995. Around it and behind it are multiple commercial developments providing the space for many major multinational employers to arrive in Ireland, especially on Burlington Road and the Burlington Plaza. Johnny Ronan had the foresight in 2016 to develop the 172,000 square-foot Vertium Building with support from English investors U+I, which is now let in full to Amazon as its European HQ. Amazon has also taken other space at the Shannon Building. There have been multiple changes of ownership of the Burlington Plaza, but the most recent, in 2021, saw Blackstone pay Colony €292 million for its share in the development (the headquarters of Three Ireland on Sir John Rogerson's Quay was also part of the deal). Nearby is the Baggot Plaza property, which Bank of Ireland has rented as its HQ since 2015. The building was purchased by Kennedy Wilson for less than €25 million and modernised at a cost of around another €40 million. It was sold then to Deka for a reported €141 million in 2021.

Back on the city side of the canal, at the corner of Wilton Terrace and Baggot Street, Irish Life received permission to redevelop the former Bord Fáilte headquarters, a 1960s five-storey building it bought in 2015 for just €4 million. The property had been vacant for eight years before permission was granted to replace it with a six-storey, 7,000 square metre building, more than three times the size of the original. The next stop is Hibernia Real Estate Group's Clanwilliam Court on the corner of Mount Street and Clanwilliam Place. The former Hibernia REIT changed its name when it changed ownership and left the stock market in early 2022, when it was sold to Brookfield, a Canadian investment fund, for €1.1 billion. It filed plans to demolish a row of buildings along Clanwilliam Place and replace them with a new eight-storey commercial development. It received permission from DCC, but last-minute complaints about the project stalled development. Irish Life, owner of the adjacent Velasco Building, an eight-storey office block leased by Google, objected on the basis that 'reasonable levels of privacy and amenity are important for the occupants of Velasco'.

The Velasco building marks a starting point on the map of Google's extraordinary expansion in Dublin. At Grand Canal Street bridge there are two options, left and right, because it is no longer possible to walk straight ahead. If I went right, a subsequent quick left turn onto Barrow Street reveals the centre of Google in Dublin. It was in 2011 when Google purchased what would become its European HQ, the

Montevetro building, from one of Johnny Ronan and Richard Barrett's companies via NAMA for €100 million and began an expansion that would see it create over 8,000 jobs in Dublin and act as a centre for taxable profits that would bring hundreds of millions of euro to the State coffers. However, in 2023 there came a limit to the company's civic-mindedness. Google and DCC had an agreement in place for a €7.5 million refurbishment of the public streets around Barrow Street, involving improvements to roads and footpaths, planting and bicycle parking and new traffic signals, to which Google would have contributed an unspecified amount. It had pitched in €2.4 million before it withdrew from further funding in early 2023, one of the world's richest companies saying it didn't have the money anymore as it had to pay for redundancies instead. Barrow Street is linked by a walkway to the Gasworks site where there is one of the most striking apartment complexes in Dublin, a circular structure that hosts 210 one- and two-bed apartments. Developed by Liam Carroll, Kennedy Wilson bought it in June 2012, its first-ever acquisition in Ireland, for just €40 million, in a 50-50 partnership with Fairfax.

The area is known to many as Googletown or Google Docks, especially given what it has done at Boland's Quay. Here, running onto Barrow Street, is where the Boland's Mill remains intact. Alongside it, three landmark residential towers have been purchased by Google in a €300 million deal with receivers acting from NAMA, which had taken the site from Benton Properties, a company owned by Sean Kelly. The three towers, which are visually remarkable and ultra-modern alongside the old mill, rise to 53 metres, 49 metres and 47.8 metres. The area is due to open to the public in 2024, marketed as 'Dublin's new destination for food, community and culture'.

If I hadn't taken the right turn at the bridge going onto Grand Canal Street Lower, I would have gone left and then quickly onto Grand Canal Quay, past the Malting Tower, parallel to the canal until the water is visible and then alongside again. This is where Denis O'Brien owns much of his Dublin property portfolio, which in 2023 was the site of major expansion. It is also where Google rents significant extra office capacity, bringing its total space around the area to over 650,000 square feet.

As Grand Canal Quay meets Pearse Street I would cross the road and occasionally sit with coffee in hand on Grand Canal Square, overlooking the basin where organised water sports often take place and the *Celtic Mist* yacht – once owned by Taoiseach Charles Haughey and funded by Dermot Desmond in highly controversial circumstances – sits moored. The anchor of the square is the stunning Grand Canal Theatre, Ireland's largest fixed-seat venue, sponsored by Bord Gáis and opened in 2010 having been built by Joe O'Reilly under the direction of local entrepreneur Harry Crosbie at a cost of about €80 million. It was designed by star Polish-American architect Daniel Libeskind, best known for his role in the masterplan for the rebuild of the World Trade Centre post-2001. Crosbie lost control of the theatre – and his other assets – in 2014 when he couldn't service his debts of €431 million with NAMA. The theatre is now owned by Crownway Investments, the investment vehicle of the former owners of Jurys Doyle Hotel Group, John and Bernie Gallagher, who bought it for €28 million. They beat a bid from multinational Live Nation, thanks to the wealth they had accrued from the sale of their large shareholding in the Jurys Inn hotel chain to Quinlan Private (for €1.16 billion in total) in 2005.

TikTok became a major tenant in the docklands area when it signed a 15-year lease in December 2021 for the Sorting Office, on Cardiff Lane, at the back of the Grand Canal Theatre, which had been purchased by Singapore-headquartered real-estate investment trust Mapletree Investments for about €240 million from Marlet and its backer M&G Investments in 2019. Mapletree apparently put the block up for sale in early 2023, seeking a €40 million profit. TikTok also agreed to occupy 85,000 square feet at the Tropical Fruit Warehouse, a six-storey riverfront building developed by Iput on Sir John Rogerson's Quay. But it pulled out of a deal to take more space alongside at Marlet's Shipping Office, one that was double the size of the Iput building. One of its neighbours there is the law firm Matheson, which rents its headquarters from Deka, which bought the building from Irish Life for about €125 million.

Immediately to the left at the front of the theatre are the Marker Hotel and Marker Residences. In 2009, with the hotel only three-quarters complete, Bank of Scotland (Ireland) (BoSI) stopped supplying funds to the original developer of the complex, Terry Devey. A year later its builder, Pierse Construction, went out of business. In 2011, BoSI appointed a receiver.

Kevin McGillycuddy, a former US Marine Corp reservist who had quit his job with AIG to join with Devey in the development had split with Devey by this stage and, with the backing of MHL, a Swiss entity, bought the 187-bedroom hotel's debts for €45 million. They also got the adjoining apartments, the Marker Residences, as part of the deal and soon struck another deal to sell them for over €50 million to I-RES, a stock market-quoted investment fund. Effectively, the sale of the apartments covered the cost of buying the hotel and continuing the fit-out, providing a five-star hotel for free. Covid seemingly changed the projected economics of the hotel sector, but even during and after Covid lockdowns trade in hotels was active. In 2021 McGillycuddy sold the Marker (remarketed as the Anantara) for €134 million to Deka, a deal that set a new 'key' record for Dublin, at €700,000 per room. In 2023, I-RES, suddenly under financial pressure as growth in the property market cooled and its level of debt became an issue, offered the Marker Residence, its 84 two-bedroom apartments, commercial units and 113 basement-level car parking spaces for sale.

Just up from the Marker, Pontegadea, the family firm of clothes retailer Zara founder Amancio Ortega, paid €101 million in early 2023 for 120 luxury rental apartments at the Opus building at Six Hanover Quay, more or less the same price as New York-headquartered investor Angelo Gordon and its local partners, Carysfort Capital, had paid Cairn Homes for the apartments four years earlier. Cairn had bought the site from a consortium involving NAMA, Bennett Construction and Oaktree Capital for €18 million in 2016 and spent about €40 million on its development before turning an enormous profit in selling. Underneath there is Mackenzie's, which is a Press Up restaurant, and a Wetherspoons pub. Park Developments developed the Reflector, an eye-catching 11,500 square metre apartment block on Hanover Quay that Deka bought for €155 million in 2019.

At the end of Hanover Quay, at the junction of the Liffey and Dodder rivers and Grand Canal Dock, sits land earmarked early in the twenty-first century for the U2 Tower, set to be the highest building in Ireland. It was to be an apartment block in which U2 would have new recording studios, built by Paddy McKillen and Sean Mulryan, personal friends of the band. There is a tower there now and even if smaller in size than envisaged, it is still a highly visible Dublin landmark at 23 storeys high and containing 190 expensive rental apartments. Capital Dock Residence was built by Kennedy Wilson, which came to the site after one of the main office blocks had been constructed by Liam Carroll in 2009. It was 2012 when Kennedy Wilson bought that office on Sir John Rogerson's Quay, let on a long lease to US investment bank State Street. Kennedy Wilson's partner on that purchase was Fairfax, which boasted publicly of getting the office building for one-third of its construction cost. The pair also got 3.5 acres of vacant land and in 2014 did a deal with NAMA for an adjoining 1.5-acre parcel of land. NAMA didn't take cash but instead a 15 per cent stake in the venture, which went on to build high-end offices behind the retained triple gables of an old warehouse, and the apartment block. Between 2015 and 2018 Kennedy Wilson built

Across the basin is the Alto Vetro tower, built in 2004 by Ronan and Barrett. NAMA took over the Anglo Irish Bank loans that had funded it and in 2014 receivers sold the 26-apartment, 16-storey tower for €11.5 million. Kennedy Wilson bought it, initially on its own, but later it was transferred into a joint venture with Axa, the insurance company. It was to be just one part of Kennedy Wilson's overall commitment to the area.

quickly, and by the end of 2018 said it had invested €350 million in the project. Kennedy Wilson sold one of the office buildings to US bank JP Morgan in advance of construction and the online recruitment firm Indeed leased the other two for 20 years at an annual rent of €11.9 million. NAMA and Fairfax sold their shares, the State entity apparently making a near €19 million profit and the Australians over €53 million. A fund managed by the French insurance and financial services group Axa entered a 50-50 partnership with Kennedy Wilson as the new owner. The apartments became highly controversial as they were slow to fill, high rents being blamed for the seeming construction of a 'white elephant'. However, by 2023 the building appeared to be fully occupied, notwithstanding charging some of Dublin's highest rents, starting at about €3,000 per month for a one-bed unit.

Crosbie's friendship with the members of U2 had been central to their using a studio at Windmill Lane for the recording of some of the rock band's most famous albums. The studio became something of a shrine to fans and when Hibernia built the Windmill Quarter of office blocks it embedded the covers of 21 albums recorded there – not just by U2 – into the footpath to create a 'vinyl walkway'.

In front of the theatre that was his pride, Crosbie has his own home, an old warehouse that he converted decades ago into a beautiful residence and from which he formulated much of the vision for the regeneration of the area. I spent one afternoon with him there in 1997 as we worked on our parts for an RTÉ television series *Start Me Up*, aimed at encouraging entrepreneurial business, but also listening to him talking about plans for the area that he would be central to delivering. He hasn't stopped dreaming up ideas despite becoming one of NAMA's biggest creditors and having engaged in a bitter and unsuccessful court dispute with it. In 2016 he lost a Court of Appeal judgment over his debts, having claimed 'a gross injustice' had been done because NAMA failed to honour an agreement that certain personal assets would not be part of the enforcement of a judgment against him for a remaining

€77 million commercial debt. NAMA said there was no concluded agreement and Crosbie feared the loss of his home. The High Court found the letter was not a binding agreement and, even if it was, it was no longer in force because Crosbie had not fully performed the purported agreement he now sought to enforce.

Crosbie has friends still prepared to back him – such as Bono and Bob Geldof – in what Crosbie admits will be his last big pitch for the area. There are still three abandoned docks in the area, in the control of Waterways Ireland, and he wants to use them for a community project he calls Slip Depot instead of the land being 'sold to the highest bidder' and turned into 'apartments for rich guys'. He wants to set up a boat-building community enterprise in what he describes as a 'beautiful cut-stone, eighteenth-century dry dock' and then in the second dock 'a double-sized Vicar Street' where the stage would be up against the lock gates and performers would play with the water twenty feet above their heads. The third piece of land, which he said was filled during the 1940s, would be a public space with a very light carbon fibre, see-through roof, open at the sides, which he called an agora. NAMA, however, has a lease on the area.

Whether bridges can be mended even at this late hour, with Crosbie now in his mid-70s, is doubtful, even though NAMA's new interest in dealing with Johnny Ronan suggests anything is possible. But Crosbie's proposal seems worthy of at least serious consideration: a sizeable area such as this cannot nearly all be about office spaces and restaurants and coffee shops to service them. Attractive as it is to sit out in the Grand Canal Plaza on a sunny day, as I often did with my dog before returning home, and fine as many of the shows at the BGE Theatre are, an area such as this needs other cultural attractions to make it a thriving community. Crosbie's imagination brought us the theatre (and other venues in Dublin) and even if his management of finances left more than something to be desired, it often takes maverick thinkers, rather than politicians, planners and committees, to come up with ideas for things that people will want and use.

THIRTEEN

DUBLIN DOCKLANDS: THE LANDSCAPE NORTH OF THE LIFFEY

On a sunny Saturday afternoon at the start of October 2022, I left the dog at home and walked further than usual, this time over to the north side of the River Liffey across the Tom Clarke Bridge. The bridge, formerly known as the East-link, was renamed in Clarke's honour in 2016, in recognition of being one of the seven signatories of the Proclamation. I was to participate on stage in one of the sessions of the Ireland's Future event, a political rally discussing the potential for Ireland as a 32-county entity at some yet-to-be-decided date.

The event took place at the 3Arena (still known to many as the Point Depot), Harry Crosbie's extraordinary conversion of a vast disused warehouse into the country's premier indoor arena for concerts. It has played host to some of the world's biggest acts, including U2, Elton John, Beyoncé, Dua Lipa, Robert Plant and Jimmy Page. The thousands attending the event at the 3Arena, just like those who go to the concerts, must be taken by the incredible modern development in what was until recent decades one of the most rundown and depressed parts of the city. It is now full of the most modern office blocks, vast apartment complexes, hotels and restaurants and an albeit limited set of social amenities, making it a desirable, if expensive, place to live and work. There are still serious social issues to be addressed in the adjacent social housing complexes where, despite the emergence of heroes such as Olympic boxing gold medallist Kellie Harrington, crime and drug use have been a scourge, contributing significantly to the murderous so-called Kinahan–Hutch feud and efforts by the State to rejuvenate the area through the work of the north-east inner-city task force.

Meanwhile, the building continues at pace. There are now six hotels in North Docklands, including the Spencer, Gibson, Hilton Garden, Mayson and Becket Locke, with more planned. The area is also serviced by a Luas line from Connolly Station and, given the north–south social divide of the city is normally biased towards the latter, is arguably more prosperous and with greater room for development than the south side of the river. This is what modern Ireland has delivered for now and for the future, despite the gloom that enveloped us from 2008 to 2012 or so, when property development was blamed for all our ills and woes.

The development of the area also offers a testament to the changing fortunes of local developers and the arrival of foreign capital. The signs of what might have been for Crosbie are visible to him each day as he looks from across the river. As part of his financial collapse, Crosbie lost control of the 3Arena to Live Nation. He also surrendered the Point Quarter complex, a development that had been partially completed when Dunnes Stores delayed in fitting out a supermarket crucial to the viability of the complex. Most visible of all is the Exo, now the most prominent building at the entrance to the docklands from the port side, but still not as big as Crosbie had planned. He envisaged what would have been Ireland's tallest office block, the Watchtower, at 120 metres in height. The Exo still became Dublin's tallest office block, at 73 metres. The Exo was bought from NAMA in December 2017 by a European fund managed by Tristan Capital Partners and its local operating partners, SW3 Capital, at a price believed to be around €75 million. An Post moved in as the main tenant of the 17-storey building in 2023, taking its management and support staff from the GPO at O'Connell Street. The

GPO remained open as a working post office and as a visitor centre for those interested in history but in the absence of a revitalisation of the capital's main thoroughfare a move to the docklands, part of Dublin's past, now seemed a better home for the future.

An Post may have been a more unusual addition to the area – a semi-state commercial company rather than one that is privately owned – because the docklands have become home to tech and financial services companies and to those who provide white-collar support, such as legal firms. To get the new jobs of the modern tech era, Ireland needed suitably modern office space to attract demanding companies ... and lots of it. The tech giants thinking of Ireland as a suitable location for European headquarters needed space for thousands of employees in one location. So Irish developers – that maligned class – pushed to resume building.

John Mulcahy of NAMA was a man with a colourful turn of phrase who was not afraid to use it in public situations. One of the buildings NAMA inherited was in the docklands between the concert arena and the Convention Centre, a shell of the edifice that was due to have been the new headquarters of Anglo Irish Bank. 'We sold the old Anglo headquarters to the Central Bank on the basis that every film crew that came to Dublin wanted to shoot the Anglo building. It was like a burnt-out tank on the road to Kuwait as a symbol of our failure,' Mulcahy told a conference in 2013. 'We decided we had to get this bloody thing off our stocks. So, we sold it to the Central Bank and I thought they would have started work by now but they seem to have got a puncture somewhere along the way.' It got built eventually and it was the catalyst for much to follow.

The Central Bank is clustered with Dublin Landings, a million-square-foot scheme of five blocks of apartments and offices, developed by Sean Mulryan's Ballymore and its Singaporean partners, Oxley Holdings. The National Treasury Management Agency (NTMA) and WeWork also became tenants and one of the buildings, later let to Microsoft, was sold to Iput for €115 million. Oxley has said the development and sale of the commercial and residential buildings at Dublin Landings generated €745.4 million, and of that, NAMA received €153.9 million. Oxley sold the residential element of its Dublin Landings development for €154.6 million to Greystar, which got 268 residential apartments and 210 car-parking spaces. This encouraged other big purchases in the area. German company Commerz Real AG spent €152.3 million on a pair of buildings from the 1990s, One and Two Dockland Central, which it bought from Hibernia REIT. Johnny Ronan's Treasury had built PwC's nine-storey headquarters, over three blocks, on Dublin's North Wall Quay in 2007 and it was sold in mid-2016 through London-based AGC Equity Partners on behalf of unnamed middle-Eastern investors for €242 million after Hines withdrew from its purchase. It was put back for sale in 2021 for €265 million but does not appear to have sold.

In 2018, Kennedy Wilson's North Bank apartment complex served as a springboard for the acquisition of Liam Carroll's remaining north docklands assets from NAMA, a 5.91-acre site between Sheriff Street and the Luas red line on Mayor Street, behind the Central Bank, to be developed under the Coopers' Cross brand. There was a residential portion of the site, with planning permission for 347 apartments, and a commercial section with more than 330,000 square feet of office and retail space permitted. Kennedy Wilson bought both for €113 million. It then sold half of the residential to Axa and half of the commercial to US property investment firm Cain International.[7] Kennedy Wilson then got permission to expand the project to 472 apartments, 395,000 square feet of commercial space, a crèche and a public park. The buildings, in seven blocks, range from two to seven storeys. Most of the apartments are one-and two-bedroom homes and all are rented. However, not everyone

---

7   Cain is a subsidiary of Eldridge Industries, the investment firm of US finan-
    cier Todd Boehly, which then became a shareholder in Kennedy Wilson itself.
    Boehly has become better known since on this side of the Atlantic as the main
    investor in the consortium that bought the London football club Chelsea from
    Russian oligarch Roman Abramovich in 2022.

is convinced about the remaining value in the area. When Lone Star sold its 25 Irish hotels to Israeli-backed LRC Group for €676 million, it included the Hilton Garden Inn on Dublin's Custom House Quay at a value of €100 million.

But of all the men with big ideas for the redevelopment of the Dublin docklands and beyond, the one with the biggest of all was the diminutive Johnny Ronan.

FOURTEEN

SMALL IN STATURE, BIG ON IDEAS: JOHNNY RONAN

Many developers were held responsible by the public, rightly or wrongly, as the villains of the 2008 crash, as much as the bankers. Some gained notoriety because they were as well-known already from the gossip pages of the newspapers in the Celtic Tiger era as they were for featuring on the business pages. Johnny Ronan, the so-called Bearded Buccaneer because of his pony-tailed jet-black hair and big beard, his driving of a €650,000 Maybach car and his dalliances with high-profile models half his age, played and partied hard and became synonymous with so-called developer excess. Although he owned an estate in Wicklow, he also built for city living, in garish pink, a Venetian-style palazzo on Burlington Road in Dublin 4. At one stage he was reckoned to be a billionaire. He became a lightning rod for much of the public anger but many banks, rival developers, judges and, in time, NAMA came to regard his often aggressive approach to business with some disdain too.

Prior to entering NAMA, the website of Johnny Ronan and Richard Barrett's Treasury boasted control of more than 131 property projects with a total value of over €4.6 billion. It also had debts of more than €2.7 billion, of which more than €1 billion was owed to NAMA. The end of Treasury – as a result of a liquidation application in the High Court by one of its creditor banks – was mired in controversy and legal recrimination. The liquidator, Michael McAteer of Grant Thornton, accused

Ronan and his business partner Richard Barrett of two asset-stripping moves in China in the last days of the company's existence, a fraud against the company's creditors as far as McAteer was concerned. Eventually, McAteer agreed to a settlement proposed by Barrett that involved a Hong Kong property company paying the liquidator for the assets ... and giving €5 million to Barrett and another large, undisclosed payment to Ronan. Justice Peter Kelly approved the deal in the High Court as being in the best interests of creditors but decried the payments to the defendants. There was speculation about possible action disbarring Ronan and Barrett from being allowed to serve as company directors, but this came to nothing.

Barrett went to China, but Ronan wanted to continue in the development business in Ireland. He identified a site near his 'pink palace' on Burlington Road for a major office redevelopment and outbid several international investors to get it. Development Securities, a London-based firm later renamed as U+I, was the main backer of a successful €42 million bid by Ronan for the property. And then, fatefully, Colony Capital, an underbidder for the same site, became involved. Colony was to embark on a major investment spree in Ireland, spending about €1 billion in a couple of years, with Ronan as its local partner. Colony was controlled by American billionaire Tom Barrack – a close friend of Donald Trump's – and had nearly €20 billion in assets. An old friend of Ronan's, Paddy McKillen, with whom he had built the Treasury Building more than 20 years earlier, organised a dinner in London, at Richard Corrigan's Mayfair restaurant, at which Ronan was introduced to Colony. Having bought the site, Ronan needed more money to develop the Vertium office block, which in time would become a 172,000 square foot building that would be let to Amazon in the largest letting in Dublin since the crash. Colony agreed to provide that funding.

Ronan's share of the profits from that development got him started again – and it also started a highly profitable relationship with Colony. It was Colony, alongside M&G Investments, a UK-based firm that managed €340 billion in assets globally, that funded Ronan's exit from NAMA, lending him the money to pay off his loans with NAMA in full. His exit was confirmed in April 2015 and he celebrated with a huge party at the pink palace. 'It was like getting me mickey out of a bear trap,' he was quoted as saying.

Colony backed Ronan because it decided that Ronan's ambitious, albeit aggressive, approach would help to identify and deliver the best sites for huge office complexes in Dublin and the best quality builds on them. That would deliver the highest returns on investment. Ronan also had a way of persuading good tenants to commit and had a positive relationship with a different state agency, the IDA. The nature of the financial relationship between Ronan and Colony remained private and there was speculation that he was merely a hired hand, even if his name was at the forefront of all subsequent developments. In reality, Ronan received hefty fees but also got small equity stakes in each development, which were increased depending on the returns he achieved. The relationship with Colony developed so well that M&G was eased aside in time.

Colony wanted peace with NAMA too because it wanted to buy more sites from it and didn't want its Irish partner to be in conflict with such a dominant seller. Ronan remained very bitter about what he perceived as mistreatment – especially its insistence that he sell valuable London assets that he believed, with some merit, could be developed to provide enough profit to clear his debts, much as Sean Mulryan of Ballymore was allowed to do. Ronan's daughter Jodie, who had become central to running the business, agreed with Colony that continued warfare was counter-productive and her influence on her father provoked a mellowing. However, Ronan couldn't resist a last shot at NAMA in a submission to the Oireachtas Banking Inquiry in 2015, in which he claimed that NAMA had a 'prejudicial approach' towards Treasury.

'I firmly believe that certain individuals within NAMA decided that they did not want to work with Treasury Holdings, its shareholders and/

or its management team and that they would take it down, whatever the consequence,' Ronan stated, adding that this had a 'stifling effect on the Irish property market'. This was more polite than his previous claims comparing NAMA's bosses to 'butchers performing heart surgery'. NAMA responded that 'these and other contentions have been comprehensively considered by the High Court which ruled in NAMA's favour'. His submission backfired somewhat, however, when he concluded it with the use of the expression *arbeit macht frei*, which translates as 'work will set you free'. That was the slogan emblazoned over the gates of Nazi concentration camps during the Second World War. He later apologised and the phrase was removed.

Simultaneously, however, Ronan went to war with other State agencies. If he had ceased hostilities with NAMA out of necessity, he regularly and deliberately clashed with the planners and politicians of Dublin City Council, even if he found An Bord Pleanála more sympathetic to his sites when it came to building upwards. He believed that the potential of the docklands was being restricted by planners. 'Dublin City Council saw to it that we're the only convention centre in the world without a dedicated hotel attached,' he raged in one interview. 'Our docklands are an arbitrary six storeys of low-density mediocrity. Why do we constrain our potential with small thinking?' Eoghan Murphy, during his tenure as Minister for Housing, was another who was sympathetic to Ronan's skyward ambitions, albeit for all and not just the diminutive developer.

The rejuvenated Ronan became somewhat obsessed with statement buildings. For developers, commercial buildings should be about the cost of building and the subsequent rental income and capital value for sale, but occasionally egos are overly dependent on praise for the scale of completed structures. Nobody else had ever thought of going as tall as Ronan wanted for his confusingly named Waterfront South Central towers on the north side of the River Liffey.

'We need the vision to realise more efficient use of spare space,' Ronan argued in an interview with *The Currency*. 'We need greater heights, greater densities and lower car parking ratios in appropriate locations – particularly those well served by public transport – the most suitable of which are unquestionably Spencer Place and Waterfront South Central.'

Ronan had a Manhattan-style vision for Waterfront South Central on North Wall Quay on a site that had been occupied by Tilestyle's warehouse and Tedcastle's coal yard. He proposed to planners that two of the three residential towers would be more than 40 storeys tall. The taller tower, 44 storeys, would rise to 167 metres in height – nearly three times the height of Liberty Hall further up the river. The second tower – just 12 metres away – would be 20 metres lower, but still 26.5 metres taller than the Spire on O'Connell Street. Comparisons were drawn with the Poolbeg stacks. Ronan argued that the height was permissible under the 2018 ministerial guidelines on building heights and that precedent had been set by the 22-storey Capital Dock across the river. Ronan proposed that there would be 1,005 apartments in his towers, of which 490 would be one-bedroom units, 500 two-bedroom and the remainder three-bedroom. Only 431 of the apartments would be 'dual aspect', with views out in two directions, and 101 units would be offered as social housing, to meet legal obligations under the Planning Act 2000. These would be on lower floors and would have lower floor-to-ceiling heights, but DCC was told these would cost it €70 million upfront plus contributions to service charges. Ronan said half of the private sector apartments would be build-to-rent and the rest would be for sale. Those prices were not disclosed but many promises were made as to the facilities, including a 'matrix of vertical and horizontal gardens and terraces … hanging winter gardens and atria, and the ground-level urban copse' that, together, would make Dublin's tallest-ever tower 'the greenest building in Ireland'.

There was a description of 'a high-rise garden village in the heart of Dublin's new riverfront district [and] a symbol of the future of living and working in Dublin', with roosting boxes for bats and birds as well as 'bug hotels' to attract bees and butterflies. Residents would be offered the chance to tend allotments as well as planted terraces, each one with a different 'theme'. At the entrance, it was proposed there be an 'edible street' lined with trees and shrubs yielding fruits, nuts and berries. 'What we're trying to achieve at Waterfront is exactly what Paris has successfully delivered at La Défense: a modern evolution of a characterful city in the appropriate location – brownfield urban regeneration at scale, at a remove from the city core,' said Ronan. The planners said no.

Ronan did, however, begin work on the office part of the development, with Citibank agreeing to take 300,000 square feet of space from 2026, at which point Ronan will begin redevelopment of Citibank's existing offices on North Wall Quay.

Spencer Place was Ronan's other major development for the north docks, further advanced than his plans for Waterfront South Central. In 2016, using cash sourced mainly from Colony Capital, Ronan paid NAMA €43 million for the site. It was the start of a €3 billion investment over the next four years as Colony became his primary partner. At Spencer Dock, Ronan got permission for two blocks of seven and nine storeys of offices and did a deal with a major multinational tenant on a long lease. Salesforce is a US cloud computing software as a service (SaaS) company that focuses mainly on customer-relationship management and it had chosen Ireland as its European hub. It also likes height. Its offices in London are located in a 230-metre-tall building, while in Chicago the office is 247 metres tall. Its San Francisco hub is higher than 300 metres.

Knowing this, Ronan sought an increase in the permitted height of Salesforce Towers to 11 and 13 storeys, which would have given him a further 100,000 square feet of space at least, sufficient to accommodate another 1,000 Salesforce personnel on the site in addition to the 4,000 already planned. Despite the job possibilities DCC refused on the basis that the proposed height addition 'would not be consistent with the provisions of the [North Lotts and Grand Canal Dock SDZ] planning scheme'. A furious Ronan responded that DCC was going against the

State's own guidelines, something he called 'idiotic, ridiculous', highlighting how he believed Spencer Dock was the most suitable site in the country for tall buildings, close to the Luas, the planned Metro underground and the Convention Centre (which he and Barrett had built, with Crosbie also in their consortium and which features later in this book).

He managed to sell the Spencer Place development, including the Samuel Hotel, for €500 million to Blackstone, one of the largest single-asset office investments in the State's history. It was an important deal because 2021 was a difficult one for Ronan. Colony's Tom Barrack became embroiled in legal and political controversy in the US because of his connections to Donald Trump and shocked Ronan by selling his property interests to Fortress Investment Group in 2021 without much warning. Fortress Investment Group is a business ultimately owned by the Japanese investment giant SoftBank and it got the Irish assets as part of a portfolio of approximately 40 positions encompassing over 100 properties in Europe and the US. Ronan apparently had wanted Colony to sell to Oaktree, the US investment firm, but that option wasn't granted to him. Ronan now faced a future where Fortress would seek to sell what it had bought from Colony, meaning he needed new partners for other deals.

The north bank of the Liffey wasn't the only location where Ronan wanted to go towards the sky. He wanted to build an 88-metre, 23-storey building beside Tara Street Dart station in Dublin city centre. DCC rejected him twice on the basis that the building was too tall. A series of anonymous adverts, which called for changes to building height regulations in Dublin, started to appear in newspapers. It was revealed quickly that Ronan and Colony Capital were behind the #GrowUpDublin campaign.

There are arguments, however, that once anything goes above six storeys in height the costs of building escalate, and that this then feeds into the rents that must be charged to recover those costs, or the prices to buy the completed buildings. In a tall building it's reckoned about one-third of the floor space will be taken up by lifts, stairs and service ducts for water, sewage, air-conditioning and cabling. Greater height also leads to increased structural and fire safety requirements. Pricey to build, they are also expensive to maintain and operate. Depending on the width of streets below, they can overshadow and create wind down-draughts. However, arguments that high-rise buildings, beyond the five- to nine-storey limits set by DCC, are unsuitable for family living do not stack up with the experience of many cities around the world.

In 2018 Minister Eoghan Murphy issued a directive to councils to encourage towns to grow 'upwards, not just outwards', saying 'arbitrary height caps don't make any sense'. Murphy may have had apartments in mind when saying this, but developers like Ronan pounced, using the endorsement as a basis for applications to ABP. It approved his plans for Tara Street, for offices in the tower but also a luxury hotel.

Critics of Ronan's proposal were enraged. Some claimed it would detract from the character of James Gandon's neoclassical Custom House directly across the river. Ronan had his answer for that. The city's historic Georgian core should be protected and celebrated, he countered, but locating well-designed taller buildings in appropriate locations did nothing to compromise the city's character: 'Cities are dynamic. They are living, breathing things that over time, must evolve.'

His plans for the tower evolved because of Covid. He applied in 2021 to change the use of the building, wanting to abandon the four storeys that would have made up the hotel and turn the entire building into offices. He said the market for hotels had faltered – something that subsequent activity disproved – and that they couldn't be built 'for the craic' if the money wasn't there for them. He said there was no likelihood of receiving a commercially viable proposal from a hotel tenant.

He won the appeal in March 2021. An Taisce was appalled, describing the decision as a 'catastrophic error'. It said removing an upmarket hotel from the tower could turn the corner of George's Quay and Tara

Street into a 'dead after dark' area: 'The development was permitted in good faith on the basis of providing a mix of uses in this prime city-core location. By removing the hotel use and changing this to office, the development would now be overwhelmingly office use, apart from the retaining of a minor level of associated restaurant/retail use.'

As it turned out it would be office space that would subsequently suffer, but there was logic to Ronan's reasoning.

It wasn't just in the docklands that Ronan showed vision and a willingness to take new risks. In 2016 he purchased part of the enormous site occupied by AIB's Bankcentre in Ballsbridge, Dublin 4, focusing on the front four buildings facing onto Merrion Road, which were owned by Aviva, directly across the road from the RDS. Ronan assembled a consortium with Colony, alongside Siobhán Quinlan, wife of bankrupt Derek, who invested €7.5 million, and the WLR Cardinal Mezzanine Fund, which also included the Irish Strategic Investment Fund (ISIF) as an investor. As Ronan began a €350 million redevelopment of the site, he and Colony purchased the WLR Cardinal and Quinlan stakes, giving them quick profits. He then persuaded Facebook that the renovated buildings would be suitable for its European HQ and he persuaded it to sign a 25-year lease on what was now called Fibonacci Square – and 375,000 square feet of office space – for €600 million in rent to Ronan and Colony over that period. It was a remarkable coup – the largest single office letting in the history of the State – more so given that Facebook already had more than 4,000 employees in Ireland across four locations: Grand Canal Square in the Dublin docklands, the Samuel Beckett building on East Wall Road in Dublin 3, Nova Atria South in Sandyford, and, in Cork, Facebook Reality Labs. The American giant ploughed on to do further deals behind the Fibonacci site, for properties owned by the Serpentine Consortium and Davy, with the intention of having more than 60 Facebook teams located in Ballsbridge, from Facebook itself to WhatsApp, Instagram and Messenger, and its Oculus virtual reality unit. It was to be Meta's second-largest campus globally, with only the global headquarters at Menlo Park in California bigger. (Facebook was renamed as Meta in mid-2022 to suit Mark Zuckerberg's idea of adapting the group for a future in the 'metaverse'.)

Ronan and Colony weren't the only ones to bet big on Ballsbridge and the Meta expansion. Blackstone paid €395 million for 340,000 square feet of office space across four existing blocks to the rear of the site which had been built by the Serpentine consortium, a syndicate of private individuals and companies assembled by AIB Private Banking and Goodbody Stockbrokers in the first decade of the century.

However, alarm bells rang in late 2022 when Meta halted the fit-out of the Fibonacci Square part of its new campus. It had become clear that Meta had over-extended and it began a series of redundancies. It wouldn't need all of the space. Instead, Meta decided to sublet all four of the newly developed blocks it had taken from Ronan to a new occupier or occupiers.

This had implications for Fortress Investments, which had taken over ownership when it bought Colony. It was prepared to sell to Pontegadea, the family firm of Zara founder Amancio Ortega, for between €525 and €550 million. However, the deal did not proceed. The locked-in rental from Meta meant that Ortega's returns from a purchase at that price – the yield – would be 4 per cent per annum. However, rising interest rates meant that US government bonds could provide the same yield – and without any fears of possible missed or non-payments. There would be limited opportunity to raise the rent, at least not for many years, so the only way the deal would make sense would be for Fortress to drop the price. Or else just wait things out.

As Ronan approached the age of 70, his involvement in the belated development of the Irish Glass Bottle site (see Chapter 34) would become the main reason for public interest in him. Some wondered if he would now look towards retirement. He took a fall off his racing bicycle in Spain in late 2021 and broke his hip. Although he was still seen occasionally in Enniskerry, County Wicklow, in 2022, he had become a resident of Birżebbuġa, a seaside town in Malta, according to corporate filings, presumably to avail of tax advantages. His three children, John junior, Jodie and James, all remained in Ireland as shareholders and officers in the family business, but few expected a contest among them to replace their father in the style of the TV show *Succession*. The expectation grew in property circles that their ambition did not meet their father's and that any future activities would be far more modest in scale and might be left to outside professional managers.

FIFTEEN

ROOMS AND VIEWS: HOTELS

For some years now, it has been easier to find somewhere to stay short-term on Airbnb than it has been to find a house or apartment to rent for a longer period. The reason was not directly related to either sector: it had more to do with the shortage of hotel rooms. This provided an opportunity for some enterprising landlords to let rooms, apartments or houses via Airbnb – even though many of them did not apply for planning permission for short-term letting use. It helped to plug the hotel accommodation gap, but it made Dublin's housing crisis worse.

Airbnb originated in the US ostensibly as a way for homeowners to let a spare room for a night or two at a time to different guests who booked through the platform. However, some owners offered rental properties instead, reckoning there was way more money to be made when all this added up than in charging long-term tenants who would also gather legal rights the longer they stayed. Airbnb regulations restrict the use of existing residential stock for short-term lettings, but the suspicion has been that the company ignores the rule.

Many local authorities have confirmed that the number of applications for planning permission required by those running short-term lets in rent pressure zones (RPZs) has been low. This application is required if a person's primary residence is being let on a short-term basis for more than 90 days in the year, or if a second property is being rented as an Airbnb within an RPZ. Dún Laoghaire–Rathdown County Council said that 'no applications to operate a property as a short-term let have been received since the introduction of the short-term letting regulations' yet the Airbnb website has over 1,000 properties available in Dún Laoghaire. DCC said it received only 27 change-of-use planning applications between 2019, when the legislation came into force, and 2022. The same is found around the country. Killarney is Kerry's only RPZ. Airbnb's website claimed there were more than 1,000 properties to rent in the tourist town. Kerry County Council said it granted planning permission for change of use in ten cases. Wicklow County Council said it has received 15 planning permission applications for short-term lets. Cork County Council said it has issued warning letters 'in relation to allegations of short-term letting for a total of 60 cases since legislation for same was introduced in 2019'.

Airbnb became popular with tourists for a number of reasons: it could be cheaper than staying in a hotel or bed and breakfast establishment; it might be a better venue for larger groups and parties; hotel rooms simply weren't available at all. In the decade after the Great Recession, between 2008 and 2018, there was no meaningful increase in the number of new hotel rooms across the country, even as visitor numbers continued to grow at a far faster rate than had been expected by almost anyone. Operators were delighted with the high occupancy rates this implied and the higher revenues that could be demanded. The period of bargain prices for customers at hotels that followed the crash proved to be short-lived.

Only four new hotels opened in Dublin in the eight years to the end of 2015: the Gibson, the Temple Bar Inn, the Dean and the Marker. In 2016, the 182-room Clyde Court closed and the 198-bed Holiday Inn Express on O'Connell Street opened. The activity in distressed asset sales came to an end and there was a realisation that Ireland, and particularly Dublin, needed new hotels. In January 2018 Fáilte Ireland wrote to urge planners to sanction developments because tourism 'is being threatened due to a shortage of hotel bedrooms'. It also highlighted how it had become more difficult to attract major conferences – which brought high-spending delegates to our restaurants and shops, such as at major aviation industry events each January – if enough hotel rooms weren't available.

Suddenly there was a burst of activity, as developers saw an opportunity and hoteliers expressed interest in operating new facilities. Four new hotel openings accounted for the bulk of new rooms delivered in Dublin in 2018, with some extensions too at existing outlets, while there were eight new hotels opened in the city in 2019. The number of planning permissions may have given the impression more hotels were being built than was the case. Pre-Covid there were plans for more than 80 new hotel proposals that, had they all come to fruition, would have added 18,000 bedrooms to Dublin's existing complement of 23,000. That was too much, but proof again that having planning does not necessarily mean that it will be acted upon, especially if others in an area get to start building first. But the perception led to something of a public backlash, based more on emotion than fact, and a campaign called #nomorehotels trended regularly on Irish Twitter.

Hotels were blamed for unrelated planning shortcomings, such as a lack of affordable housing or cultural venues. Dublin city councillors voted in September 2020 to curb new hotel projects in favour of more residential and cultural spaces, ignoring the fact that so few had actually been built, that there was a genuine need and that denial would not lead to more houses or apartments in their stead.

Although thousands of pubs had closed nationwide in the previous decades the announcement that the George Bernard Shaw was to close at the end of October 2019 became an opportunity for a social media campaign to condemn the government for apparently failing to protect the capital's culture, that Dublin was 'losing its soul'. The likes of podcaster Blindboy and singer Hozier led the charge on Twitter. 'They're closing The Bernard Shaw? Are you fucking serious? Where is left for Dublin pints and daycent tunes with like mind?' lamented Blindboy. 'What is most special and unique about Dublin are Dubliners themselves, and spaces like this where culture and community is fostered and grows,' tweeted Hozier. 'Without interesting places like these, the city loses its heartbeat.'

The venue on Richmond Street in Portobello, Dublin 8, was not an old traditional iconic venue with a so-called vaunted history. It was 13 years old. Bodytonic's Trevor O'Shea took on the existing pub in 2006 on a one-year lease until the Richmond Partnership, owned by the family of the late Ray Kearns, the founder of the Institute of Education school, was ready to redevelop its expanse of land around it, much of the rest of which was owned by Clancourt Holdings. There had been no applications at this stage for the construction of a hotel but that didn't stop the narrative being spread on social media.

As it happens, the building, dating from 1859, is a protected structure. Temporary planning permission was granted in 2008 for a smoking area adjacent to the pub, which in 2011 was changed into an open-air beer garden and dining area. DCC permitted the beer garden, dining area and Big Blue Bus Pizza Kitchen for a further three years. However, this was overturned by ABP, who decided the outdoor area would likely delay the regeneration of the area and refused permission. It was a bit different from the conventional pub but traded on the fact that it had 'popped up' and made use of what would otherwise be unused space during the recession years. It provided space for art exhibitions. It was very colourful, with murals abounding. And music was played there, sometimes with DJs doing live sets. Many of its clientele might have fancied it as something more and themselves as a cool crowd, somewhat more sophisticated and modern than the yokels who drink elsewhere, but its cultural significance was somewhat exaggerated. And the prices were quite high (as I noted on occasions when I was there with friends or family). It was not run by some kind of hipster cooperative as a sort of not-for-profit organisation.

Bodytonic, as the parent business is called, was in operation to make a profit and had four other pubs in Dublin. It had spotted an unconventional niche in the market and it served it, but it was nothing more special than a conventional business offering a slightly less-than-conventional service. In early 2023 the rest of the site around the old pub was demolished, including the long-closed Manhattan diner, a staple for early morning drinkers on their way home from a long night out and who wanted a fry-up. But the George Bernard Shaw remains a strange-looking and redundant anomaly alongside the new clearance work around it.

Plans to further gentrify part of the northside, at Smithfield, not far from the Four Courts ran into similar #nomorehotels opposition. The Cobblestone pub in Smithfield sits among a host of derelict buildings in one of the few parts of the area that has not been redeveloped. The pub was leased by a family, the Mulligans, for over 30 years and was well known as a venue for traditional music performances and, in its back rooms, teaching. In 2021 the owner of the property and surrounding land, the Marron Group, applied to build a hotel that would partially incorporate, but change, the pub.

The pushback was bigger than anyone had expected. Almost 700 objections were lodged with DCC. An online petition, Save the Cobblestone, gathered almost 35,000 signatures and public rallies in support of the pub were held. Objectors to the proposals included local TDs Mary Lou McDonald, Gary Gannon of the Social Democrats and Neasa Hourigan of the Green Party. The campaign was successful. The removal of the back-room area of the pub – a space for teaching, rehearsal and performance of traditional music – was a specific ground of refusal by DCC, who believed its loss would be contrary to the city's development plan provisions in respect of culture in the capital. The Dublin Is Dying campaign group said this was 'a major victory for people power' and asked that Dublin City Council 'safeguard our wonderful cultural bastion for all to enjoy'. Gannon said the council had an opportunity 'to put some life and heart back into the city' by enhancing what already exists at the Cobblestone site and said there was 'real merit' to the idea of a compulsory purchase order (CPO). 'The Cobblestone not only brings vibrancy to Dublin but it also gives people cause to come into the city,' he argued. 'Investing in culture should not be an alien concept to the State. We should have city managers falling over themselves to preserve these types of institutions for Dublin.'

After the public protests the developer, Marron Estates, revised its plans for the Cobblestone, proposing a seven-storey scheme instead of nine and to retain the entire Cobblestone pub over all floors at the basement, ground and first and second floors. It offered to relocate the back room to 'a purpose-built performing space contained within the retained historic yard to the rear of the site ... This, along with the reduced proposals of maintaining all other uses at first and second floor above the existing Cobblestone pub, would ensure that the important cultural offering would be maintained.' It argued that 'this application offers an opportunity to redevelop this important site, one that has lain vacant and in disrepair for a substantial number of years.' However, it subsequently withdrew the revised application and at the time of writing there are no known plans for development.

The protestors may be happy that all is left alone, but there is plenty of evidence there and elsewhere that leaving things as they are because of a distrust or dislike of change often leads to decay; while change may not always work as intended and may be disruptive, the creation of something new may help an area to prosper for longer.

DALATA

Pat McCann is one of the most ebullient figures in Irish business, not someone prepared to leave things as they are. He has needed to be. He became chief executive of Jurys Doyle Hotel Group in 2000 but retired in 2006 when the group was largely broken up in a series of Celtic Tiger property-inspired plays, such as the Dunne purchase of the lands at Ballsbridge where the Jurys and Berkeley Court hotels stood. He received private equity backing to set up what became Dalata, buying 11 Quality Hotel and Comfort Inn properties in 2007 just before the crash caused him to dramatically reassess his options.

Not for the first or last time McCann pivoted. Dalata offered management services to banks and receivers, operating hotels on their behalf once the original owners had been ejected. One of its biggest contracts was with Blackstone, to manage the Burlington Hotel in Dublin 4. McCann assembled money to buy hotels at low prices from receivers and liquidators, the key being the price paid was below what it would cost to knock and rebuild the hotel. He launched the Maldron Hotels brand in 2008 and then the Clarion, subsequently renamed the Clayton, in the three- and four-star markets.

Having established the group's reputation, in March 2014 McCann raised €265 million by selling shares in Dalata through a listing on the Dublin stock market. Major US investment firms, such as Franklin Templeton and Pioneer, became significant shareholders. With this money – and additional borrowed funds – Dalata bought the Red Cow group of ten hotels, with 2,627 rooms, from Tom Moran and his family, giving it properties in Dublin and Cork, and in London, Leeds and Manchester in the UK, although he sold the title property, located at a junction on the M50, back to Moran. Dalata bought a business that was trading successfully, at least before it had to make its debt repayments because it had bought the Bewley's hotels chain six years earlier for €580 million in a spectacularly bad piece of mistiming.

McCann believed the days of small, family-run hotels were numbered and that local properties needed to club together and pool resources to survive. He told investors of the cost savings larger hotel groups could have with centralised back-office support and booking systems. The biggest factor was the ability to buy hotels cheaply. In time, Dalata became a builder itself, at the former Charlemont Clinic along the Grand Canal and on Kevin Street in Dublin 8, just minutes from St Stephen's Green. Having equity helped because two of the sites it bought in Dublin came from developers who had full planning permission but couldn't get the money to build.

McCann and his board decided that the company had to diversify out of Ireland. It continued to expand in Dublin – at the IFSC, in particular, and with plans for a new hotel near Croke Park – but focused the bulk of its expansion outside the country. When I interviewed him during the depths of the Covid lockdown, McCann was confident that business would return to normal in time. During his career he had seen the impact on tourism of the 1970s oil crisis, the recession of the 1980s, the Gulf War of the early 1990s, the terror attacks on the World Trade Centre in 2001 and then the Great Recession. He felt that he would be justified in building new hotels. He was correct.

By the end of 2022, Dalata had 10,659 rooms and its revenues were over €500 million annually. Less than 500 of the rooms were in Dublin, with 1,800 in the rest of the country. McCann retired, having turned 70, leaving his long-term deputy Dermot Crowley to take over the running of what had become a major organisation. As a major operator in Ireland, Dalata also had to find overseas markets to diversify and protect itself from over-reliance on local events; just as foreign operators spread their own risks and opportunities geographically across different markets, which includes coming to Ireland.

TIFCO

Tifco was second only to Dalata as the largest hotel group in the country, and it also profited from taking on management contracts on behalf of banks and receivers after the crash. Tifco's original founders were businessmen Aidan Crowe and Gerry Houlihan, the latter the owner of the high-profile DID Electrical retail chain. Their hotel interests started with Clontarf Castle in Dublin but expanded to include the 204-bedroom Crowne Plaza Hotel at Northwood, Santry, near Dublin Airport, as well as Crowne Plaza hotels in Blanchardstown and Dundalk, the 114-bedroom Holiday Inn Express at Northwood and the 120-bedroom Hilton Hotel at Kilmainham in Dublin. This was funded by debt held by IBRC, which provided Goldman Sachs with the opportunity to take control for an undisclosed price. The American investor decided to work with the management and added 12 Travelodge hotels to the portfolio to make for a bigger entity.

By 2018 Tifco controlled about 1,800 bedrooms across 18 owned hotels and other management contracts. It was sold to US fund Apollo Global for a little more than €200 million, about one-third of the initial suggested sales price, which was based on estimates of the value of the properties instead of the profitability, which was low. It continued to expand, developing the country's first Hard Rock Hotel on Parliament Street. In May 2019 it spent €100 million on a 393-bedroom venue built on Townsend Street by Tetrarch which became a Travelodge.

THOMAS ROEGGLA

Roeggla is an Austrian who set up AktienInvestor.com, a Vienna-based 'international equity investment organisation' that invests in the resources, tech and industrial sectors by targeting 'undervalued companies with outstanding potential'. His initial fortune seems to have come from bets on resources companies in Australia and Canada in the late 1990s. He was introduced to Ireland through some successful early investments in government bonds.

He also bought the Quayside Shopping Centre in Sligo, apartment blocks in Limerick and office buildings in Dublin and Cork. He bought the Fitzwilton Hotel in Waterford out of receivership in 2014 and then spent over €26 million to acquire the Farnham Estate hotel and golf resort in 2016. It had been operated by Radisson, a 158-bedroom hotel on a 1,250-acre estate, which had been developed by Roy McCabe, founder of the McCabe pharmacy chain, during the property boom at a cost of about €85 million.

Roeggla bought the four-star McWilliam Park Hotel in Claremorris, County Mayo, for €9 million after it went into examinership in 2016. It was developed in 2006 at a cost of more than €20 million. It has one of the largest concert hall venues in the west of Ireland, frequently attracting 800 guests to country music functions. He also bought the four-star

Anner Hotel in Thurles – well known to hurling fans on Munster senior championship days – the luxury Aghadoe Heights in Kerry, which overlooks the lakes, the Cavan Crystal Hotel, the Diamond Coast Hotel in Sligo, the Clarion in Limerick, Mount Wolseley golf resort in Carlow, the Connemara Coast near Barna in Galway and Harvey's Point hotel in Donegal.

He also acquired 10 Ormond Quay, a carefully preserved Georgian mansion on Dublin city's quays to use for private functions. He bought the 186-bedroom Tallaght Cross hotel in west Dublin in 2019, to add to the TMR Hotel Collection. It was sold to him by an unnamed private investor who had bought it from NAMA in 2014 but didn't reopen it. It had been developed by Liam Carroll in 2008. He has continued to add assets, buying the Ballymascanlon House hotel on the Cooley Peninsula in 2022. Roeggla, who lives on a lakeside home with its own helipad near the ski resort of St Moritz in Switzerland and who posts on social media regularly from luxury resorts around the world, used Davy Real Estate to assemble his portfolio and Windward Management, run by former Gresham hotelier Patrick Coyle, to manage them.

THE WATERS BROTHERS

Of the new Irish money investing in hotels, perhaps the most interesting was that of Eamon Waters. He and his brother Noel started the waste management company Panda in 1990 with three trucks and a patch of ground behind the family's petrol filling station in Beauparc, near Slane in County Meath. They ran waste collection routes in Louth and Meath before expanding into Dublin.

Panda's real breakthrough came in 2005 when Dublin's four local authorities handed all collection responsibilities to private operators. Panda was the only company operating in the four Dublin districts. Waste collection isn't just domestic waste from people's homes. Panda became the capital's largest skip operator when the owners of A1 Waste went out of business and it also did significant business in collecting and disposing of construction rubble during the boom years. It also became an expert in sorting and recycling and reselling waste, where more money can be made.

During the Great Recession, many waste operators suffered badly as demand suddenly evaporated (due to the lack of construction waste to be removed from sites) and a price war for domestic refuse collection put some out of business. Panda continued to prosper and in 2016, in partnership with Blackstone, Waters merged Panda with its biggest rival, Greenstar, creating the country's biggest waste company, Beauparc Utilities. Greenstar had entered receivership in 2012 with an estimated deficiency of €250 million. Its banks were owed €82.3 million. It was bought by US investment fund Cerberus for just €12.7 million. But the losses continued and Cerberus was happy to sell for a small profit to Waters and Blackstone.

By 2020 the expanded company was the biggest in the Irish market, with over €500 million in revenue and €34.74 million in profit, employing more than 2,000 people not just in Ireland but in Britain and the Netherlands also. In 2021 Beauparc Utilities was sold to the asset management arm of Macquarie, the Australian investment bank, for more than €1.3 billion. Eamon Waters was reported to have made €367 million from the deal. He began spending it, mainly on property.

Waters acquired Royal Hibernian Way, a mall complex on Dawson Street, Dublin, for €74 million. The brothers bought the Grafton Plaza hotel on Digges Lane, near St Stephen's Green, for about €15 million and closed the Break for the Border pub as they expanded the hotel. That project had been an O'Dwyer brothers' creation and when Waters bought No 8 Dawson Street, beside the former Waterstones bookstore, the O'Dwyers advised on turning the building, which has a defunct church at the back, into a restaurant venue.

A Waters company bought a building on Pembroke Street in Dublin, which had full planning permission for a 108-bedroom hotel, bar and restaurant. The building was the former office of the Commissioners of

Irish Lights. It had been acquired for €26 million in 2006 by developers Gerry Deane and Paddy Fitzgerald but was purchased by companies linked to Brian Clingen, a Florida-based businessman, for just €3.5 million in 2013. Meanwhile, Waters received permission to build a €30 million hotel at Ship Street in Dublin 8, almost next to Padraic Rhatigan's Radisson Blu at Golden Lane.

COVID AND HOTELS

Once Covid passed there was further economic uncertainty caused by the Russian invasion of Ukraine in early 2022, which brought tens of thousands of refugees to Ireland. The hotel sector was not as imperilled by Covid as it had been heading into the 2008 crisis, however, because it was less indebted than before; much of its recent investment was provided by equity funds, although many outlets were very dependent on State financial supports to carry them through the Covid shutdowns.

The Russian invasion created new options for some hoteliers as the State faced an accommodation crisis and turned to them. Many hoteliers, particularly in the lower price range, still suffering from accumulated Covid losses, usually in rural areas, saw an opportunity for guaranteed revenues at a time of dramatically rising costs as electricity and gas prices soared; they feared not only their own rising costs but also the ability of customers to afford their prices. About 140 hotels and guesthouses provided about 8,400 beds overall to accommodate some 14,000 people, beneficiaries of temporary protection (BOTP) – the EU-wide scheme in which Ireland participated. By the end of the first annual contract, however, many hotels withdrew as hoteliers faced a push from locals in tourism-reliant areas to provide beds for visitors instead. Some feared being too publicly associated with refugee accommodation as small numbers of demonstrators fermented dissent in their local areas.

It was an indication of the uncertainty caused by the Russian invasion that in February 2022 the JMK Group converted the 421-bedroom Holiday Inn at Dublin Airport it had opened just seven months earlier into an asylum centre, guaranteeing it a stable income for 12 months. JMK Group also owns Hampton by Hilton and Holiday Inn Express (which it wants to extend) in Dublin city centre and Waterford Marina Hotel. It is developing an Adagio aparthotel in Cork city and a Moxy Hotel and Residence Inn in Cork city. JMK is owned by Londoner John Kajani, who moved from textiles to the property industry in 2009 by opening a small boutique hotel in Kensington. But by 2023 Dublin Airport hotel had returned to normal functioning.

The HSE paid Tetrarch (an Irish-controlled company that had been formed after the crash to pick up assets cheaply) at least €25 million for the use of Citywest as a Covid-19 isolation facility and field hospital. As well as leasing the hotel at a cost of €22.63 million for seven months at a rate of €142.50 a room per night, the HSE deal included leasing the Citywest convention hall for nearly €2 million. The hall was prepared as a field hospital, with 350 beds for recovering Covid patients. It was never used as it wasn't suitable for frail patients due to the lack of privacy and the distance from beds to toilets and showers. There was also considered to be an increased risk of hospital superbugs, such as MRSA and CPE, due to it being below normal hospital standards. Citywest Hotel Group recorded an operating profit of €3.34 million for 2020 after recording an operating loss of €222,599 in 2019. Citywest got new tenants subsequently, once the Covid crisis passed: it became one of the country's main reception areas for refugees arriving in the country.

It was an interesting turn of use for Tetrarch, which is chaired by financier Paul Connolly, a close associate of Denis O'Brien's.

Citywest had been developed by the late Jim Mansfield, a controversial character whose wealth was often quietly linked to criminal elements in gossip but not in the media because of libel laws. The extent of the family's interests in criminality became clearer in the years after his death when his son was imprisoned and connections to money-laundering for the criminal Kinahan empire were aired in court cases. Citywest featured 764 rooms, 30 different meeting and/or event venues, a convention centre with physical capacity for up to 8,000 people and an 18-hole, par-70 championship golf course. Bank of Scotland (Ireland) seized the property in 2010 when Mansfield couldn't meet loan repayments.

Citywest was acquired out of receivership by an Irish company called Brehon (later renamed Tetrarch), in partnership with the giant US fund Pimco, in September 2014 for about €30 million. They then spent another €12 million in upgrading the four-star property. Brehon then bought Mount Juliet hotel and golf estate in Kilkenny with different partners, including Denis O'Brien's nephew Emmet O'Neill and Stephen Grant of Grant Engineering.

Tetrarch scaled back on its hotel ownership ambitions after it abandoned the idea of a stock market flotation in late 2018. It had intended to buy 100 per cent ownership of Powerscourt in County Wicklow by buying the half belonging to its partner, the Swiss company Midwest Holdings, but instead sold its share. It sold Mount Wolseley resort in County Carlow and having bought the four-star Clonmel Park Hotel in 2015 it sold it for about €7. 5 million to Talbot Hotels only a few years later. It sold the four-star Killashee Hotel in County Kildare, a 141-bedroom hotel with conference, wedding, spa and leisure facilities located 30 kilometres from Dublin city centre, between Naas and Kilcullen, for €25 million to FBD Hotels & Resorts in 2022.

———

Various estimates had the total number of hotel rooms in County Dublin at 23,006 at the end of 2022. About 60 per cent of Dublin bedrooms were in four-star hotels and only 1,752 were five-star. There is clearly room for more, but just how many more hotels will be built is debated. The rising cost of borrowing money during 2023 suggested that many planning applications for 8,000 room keys would not be activated. Some suggested 3,000 more rooms would be supplied between 2023 and 2024, others less than 1,000.

The building costs for hotels – at the end of 2022 – ranged from €147,000 to €256,000 per room and aparthotel costs ranged from €135,000 to €223,000 per room. Room sizes range from 19 to 21 square metres for three-star hotels to between 21 and 23 square metres for four-star and 24 to 26 square metres for five-star hotels. This explains why developers are more eager to build hotels than apartment blocks, and why they are keener on smaller room units than bigger ones. It is cheaper. For the same site, where a five-star hotel may have 100 rooms, a compact luxury could accommodate as many as 180 keys. It is estimated that about three-quarters of hotel openings in 2023 would be in the budget segment. However, the sums still have to be done as to how much income each room could bring, as against the rent for an apartment, and some developers have opted to sell their hotel sites or make arrangements first with operators rather than speculatively develop them. A slowdown in construction, especially in urban locations, might not be good for the economy.

We need the hotel rooms to deal with increasing tourist numbers and to force Airbnb venues back into the rental housing stock. The realisation about the importance of hotels was emphasised when up to a third of them were converted temporarily in 2022 for use as emergency accommodation for refugees; it became evident that refugees did not have spending power in the local economy whereas, according to official figures, tourists tend to spend about €2.50 in the community for every €1 they spend in accommodation costs. In addition, the hotels are not using locations that could otherwise be used for housing: there is plenty of unused over-the-shop space that can be used for that purpose as well as land zoned for housing that has not been used.

SIXTEEN

PRESS UP: THE INSTAGRAM GENERATION

The twentieth-century pub landlord (it was nearly always men but sometimes widows) had the opportunity to live a comfortable lifestyle if he
ran his house well – and didn't drink the profits. The pub was the centre
of Irish social life for many during the last century. Many people had
few other social outlets and visited regularly, providing a regular and
reliable cash flow to publicans. Owning a well-located pub was deemed
a good investment because while the licences issued by the State were
restricted in number, they could be traded, and as long as the publican
remained in good standing with the Gardaí, then a licence was a valuable asset that could be put to profitable use.

Much changed in the twenty-first century. Although alcohol use
remained popular, consumption per head peaked in the early years
of the first decade and declined thereafter. People began using their
money for other things, such as eating out or foreign holidays. People
became more demanding of their pubs: they wanted a better choice of
food and more quality, and more comfort than many pubs had provided traditionally. To cover the costs of providing all of this the price
of alcohol went up and now, for their own financial reasons, a younger
generation began treating the pub as a more occasional night out rather
than the home from home it had been to previous generations. Home
drinking, with cheaper alcohol purchased from off-licences, became

more popular and people opted for 'prinks' – a few drinks with friends at home before heading out later to spend a shorter time in the pub. Technology played its part too in changing behaviour: younger people used to go to the pub in the hope of meeting possible partners but now their options increased as they swiped dating apps on their mobile phones. Competition between pubs for custom intensified and despite a rapidly growing population our number of pubs – which had been very high to start with – went into rapid decline, particularly in rural Ireland but also in suburban areas.

Publicans had to invest to survive, in improving the scale of operations, in introducing or increasing quasi-restaurant facilities and in making premises far more visually attractive. Pubs that didn't have optimal layouts and good design and were not in locations with relatively high footfall, or were competing in areas with too many pubs, struggled. Many publicans borrowed to expand or upgrade or, if they were doing well, to buy out rivals.

As the Celtic Tiger emerged, so did vast pubs on which enormous sums of money were spent on décor and comfort. We didn't have the corporate-owned chains that dominated much of the English pub landscape, but we got local operators who sought to expand by owning many properties, presumably to benefit from operational economies of scale.

The extent to which the banks effectively owned and controlled the pub trade was emphasised in 2015 when Ulster Bank put loans of €500 million connected to 66 pubs – and some hotels – up for sale at a price of €166 million. Sankaty Advisors – an offshoot of the former US Presidential candidate Mitt Romney-founded $75 billion Bain Capital – bought them. Other banks also had large loans outstanding with publicans and in some cases had sent in new managers to run the bars instead of original owners, looking to maximise cash for repayments before they looked to sell to new owners. Some existing owners continued to manage their relationships with the banks, and hold their properties, often with some difficulty, especially when cash was required for continued updating of venues to cope with the contraction in the market.

New investors launched new venues or took over old ones and revamped them to suit new customer demand. One of the fears was that during this change we would lose the distinctiveness of our pub culture, especially if UK chains moved in to buy loans from the banks. The arrival of JD Wetherspoon in 2013 terrified some existing publicans and even health campaigners. The British chain – led by high-profile Brexit campaigner Tim Martin – has nearly 800 pubs in the UK and is regarded as 'cheap and cheerful', attracting its clientele with lower-priced alcohol. However, it expanded slowly in Ireland – opening pubs in Dublin (city centre, IFSC, Blanchardstown, Blackrock, Swords and Dún Laoghaire), Cork, Carlow, Waterford and Galway. It has been prepared to invest significant sums and did an excellent refurbishment on the long-abandoned buildings of the former convent of the Little Sisters of the Assumption at Keaven's Port on Upper Camden Street, spending €33 million on the construction of an 89-bedroom hotel and pub, removing what had been a significant eye-sore. It opened a €4 million outlet on Hanover Quay in the docklands, close to the plaza outside the Bord Gáis Energy Theatre, and paid €9 million for a site in Temple Bar, Dublin's tourist quarter. It sold its first Dublin development, in Blackrock, to a consortium led by publican Noel Anderson with investment support from former Irish rugby internationals Jamie Heaslip, Sean O'Brien and Rob and Dave Kearney.

Funds also arrived. Attestor Capital, a London-based fund that is believed to have made a lot of money during the financial crash buying distressed assets across Europe, became an active purchaser of pubs in Ireland. It purchased the Brazen Head on Bridge Street – across the River Liffey from the Four Courts – for €15 million in 2021, a price that surprised many given the uncertainty for the entire business caused by Covid, although it seems that other property was included to allow for expansion. The Brazen Head's previous owners, John Hoyne and Tom

Maguire, had bought the premises for €5.5 million in 2004. The pub is reputed to be the oldest in Dublin, at its location since 1198 with the current building constructed in 1754, something that is marketed strongly to tourists along with its traditional music credentials. Attestor's confidence was emphasised by its acquisition in December 2021 of Camden Palace, on Camden Street, and Lundy Foot's in Temple Bar from publican Ross Murray for a rumoured price of about €27 million.

The sale of the Camden Street business by Murray was something of a surprise as it had bought the Palace nightclub, which was part of the Camden Deluxe Hotel, and revamped it as the Camden premium sports bar and multipurpose venue with a €10 million-plus investment. Attestor then bought The Bleeding Horse, Camden Street, for a price in excess of €9 million from David L'Estrange, a publican who still held eight pubs around Dublin. Attestor also bought five well-known Dublin pubs from the Smith Pub Group (owned by brothers Peter and Thomas) for a price of over €35 million: the Auld Dubliner and the Norseman in Temple Bar, TP Smiths on Jervis Street, the Lagoona in the IFSC and the Forty Four in Swords.

Irish investors also bought. Architect Paul Clinton, best known for his convention centre efforts on O'Connell Street decades earlier, bought O'Donoghue's on Westmoreland Street in 2011 and Flannery's on Camden Street in 2014, benefiting from knock-down prices and, in the latter venue, from the emergence of the area as one of the most active in the country in which young people socialised. Mixed martial arts star Conor McGregor also got in on the act, albeit later and with prices higher. He had become one of the richest people in his sport and one of Ireland's richest men, partly because of investments in bottled whiskey sales. Some of his fortune, estimated in the hundreds of millions of euro, has been reinvested in pubs: he has purchased the Black Forge Inn in Dublin 12, the Marble Arch pub in Drimnagh and the Waterside Bar beside Howth Yacht Club.

Michael Breslin from County Meath made a fortune in scaffolding in the US. He employed former Anglo Irish Bank boss David Drumm as a consultant for a period and then teamed up with Maurice Regan (who owned Opium, also on Camden Street). After a series of deals with local publicans, Breslin and Regan engaged in a €30 million investment programme, including a €4 million renovation of Café en Seine on Dawson Street and a €3 million revamp of NoLita on George's Street. Café en Seine was something of a trailblazer in the early part of the century, the creation of the late Liam O'Dwyer, and continues as one of Dublin's most popular venues, one of those that draws people into Dublin's city centre, albeit not in the numbers of previous decades, as the more health conscious younger generation eschew excessive alcohol consumption and more people look for restaurant alternatives.

One of the most active buyers was Alan Clancy, from County Westmeath, a former manager for Michael Wright of the Wright Hospitality Group; it had owned The Wright Venue in Swords, an enormous venue in an industrial estate near the airport in the Celtic Tiger years and which had once hosted the superstar singer Rihanna as a guest. Clancy emerged as one of the most enterprising of the new pub owners, seemingly in partnership with a range of investors, both individual and private equity. He established House, an upmarket pub and restaurant on Leeson Street, followed by 37 Dawson Street. House then expanded into outlets of the same name in Limerick and Belfast. Clancy turned the Baggot Inn into Xico and opened a basement venue, 9 Below, in St Stephens Green and took over the Oyster Tavern on Patrick Street in Cork and Mrs Robinson's in Greystones.

In his earlier years in business, Clancy was backed by Irish financial group Warren Private and also by Kish Capital, established by former Merrion Capital stockbroker Dan Ennis, which bought Thomas Read's on Dame Street. In 2018 he teamed up with property developer Gerry Conlan. There was speculation that wealthy friends, such as former footballer Robbie Keane and golfer Shane Lowry (who was best man at Clancy's 2022 wedding), might also be investors. Indeed, in December 2022 he and Lowry announced a joint venture to open a bar, restaurant and café in Tullamore, County Offaly. He continued to expand, opening The Gables in Foxrock in December 2021 and Beckett Locke in Point Square Village in October 2021. But he was very much in second place when compared to the expansion of the Press Up Group.

THE VISION OF MCKILLEN

Paddy McKillen senior featured prominently in one of my previous books, *Who Really Runs Ireland?*, particularly for his involvement, alongside Derek Quinlan and others, in buying the Maybourne Hotel Group, which included the famous and elite Claridge's, Connaught and Berkeley hotels in London, during the boom years. The legacy of that deal remains: he sold his 36 per cent shareholding to members of the Qatari royal family in 2015 under a profit-share arrangement. His seven-year contract to manage and redevelop the London portfolio ended in April 2022 and was followed by a legal action against the Qataris in which he claimed he was owed 'billions of pounds'. In late 2022 he began legal proceedings in California claiming the Qataris had cheated him out of 'tens of millions of dollars' in fees on work carried out transforming the Maybourne Beverly Hills hotel in Los Angeles into a 'world-class establishment'. He also started legal action in France, claiming €19.6 million of unpaid project management fees in relation to the Maybourne Riviera, formerly the Vista Palace, over-looking Monaco and the Mediterranean Sea.

McKillen is understood to have homes in London, Paris and Los Angeles, but most notable is the 600-acre Château La Coste vineyard in Provence, in the south of France; it is not an actual château but an elegant seventeenth-century bastide, or lodge, alongside which can be found the Villa La Coste hotel. Artworks in the lobby of that hotel include three sculptures by Damien Hirst, two drawings by Matisse, a Picasso mosaic, a Le Corbusier tapestry and paintings by Sean Scully. There are more than 40 art and architectural sites scattered across the property and new shows for the five galleries located there every three to four months.

When Lara Marlowe visited for the *Irish Times* in 2022, she wrote about how 'Bob Dylan was exhibiting his brightly coloured, French-influenced paintings when I visited. Dylan has also welded a permanent sculpture of a decorative railway boxcar up the hill.' Marlowe described a 'work in progress, with at least seven construction sites underway, including pieces by Norman Foster and Paulo Mendes da Rocha, bringing to eight the number of Pritzker Prize winners whose work is featured at the property.'

McKillen senior has said he owns 23 hotels globally as well as prime residential and commercial properties in the US, Dubai, Germany, Japan, Hong Kong, Vietnam, Argentina and Kazakhstan. He doesn't spend much time in Ireland but even after legal battles with NAMA – which he fought in the courts to prevent taking his loans under its control – he proclaims himself a proud Irishman. He repaid over €1.3 billion in loans, both personal and corporate, to IBRC as successor to Anglo Irish Bank and its chief executive, Mike Aynsley, supported him in his legal action against NAMA. McKillen co-owns the Jervis Street Shopping Centre in Dublin with Padraig Drayne through an Isle of Man-registered company, having moved ownership there in 2013 as part of a refinancing out of IBRC with UK firm M&G Investments. The loan was later refinanced by AIB, but the asset was left sitting in its tax-efficient structure in Douglas. McKillen also co-owns the Powerscourt Town Centre, in partnership with Tom Leonard.

In Ireland his son, Paddy McKillen junior, has come to prominence, albeit even more rarely photographed than his father, who has over-come his reclusive nature only in recent years. McKillen junior and Matt Ryan established the Press Up Group in 2009 in the depths of the Great Recession and also a development company called Oakmount. Together, these companies established a sizeable presence in hotels, restaurants and pubs around the country, if mainly in Dublin, as well as a sizeable portfolio of commercial office buildings.

There was some envy in the hospitality trade as to the pace and scale of the expansion of the Press Up Group. Many wondered how it was funded, with assumptions being made that the extremely rich father – with personal wealth estimated by the *Irish Times* in 2016 at €3.5 billion – was either bankrolling or guaranteeing the expansion. But McKillen senior has said he leaves it all very much to his son.

The development company, Oakmount, is operated independently of the Press Up Entertainment Group. McKillen junior and Ryan frequently use the development arm of their business to deliver buildings that Press Up can then occupy as a tenant. Oakmount either continues to own it or sells it to an investor, such as a pension fund. Once established in 2009, Press Up developed new or revamped existing entities to get to 20 venues by 2016. It claimed it was probably the only business that brought new concepts to Dublin over a five-year period from 2011 to 2016 and that is probably correct. Property was relatively cheap at the time and few others were taking risks. Press Up took control of restaurant brands already in the McKillen family ownership, such as the long-established Captain America's on Grafton Street and the Wagamama franchise for Ireland, as well as introducing the Wowburger chain and buying the Elephant & Castle in Temple Bar, a brand it then applied to multiple locations across the country. It opened the Vintage Cocktail Club, the Workman's Club and the Dean Hotel on Harcourt Street – home to what became the most celebrated swing in Irish politics when Fine Gael TD Maria Bailey fell off it one evening while taking photos and was ridiculed publicly for taking legal action to claim compensation.

Many of the new restaurants were given women's names for some reason, such as Sophie's (at the Dean Hotel), Angelina's by the Grand Canal, and Roberta's in the heart of Temple Bar at the Clarence Hotel. Highly stylish and well-finished and, importantly for the Instagram age, very photo-friendly, they were aimed at affluent millennials, with a less formal atmosphere than traditional outlets. The emphasis was on expensive cocktails and there were criticisms that the food was relatively bland and crowding out smaller, independent operators.

It branched into ethnic offerings, with 154-seater Chinese restaurant Mama Yo on Camden Street in Dublin and a large Indian restaurant,

Doolally, in Portobello, directly across the road from the George Bernard Shaw. Doolally occupied the ground floor of an office block called the Lennox Building, which Oakmount sold for €27 million to a fund managed by Swiss Life Asset Managers. Oakmount had acquired the building's long undeveloped 0.35-acre plot from developer Pat Crean's Marlet Property Group for €7 million in 2017 and is understood to have spent in the region of €10 million on its development. It financed that deal with Core Capital, run by Derek McGrath, which had become one of its main financiers, on schemes such as the Clerys Quarter, the refurbishment and extension of the former New Ireland Assurance Building on Dawson Street, and the delivery of a 40,000 square foot office block at 73 North Wall Quay in the Dublin Docklands. It was backed also by AIB and real estate specialist lender Greenoak Capital, which describes itself on its website as 'quintessentially British'.

Press Up added Dean Hotels in Cork and Galway and the Devlin Hotel in Ranelagh in Dublin 6 and operated the Clarence Hotel in Dublin's Temple Bar, having acquired the lease on the property in 2019, which continues to be owned by U2's Bono and The Edge with their friend Paddy McKillen senior. It also owns the Glasson Lakehouse near Athlone in County Westmeath. This is a 78-bedroom hotel with a bar, restaurant, 18-hole golf course, 400 metres of lakefront at Lough Ree, a marina and a wedding venue. It surprised many when it acquired the 60-bedroom Butler Arms Hotel in Waterville, County Kerry, for an undisclosed amount. The hotel has been in operation for more than 100 years under four generations of the Huggard family. Charlie Chaplin holidayed there regularly and Walt Disney stayed in 1946. Legendary financier JP Morgan liked the food so much that in the early 1900s, he hired Kathy Buckley, the head chef, to work at his mansion in Connecticut, USA.

Another surprise purchase was Loftus Hall on Hook Head in County Wexford, which has attracted attention because of its reputation for being haunted. Oakmount plans to rename it Ladyville Hall. As well as the conservation of its sash windows, other work will include the preservation of its famous staircase, which is one of only three of its kind ever made, the others being for The Vatican and the RMS *Titanic*. The 84-bed Dunboy Castle estate in Castletownbere, County Cork, is earmarked for conversion to a luxury hotel.

Back in Dublin, Oakmount constructed a 54-bedroom boutique hotel, The Leinster, on the site of the former Howl at the Moon venue on Lower Mount Street, having bought the property from the Mercantile Group for €3.2 million in January 2017. There are also plans to open Dean hotels in Belfast and in Birmingham, UK.

The idea of conservation of these buildings almost certainly appeals to McKillen junior and Ryan. The Stella Cinema renovation at Rathmines is one of the finest examples of a private enterprise sensitively and imaginatively putting an old building to good use while maintaining its best physical and aesthetic attributes. The century-old building – used originally as a ballroom as well as a cinema – had closed in the late 1990s after falling into disrepair. It was listed for demolition, with planners agreeing that it could be replaced by an apartment block. Oakmount saw different potential. When it removed a 1970s concrete screen wall it found the beauty of the original façade behind with many hidden 1920s features, including Art Deco designs and highly ornate ceilings. It spent heavily on restoring the premises to its original, single large space and created a luxury cinema experience. In 2021, *Time Out*, the entertainment platform, named Stella Cinema as the number one Best Cinema in Britain and Ireland and in the top 20 of the world's most beautiful cinemas. It has a cocktail club upstairs and a steakhouse in the next-door building.

McKillen and Ryan believed that the best way of conserving a historic building was to keep it in active use. At North Wall Quay in Dublin, they took a former pub and warehouse, both protected structures dating from the latter half of the nineteenth century, and repurposed them as the 94-bedroom Mayson hotel, which opened in December 2019 with a gym, swimming pool, Elephant & Castle restaurant and other amenities. The Lucky Duck on Aungier Street, near St Stephen's Green, was derelict for over 20 years before Oakmount restored the Victorian public house with original decorative shopfronts, original Victorian men's toilet urinals and reinstated a missing staircase.

It has also developed modern creations, such as at Bray in County Wicklow, where the population is fast expanding because of more affordable housing prices than in the nearby south Dublin suburbs. Oakmount has built where others talked about it. A 2.4-acre site in the town centre, known as the Florentine Centre, had been the subject of several planning applications by Ballymore Properties since 1997, but none was acted upon and the land was used as a car park before Bray Town Council acquired it in late 2013. Oakmount was appointed as a development partner in March 2018 to realise the site's potential. Its Bray Central scheme is over 270,000 square feet with a five-screen Stella cinema, bowling alley and restaurants (including Elephant & Castle), three anchor stores and 250 car-parking spaces.

The group has expanded to 17 pubs and continued to buy even during the Covid pandemic, establishing Thomas Rody Maher's pub on Baggot Street, which replaced Larry Murphy's after the latter was bought for about €1 million, and revamping the Foxhunter pub in Lucan. Lamb Doyle's on Blackglen Road in Sandyford was also purchased; its 1.21-acre site presumably offers development potential.

But of all the acquisitions it is one in County Wicklow, on land that serves as the route to Magheramore beach, a celebrated cove much loved by swimmers, that caught the most attention in 2023. Oakmount had spent €700,000 on it in 2021, beating off competition from a series of bidders, including Wicklow County Council, which was left to make a decision on ambitious planning permission.

Oakmount applied for permission to develop a boutique holiday resort and surf school on the clifftop, what it described as an integrated tourism and leisure and recreational (ITLR) complex, along with 48 accommodation pods and a surf school facility on just over seven of the 21 acres it had purchased. The two-storey lower ground-level building was to contain a gym, sauna, cinema and an outdoor swimming pool at lower ground level, a reception, bar and restaurant, washrooms and outdoor terrace at ground level, and an event room at first-floor level. It also sought permission for 49 car-parking and 13 bike-parking spaces to serve the development's main complex but promised 'the enhancement and supplementation of planting' to protect its existing ecology. Magheramore beach itself is part of a large special area of conservation.

The land had been owned by the Missionary Sisters of St Columban before it was sold in the 1980s, and then several sales thereafter. It was a member of the order, Sister Kathleen Melia, who in her objection described the 'grandiose plan' as 'the height of folly', a grave threat to species and habitats. Others were more worried by human access to the beach. Oakmount promised that the 'existing public pedestrian access to the beach will remain unaffected'. However, it was proposed that access to the beach would be barrier-controlled by the operators of the complex, at least if planning as applied for was agreed.

Just how much further Press Up expands remains to be seen. At the time of writing it was reportedly pulling back from a plan to create a new venue on St Stephen's Green and was engaged in refinancing of its balance sheet, having offered some of its more prominent hotel properties to investors for sale and leaseback arrangements.

PART 5

OWNING THE HOMES

There are a few basic needs that all humans share and one of them is shelter. Housing has become arguably the most emotive issue in Irish society over the last decades. The cost, availability and standards of what we live in have all provoked disquiet, dissent and, in some cases, despair. Environmental requirements have entered the equation too, impacting matters of personal choice as to where people can live as well as the provision of these homes. Ireland is not alone in what has become a major international debate, as to where and how people live affordably and sustainably, and who holds ownership. All of which has the potential to cause major political disruption that may not lead to acceptable or workable practical solutions.

SEVENTEEN

CHEAP MONEY AND OVERVALUED ASSETS

The early years of the twenty-first century saw the introduction of the euro and Ireland's membership of the new single currency. Interest rates tumbled to previously undreamt-of lows, the availability of apparently cheap money giving more people an incentive to borrow larger sums of money, especially when saving was no longer being rewarded by high deposit interest rates. Developers and speculators borrowed money from the banks to buy land and build on it; the banks then lent to individuals and couples to buy the houses and apartments that were newly constructed; and that gave the developers the money to repay their original loans. Land values and properties soared to previously unimaginable levels.

This was not a purely Irish phenomenon by any means, but we surfed the international wave of residential property speculation enthusiastically. International banks, even British ones outside the eurozone, rushed to join the Irish banks in offering loans to both builders and buyers. One hundred per cent – and even higher – mortgages became commonplace, either to buy homes or investment properties, encouraging the better-off to become small-scale landlords. Everyone, it seemed, was able to get a loan, sizeable deposits and proof of ability to repay was seemingly unnecessary.

Between 1994 and 2007, house prices rose by nearly 300 per cent but private debt rose by 400 per cent while incomes only increased by about 70 per cent. The economy was booming, and everyone seemed happy. In 2006, more than 90,000 homes were constructed and about 80,000 again the following year. Apparently, we needed them for all the people who were in jobs and to house those coming into the country as immigration replaced emigration as one of the defining features of modern Ireland. We even started building houses to home the foreigners who had come to Ireland to build houses for us. We also built lots of second homes, because people seemed wealthy enough to indulge in holiday retreats, and left empty ones in areas where people didn't really want to live because planners and buyers weren't realistic about what was really needed. Despite such a large supply, prices kept going up, caused by the availability of cheap money and artificial demand. It couldn't last. And it didn't.

When the crash came – and jobs were lost in their hundreds of thousands – many people discovered that they couldn't meet their monthly loan repayments. Many feared the loss of their homes, particularly those who had paid inflated prices in the last four to five years of the boom. A concept called 'negative equity' became a talking point, which referred to owing more on a loan than the property could be sold for, wiping out the perceived and temporary wealth that many had enjoyed. Those who had to sell were in trouble if they couldn't raise enough through the sale to clear the loan. If they were forced to sell, or opted to do so, they were left with a debt outstanding once all the sale proceeds had been applied to repaying the mortgage and they had no other way to raise the remaining money. Even those who didn't have to sell suddenly felt less wealthy and were more cautious about borrowing and spending, exacerbating the recession. Mass emigration replaced the net immigration of the early twentieth century when we had attracted hundreds of thousands of workers and their families, especially from the new EU accession states of eastern Europe. Now many of those who had arrived left again, to be followed by another generation of the Irish-born, a very sore point given our history of forced emigration from which we thought we had escaped.

The State faced something of a dilemma when it came to what to do with mortgage holders in arrears given the power that lenders held over borrowers and the stress that the potential loss of a home causes. The level of family-home mortgages in arrears of 90 days or more peaked at 12.9 per cent in September 2013. The government didn't want the banks it controlled to pitch people out of their homes, not just because of the public anger that would have caused but also because of the need for additional social housing it would have created. The number of properties repossessed was only a small fraction of those who were not making repayments – way lower than the European average – and judges in the courts showed great reluctance to grant repossession orders to lenders or even to enforce ones that had been granted. Memories of the nineteenth century remained in the folk memory.

The length of time the repossession process took – and the likely imperfect outcome, as they saw it – persuaded the banks that they might be better off improvising. Instead, they found ways to reduce monthly repayments by extending the length of time over which a mortgage could be repaid or by splitting mortgages into different portions to be repaid at different times. One scheme involved a so-called 'mortgage-to-rent' system, which required borrowers to give up ownership of their homes and become social-housing tenants in the same property. If borrowers played ball, then it was likely they could find a way to stay in their homes, albeit not without some pain; if they ducked and dived too much, they ran a greater risk of losing their homes.

Not everyone agreed with this strategy. Some felt it was unfair on those who did everything they could to meet their monthly repayments, often denying themselves other things they now couldn't afford. Why couldn't everyone get a write-down of their debts? Another argument was that it led to higher mortgage rates being imposed by banks on compliant payers and that it slowed the repair of the balance sheets of the banks. The ECB agreed with the latter and insisted that the banks sell as many mortgages as possible to non-bank lenders, many of whom were not regulated by the Central Bank. The new owners got bundles of loans put together at a discount to their original price, irrespective of whether the borrower wanted a switch in lender or not. As it happened, it worked relatively well in the low-interest rate environment. Having bought cheaply, these funds were more likely to restructure a loan and enjoy the reliable new income stream than force the sale of a property. Research from the Central Bank suggested that there was 'no material difference in the number of properties being taken into possession by unregulated loan owners compared to regulated lenders'. However, a problem emerged in 2022 when some of the new owners of these mortgages reacted to higher ECB interest rates – designed to deal with inflation – by pushing variable mortgage rates up much higher and refusing to allow customers to fix at lower rates. It became a crisis for tens of thousands of borrowers in 2023 as interest rates soared.

In 2016, as an opposition spokesman, Fianna Fáil's Michael McGrath introduced a bill designed to give the Central Bank the ability to cap variable interest rates of mortgages. It got nowhere. Patrick Honohan, the Central Bank governor of the time, said it would not be a good idea and suggested that it might be a better idea to give the Central Bank the power to restrict the rates charged by financial institutions that purchased loans from banks. The regulated banks continued their strategy of selling portfolios of home loans – not all of which were held by customers who had issues making repayments – to non-bank financial institutions. It has meant that many customers suddenly were charged excessive interest rates by those who now held their mortgages and struggled to meet their monthly bills.

McGrath became Minister for Finance in late 2022 but didn't act. 'A lot has changed since I introduced my own bill,' he said. 'Irish rates are now the third-lowest in the eurozone, whereas once they were among the most expensive. We also have a situation now where over 90 per cent of new mortgages being written are fixed-rate in nature. We have also seen an uptick in mortgage switching.'

All of which was true, but only part of the story. Many of those who have seen their mortgages sold by their banks were unable to secure a switch in their mortgage to a different provider who would charge a lower rate. They couldn't get fixed-rate mortgages from their new loan holders. There are over 100,000 borrowers who were affected in this way. The Central Bank maintained its position and these people were left to fend for themselves.

THE BLIGHT OF EMPTY HOUSES

The crash left us with empty houses. Most of them have gone now, but at the start of the 2010s Ireland was afflicted by what was called the 'ghost estate'. We had large new housing estates, usually in rural areas but sometimes urban, where building of all the planned units hadn't been completed when the developer ran out of money. Partially finished and unoccupied units abounded, some with the roofs on and windows in, others not, some with little more than foundations set down. Some units were finished but nobody moved in.

The April 2011 census counted 289,451 vacant properties – 14.5 per cent of the total stock in the country – of which just 59,395 were classed as holiday homes. It was estimated that around 120,000 of the vacant homes were unlikely to ever be sold. That year the number of unfinished estates was reported officially as 2,876. The blight covered the country from Cork to Donegal but was particularly prevalent in the upper Shannon area of Cavan, Longford, Leitrim, Sligo and Roscommon; the latter county alone had 35 ghost estates. The State was as much to blame for this mess as the greedy developers. The availability of myriad tax incentives had resulted in massive overdevelopment at entirely unsuitable locations.

This all took place in plain sight. In May 2005, I presented an RTÉ documentary called *Tax Me if You Can* in which we filmed in Keshcarrigan in County Leitrim, a small rural village that suddenly had a large housing estate in which hardly anyone was living. We (my producer Brián Páircéir and I) argued that tax breaks were encouraging the construction of houses in inappropriate areas, which would remain empty, just because investors wanted the tax breaks over 10 years for buying them. This, effectively, was subsidising the better-off to reduce their tax bills, even if they were to be mistaken in their belief they'd be able to sell the houses ten years later for profit. The programme led to some debate in the Dáil and Brian Cowen, as Minister for Finance, was forced into curbing and abolishing some of the construction-based tax relief, but most of the damage had been done. Various county councils weren't particularly interested in stopping the practices as they were getting development levies in return for new houses built. For a period of time, everyone involved in the process was making money from building homes of no use to anyone and so had no motivation to stop.

Until the crash came, and then there was little or no interest in finishing the remaining units. The developers didn't have the money and the banks wouldn't lend it to them, sometimes reckoning that whatever eventual sales price was achieved for finished units would not cover the repayment of existing debts, let alone bigger ones. The developers also needed money to connect services, such as water, sewerage and electricity, and to finish roads and common areas on estates. The State didn't step in, and often local authorities refused to take estates 'in charge' until the developers had finished their work. It was a cynical cop-out.

There might have been the potential to sell units at lower prices, but the banks didn't have any money to lend to potential homeowners either and most didn't have the means to make repayments. There was potential for social housing, but few seemed interested in living in many of these places: most of the new locations were too remote from places of work and potential tenants would need cars because of an absence of public transport. They also lacked basic facilities, such as shops and playing pitches. The government was short of the money needed for so-called 'site resolution': what little was made available went mainly to fencing off dangerous areas and the worst of the potholes. All of this had enormous consequences for those who lived on those parts of the estates that had been completed. The unfinished buildings were not just eyesores, especially as they became overgrown, they were dangerous to children and young adults who got beyond the fences. They drew squatters and anti-social elements who used them for drug-taking. They attracted vermin. Buyers in completed homes had overpaid already; now the remaining value of their properties was being eroded further by the proximity of these messes. All of the financial, legal, health and safety and technical issues seemed beyond the ken of those who had responsibilities. The solution in many cases was simply to demolish instead of trying to finish or repair.

There was so much to learn from all of this, particularly when it came to deciding where we would locate future home-building and what type of properties we would encourage people to rent or own. The fear of excessive borrowing by individuals as much as by developers, and of excessive lending by banks, as well as the practical absence of money, drove what was to happen next.

EIGHTEEN

LANDLORDISM: ACCIDENTAL, RELUCTANT AND DELIBERATE

A house or an apartment is a permanent home, temporary perhaps to people who see it as a staging post to somewhere else, somewhere better, at some other time, but still a ballast for day-to-day activities, a place of certainty to go each evening, often an emotional harbour. But to some people houses or apartments are simply assets that produce income and that have a value they seek to protect or enhance. They are transactional vehicles rather than their homes.

We've all heard the stories of the Garda with a string of flats or the local pharmacist or shopkeeper who bought a property for income, with the intention of selling it later on to raise cash to cover their pensionable years. Tradesmen who dealt in cash, particularly in the building trade, would buy properties, 'do them up' and then rent them out instead of selling them. The professional classes – solicitors and accountants – hosted some of the most eager investors. For those renting these properties, sometimes there was an insistence that the rent be paid in cash, with the intention that the income be kept away from the reach of the Revenue Commissioners.

During the first decade of the twenty-first century, the banks eagerly encouraged this speculation. They advanced 100 per cent loans to cover the cost of purchase of houses, apartments and office suites that would be let. Sometimes they even lent up to 120 per cent of the supposed value of the asset to be acquired, encouraging the borrowers to spend the rest. People borrowed to invest in second or third properties, with the intention of having a separate income through rent to their main one or, if the income didn't cover mortgage repayments, being able to sell at a later date with the mortgage paid off, to provide a major capital nest egg.

In 2006 alone, Irish individuals took out more than 28,000 buy-to-let mortgages. By March 2013 the banks held 150,000 residential mortgages for buy-to-let properties. The amounts secured on these mortgages totalled €31.1 billion, the market value of the properties considerably less. Those who had become deliberate landlords for investments now regretted that decision. Some of these landlords struggled to find or keep tenants and rental income dropped, making it hard for some to cover their monthly mortgage repayments. The banks, who had eagerly pushed loans to these people, were often aggressive now in dealing with them. They were less sympathetic when it wasn't the family home involved and used their legal powers to demand sales at amounts that wouldn't cover the full repayment of the money owed. While repossessions and evictions would not happen at the scale that had been predicted, the fear of them hung over many people who struggled to get their lenders to cut them fairer deals over lengthy periods of repayment.

There was another class of landlord that the banks had to worry about, too. The phrase 'reluctant landlord' entered the lexicon: those who couldn't afford the mortgages on places they had bought to live in and who instead rented to others who could cover those bills. Those landlords then found somewhere cheaper to rent. Some, because of family circumstances, such as children being born, had to move to get more space and, while they paid reasonable rent elsewhere, were unable to get rid of a unit they may have wanted to sell. At the mid-point of 2013, it was estimated that about one-third of mortgages were larger than the value of the properties they supported. More than 100,000 people were failing to make their monthly mortgage repayments at all and were at risk of losing their homes.

A NEW PHASE

Successive governments over decades encouraged owner occupation and made it more affordable through grants and subsidies, including tax relief on mortgage interest payments. However, ownership peaked in 1991, when 79.3 per cent of Irish people were homeowners. Many of the homes owned were previously social housing that were then sold to private ownership at often generous prices. The subsequent decline in home ownership was confirmed in the 2016 census: it put the rate at 67.6 per cent, lower than the EU average of 69.2 per cent. It was an ongoing trend: we had fallen to 74.7 per cent in 2006 despite the house-building boom, implying much of that era's new stock was going into the rental market.

It was late in 2014 when TV3 broadcast a television documentary called *Ireland's Housing Crisis – What's Next?* that I presented and co-wrote with producer Lydia Murphy. We made the argument that the economy was showing signs of recovery and that a new housing need was developing. The public finances had been stabilised during a very difficult five-year period in which successive governments were forced to increase taxation dramatically at the same time as reducing public sector pay, social welfare entitlements and public services to the general population. The government had succeeded in the most difficult of circumstances to persuade foreign employers to come to Ireland. The strategy had largely worked and the Troika handed back control of the State's economic management – and essentially our economic sovereignty – to our democratically elected government. The economic recovery would continue at pace after that. Jobs would be created almost as fast as they were lost during the crash and then faster as money flowed back into the economy. Immigration instead of emigration would return and that would mean that yet again we would have a need for new housing stock to cater for a growing population, especially in our major cities. We did not anticipate the speed of what would happen, or how far the recovery would go, but it was clear even then that the worst was well over and that there would be a need for construction, no matter what distaste the public still held for developers.

Conor Skehan, chair of the Housing Agency, oozed confidence as he sat in front of our cameras and answered my questions. 'In Ireland, we have a culture of wanting to own our houses,' he declared. 'It's changing rapidly and we're seeing quite a marked shift as we move into the next generation, people who are well able to buy choosing not to, where we have a voluntary rental sector as opposed to an involuntary one.'

That was a big assumption. Renting was regarded by many as 'dead money'. It purchased a month's accommodation and nothing more, whereas a monthly mortgage repayment was a down payment on the eventual debt-free ownership of a valuable asset. However, a consensus developed that too many people on insufficient incomes had overstretched themselves by buying during the boom, that in other EU countries people were content to rent their living accommodation instead of seeking to own it and that they were better off financially over the long run because of this. The new arrangements were presented to the public almost as a *fait accompli*, but to rent or to own is a fundamental question for any adult individual, couple, family and, on a wider basis, Irish society. For some, the issue is one of status and security: home ownership suggests self-sufficiency instead of dependency. There are other, more practical issues: ownership is also potentially a protection against poverty in retirement years. Being in a position of having to rent when unable to earn extra income beyond a pension is a major concern to many people in their older years. In other jurisdictions people can often expect a high percentage of their salary in pension, enabling them to keep paying some form of rent until they die.

There may be health implications too. A study by the ESRI in 2023 found 'significant variations' in health outcomes between homeowners and renters, across all age groups, with renters in the private sector having poorer health outcomes compared to homeowners. Individuals in the supported rental sector had the poorest health outcomes. 'Less than half of employed supported renters possess a medical card, despite facing a high risk of poverty and having incomes that qualify them for public housing assistance,' the ESRI report said. 'Regions and local housing developments with high rates of social housing and indirect housing supports will require more healthcare services on average than regions and local developments where private renters and homeowners make up the majority of the population.'

Other benefits of home ownership – such as releasing equity to fund a child's education, using it to finance nursing home care, or having something to bequeath upon death – will remain out of the reach of renters.

In 2014 the Department of Finance estimated 600,000 households had been formed since 1996, of which about 400,000 comprised either one or two people. Average household sizes at 2.75 people were still ahead of European averages but the Department of Finance believed 'there is no obvious reason why Irish rates will not continue to converge with the European norm'. Those who bought their homes were more likely to be in their thirties now than twenties, which also meant many young adults in their twenties were living at home with their parents, whether willingly or not for either party. By 2017 the number of Irish people aged 25–29 living with their parents grew to 47.2 per cent, one of the highest rates in Europe. A decade earlier the figure had been 36 per cent. It wasn't as if they had somewhere to buy. If they moved out, it was to rent. The number of buyers was falling as we developed a generation seemingly doomed to living in rented accommodation, never to own their own homes, unless they had extremely large incomes or were in receipt of gifts or inheritance from their families. Research by the Economic and Social Research Institute (ESRI) found that 60 per cent of 25–34-year-olds in 2004 owned their home. By 2019 that number would fall to 27 per cent.

Skehan went further: 'The three-bed semi in Ireland has much less of a future, if I can put it like that, than it did in the past, mainly because of changes in demographic structure. We reckon that less than about a third of the market requirement is going to be satisfied by those going into the future, that the household formation that's taking place is of more and more units with fewer and fewer people in them, very large numbers of people living on their own voluntarily. People are deferring starting their families until well into their thirties, so their need for a two-bedroom apartment remains. There's a very large number of people looking for what my kids call the *Friends*-type accommodation, like the TV show, where they can each have their own individual bedroom but share a communal living room and kitchen area. These are markets that are supplied by the development sector in other parts of Europe. We haven't started doing them here yet and the developer who starts doing them will have his arm taken off.'

While it was true that family formation was changing, there was scant evidence to suggest the desire to own had diminished, or that people wanted apartments instead of houses, even if most planners believed it was better for everyone if more people lived in urban apartments. The reality was that potential buyers were stymied by the lack of finance and a shortage in the supply of housing they wanted. It was not necessarily their choice to rent or to live in apartments, it was being forced upon them. It meant that home ownership among young adults – or at least those aged between 25 and 39 years – fell sharply in the first years of the Great Recession, going from 22 per cent in 2011 to 16 per cent in 2016 (and then to 12 per cent by 2020). Even with prices lower than less than a decade previously, those prices were still too high for those who didn't have ready cash and had to borrow by way of a mortgage. They were in competition with wealthy people who still had cash after the crash and who saw the opportunity to buy, sometimes to rent to others, sometimes to gift homes to family members. While there was a realisation of the growing numbers of single and separated people, or single parents with one or more children, the reality was that two salaries were needed to get a loan for a purchase.

If the Housing Agency recommended fundamental policy shifts, then the Central Bank implemented measures that would effectively enforce some of them, introducing mortgage rules that limited the amounts individuals and couples could borrow to buy their own homes. There would be no more 100 per cent mortgages; instead, deposits of 20 per cent would have to be saved and produced first. Further, the amounts borrowed would be restricted to three-and-a-half times the income earned annually. If people couldn't afford that, they could rent instead. The action appeared to be motivated with the safety of citizens in mind, to prevent another generation from getting into financial trouble by overstretching in their ambitions, paying what they couldn't afford to buy houses. It was paternalistic but was to have unexpected consequences, based on many poor assumptions: that purchase prices had flatlined at a new lower level and would not climb; that sufficient rental properties would be available; that people would actually want to rent and not own.

When I asked Skehan about the perception that many people have of rent as 'dead money', and that they would prefer spending money on something they'll eventually own, he replied: 'Well, I'm the chairman of the Housing Agency and I will never buy a piece of property again. I rent.' Skehan wasn't paid as chair of the Housing Agency, to which he was appointed in 2013. He had been a policy advisor to Fine Gael previously, but his private business advised local authorities and public bodies on planning and environmental issues.

His prediction turned out to be ruinously incorrect.

Rents had fallen to more affordable levels during the crash, but they would now go up due to rising employment and population levels and a shortage of supply. In normal circumstances, a monthly rental payment should be less than a mortgage bill. Now, to the frustration of eager would-be purchasers, the monthly rent was to become much higher than the mortgage repayments the authorities had deemed to be unaffordable. Their ability to save towards the required deposit was compromised also.

Skehan also predicted that 'house price rises in Ireland are coming to an end', something else that turned out to be wildly incorrect. His suggestion received support from TCD economist PJ Drudy: 'If you look at the price index since 1991, housing is still something like 250 per cent higher, compared to the consumer price index, which is only about 70 per cent. Housing is still massively overvalued.'

However, economist Robbie Kelleher of Davy told us property prices were already too high again. 'Even though house prices are a good deal off the peaks we saw in 2006–07, they are not cheap by most measures. If you look at, say, the ratio of average house prices to average incomes in Ireland, now it's about 5.6, which is much higher than the UK and much higher than the long-term average. Many people say a sustainable rate is 4 or 4.5, so house prices are already quite high. So, I think it is important to try and do something at this stage to at least limit the rate of price increases going forward.'

We made the documentary at a time when there were clear signs that the economic crisis was ending, emphasised by a nascent recovery in the prices of a limited amount of traded housing stock. I suggested the government would be happy if prices went up for both new and second-hand houses as it would help lift the valuations of houses that weren't trading and reduce the negative equity of those who had bought overpriced houses during the boom. Rising property prices – and improved levels of repayment on loans – also improved the balance sheets of the banks, still impoverished despite shifting their biggest non-paying loans to NAMA, and increased the chances of the State recovering some of the money it had 'invested' in the banks at the same time as the European Central Bank (ECB) applied pressure for banks to get rid of loans that were not producing the required repayments.

In our TV interview, economist Ronan Lyons argued that Ireland was 'trading off the needs of those people who bought in the last 15 years against the needs of those who will buy in the next 15 years. We should have a policy of cheap and affordable and abundant good quality housing, not getting house prices up because you think it will help you get re-elected.'

But the recovery in house prices was being driven by a lack of supply of both new and second-hand homes. Potential vendors preferred to wait until prices rose higher before they would sell, particularly if the proceeds from a sale at existing levels would not clear their mortgages. The banks were still desperately short of money to lend as they tried to sort out their balance sheets under pressure from the ECB. Restricting the ability of individuals and couples to borrow took attention away from the inability of the banks to provide loans even when the demand was there.

In that 2014 TV documentary, I argued that this was the time to make long-term fixed-rate mortgages – of 10–20 years in duration – the norm for borrowers, as in continental Europe. The timing was perfect as ECB interest rates were at zero. The banks, in theory, would be able to borrow themselves long-term at those rates and then fix for borrowers, guaranteeing the banks a small margin of profit and the borrowers the certainty of repayments over the long term. This rare opportunity – when prices of loans were low – was denied to many of them because the banks weren't capable of or interested in promoting such offers. Instead, they maintained the highest variable interest rates for customers in the EU as a way of extracting as much profit as possible to recoup previous losses. They also fraudulently denied many people interest rates to which they were entitled as they moved off tracker mortgages, a scandal that later resulted in massive compensation to victims and hundreds of millions of euro in fines by the regulator, but too late to save customers enormous stress and, in too many cases, their homes.

Within three years we needed to build houses, though many people took persuading of that fact. The State's policies assumed that the pipeline of new homes built for sale would remain low for many years to come, even though it simultaneously wanted the new owners of land bought from NAMA to make use of it quickly. The State couldn't see how the banks would provide private sector developers with the finance they needed to build, but also assumed that the new owners of land would somehow get money internationally to make productive use of their purchases instead of holding them to increase in value. This underestimated the immediate need for new homes and failed to anticipate the rapid recovery in the economy and the job creation that resulted. In fairness, almost nobody predicted the strength of the recovery or, when it seemed to be happening, believed it could continue. People feared being fooled twice.

The lack of new building fed into higher rents: in 2014, rents across Ireland increased by 11 per cent on average and in Dublin by 14 per cent, a precursor for far worse to come. This led to widespread demands for the introduction of rent controls. However, the Private Residential Tenancies Board (PRTB) published a report from DKM consultants arguing that the introduction of rent controls could lead to landlords exiting the market and further curtailing already limited supply as well as pushing up rents. The government played along. Economically it may have been the correct intellectual approach, but politically and, more importantly, socially it was to prove highly divisive, as rents would climb over the next decade to levels even higher than during the Celtic Tiger era – and left people in the remarkable and previously unheard-of position of having to pay more to rent a home than to own one.

NINETEEN

HOUSE OR APARTMENT?
THE STATE DECIDES

The worst type of apartments were bedsits, rooms in old houses, mostly built before 1963 and reformatted internally to provide accommodation that allowed tax breaks to landlords. The standards of some of the bedsit accommodation in early twenty-first-century Ireland were atrocious – and damning of many of the landlords who profited from their provision. Individuals – and in some cases couples – lived in a small room, often in an ageing and not particularly well-kept building, with a bed, cooking unit, chairs, small table and maybe, if lucky, a sofa. They shared toilet facilities outside of this room with others who lived in similar rooms. If they were fortunate, the landlord kept the house and their room in good condition and turned on the heating, all for an affordable rent. Unfortunately, some landlords overcharged for damp, mouldy and unsuitable living con-ditions that did nothing for the health of their tenants and refused to spend money on improvements. They were for people on low incomes who were not provided with social housing. These buildings were the successors of the detested overcrowded tenements. At the creation of the State, it was estimated that over 20,000 families, of all sizes, lived in single rooms within large houses with shared sanitation facilities. We had come a long way from that, but not far enough.

The idea behind getting rid of bedsits seemed noble. As Minister for the Environment in 2009, Green Party leader John Gormley brought forward legislation to effectively ban bedsits – or studio apartments as some tried to describe the better-kept ones – following a lengthy campaign by charities such as Threshold. The new regulations, enforced in 2013 after a transition period, required all rented accommodation to have sanitary facilities in a separate room unique to the renter and to have control over their own heating. The hope was that the new minimum standards would persuade landlords to upgrade. The complaints of some landlords that this would reduce supply were dismissed as selfish self-entitlement and duly ignored.

The law of unintended consequences quickly took hold. Nobody can provide the number authoritatively, but it is possible that anything between 10,000 and 20,000 living units were eliminated by the measures. Some large period houses in which these bedsits were accommodated – often just outside the two canals in Dublin 6 and 7 – were bought by wealthy people who renovated them to become luxury family homes in which the owners enjoyed considerable personal space. Others were purchased by investors who renovated them but only after evicting all of the existing tenants, who often had nowhere else to go. The new owners met the new regulations, but not necessarily by giving each room its own toilet. There was nothing to prevent tenants from organising their own 'house shares' – maybe a group of friends coming together to take a room each but with a commonly used kitchen and toilet facilities. Or maybe they weren't friends at all but came together in a 'share' or joint tenancy organised by the landlord. House-sharing was legal but bedsits were illegal. A grey area emerged. The price of accommodation in such refurbished houses went up sharply during the rental boom in the decade from 2012 onwards. There were also published examples of unscrupulous landlords putting bunk beds into rooms and renting them to migrant workers in numbers wholly unsuited to the available space, a new form of tenement living worse than the bedsits they replaced.

Meanwhile, people on low incomes who wouldn't accept such 'house shares' and who wanted to live on their own were left to look for different accommodation to rent. Much of what was on offer was beyond their financial means. In 2014 the government introduced the Housing Assistance Payment (HAP) to top up what people on low incomes, or on social welfare, would pay to private sector operators if they were unable to secure low-cost social housing from the State or an approved body. Questions were asked about the wisdom of the policy: why not just build more social housing instead of providing what were effectively subsidies to private landlords? Labour party leader Joan Burton, Tánaiste and Minister for Social Protection since the summer of 2014, argued strongly that private landlords would not make the accommodation available to lower-income people without the extra State money to bring whatever they could pay up to market rents. She also said it would be a temporary measure, phased out as the State supplied more social housing. The State's expenditure quickly ran to hundreds of millions of euro annually, a big transfer of public money to landlords of all sizes, as did the Rental Accommodation Scheme (where the local authority arranged the lease directly itself for people). It was calculated that over 60,000 families became dependent on it – even if many households in need of social housing didn't receive it. Over one in five renting households registered by the Residential Tenancies Board were supported by HAP.

The ban on studio flats was overturned in 2015. Minister for the Environment Alan Kelly allowed their reintroduction, as long as they were no smaller than 40 square metres in size. He said that he would not allow 'shoeboxes' as homes: 'We have made changes to ensure that there can be apartments built, particularly in the city centre locations, that are actually affordable.' He also declared at least one-third of new-build apartments in a block would have to be dual-aspect, whereas the figure for DCC's guidelines at the time was 85 per cent of units. By 2017 Eoghan Murphy of Fine Gael was the Minister for Housing. He said that outlawing bedsits 'probably' had been a mistake and that it had contributed to a record number of homeless individuals and families, many of whom now found refuge in charity-provided accommodation or in short stays in hotels paid for by the State. It was expected that newly provided single-room bedsits would be of a higher standard than their predecessors and that tenants would have adequate access to clean sanitary facilities, proper heating appliances and proper food preparation areas. He put into law that new-build studios would have to be a minimum of 37 square metres in size.

There were also developers who saw the revamping of large old houses into modern bedsits as an investment opportunity that could be sold to institutions. In January 2023 reporter Killian Woods of the *Business Post* wrote of one extraordinary example. He revealed how Nassarius Capital, a company in Liechtenstein controlled by the Swiss-based Monterosa Group, purchased 24 Irish properties – all subdivided into four to seven bedsits – in 2022 for €50.6 million. The majority of the properties had been bought from Mary Moloney and Sonia Gleeson, two Irish property investors, for €45.7 million. The duo had assembled the portfolio over the previous three years at a cost of €13.5 million in a series of one-off deals. Woods gave the example of a house bought in October 2021 on Whitworth Road in Drumcondra for €550,000 that was subdivided into seven bedsits and sold to Nassarius Capital for €2.1 million in July 2022. The State would have captured some of the profits made by the duo by way of capital gains tax, but the purchase price created its own problem for Nassarius. It was based on the presumption that bedsits would be rented, depending on their location, from €1,500 per month to over €2,200. Having spent so expensively on buying these 'assets' the new owners could not allow the rent – their return on investment – to fall.

As many as half of the apartments built between 1990 and 2008 may have fire safety or other construction issues because of a lack of proper regulation. The new standards are higher and more rigorously enforced, which is necessary because the post-crash State wanted to encourage apartment living in urban areas, instead of houses in suburban and rural Ireland. Whereas apartments accounted for 30–50 per cent of the housing stock in most European countries, they yet had to account for 10 per cent of all housing in Ireland. There were environmental reasons for the push as well, based on the belief that it would lead to much better use of public capital. The Irish public would be hard to convince.

Robert Watt, as secretary general of the Department of Public Expenditure, said Ireland needed to build cities 'in a much more compact, densified way', which could only mean building upwards. He believed having a mass of the population in our cities would provide a cost–benefit rationale for infrastructural projects like the underground rail line Metro North for Dublin, given that major expenditure on big transport projects needs a critical mass of users.

While Watt and John Moran (his counterpart at the Department of Finance) did not always agree when they were in their respective positions, they concurred on the social and environmental benefits, as they saw them, of large-scale apartment living in cities. Moran was a strong advocate of higher-density accommodation to save the rural environment, reduce pollution and allow easier access to government services in large population centres. He condemned what he described as the Irish 'obsession' with owning a suburban house with a front and back garden. 'Overly concentrated activity in our capital has meant a congested and unaffordable Dublin for many and sprawling car-dependent living for others,' he said. He believed this perpetuated great inequality and resulted in a lopsided economy centred around the capital, just as unregulated, unplanned one-off housing in the countryside reduced the quality of rural services and added to the costs to the State for providing things like rural broadband. He wanted to grow competing regional urban centres outside of Dublin, with a particular emphasis on his native Limerick, but also the other cities like Cork. 'Building for the future in Ireland requires a clear rejection of the car-dependent suburban house model, with Dublin as an overgrown city state.'

Moran was thinking decades ahead. 'The prospect of having an additional two million people in the country by 2050 necessitates a complete rethink of how people live,' he said. He wanted incentives and taxes to convince people to move out of the open countryside and into villages and towns, where they would have better access to health and other services. 'In rural France, houses are concentrated in the village. The local nurse can visit five or six people without ever having to drive a car. Everyone benefits from an easy access to services,' he said.

He conceded that there was 'an emotional appeal' to the idea of someone giving a house to their children in rural areas, but that many of these houses were being left empty.

People who owned their own land – or who had it provided to them by their families – built for themselves. This led, in the 1960s in particular, to the so-called bungalow blitz in rural Ireland, the proliferation of privately built low-slung units, and in the late 1970s and early 1980s to 'Southfork style' large houses that aped a large, detached unit that was central to the hit US television show *Dallas*. In subsequent decades they were called McMansions.

This one-off housing is regarded in rural Ireland as the exercise of a traditional right to the use of privately owned land, with 'frontage' – a driveway onto a rural road – seen as a prized asset. But even in the mid-to-late twentieth century, Ireland was regarded by environmentalists as addicted to damaging 'ribbon development' that creates carbon because of the dependency on motor transport. It also brings extra expense to the State in the provision of water, sewerage, electricity, telephones and, in recent decades, broadband delivered to their doors. Various councils have tried to dissuade such development in recent decades, leading to many political rows at local and national level as rural Irish people fought for permission to develop on their own land, with all of the financial advantages accruing to them from that.

Those who didn't own land but who could afford to borrow to buy usually opted for newly built houses on the growing number of private estates in the major cities and towns, although some chose to purchase and revamp existing houses in the second-hand market. The new housing estates were built on privately owned land. This made the owners of such land very rich if they received zoning for their land to be used for residential purposes or had services such as water mains or sewerage pipes laid on their lands. This led to many allegations of corruption, that those in the know, or who paid for it, benefitted from zoning or the provision of services.

In the late 1960s rising house prices caused the Fianna Fáil government to commission a report on ways to improve the supply of land for development at affordable prices. *The Report on the Price of Building Land,* known as the Kenny Report after its chairman, High Court judge Mr Justice John Kenny, was published in 1973 and has since become arguably the most celebrated non-implemented report in Irish economic history. Its contents were too radical for a conservative Irish State, even if Kenny himself was no radical. Kenny's committee was asked to consider possible measures for controlling the price of land required for housing. Importantly, it was asked to ensure that at least a substantial part of the increase in the value of the land would be secured for the benefit of the community. Kenny's report – although there were dissensions on the committee – recommended that local authorities be given the right to acquire undeveloped lands at 'existing use value' plus 25 per cent by adopting Designated Area Schemes. This was recommended as 'a reasonable compromise between the rights of the community and those of the landowners' because the local community had a legitimate claim to all profit accruing to land that had been serviced at the expense of the State. It never happened.

Moran believed property tax was far too low. 'People keep rural homes as a second-home luxury and there are an awful lot of second homes. There is bungalow blight and our property tax is having very little effect,' he said.

We have a great reluctance in Ireland to levy taxes on property, depending instead, to an unhealthy degree, on taxing income. The government's taxation of domestic, residential property is limited. A local property tax – to fund the provision of local services – was introduced in 2013 to widespread opposition, most especially and bizarrely from those on the political left. Ever since then, the majority of local councils have sought to reduce the amounts levied wherever possible, wilfully reducing their own budgets. The government held off for eight years against the revision of baseline valuations despite a known surge in the price of second-hand properties in the years after the Celtic Tiger crash that should have allowed for bringing in more money. Property is also the basis of much inherited wealth, offering riches rarely obtained through working and saving. Again, however, governments regard it as imperative to tax property inheritance relatively lightly for fear of backlash from the public.

This line of thinking from two of the most influential public servants in key government departments – Watt and Moran – suggested moving to a system that would save us from the building of ghost estates in rural areas, and one-off houses, too far away from amenities and jobs. But how public servants and politicians think is not always the same. Given the visceral reaction to the imposition of local property taxes and the anger about the restrictions on allowing further one-off housing on privately owned land, it was always most unlikely that vote-conscious politicians would take control of such intellectual arguments to suppress them.

Nor were experienced developers, such as Michael O'Flynn, convinced by this planning-led approach. 'The planning lessons are not being learnt, producing densities that are unsustainable in terms of what the market needs,' he told me in an interview in 2014. 'Gone are the days when you fund developments that the market doesn't need. This was one of the mistakes that we made: there were duplexes funded in country villages. It was mad but they were built because the planners insisted on them. We have to get the planners out of the ivory towers. We can't have developer-led planning before anyone screams at me, but we have to have developer-involved planning and we have to have market-involved planning.' In response, Ali Grehan, then the DCC architect, said, 'We can't continue with this very simplistic response whereby we carpet the suburbs with semi-ds and we build shoebox apartments in the city centre. That's not sustainable.'

But what sort of apartments should we have, either owned by occupants or rented? Many of the modern apartments built in the last decade of the twentieth century and the first decade of the twenty-first century earned a bad reputation for design and construction standards. Many had small rooms, low ceilings, poor storage, barely basic kitchens and limited natural light because they were single-aspect, with windows on just one of the four sides of the unit. Walls were often paper-thin, allowing for uncomfortable audibility of what was happening in the adjacent unit. Fears about inadequate fire safety would be later confirmed. They were smaller in floor space than houses, without the benefit of gardens. Many found them unattractive to rent, let alone buy, but had used them during that era as a stepping-stone towards buying a house, not expecting that they would collapse in value and that couples, as children arrived, would be stuck with these bad investments.

Michael Stanley of Cairn argued for years that residential development in Dublin was not viable or profitable for the builders. In 2017 Stanley said offices capable of housing 80,000-plus workers would be built in Dublin over the following five years but that just 6,000 apartments would be added, with room for 14,000 people. 'We have made appalling use of our land [in Dublin] as a city for the last 50 years, particularly in central locations,' he said. 'If you look at even the last five years, an awful lot of the available land was used for office development.'

Land is more expensive when it is part of or near existing infrastructure and population clusters and has zoning for particularly valued uses. If it is cheaper to build on greenfield sites outside urban centres than on brownfield ones in cities and towns, that does not necessarily take environmental costs into consideration. The Irish Green Building Council (IGBC), a non-profit organisation that advises professionals involved in sustainable construction, has argued the State cannot meet its climate action goals if it continues to allow the development of large, detached houses. They may be cheaper to build than apartments – and therefore better priced to buy or rent – but that doesn't allow for the cost to the owner or tenant of needing a car because of its location, the damage to the environment of driving one and of the permanent loss of agricultural land and hedgerows. As one summary, by Claire McManus of the Royal Institute of the Architects of Ireland (RIAI) put it: 'Affordable housing isn't sustainable and sustainable housing isn't affordable.'

UPWARD PRESSURE ON PRICES

If the land in cities is already expensive, the requirements imposed by the State on building standards for apartments made things even more expensive. While the desire to improve on the poor building quality and size of many of the apartments built in the late twentieth and early twenty-first century is laudable and essential, the new regulations have pushed prices to buy or rent up dramatically.

Apartments are much bigger too, as much as 40 per cent bigger than in the early Celtic Tiger years, despite the claims of many critics that developers are trying to slam in as many units to developments to maximise profits. A two-bedroom apartment must be at least 73 square metres, and a three-bedroom unit must be at least 90 square metres and if a development contains more than 100 apartments, the average size must increase by 10 per cent. The local authorities are likely to insist on bigger than the minimum, but this all adds to the cost and, eventually, to the prices charged. The standards also require at least half of all apartments in a development to be 'dual aspect', which means windows on two sides. They also demand no more than eight apartments per 'core', which means a lift shaft or stairwell per floor, whereas developers argue that buildings could easily have 12–15 units per core. Car-parking spaces cost a further €25,000 per unit. It means that a three-bedroom apartment will cost more than €500,000 to build, whereas a Dublin three-bedroom, semi-detached house could cost less than €350,000 to construct.

Developers were accused of maximising site values by squeezing a higher proportion of smaller units into planning applications. Dún Laoghaire–Rathdown County Council considered mandating developers that three-bed units make up at least 40 per cent of new apartment blocks. Property developer Quintain Ireland responded that three-bed apartments could only be built in south Dublin at affordable rates for families with a household income of €157,000 or more. Almost everyone making that money wanted a house, not an apartment.

BUILDING APARTMENTS

The State doubled down on its belief in apartments when it set the 2016 National Planning Framework. Developers were told that they must build at least 35 homes per hectare or 14 homes per acre. That meant apartments had to be included in what was being built, even in areas where there was little or no demand for them. Developers claimed it was uneconomic to build apartments for the sales market because people on average incomes and even above-average incomes would not be able to afford them. They said they applied for permission for them because if they didn't, they weren't allowed to build anything.

'Everyone is saying it's the developer that is driving this,' said Stephen Garvey, managing director of Glenveagh Properties. 'I would actually say it's the exact opposite. It's policy that's driving this and the developers are responding. We have recklessly planned apartments which are too costly to deliver and out of favour at the expense of own-door homes which are more affordable, sustainable and, most importantly, will be built.'

Cairn and Glenveagh disagreed on the optimum height of apartment blocks in Dublin. Stanley argued that land costs and basement costs are the same irrespective of height, so it makes sense to use more 'air space' and that the cost of Dublin apartments could be lowered by about 20 per cent by going higher. However, Garvey believed that 'once you breach 18 metres in height, your fire regulations become much tighter, the amount of fire stopping, sprinkler systems, exit plans, all of those increase and become more expensive. So, the higher you go, the more expensive it actually gets.'

Apartment blocks have structural requirements that don't apply to houses – and these increase the higher the apartment becomes. An apartment block needs lifts, for example, and the higher it goes the more car-parking spaces are needed in a bigger basement – assuming those are provided. In one report, the Society of Chartered Surveyors Ireland (SCSI) put the cost of delivering apartments in urban Dublin at around €500,000 for a two-bedroom unit in a medium-rise development and at over €620,000 for a two-bedroom unit in a high-rise development. That's before profit for the developer, adding to the price to the buyer.

Garvey also complained about the amount of capital required for apartment development. 'If Glenveagh was to build 3,000 apartments every year and sell them to the public, we would need about €1 billion finance for work in progress,' he said. 'If I was to build the same number in houses, I'd need about €350 million.' People can move into completed houses on estates while more are being built on the larger site. All apartments must be completed before the first residents can move in. 'We're able to turn housing within about 16 to 20 weeks,' Garvey said. 'In an apartment, the timeline is somewhere between 18 months and three years. The capital needed is a massive constraint.'

Garvey believed that buyers wanted own-door houses, even if there were more houses on an estate as a result because there was 'no appetite for owner-occupied apartments outside of the M50'. He also believed the demand was limited within the M50. Developer Michael O'Flynn built apartments too because land use restrictions have forced him to do so, but like Garvey, he was keen to build more houses. It was telling that only 17,000 of the 81,000 apartments granted permission between 2017 and 2022 were built, almost all purchased by institutions. There were two main reasons: the institutions wanted them and could afford them, whereas individuals and families didn't and couldn't.

TWENTY

VULTURES, CUCKOOS AND FUNDS

Mortgage debt among Irish householders fell enormously after the crash. In the first quarter of 2011, the money owed amounted to nearly €155 billion. A decade later it was down to just below €70 billion. Household deposits reached €152 billion by 2023, having been under €84 billion in 2011. Ireland had moved from a culture of borrowing to one of saving. Borrowers didn't want to get burned again; they used what they earned to pay down debt and were prevented from taking on too much debt. The banks simply didn't have the capacity to lend because of restrictions forced upon them by the European Central Bank and the government; they were also highly reluctant to do so, unless on far superior terms and to customers with deeper reserves.

It may have been something of a missed opportunity. There was plenty of Irish money that could have been invested as equity – not debt – in purchasing houses and apartments, instead of looking for money to come in from abroad. For all of those who got into financial trouble, there still were private citizens with cash prepared to seek bargains, or who were buying for their adult children. However, many became more cautious as prices went up and preferred, perhaps scarred by the experience of the crash, to keep their money on deposit or in low-risk investments despite low interest rates and returns. Institutional fund managers were limited by their own rules and by EU laws as to how much they could invest in Ireland. There are good reasons for that; it would have caused great trouble if massive sums of money were to be invested in Irish property and then prices were to fall again. The Central Bank put in new rules that made it tougher for Irish individuals to borrow to purchase buy-to-let properties. It installed a requirement of a minimum deposit of 30 per cent for nearly all such loans, a major disincentive for all but the wealthiest to buy property that could be let to renters.

So, the institutions, mostly foreign, stepped in, with active State encouragement. The arrival of these so-called vulture funds was a deliberate strategy on the part of the government – which used taxation as an inducement – and was actively facilitated by the actions of NAMA, which sold loans and land to the new arrivals. It was known what they would want: these professional landlords, so prevalent in Europe, were interested in scale and didn't want to buy individual units in small villages and towns across Ireland. They would want entire blocks. They would become major presences in our major cities, especially Dublin. Individuals who owned residential property to let to others would not be actively encouraged in the future. We were told that we needed professional landlords to own large tracts of apartment and housing accommodation that they would rent on a long-term basis to tenants, on legally secure terms. These professionals would be in the financially strong enough position to ride out any ups and downs of the economic cycle.

It was made easier for foreign investors to take control of assets that could be rented to us. Individuals and families were handicapped at the very time the institutions were given preferential treatment. If the tax system had been gamed during the 2000s to encourage domestic property speculation, it was used in the post-crash era to entice foreign money. The country's much-vaunted 12.5 per cent corporation tax rate – which has attracted billions in productive investment – applies to trading income. It's not so well known that if profits are made by a company from rent or trade on an investment property, it is regarded as 'passive income', with tax charged at 25 per cent. That rate may not be onerous – particularly to any income tax-payer – but it was still something that may have deterred some foreign providers of capital. The new institutional investors looked for ways to reduce their tax liabilities and the simplest of the early tax breaks they got – for property bought between 2011 and 2013 – was the ability to sell without any capital gains tax (CGT) liability if they held these property investments for at least seven years. As Minister for Finance, Michael Noonan cut stamp duty on commercial transactions from 6 per cent to 2 per cent in an effort to encourage trade. When buying loans, land or properties from NAMA the institutions didn't have to pay stamp duty at all.

But these investors still sought ways to further limit their tax on income and profits, too, and clever Irish accountants and solicitors, who knew the system and the laws that supported them, saw many ways to service their wealthy clients, sometimes outfoxing and surprising the Revenue Commissioners. The most popular mechanism involved Special Purpose Vehicles (SPVs) – so-called Section 110 companies – which had been created in the tax laws two decades earlier to boost activity at the International Financial Services Centre (IFSC). SPVs were allowed to hold a wide range of financial assets, commodities, plants and machinery in a 'tax-efficient' manner. The SPVs couldn't hold property, but what nobody had envisaged was that they would be allowed to hold loans acquired from NAMA or the foreign banks that were selling loans. One Section 110 company called Promontoria Eagle, set up by Cerberus to hold a loan book bought from NAMA, paid corporation taxes of just €2,500 one year despite earning a net interest income of €50 million on the loans it owned.

There were serious opportunities to make a profit. Bill McMorrow of Kennedy Wilson, as one of the early beneficiaries, said publicly that his company could 'push rental rates' in Ireland, even though he already regarded rents as 'very high' because possible buyers were being forced into the rental market. His colleague Mary Ricks referred specifically to the Central Bank's plans to impose 80 per cent loan-to-value on mortgages. 'That's making it very difficult for young people to borrow money and take out mortgages to buy houses,' she said. 'We're seeing double-digit increases straight to the bottom line in rent.' McMorrow also related how Kennedy Wilson got financing to purchase Irish property from international sources at 'sub-3 per cent interest-only for ten years'. In other words, low-interest repayments now and capital repayments to be made many years away, very similar to the type of debt that had created the Celtic Bubble. Such generous loans were not available to Irish individuals or families.

In September 2016, amid much public commentary, Noonan closed the Section 110 loophole for SPVs to ensure they would be taxed at 25 per cent. Noonan also changed the rules for Irish Collective Asset-Management Vehicles (ICAVS), which held either the property assets or the loans connected to them, and Irish Qualifying Investor Alternative Investment Funds (QIAIFs), two other favourite holding mechanisms. The ICAV, also known as the IREF (Irish Real Estate Fund and not to be confused with a REIT), only paid tax of 20 per cent each time a distribution was made from the fund to owners and paid no corporation or capital gains taxes. Kennedy Wilson, for example, held its assets through two Irish QIAIFs and noted in its 2018 annual report that 'during the year these funds were exempt from any direct Irish taxation on income and gains'. The discrimination was notable: an Irish non-corporate landlord had to pay tax every year on rental income of up to 55 per cent and faced a CGT bill of 33 per cent on the profits of a sale of a property.

Insult was added to injury when it emerged many of the funds were somehow (legally) registered as charitable trusts, which meant they were exempt from tax. 'I believe these vulture funds are about to pull off the largest avoidance of tax on Irish profits in the history of the State. The scale is likely to be in the tens of billions of euros in missed taxes,' said Stephen Donnelly during his time as a Social Democrat TD. He subsequently joined Fianna Fáil, became Minister for Health, and, if he has been saying anything about housing matters, it has been quietly or in private rather than with his old loudhailer. Meanwhile, €55.6 billion worth of assets in Irish Section 110 companies were transferred to foreign companies following the 2016 change.

Their ultimate owners did not surrender control of the underlying property assets. They just found new ways to take ownership and control of properties and to structure their tax accordingly. They could buy so-called standing stock (second-hand properties) or they could finance the construction or guarantee the purchase, once completed, of new apartment blocks. They had the whip hand as the domestic banks resiled from taking the risk of financing properties that might not sell once built because of their high price.

THE RISE OF THE REIT

Bill Nowlan, a veteran property investor who had worked for Irish Life for many years, was an eager and public promotor of the idea of Real Estate Investment Trusts (REITs), regularly in the ear of government officials and using a platform of occasional articles in the *Irish Times* to argue the merits of a way of keeping the private investor involved in the property market but in an apparently much safer way. A REIT would gather capital, or equity, from investors, both large pension funds and insurance companies and from smaller individual investors, through the issue of shares. It would be a consortium of sorts. Any investor would get annual income by way of a dividend from the profits and could buy and sell shares whenever they needed their cash back, or to take a personal profit. It wouldn't be just for housing either; this would be a way for people to share in the investment in commercial properties and office blocks too, assets they couldn't afford to buy on their own unless exceptionally wealthy.

Nowlan said that he saw property ownership as 'an equity play' – where people or institutions invested their own rather than borrowed money – and that 'we lost the plot' during the 2000s. He also believed that Ireland was too reliant on its own wealthy people and institutions to fund this equity and that we needed more international capital that wasn't reliant on debt. He used France and the Netherlands as examples of where REITs were used extensively. 'It is one of my biggest sources of professional pride to have led the campaign for the introduction of REITS to Ireland.'

Nowlan found a receptive ear in John Moran, who in turn was encouraged by John Mulcahy at NAMA. Moran also wanted to make property investment less risky. 'We see this as producing a way for the Irish obsession with property, historically so individualised, to be more professional,' Moran said. He also saw it as a way to help NAMA shift unwanted property that could pay off loans. Moran promoted REITS as 'a tax efficient way to enjoy the benefits of owning investment properties without the hassles of being a landlord'. The tax 'efficiency' was held up by critics as being controversial when it emerged that REITs would be exempt from corporation tax, as long as 85 per cent of annual profits were distributed to shareholders as dividends. There was a logic to this, even if it was not easily explained or understood: the dividends would be taxed in whatever country the shareholders paid their tax, therefore to tax the profits first would effectively be double taxation, something that would dissuade investment. Once the legislation had been put in place, the issue for government officials was finding the people who would set up and manage these new REITS on behalf of investors.

While two major commercial REITs – Hibernia and Green – were established and went on to make significant returns for their owners from their investments in office blocks, the first, and surprisingly only, REIT to enter the residential market as an apartment landlord was the Irish Residential Properties Real Estate Investment Trust, which became known as I-RES REIT. It was an offshoot of the Canadian investment group Capreit, which owned and rented about 48,000 apartments in Toronto, Montreal and Vancouver. It entered the Irish market in 2014 by buying 338 apartments in Dublin, from Lloyds Banking Group, in

Smithfield, Sandyford, Inchicore and Tallaght, at a price of €42.2 million, an average of less than €125,000 per unit. That same year I-RES REIT joined the stock market, Capreit allowing its share to fall to just over 15 per cent of the overall amount of stock. I-RES raised €200 million from shareholders and another €215 million the following year as it went on a buying spree of almost 2,450 apartments.

I-RES was run initially by a New Jersey-born lawyer David Ehrlich. 'We saw an opportunity that the Irish economy would rebound; the housing statistics in terms of supply and demographics looked very good, things like the highest birth rate in Europe,' he said. The opportunity for the Canadians, as he saw it, was that Ireland had never had a professionally managed apartment sector. There was also the opportunity to assemble critical mass quickly, buying from the departing foreign banks or, more and more as time went on, from NAMA. Ehrlich was somewhat sensitive to how he and others were described. 'There is nothing wrong with vulture funds,' he said. 'They perform a valuable service when banks need to unload a lot of debt off their books. But we are the opposite of a vulture fund. We are in Ireland for the very, very long term.'

I-RES publicly entered the debate with the government whenever the issue of restricting rent increases was raised. It claimed that rent controls would limit the willingness of investors to finance new construction. When Simon Coveney as Minister for Housing introduced rent pressure zones, limiting increases per annum to 4 per cent in certain areas, Ehrlich claimed the move was 'poorly timed' and left investors feeling 'burned'. However, he also boasted to investors that Ireland was a 'great market' and that 'we've never seen rental increases like this in any jurisdiction that we're aware of'.

It is estimated that in 2017 half of all new builds would have been available for purchase by members of the general public. One of the earliest examples of the change that would take place came in 2018 when more than 1,000 hopeful buyers on a waiting list for 262 apartments in

Churchtown, south Dublin, at the location of the old Notre Dame private school (where Mary Lou McDonald had been a pupil), discovered themselves gazumped by Irish Life (now Canadian owned), which paid €138.5 million for the entire estate. This was possibly the first time the media prominently featured what was to become a controversial trend.

However, it wasn't until 2019 that the surge of activity in apartment buying really began as others followed the lead of long-standing investors such as I-RES and Kennedy Wilson, both of whom continued to actively add to their numbers, and who at one stage held 40 per cent of all institutionally owned homes. The profits made by I-RES were publicly disclosed and acted as a beacon to others.

In 2019, I-RES reported a total profit of €86.3 million ... and paid no corporation tax. By the end of 2022, I-RES had 3,938 homes, nearly all apartments, 99.4 per cent full and each paying an average rent of €1,750 per month. I-RES recorded a net loss of €12 million in 2022 after revaluing some of its properties downwards. Revenue at the company rose from €80 million in 2021 to €85 million in 2022, with just 130 additional homes on the books that cost €70 million to buy. 'There is a significant shortage of good quality private rental accommodation available, as highlighted in recent reports, to service a continually strong and growing population, economy and jobs market,' said Margaret Sweeney, an Irish accountant who had replaced Ehrlich as CEO when he returned across the Atlantic.

If I-RES and Kennedy Wilson initially had dominated the landscape of institutional residential landlords, others came to the fore. Greystar, the creation of its chief executive Bob Faith and headquartered in Charleston, South Carolina, USA, manages more than $250 billion of real estate in 227 markets globally throughout the USA, UK, Europe, Latin America, and the Asia-Pacific region. It is the largest operator of apartments in the US, manages nearly 794,000 units/beds globally, and has over $26 billion of assets under development. When it arrived in Ireland in 2019, it spent €240 million buying 342 apartments in Dublin 9 at Griffith Wood from Cairn and €175 million buying 268 apartments at Dublin Landings from Ballymore.

A lot of German money was quietly invested. DWS, a subsidiary of Deutsche Bank, bought a portfolio of 317 homes over four schemes on the north side of Dublin, while German fund Patrizia spent €93 million on 166 apartments developed by Marlet Property Group at Mount Argus in Harold's Cross, Dublin. The German-owned Union Investment paid €200 million to Ballymore for 435 apartments at 8th Lock, Royal Canal Park, Dublin 15. Lugus may have paid as little as €8.45 million for the Leeside apartment block in Cork in October 2017 before selling it 18 months later for €20 million to Clúid Housing Association and Cork City Council. Macquarie, an Australian bank, set up a €100 million fund to buy homes and started with second-hand homes in Carlow, doing deals with Japanese and Italian banks to finance future deals. It set up a €120 million deal with Tinc Commercial Partners, a Dutch infrastructure fund, to build more than 530 social housing units in Dublin and the east of the country.

Having succeeded with a company they named Hibernia REIT in the commercial market, Bill Nowlan and Frank Kenny turned their attention to the residential sector and formed Urbeo Residential in 2017. They created a fund made up of institutional investors who would invest in the lower end of the property market, with a focus on affordable housing that would be rented to tenants on a long-term basis. Nowlan believed that countries like Germany and the Netherlands depended on private capital for social and affordable housing projects, attracted by secure long-term yields. As CEO, they hired Felix McKenna, who had worked on property at Eircom and then at NAMA, where he was an expert on ghost estates. House-building company Durkan and the directors of MKN Property Group invested too, but the main funding came from Starwood Capital, an American firm with $60 billion of assets under management, and the State, through the Irish Strategic Investment Fund (ISIF), which put in €60 million.

Urbeo sought to put together a €1 billion portfolio of build-to-rent assets and spent half of that in its first 12 months in purchasing 1,500 rental apartments, focusing on homes in the greater Dublin area in what it called 'under-served segments' of households with a low or mid-range income. Urbeo proposed offering about 30 per cent of its schemes for rent as social and affordable accommodation, with the balance to private occupiers, on leases up to six years, to mimic many European countries.

It never intended to be a developer itself, seeking instead to partner with builders and housing associations to deliver 'new rental housing projects in non-prime but well-serviced locations'. Its sites in Dublin include Citywest, Hansfield, Finglas, Tallaght, Rathborne Village and two projects in Maynooth, County Kildare. In 2019, Urbeo bulk-purchased nearly two-thirds of the 143 new-build homes in Carton Grove housing estate in Maynooth. The same year, it bought an entire phase of 151 homes in Mariavilla, another Maynooth housing estate, for €53.5 million.

Other Irish funds emerged. Ardstone Capital, founded by former executives at Friends First, spent €450 million in 2021 on more than 900 residential units under development or due to be developed in various schemes across the greater Dublin area. Avestus was responsible for the second largest deal of 2021 when it acquired a portfolio of 382 rental apartments distributed across two high-end developments in south Dublin for €216 million. As well as being called vultures, these funds became known as 'cuckoos': they entered and took over the nests that could have been purchased by individuals or families. To make it seem more acceptable, the private rented sector (PRS) or buy-to-rent (BTR) got a new name among its promoters: the multi-family sector. It was almost an amusing description as the preponderance of one-bed apartments limited the number of couples with children in these apartment blocks.

It was estimated that between 2016 and 2021 more than €7 billion was spent by PRS investors on 12,000 new homes that would house at least 25,000 people, with another 6,000-plus second-hand homes traded. A marked bias in favour of buying newly built apartments rather than standing stock became entrenched in later years because higher rents could be established from the outset at a new development. The buyers were stuck with lower rents at existing blocks, although that did mean some could be purchased relatively cheaply compared to new developments. In 2019 it was calculated that the investment in PRS in Ireland was almost the size of that in Britain, the latter being a market twelve times our size. It also accounted for 44 per cent of all property investment in 2019, ahead of offices, warehouses, hotels, pubs and shopping centres, when in 2016 its share was just 4 per cent. Not surprisingly, Dublin became one of the top 10 cities in Europe for PRS investment. It is true that institutional investors were attracted by high rents, but without that investment new apartment blocks would not have been built.

However, the extent of the involvement by foreign investors may have received more attention than it deserved because of the amounts of money being spent on individual deals and because they were buying the vast majority of new apartment blocks. In total, they were buying not much more than 10 per cent of the entire new housing stock coming on stream, while affordable housing bodies and councils backed by the government bought around 20 per cent.

By 2021 the number of new builds available for general purchase was down to about a quarter despite increased supply. The State acquired social housing for at least 4,400 of the 21,000 new homes built in 2021, while investment funds bought 95 per cent of the 3,644 apartments built. About 5,000 of the new homes were one-off houses, mainly built on their own land by their owners and not offered for sale.

The trend wasn't as far removed from the past as it seemed, though. In the boom-time era, a third of new properties were bought by buy-to-let investors who shut out prospective homeowners. Essentially, they were replaced by institutional investors who received more opprobrium because of their size and because they made their acquisitions in bulk.

If housing has become a speculative investment asset, removed from its primary social function, then that trend was in place before the Celtic Tiger crash and did not emerge, as some have suggested, subsequently. Nor was this unique to Ireland: it was an international phenomenon.

Prices went up because, in the decade after the crash, we built only a fraction of the new homes we needed. For all the complaints of a shortage of houses to buy, we didn't build enough apartments to rent either, notwithstanding all the criticisms about the institutions taking control of the new ones and charging high rents. They were able to put up the rents because of the shortage of supply. Economist Ronan Lyons has estimated a need for 500,000 homes but calculated that just a quarter of that was built between the start of 2012 and the end of 2021. We still built 40,000 new one-off homes in a decade, either owner-occupied or holiday units. Of the remaining 87,000, only 20,000 were apartments, the most likely candidates for new rental homes, while the other 67,000 were 'scheme developments', in other words in housing estates.

It is arguable that the rental sector in Ireland is no larger now than it was a decade ago, even though demand for rental accommodation has risen by perhaps one-quarter in that time as the population surged to over 5.1 million, as disclosed in the 2022 census. We needed social housing and new owner-occupied homes, therefore the shortage of supply led to an understandable, if nasty, increase in all prices. There simply weren't enough apartments built in the urban areas of Dublin and Cork, and short supply saw a doubling of rental prices over a decade. Rents had exceeded their Celtic Tiger-era peaks long before institutional investment stepped up in 2018. The investors came because of the rental opportunity; the failure to provide alternative supplies allowed them to push rents up further. Unfortunately for tenants, incomes didn't rise to match soaring rents or come anywhere close to doing so. Those who already owned their own homes escaped the awful reality of those who couldn't get to buy.

When the government announced its latest housebuilding plan in September 2021 – Housing for All – it defended the dependence on foreign money to create a housing supply and admitted that the role of the Irish banks would be limited by a lack of resources. Its document stated: 'A proportion of this funding will be provided by the domestic banking sector, however, the vast majority will be required from international sources, underlining the critical importance of institutional investment in generating additional housing supply. Without such investment, activity in the housing market would be much reduced and would increase the significant pressure already facing renters and prospective home-owners.' Political opponents didn't want to listen or concede to this financial reality.

Unfortunately, the government's long-term ambitions were deflected sometimes by a need to respond to controversy. In the summer of 2021, the government introduced a 10 per cent stamp duty on the purchase of 10 or more houses in a 12-month period. This was a reaction to the realisation that the investment funds weren't just buying apartment blocks within the M50 but also houses on new estates in commuter towns. People didn't want to buy the apartments, but they did want the houses and were not happy to lose out to these buyers.

It was the publicity about a single proposed transaction that prompted the change: the purchase of more than 100 houses on the Mullen Park housing estate in Maynooth, County Kildare, by UK property investor Round Hill Capital. Minister for Housing Darragh O'Brien introduced new planning regulations that ringfenced a portion of houses in any new estate for individual buyers, but not apartments. Kelston Properties, the Irish developer of Mullen Park, cancelled the sale to Round Hill Capital and offered the 115 remaining homes for sale individually, at prices near to €500,000, almost 25 per cent more than the original asking price in April 2021. Round Hill Capital had also bought family houses at Hollystown, Dublin 15, but it wasn't the only investment fund buying houses. And the funds didn't stop either when the new stamp duty measures were introduced. Property investors and institutional funds bulk bought more than 350 houses at a cost of over

€100 million after that, prepared to pay levies of more than €30,000 per home, ten times the regular stamp duty levy owed when a property is purchased.

John Moran believes now that the State should have moved in 2014 and 2015 to limit the ability of foreign investment funds to outmuscle individual buyers, and Robert Watt concurs. It's easy to understand why they would think so, but at the time of their arrival, the foreign institutions were largely the only show in town.

One of the attractions was rental yields – calculated by dividing the purchase price by the annual rent – of close to 4 per cent, higher than was being achieved elsewhere in Europe. Institutions were prepared to invest on that basis as long as returns on safe assets, like government bonds, were low because of low interest rates. That changed as 2022 progressed and the ECB reacted to soaring inflation with concerted interest rate rises. That meant government bonds paid debt-holders an acceptable return and reduced the potential for future investment in housing. This came at just the time vocal political opponents of the government were saying we didn't want foreign funds, and they disregarded the arguments of the likes of Brian Moran from Hines who said: '... we now have longer-term, patient capital that has for the most part replaced speculative, or short-term, highly leveraged capital.' Many didn't want to listen or appreciate that foreign capital is a fact of international commerce and that it provides where the State can't afford it.

Bill Nowlan weighed in and warned about the cost of the State paying for all of the new housing itself: 'We are reaching an Orwellian point of promoting the idea that capital that produces jobs is good, while capital that produces housing is bad and therefore should be forbidden or penalised by penal rates of taxation.' He pointed out that if these institutions didn't do the building then the State would have to do so and the costs would be tens of billions of euro per annum.

TWENTY-ONE

THE HOUSEBUILDERS

The country didn't just need investors in housing: it needed major house- and apartment-builders with a solid financial foundation. The first picks were made by NAMA and some of those were controversial considering the financial record of those it favoured.

NAMA's remit expanded many times in the decade after it was created. If its initial priority was to recover as much money as possible – something that remained its overriding ambition – it was given additional mandates by politicians to provide housing and to develop infrastructure, something most of its senior executives had limited knowledge of doing. As well as picking losers among the developers – who it would put out of business – it would have to select potential winners with whom it would work.

The extent of the lack of ambition on the part of the government – which was attributed initially to the lack of money available to a near-bankrupt State – was demonstrated by the announcement in the October 2014 budget of €2.2 billion in new funding for housebuilding. The money seemed significant given the condition of the national finances at the time but wasn't all that it seemed. It was only meant to provide 1,000 new homes between 2015 and 2017, with the bulk being used for refurbishments and the renting of existing facilities. The actions did almost nothing on the supply side, something Robbie Kelleher of Davy Stockbrokers described as 'inexplicable'.

A year later and the government, facing an election in early 2016, belatedly realised improvements had to be made. In December 2015, Minister for Finance Michael Noonan and NAMA officials held a press conference at the Aviva Stadium to announce plans to build 20,000 houses, 15,000 of them in Dublin, by 2020 at a cost of €5.6 billion. 'It isn't a pie-in-the-sky announcement,' said Noonan. 'This is real and this is happening already, and I am quite confident it will be delivered on time.' Noonan said the plan was a response to a 'market failure', and that houses built would be as entry-level starter homes. Chairman Frank Daly claimed NAMA would deliver more houses annually than all the UK-quoted builders combined, although NAMA also admitted that its programme would meet only 20 per cent of the private housing need in Dublin.

Developers outside of NAMA reacted with horror to the idea of having to go into competition with it, or rather with rival builders who would be funded by it as banker and backer. They claimed NAMA had distorted the market by charging its builders significantly lower interest rates than were available from commercial lenders and that NAMA's role had changed in September 2015 from a bank set up to deal with toxic loans to a 'fully-fledged' property developer. It said the agency had also illegally benefitted from state aid. In early 2018 the European Commission found in NAMA's favour.

NAMA selected eight key locations for new housing and a number of developers with whom it believed it could maintain good relationships as a quasi-financier. One of the most extraordinary decisions was to become the banker to Bovale Developments and its owners, Michael and Tom Bailey. Bovale became one of the most infamous developers in the country before 2000. In 1998 I wrote the story in the *Sunday Tribune* of how Michael Bailey personally handed Minister for Justice Ray Burke a payment of IR£40,000, something that became central to the investigations of the Planning Tribunal. It later established that Bailey also paid former assistant city and county manager for Dublin George Redmond three cash payments amounting to between IR£16,000 and IR£20,000 in the 18 months prior to July 1989.

THE BAILEY BROTHERS

In 2006 the Bailey brothers made the biggest tax settlement in Irish history, amounting to €22.7 million and made up of unpaid tax, interest and penalties. The Office of the Director of Corporate Enforcement (ODCE) had taken an action against them, seeking to have them disqualified as directors. The action took seven years to wind its way through the courts because the brothers objected successfully to the use of the Planning Tribunal report in evidence against them. It meant that the case successfully taken against them focused only on two years, July 1996 to June 1998, instead of the twelve-year period from 1988 to 2000 as the ODCE wanted.

The case taken was civil, not criminal, and as a result, the sanctions could not include imprisonment even though the Planning Tribunal had found them to have made corrupt payments. Instead, the High Court found them guilty of 'particularly serious' misconduct and fraud in their operation of company finances, including understating their gross remuneration in that period by €6 million. Ms Justice Mary Finlay Geoghegan said the 'particularly serious' misconduct, involving 'systematic falsification' of books of account, left them unfit to be directors of a company. She noted that a managing partner with accountancy firm PWC gave evidence of how during his 35-year career in public accounting in Ireland he had never encountered such a failure to maintain proper books and records 'that compares with the extent and gravity of the failures in respect of Bovale for the two-years ended 30 June 1998'.

Justice Finlay Geoghegan disqualified both Bailey brothers from acting as company directors for seven years, although she could have done so for 14 years. The brothers did not oppose the disqualification orders but successfully argued mitigating factors to reduce the period, arguing that they had 'learnt from their mistakes', intended to set matters right and had been tax compliant since 2001 now that they kept proper books and records. The judge agreed there was 'some objective support' for those sworn contentions arising from a 'forensic review' of Bovale's accounts conducted by PWC and from their cooperation with NAMA.

NAMA financed the Baileys in 2015 when they completed their first housing development since the crash, the Coill Dubh development at Broomfield, Malahide, County Dublin, with 74 three-, four- and five-bedroom detached and semi-detached homes opposite Malahide Community School and next-door to St Sylvester's GAA club. In mid-2018 it sold a site in Kilcock, County Kildare, with the capacity for 400 new homes, to Glenveagh for €20 million.

The most conspicuous development was on a prime one-acre site off Anglesea Road in Ballsbridge, which Tom Bailey had purchased in 2005 for €6.2 million. There now stand four cubist apartment blocks of 24 expensive units, called Dunluce, each of which had three-bedroom penthouses that sold for €1.8 million each, built by a company called Blackhall Green.

GERRY GANNON

Another controversial figure to be backed by NAMA, albeit not one who faced court proceedings but who was a key witness in a major Celtic Tiger trial, was Gerry Gannon. Born in Roscommon in the 1950s, Gannon became one of Dublin's biggest housebuilders and is reckoned to have built over 10,000 homes since 1984. His best-known developments were at Malahide, Swords and Clongriffin on the north side of Dublin and at Rockfield, in Dundrum, on the south side. He also built the €20 million rail station at Clongriffin with the intention of it serving as a spur for a new line to Dublin Airport.

Gannon made two highly notable purchases in the first decade of the twenty-first century. He partnered with industrialist Michael Smurfit to buy the luxury K Club golf estate at Straffan in County Kildare in 2005, using finance supplied by the Irish Nationwide Building Society to pay the estimated €115 million price tag. The existing revenues and slim profits from the hotel and golf course would not justify such an expenditure but the building and selling of houses around the course might. This was what was known at the time as a 'property play'.

Gannon also purchased the 215-acre Belcamp College site in North Dublin for €105 million. He had plans to build a medical campus for the Royal College of Surgeons in Ireland on 60 acres of it, to serve over 2,000 students, a 320-bed teaching hospital, a 90-bed nursing home, staff and student accommodation and a hotel with leisure facilities. The construction costs were estimated at €756 million over ten years. It never happened.

By 2010, turnover at the K Club had slumped to €10 million, and the resort made a loss of €5 million. The crash meant Gannon was unable to get cash flow from the sale of new builds there or elsewhere. His company's debts, estimated at over €1 billion, were transferred to NAMA.

Gannon later, as a witness in a criminal trial connected to matters at Anglo Irish Bank, testified he 'probably' had a net worth of around €1 billion in 2008, far more than anyone outside of his inner circle had ever reckoned. He was one of ten very wealthy clients of Anglo who became involved in a highly controversial share purchase scheme – using money borrowed from Anglo – to try and support the bank not long before it collapsed. He became a figure of some public notoriety after he was the subject of surveillance by secret cameras for an RTÉ *Prime Time* programme, the most notable images being of him lumping Brown Thomas bags full of goodies into the boot of his Range Rover in the shop's car park. He featured because he had tried to sign over assets of about €12 million to his wife, Margaret, just before his loans were transferred to NAMA.

Gannon argued, much as other moguls of the time did and perhaps correctly in retrospect, that NAMA had moved on him too quickly and that if he had been given time, the value of his land would have recovered and he would have been able to repay his debts. At the time he owned about 700 acres of undeveloped land, including a 74-acre parcel at Straffan, opposite the entrance to the K Club, which was owned separately from his partnership with Smurfit. He wanted to keep that and develop a new village. However, he didn't try to justify hanging onto his K Club shareholding. 'I can't expect the taxpayer to fund an exclusive loss-making club in County Kildare,' he said in 2010. A year later NAMA approved the transfer of his shareholding in the K Club to Smurfit when his erstwhile partner paid about €35 million to refinance the NAMA debt of €55 million.

Gannon then went to work for NAMA, at an annual salary of €170,000. He assisted in the sale of assets for about €200 million but persuaded NAMA to back him in new housebuilding. His first major post-crash venture was at Miller's Glen in Swords; when those houses went on sale in 2014 queues of eager potential buyers formed, alerting many to the potential for a return to housebuilding. It encouraged him to seek planning permission on other lands in Swords.

However, it was other, new companies that were to become the new face of Irish home-building. Cairn and Glenveagh would become the most prominent and active of these, two companies that wouldn't rely excessively on debt but on equity investment, i.e. money they raised on the stock market. One reason for the crash was how much debt developers had taken in buying land and how little equity they'd had to fall back on when things went wrong. With the exception of McInerney Properties and Abbey, two stock market-quoted companies that had been based on family businesses, most of the builders who prospered during the boom were individual or family-owned. They relied on cash flow and borrowings for funding and had little equity to provide a buffer during a downturn or crash, although the crash was so severe it still took McInerney with it. The stock market should have provided the basis for a refinancing of remaining builders, but surprisingly few sought that option.

CAIRN

Cairn was based on an established builder called Shannon Homes, owned and run by the Stanley family, which went into NAMA with big debts and a large landbank. Shannon stopped building in 2008 but the Stanleys caught two big breaks in 2014. A legal challenge to a judgment of the Revenue Commissioners, arising from the way Joseph senior transferred the business on retirement to his sons, Michael, Kevin, Robert, Conor and Joseph junior, saved them from a massive tax bill. Then they met wealthy Scottish financier Alan McIntosh, who provided help in exiting NAMA while keeping a 50-acre site at Balgriffin in north Dublin. It was the basis for a new company, Cairn Homes.

Cairn pitched to investors that it would be a well-capitalised housebuilder buying development land at low prices from 'unnatural owners', such as banks. It raised €440 million in June 2015 and a year later sold more shares for €176.5 million as it went on a land-buying spree. It teamed up with John Grayken's Lone Star to buy a major portfolio of loans from Ulster Bank called Project Clear. Lone Star took nearly 500 acres across 31 residential development sites for €125 million and Cairn paid €378 million to buy €1.75 billion in property loans, all with the purpose of taking over the development sites that the debts were secured against. Many of the sites – owned by some of the biggest names of the boom years, including Liam Carroll, Joe O'Reilly, Sean Dunne, Sean Mulryan and Michael Whelan – were already under the control of receivers appointed by the bank when Cairn bought the debt to take control of the properties. The sites were mainly in Dublin, with one in Cork and one in Kilkenny, and gave Cairn 120 loans secured against 1,200 acres of land, across 28 residential development sites, and 21 borrower connections. In Dublin, it assembled about 20 per cent of the county's zoned undeveloped land on which over 12,000 housing units could be constructed. All of its land would soon be valued at €835 million on its balance sheet, with 96 per cent of it either zoned for residential use or with live planning permission. It would not all be built on quickly, it not being possible to do so all at once, although it was also in Cairn's interest to drip-feed the stock of housing into the market. The remaining land would go up in value in anticipation of higher prices for the units when eventually built and sold.

McIntosh and two of the Stanleys, Michael and Kevin, moved quickly to take money out on joining the stock market. As well as having a large starting shareholding, they persuaded the new investors they should get 20 per cent of the business's total returns over seven years by way of additional shares. Just two years after setting up the company, they sold 2.1 per cent of the shares for €26.6 million and continued to hold more shares worth about another €100 million; if things went as anticipated, they would receive another 47 million shares in the company at a later date. Cairn had built little more than 200 homes by this stage. The Cairn founders received almost €50 million from selling more shares between September 2017 and April 2019.

GLENVEAGH

Something similar, but on a lesser scale, happened at Glenveagh. Again, it was a British individual who was the driving force in its creation. Justin Bickle was employed at Oaktree Capital Management, a major global private equity fund, and set up and ran its European Principal Group, specialising in so-called 'distressed for control investing', or 'loan-to-own'. He first arrived in Ireland in 2010 when Oaktree considered and then rejected investment in McInerney. He remained intrigued by the idea that stock markets could provide equity to builders as Oaktree went about purchasing loans and the underlying assets. What he needed was a builder.

Stephen Garvey, a young and low-key builder during the boom, had avoided NAMA, spotting the madness and shutting down most of the operations at his Bridgedale company in the nick of time. Garvey was already buying land in 2012; he'd noted how the number of properties available for rent had fallen sharply and reckoned that new supply would be needed. Bridgedale purchased its first site, in Ballyboughal, north County Dublin, from Ulster Bank, with loans provided by the bank itself. It then asked him to take on other projects, before he met up with Bickle.

They bonded over a conversation on the internal rates of return on investment, something Bickle didn't expect from someone who had left school after his Junior Cert as a 15-year-old. However, what he discovered quickly was that by the age of 20, Garvey had about 100 people working for him at his plastering contracting business, which got contracts with some of the country's biggest builders. Oaktree subsequently invited Garvey to develop sites for it in the greater Dublin area. The first big project was the marina village project at Greystones, County Wicklow, which had been a Sisk Group-led public–private partnership postponed because of the crash. Oaktree had also signed up John Mulcahy as an advisor on his departure from NAMA in 2014. Mulcahy had also become a director of Iput and an advisor to Denis O'Brien, although he insisted this was only for his overseas property interests and that he was not conflicted by his NAMA knowledge.

In 2017, Oaktree decided to partially cash out by putting much of its land into Glenveagh, which raised €550 million by offering shares through a stock market mechanism called an initial public offering (IPO). Singaporean sovereign wealth fund GIC emerged as a major shareholder. A year later it went back to the market to raise another €213 million to buy more land and fund development. Other investors were unimpressed by Oaktree's plan to sell half of its remaining 16.5 per cent stake and the share price began to fall, which had an impact on the founding trio.

The IPO involved the issue of 200 million so-called founder shares – of which Bickle and Garvey got 90 million each, the remaining 20 million for Mulcahy – set up for conversion into ordinary shares over five years, subject to the stock price rising at a minimum annual rate of 12.5 per cent. This 'founder' share scheme was meant to give them 20 per cent of total shareholder returns over five years and in the first year, they got one-fifth, valued at just €22 million between them at the time. But they weren't to get more shares. Bickle left Glenveagh in 2019 and set up Eagle Street Partners alongside Shane Scully, to spend €3 billion on 5,000 build-to-rent apartments. In 2022 Bickle died of a heart attack while on a trip to Dubai. He was only 51 years old.

The desire of institutions to invest in publicly quoted housing companies ebbed, possibly because the value of the assets – including land – on their balance sheets was more than the stock market valuations of Cairn and Glenveagh. Lone Star had looked to the stock market as a way of furthering and/or exiting its Irish investments, copying what had been done at Cairn and Glenveagh. It had gone a long way, with builder Durkan Residential, towards creating a new company called Dres with an anticipated initial stock market value of about €300 million. Instead, Lone Star introduced Quintain, its UK-based residential property brand, into Ireland to manage its assets. It allowed Durkan to retain ownership of the Dres brand but ended their exclusive construction partnership. Cairn, Glenveagh and Quintain became the country's three biggest residential landholders and developers. Both Cairn and Glenveagh focused on suburban starter homes with an average selling price of €300,000 and on apartment blocks pre-sold to investment funds for the rental market. They targeted people who wanted to own at prices where they could get access to mortgage finance. Typical customers were couples in their mid-to-late thirties, often with children, who wanted a good first home in an urban or suburban neighbourhood.

However, both companies were among a host of developers who claimed that the Central Bank rules to restrict mortgage borrowing by those who wanted to buy their own homes were too stringent. Michael Stanley complained about the 'difference between demand and realisable demand' and said Central Bank rules had displaced house price inflation into rental inflation. 'The challenge is that 75 to 80 per cent of potential customers can't get access to mortgage finance.' Stephen Garvey described the projections of up to 50,000 houses a year being needed to satisfy demand as 'irrelevant' for as long as restrictions remained in place on the amount that could be borrowed: 'The Central Bank's rules have anchored prices to incomes. It all comes down to prices and incomes, not housing supply.'

The CBI ignored the sustained campaign by developers who wanted to either increase the limit from 3.5 times income to 4.5 times or to a new measure linking earnings to their ability to service their debts, pointing out that many were paying more in rent than they would on a mortgage at a higher limit. The CBI would not relent and said that house prices would have gone up by 25 per cent more by March 2019 had its 2015 rules not been implemented.

THE CALL FOR REFORM

Meanwhile, Garvey argued for housing schemes, instead of apartments, if greater house unit density were allowed on the sites. 'I haven't seen a domestic buyer come to one of my [apartment] schemes since 2010,' said Garvey. 'They don't want them.' In mid-2022 Garvey suggested reducing the size of gardens for new houses. His idea was regarded by some critics as an attempt by a builder to shoehorn more houses onto a site, but Garvey's thinking was far more nuanced and deserving of attention instead of outright rejection.

He argued that if the land devoted to gardens were smaller, he would have more space in which to build more houses to sell to willing buyers. Garvey argued that they weren't getting private gardens anyway if they were living in apartments and that a new minimum garden space standard of 40 square metres, rather than the current 60–70 square metres, would allow for a reduction in house prices of up to 20 per cent. All of those one-third reductions would add up and, he claimed, the average rents in new-build homes could be cut by 30 per cent to €1,313, while the average price for new-builds to purchase could be reduced from €376,000 to €315,000. The lower purchase price would allow households on €75,000 salaries to buy homes in new-build residential developments.

At present, the back walls of new houses must be 22 metres away. Garvey said this could be cut to 16 metres and that would be fairer to everyone in a development. 'They would eliminate the current imbalance between apartment owners who might only get six square metres of balcony space and owners of houses who get 55-60 square metre gardens. How is this fair?'

The separation distances between houses were introduced in Britain and Ireland in 1918 for the post-World War One era when back gardens had to include outdoor toilets and coal sheds. Britain ditched these regulations a long time ago. 'You can still give everyone a drive and a back garden. You actually achieve the same density, but you give a better-quality product and you reduce the cost of doing it. Everyone in the development gets an own-door house. The public open space is better utilised for everyone in the development. Because if you go to a development today, you'll see one big green area in the front of the development and only 20 per cent of those people benefited for it. So, why not take that large space and break it up into smaller pockets?' Garvey argued.

The annual report of the Office of the Planning Regulator for 2019 found that there were 40,252 planning permissions granted, of which apartments accounted for 51 per cent, the first time ever it was in the majority. In Dublin, 86 per cent of the applications were for apartments. However, the banks wouldn't supply the finance to developers unless sure that there were guaranteed buyers for the end product. 'Banks won't lend to developers unless they're making 15 per cent gross profit,' Paul Mitchell from construction consultants Mitchell McDermott said. He said that, on average, it took a year to design, a year to get planning and two years to build, to which can be added the cost of finance and the risk of what prices the market will bear by the time they're ready for sale. 'European countries have been building apartments since the rebuilding programme after the Second World War and have established developers and structures for funding these schemes,' said Mitchell.

Glenveagh and Cairn soon accounted for about 10 per cent of annual housing output nationwide. The next eight top privately owned companies were reckoned to account for up to a further 10 per cent of further output. They had financial resources and landbanks, yet were reluctant to build unless they were guaranteed buyers for their houses and apartments at prices that gave profit.

Both companies are highly profitable. Glenveagh had revenues of €649 million in 2022 and made an operating profit of €70 million as it sold 1,354 suburban units at an average price of €330,000 in 2022, up from 902 units at €308,000 a year earlier. It had a landbank with a capacity for 16,600 units. Its aim was to produce 3,000 units per year by 2024. Cairn made operating profits of just over €100 million for 2022 on revenues of just over €600 million. Cairn was active on over 20 sites nationwide during 2022, employing over 3,000 people, and boasted that it had built and sold 5,500 dwellings since 2017. It moved beyond the greater Dublin area, where it has over 95 per cent of its landbank, beginning work on its first site in Cork, at Castletreasure in Douglas, in 2021, and has plans to build in Galway, Kilkenny and Limerick. Both were slow to buy new land, however, instead returning money to investors by way of share buybacks, as well as paying dividends.

Glenveagh spent €145 million on share buybacks and Cairn used €75 million of its cash to buy its own shares, something that increased the value to its owners of the remaining shares. That they did this rather than expand their land holdings suggested they thought land had become too expensive to buy and develop. If Glenveagh and Cairn – with their financial firepower – were reluctant to buy more land, then it didn't bode well for the smaller housebuilders without capital backing who depended on debt or pre-sales for their business. By 2022 and 2023 we reached the stage where the government was offering subsidies to builders to get them to use their planning permissions as it feared that the housebuilding recovery would stall and then falter, leaving us tens of thousands of units a year behind the new construction we needed.

TWENTY-TWO

EXPECTATIONS OF SOCIAL HOUSING

Since its creation, the State, at various times and with various emphases, has tried to provide housing for those who are economically disadvantaged and unable to provide for themselves. The 1930s saw the introduction of the first major programme in the provision of public housing to low earners, the construction of modest but solid accommodation to assist in the improvement of living standards despite the financial constraints imposed upon the country's overall finances by an inward-looking economic set-up.

After an interruption to building in the 1940s caused by the economic limitations of the Second World War, the process resumed in the late 1950s and early 1960s. There was a genuine effort to deal with the poverty of inner-city living and tenements. Unfortunately, experiments based on European models, such as modern high-rise apartment blocks in Ballymun in Dublin, for example, failed for a variety of social reasons. New public housing estates often suffered a disproportionate amount of anti-social behaviour, blamed on the absence of sufficient amenities and income deprivation caused by unemployment.

This expenditure soaked up most of the available State capital that could have been used to fund new health, educational and transport infrastructure – as was happening in the UK and elsewhere in Europe. We left much of the first two responsibilities to the Catholic Church, and occasionally other religions.

In every city and town in Ireland, there are large estates of houses and blocks of flats (before they were called apartments) that were built by the State, usually through local councils. In the early decades of the State, this comprised the majority of new housing. Private housing became the predominant new building as the country became more prosperous, but still in the 1970s and 1980s local authorities made up about one-third of all housebuilding activity, providing social housing. It's estimated that one-quarter of the country's private housing stock was built by and once owned by councils.

This housing gave people, especially families, a chance in life that might have been denied to them in previous generations. It allowed them to own and thereby feel committed not just to the maintenance of that property – even if it was more functional than luxury – but to their communities. The facilities may not have been extensive either, but in many cases there were schools and shops and playing pitches and much of what was needed for day-to-day living. It sometimes took time for estates to mature – as the people living there did – but for as many of those who complained and wanted out, there were others who were happy with what they had and who felt some gratitude towards the State accordingly.

However, some of those championing the apparent past successes of local authorities in providing social housing seem to have overlooked the many failures. The housing built was of variable quality – requiring significant upgrades in later years – and construction standards may even have disimproved in the decades before local authority-built provision was largely scaled back and then abandoned. Serious issues also arose in relation to social and economic deprivation and the provision of adequate services in the locations chosen for development. We may not have developed quite the same extent of problems as in the so-called sink estates of England and France, for example, but it would be naive and disingenuous to deny the anti-social behaviour, drug addiction and criminality that was attributed to the near ghettoisation of some social housing estates. The Ballymun towers had been celebrated as a major achievement of the modern State in the 1960s – and were built to a very high standard of insulation and space, which was underappreciated – but their location on the fringes of Dublin city led to a degree of alienation among some of the people who were moved there. Major problems of poverty, drug dependency and crime developed, to the horror of many people determined to avoid all of that and angry that the name of their local area became synonymous with those issues.

It was regarded as an achievement of the Celtic Tiger era when some of those flat complexes were demolished and replaced with lower-lying apartment blocks. Many weren't. When a renovation of Limerick city was planned, as a response to the drug gang wars going on at the time, I was brought on a tour of empty houses in St Mary's Park and Moyross that were well overdue demolition and replacement. Many of them still stand. Indeed, some of the crime problems that affect areas in Dublin today, such as Finglas, Crumlin, Ballyfermot and Tallaght, have been attributed to the lack of a sufficient mix of public and private housing, even if many of the council houses have passed into private ownership. Things did not get any better in the late twentieth-century housing schemes either – such as Jobstown and Killinarden in west Tallaght – as the local authorities contributed to suburban sprawl and displaced young families in poorly serviced locations by going to greenfield sites further and further from the city's centre. There was a deliberate element to some of this: out of sight and out of mind.

There was also a shift in government policy during the 1980s and 1990s: the provision of social housing, while not abandoned, was scaled back and the money was diverted to infrastructure such as schools and hospitals and roads, especially motorways with EU funding support. And few argued, because it accelerated the development of the economy. Politicians and planners were not blind to the failings this caused, or of social segregation, and attempted to rectify both with Part V developments, a rule that all new private housing projects would have to make at least 20 per cent available for social housing, the recipients to be decided by the council or an approved housing body. It was an effort to effect greater social integration and cohesion. However, some potential private buyers objected strenuously and the developers, conscious of protecting the prices they could demand, often paid off the local councils to avoid meeting the obligations, or offered land in unfavoured locations where they would build alternative units for social provision. Anything to keep the social housing away from their profitable private developments. While the 20 per cent social housing element of new developments has been reduced in the last decade to 10 per cent, the land swaps and cash deals that had been used to escape or minimise the social housing in new developments are no longer allowed. Mostly.

A QUESTION OF PRIORITIES

The lack of urgency in providing social housing – and the legal and political rows that delay things further – is also exemplified by the story of O'Devaney Gardens, a 1950s flat complex of 278 units near the Phoenix Park. Early this century it was acknowledged that the complex was not fit for purpose and had to be replaced. It was earmarked for replacement under the 2000–6 National Development Plan. As the area was in then Taoiseach Bertie Ahern's constituency, he gave it close attention. In 2006 his brother Noel, as Minister for Housing, approved a €180 million public–private partnership deal with property developer Bernard McNamara to provide more than 800 social, affordable and private homes, along with shops, community facilities and some offices on the site.

It was one of the first casualties of the crash as the soon-to-be-bankrupt McNamara reneged because he had calculated correctly that the anticipated profits from selling apartments would not materialise. He realised he would not have the money to cover the cost of providing social housing. Many of the tenants had left the flats and the empty units became a haven for drug-dealing and criminality. Some were set ablaze.

The council went ahead with the demolition and announced plans for a social housing site it would develop, with some land to be kept for commercial and private development whenever the economy recovered. The idea was to have the first social houses completed by the end of 2012, but the government could not provide the €32 million requested. It would be a further decade before the council provided 56 units on the edge of the land, building work that somehow took four years to complete, notwithstanding the complications of building during Covid.

In 2015, DCC came up with a new plan to develop the site for social, affordable and private housing. It took two years to persuade city councillors of its merits: the new complex would engage a private developer to deliver a housing mix of 30 per cent social housing and 20 per cent affordable housing, with the remainder available for private sale by the nominated developer. It would take another two years before the site was transferred to Bartra, a firm controlled by Richard Barrett. Remarkably, Bartra decided not to act upon the fully approved planning permission for 800 homes on the lands but to seek a bigger development of 1,044 apartments over nine blocks up to 14 storeys tall. Bartra intended to sell its 50 per cent of private homes to a single buyer, an institution that would rent the units to tenants. DCC, under pressure from its councillors, sought to stop this, but Bartra successfully defended its position in the courts. Construction work did not start until 2023.

Between 2011 and 2016 the Fine Gael–Labour government was responsible for the lowest social housing build in the State's history, just 1,300 units, of which only 75, a record low, were built in 2015. This is in comparison to 1975 when local authorities built nearly 9,000 social housing units and the private sector built 18,000 homes. The condition of the public finances was the explanation: there simply wasn't any money available for capital expenditure once the day-to-day bills had been paid. But in my 2014 TV interview with economist PJ Drudy, he anticipated the problems that were gathering: 'We have gone from a situation where 50 per cent of our homes in the 1950s were non-market, produced by local authorities and by housing associations. We will have nothing but trouble if we concentrate only on this so-called market. It is seriously problematic. Governments must take action. I would call it something other than social housing because that seems to have the wrong connotation. I would call it community housing. You have the nurse, the teacher, the garda, living next door to the person who is unemployed and on the local authority list and rightly receiving priority. But the broader spectrum, the State must take on.'

During the boom years, the local authorities had been encouraged by the Department of the Environment to buy land for the construction of social and affordable housing, despite the high prices land was commanding and the very low level of actual building being undertaken by the councils. Using loans from the State's Housing Finance Agency, local authorities spent more than €80 million on land in 2007, the year in which many developers stopped buying and tried to sell. The State, via its councils, outbid the developers in many cases, maintaining the insane price inflation, some of the worst examples being in Dún Laoghaire–Rathdown, Cork city, Fingal and Kildare. It meant that when the crash came, local authorities had property-related borrowings of about €650 million. On top of that, they incurred more debts on affordable housing that was built but never sold. In 2010, the government introduced the land aggregation scheme, which transferred the unused land to the Housing Agency for €1 with the local authority's debts forgiven. There was plenty of vacant land on the Housing Agency and local authority books that could have been used for construction over the following decade, for more than 110,000 homes according to one estimate, but wasn't.

PUBLIC-PRIVATE WRANGLING

The idea of the State leasing properties from institutions to use as social housing gained traction. Leasing not only avoided the need to buy the units outright but was regarded as an 'off-balance sheet' method of financing that would not breach EU rules that limit spending on capital projects like housing. By 2021 it was estimated that Ireland would spend nearly €1 billion in rent on the 2,400 homes due to be leased that year ... and the commitment for those homes would run for 25 years. It saved the State from having to borrow the money to build them – off-balance sheet – but raised debate about the wisdom of the financial arrangements, and not just from those on the political left.

Wealthy businessman and foreign resident Dermot Desmond claimed the policy of relying on Part V arrangements, leasing from the private sector and subsidising rents to private landlords 'is not good policy and it is not in line with the social housing policy in most other countries'. Desmond reserved particular ire for the buying and leasing of social homes from private developers and investment funds, arguing it was a 'criminal waste of money' and that the 'misguided strategy' had 'left housing in Ireland prey to greedy developers and international investors ... These funds are taking on Irish sovereign risk, but instead of being paid 0.02 per cent, they are being paid over 5 per cent,' he raged. He claimed the funds were 'delighted with Ireland's approach to funding public sector housing' and it was 'no wonder' they were 'laughing at us'.

Desmond wrote in a letter to Micheál Martin as Taoiseach: 'Allowing the private market to dictate the price of social housing is a shocking mismanagement of public funds. You might as well hand out blank cheques. It is astounding the government cannot see this, and persists in pursuing what is clearly a deeply flawed national housing model to the detriment of all.'

It seems Martin agreed because he subsequently said the State should not be leasing homes because it was not good value for money. Instead, councils were told to rely on direct builds and acquisitions to boost social housing stock. However, there were also considerable concerns about the ability of the councils to deliver appropriately and to provide value for money.

Anyone who believes councils should be given more responsibility or resources cannot have been watching how poorly it often does with what it has. Council-run social housing projects sometimes can take three times longer than outlined in government guidelines to get through planning processes. The problem is worst in local authority areas with the highest housing demand, with almost half of local authorities taking more than 100 weeks to bring schemes to the site when the deadline is 59 weeks. Cork City Council's schemes have spent 155 weeks on average going through pre-construction processes, including designing the scheme, tendering and reviews. The excuse for the delay is the administration involved in adhering to the Public Spending Code, which is applied to any development expected to cost more than €100 million (increased to €200 million in early 2023). While that is meant to ensure value for money the delays can often undermine the objective.

It can get worse when the local authorities oversee their own building. An audit of DCC's expenditure conducted in 2022 – to cover the years from 2019 – discovered that it had spent up to €150,000 more per home to build social housing compared to what it cost private developers to deliver. An examination of over 1,000 apartments across three different types of development revealed DCC costs to deliver one- and two-bedroom homes were between 11 per cent and 44 per cent higher than those from the private sector. Between 2019 and 2022, the average all-in cost of a one-bedroom apartment built by DCC was estimated at €335,000 and that of a two-bedroom apartment was €514,000. However, the average cost of a one-bedroom home provided to DCC at build cost through ten Part V projects was €250,000 and of a two-bedroom Part V apartment supplied to it was €358,000. Apartments provided to DCC by approved housing bodies were also on average cheaper, with the all-in cost of a two-bedroom apartment from that source ranging from €363,000 to €486,000. The auditors suggested the difference in costs between private developments and local authority-led schemes 'may reflect the relative scale of projects' but 'it would not be appropriate to conclude that cost differentials between public and private delivery can be explained entirely by scale'.

Further evidence of the failure of the councils was emphasised by the revelation that in Dublin the four local councils added just 200 homes to social housing stock each year between 2017 and 2021 despite there being a waiting list for social housing of 26,000 across the four councils. Architect and housing policy analyst Mel Reynolds went through all the available figures from the National Oversight and Audit Commission (NOAC); he added all the new builds by local authorities, the purchase of new and second-hand properties, those returned when tenants died, and the Part V units acquired from developers, and then subtracted units sold to tenants and demolitions of unusable stock. This suggested that nationwide just 10,108 local authority homes were added from all sources over the five-year period. Dublin City Council and Cork County Council actually reduced their social housing numbers in the period. Cork City and Kildare councils did best, albeit off a low base. Reynolds had calculated previously that there was sufficient public land for councils to build almost 50,000 homes.

The government's response was that a significant proportion of the need was met by approved housing bodies that are not part of local authority stock. While that was true, it still suggested major shortcomings that could not be excused away. It called into serious question DCC's ability to deliver more than 7,000 units directly over five years from 2023, as it had announced. Nor did it provide encouragement that the nationwide plan to retrofit 36,500 council-owned properties and introduce minimum energy standards for rental properties would be achieved.

For all of the disdain aimed at private-sector developers, they provided almost 80 per cent of all new-build social homes delivered by the State in 2021. After the crash there remained considerable opposition in official circles to the idea of returning to widespread building by local councils. 'Some people in the public-policy arena hark back to the local authority housing estate,' John Mulcahy said in one interview. 'There is a romantic notion that we should forget about the private sector and give the money to local authorities and let them start building.' Instead, he wanted the local authorities to bring in private-sector developers to develop land, with a portion to be allocated for social and affordable houses and the developer being allowed to sell a proportion of houses on the private market.

A defence of the councils was that they weren't given the budget or the chance to become major developers. That, however, does not stand up to scrutiny. The desire of councillors to suck up to the most vocal of opponents to developments in their local areas for fear of losing votes plus a mindset, not supported by evidence, that the council will always deliver a better result than profit-seekers in the private sector has meant delay after delay and the failure to deliver.

Brendan Kenny, head of housing at DCC, conceded that getting his own councillors to agree on doing things was a factor in delays: 'It's getting approval from our own councillors, even getting agreement on what a site is to be used for. We could have a site for five or six years before we even get agreement that it is to be used for housing, and everything we do meets strong resistance locally.'

For example, in the 1980s DCC bought a 17-hectare site at the Santry end of Oscar Traynor Road, just to the east of the entrance to the Dublin Port Tunnel, but didn't produce housing plans for it until 2015. It took two more years to get planning approval for Glenveagh to build 853 homes on the site, with the support of DCC's housing officials. However, councillors then refused to approve the private sale of 428 of the homes by Glenveagh, with 253 to be bought by the council for social housing and 172 sold to workers qualifying for an affordable purchase scheme. They decided that State land could not be used for private profit. A majority of councillors held out in the hope the department would approve 100 per cent public housing on public land instead. Finally, a compromise was reached, despite the 'serious reservations' of DCC chief executive Owen Keegan about no private housing being included to assist in the social mix. Instead, the council decided that 40 per cent of the homes would be used for social housing, 40 per cent for cost-rental homes, and 20 per cent would be sold to low- and middle-income workers qualifying for the State's affordable purchase scheme. The finally agreed scheme was to include 240 houses and 613 apartments and duplex units up to six storeys tall. Final approval for the government provision of €104 million in government money to build the homes came in July 2023. By the time the units would be habitable it would be ten years from the decision to use the land for residential development.

Glenveagh's involvement was notable because it emphasised how the State had decided it needed to work further with the private sector, and vice versa. Glenveagh had begun developing cost-rental units for approved housing bodies and then in 2021 contracted partnerships to deliver over 2,000 new homes at the Oscar Traynor Road site and 1,200 homes at Ballymastone for Fingal County Council. In 2020, only 9 per cent of Glenveagh's landbank was linked to housing projects being delivered for the state. By 2022, 23 per cent was connected directly to government initiatives for social and cost-rental housing. Of Glenveagh's 2022 landbank, 60 per cent was for housing designated as 'private with government support', which includes homes acquired through the government-backed First Home and Help-to-Buy schemes.

Cairn went into business with NAMA, entering a joint venture with the State institution for nearly 650 homes off the Malahide Road in Dublin 13. In early 2023, Cairn told its shareholders that it 'has become a more established delivery partner for various State entities, including Approved Housing Bodies, Local Authorities and the Land Development Agency' and one of the largest providers of new social and affordable housing. It promised to deliver over 800 new social and affordable homes in 2023.

THE MOVE TOWARDS 'SOCIAL RENTING'

The need for social housing is a reality every European country faces. At least one-third of people may never be in the position to afford their own homes and the State will have to provide. That provision isn't always popular with all citizens because those who provide for themselves sometimes disparage those who don't, ignoring income disparities. But those who pay mortgages don't like it when they hear of cheap rents on council-owned properties or of rents charged that do not cover the cost of management and maintenance of the stock. Sometimes, too, the rents remain generous in comparison even when the income of the household increases. Bill Nowlan has argued that the rent 'tenants are charged for social housing is insufficient to manage or maintain that stock. The average social-housing rent is about €200 a month in Ireland; in comparable countries, it would be between €600 and €800. Uniquely, Ireland generally charges below market rents even to tenants who have the ability to pay a viable rent.'

Whatever the shortcomings in the management of council stock there is plenty of international evidence to suggest there is a social benefit for society in avoiding homelessness. There is an ethical dimension, too. However, in recent decades the government has emphasised renting in the private sector as an alternative to having social housing. Initially, it gave people a payment towards their rental costs, called a rent supplement, if their finances met the criteria. It meant that nearly 60,000 households ended up renting privately that previously would have been in council houses and that, according to Residential Tenancies Board (RTB) research, almost 20 per cent of tenants in the private rented sector received rent assistance. Those who accepted Housing Assistance Payments (HAP) were considered housed and lost their place on the social housing waiting list, somewhat skewing the figures as to what was needed.

The HAP went to landlords of all sizes who would take it, although many wouldn't because they didn't want tenants on social welfare. Of the

€435.9 million spent on HAP in 2020, €185.5 million went to landlords with more than ten properties. Of these, corporate entities collected €162 million, with I-RES, the biggest, getting just under €13 million from HAP in 2020, 3 per cent of the government's spend and 17 per cent of I-RES's revenues. Of 3,688 homes owned by I-RES in 2020, over one in four was getting revenue from HAP. The second-largest direct HAP beneficiary was LRC Group, a Cyprus-headquartered property invest-ment firm led by British-Israeli investor Yehuda Barashi, which collected €2.1 million across 262 homes from its overall portfolio of 2,200 apart-ments. GIC, the sovereign wealth fund of Singapore's government, invested in Irish residential property through an ICAV called The Vestry, with local management provided by Irish property investors Richard Moyles and Andrew Gunne through BEO Capital. It was the registered owner of 690 properties spread across all 26 counties, and of these 144 were subsidised by HAP in 2020, generating just over €1 million in revenue.

Dutch property investment firm Orange Capital Partners and its Dublin minority partner Lugus Capital were other major HAP recipients. Lugus purchased a series of run-down, pre-1963 houses in south-central Dublin, largely laid out as bedsits, and converted them into a 265-apart-ment rental portfolio with funding from Bain Capital. The majority became eligible for HAP. Lugus Capital sold the portfolio to its Dutch partner for a reported €70 million.

Many of the other recipients of HAP were the personal investment companies of wealthy Irish people, who had residential property as a side-investment. As the market developed many of the institutional investors looked to provide long-term leases to local authorities or approved housing bodies for entire blocks of flats or housing estates.

This essentially meant that the State competed with its own citizens to procure rental properties. It also went into competition with first-time buyers to lease or buy homes, ironically keeping those people that it outbid in rented accommodation. The State's involvement in buying new housing to use as social housing went from about 10 per cent in 2016 to about 25 per cent five years later. In 2022, DCC admitted that it planned to spend €125 million on purchasing hundreds of homes, already under construction, before they hit the open market, an activity every bit as significant as that of the foreign funds in denying opportunity to private buyers.

The government's late 2022 plan to spend €36 billion between then and the end of the decade called for more than 88,000 new builds, up to 10,200 a year, that would be for social housing. DCC also issued a tender to find developers who could provide social and affordable homes as part of its programme to deliver 9,000 new homes between 2022 and 2026. It said it would consider buying up partially finished housing units already under construction or homes on sites where residential construction has not begun. It promised that more than 6,900 homes would be delivered through the council's own build programme, that a further 1,400 would be leased from developers and investment funds and 1,500 bought under Part V rules.

If people couldn't get social housing, they needed private rental accommodation. Official data from the Central Statistics Office showed that the number of rental properties in the country increased by just 4.9 per cent between 2011 and 2020, not nearly enough to deal with the population surge. That helped explain how by mid-2022 rents had risen by 116 per cent from their post-crash nadir in 2012; worse, rents were 55 per cent ahead of their 2007 pre-crash highs.

Needing more rental properties implied that we needed more landlords, but the campaign to 'professionalise' the sector was having its impact. The number of landlords registered with the RTB fell from 173,200 in the third quarter of 2017 to 165,700 in the third quarter of 2020 and is believed to have fallen further since. About 135,000 of those are reckoned to own just one or two properties. The number of corporate entities or individuals with more than 20 rental properties stands at just over 400. We needed more properties, which implies we needed more landlords of all kinds – unpopular as they are in some circles – but by 2021 the number taking out buy-to-let mortgages fell to under 1,000; people were not entering the sector or expanding their existing interests. Indeed, many seem to take advantage of higher prices to sell and clear negative equity; many of the buyers, though, looked to use the houses themselves as homes, thereby taking the unit out of the rental market.

'We drive small private landlords out of the market with high taxation on rents, then expect that market to supply large numbers of social houses for the housing-assistance-payment scheme to make up for the failure to provide extra council houses,' said Bill Nowlan. 'And after driving those landlords out of the market we get surprised that rents go up because of the scarcity of rental housing.' Nowlan also argued that taxation for private landlords was 'significantly less generous than for other forms of property income, or indeed for other forms of self-employment. This in turn aggravates scarcity and has driven more unaffordable rents.' Private landlords long claimed discrimination compared to larger institutional landlords. Local property tax was not a deductible tax expense for small landlords, and with rental income liable to USC, a marginal tax rate of 55 per cent could be applied to small landlords.

Landlords found that their ability to increase rents was limited if their properties were included in newly minted 'rent pressure zones'. They were limited to a 2 per cent a year increase each year, even if inflation was running far higher. Landlords were stopped from meeting their own higher costs by increasing their revenues. The protection was biased towards tenants. While this was seen by the majority as a social good and a reaction to the higher overall prices, it did not tell the full story: some landlords may have reduced their rates during earlier times and, if they found a good tenant, not put them back up again by as much as they could have to market rates. Now they were to be punished.

Since the second quarter of 2019, landlords must notify the RTB both of termination notices to tenants and reasons for giving them. Landlords were allowed to end a tenancy if they intend to sell the property, convert it to another use, move in themselves or allow a family member to do so, or they intend to substantially refurbish it. About two-thirds of thousands of notices were on the basis of an intention to sell the property. Tenancies can also be ended due to non-payment of rent or damage to the property, although many landlords complained about the length of time it took to secure an eviction, even when warranted, and how few of those who were instructed to pay compensation or unpaid rents actually did so.

Where the issue really came to a head was at the end of March 2023 when a temporary ban on evictions – which had been brought into place the previous October – expired and the government declined the opportunity to extend it, despite the pleas of homelessness groups and the anger of the opposition parties who said people affected had no other place to go. Thousands had already been given notice to quit by landlords who said they wanted to sell their properties. Some refused to move. Others went 'couch-surfing' with friends or relatives and did not appear anywhere in the official statistics.

'Having considered it, the government formed the view that it wasn't in the public interest in the round to extend the eviction moratorium,' Taoiseach Leo Varadkar told the Dáil. He said the government believed the moratorium was not effective in reducing homelessness as the number of people being provided with emergency accommodation by the State increased every month for which the moratorium was in place. He argued that people have been unable to move back from abroad into properties they own or to move a son or daughter into an apartment they had bought for that purpose. He also claimed leaving the measure in place would reduce the availability of places to rent and would drive up rents as it would discourage new landlords from coming into the market.

The government's response was to provide funding to local authorities to purchase up to 1,500 homes from landlords who were selling so tenants could remain in them. Private tenants were also to be given the first right of refusal if their landlord was selling. By the end of April, the number of people recorded as homeless increased to 12,259, including more than 3,500 children, an increase of 271 people. These people were left to live in emergency accommodation, such as hostels, family hubs, hotel rooms or bed and breakfasts. Single-parent families, those on social welfare and in receipt of HAP were at the greatest risk.

TWENTY-THREE

HOMELESSNESS: THOSE LEFT BEHIND

The campaign against homelessness started long before 2023. In late 2016, the Home Sweet Home campaign found an unlikely focus. Activists supported by musicians such as Glen Hansard and Hozier, movie director Jim Sheridan and trade unionist Brendan Ogle occupied a NAMA-controlled building, Apollo House, near Trinity College and turned it into emergency accommodation for up to 40 people. Their aim was to provide shelter for rough sleepers, while simultaneously highlighting the homelessness crisis. The Home Sweet Home campaign got plenty of publicity but, as Ogle admitted subsequently, it did little practical good.

The idea of people sleeping, and freezing, in the streets is and was unconscionable but it wasn't true that there was no accommodation provided for people in these circumstances: it was, but the State struggled to provide enough that was functionally designed and staffed appropriately. Apollo House was unsuitable as a venue to provide proper and safe accommodation for the people who went there. It was an office block that was never designed to have sleeping quarters. Reinstating the hot water and electric light, putting on the heating and throwing down some mattresses for beds was better than nothing, but it was not sufficient. The efforts of the volunteers were highly laudable, as were the good intentions of the campaigners, but they provided no real solutions.

The choice of building made a point, however. Six years earlier, NAMA had taken control of Apollo House and two adjoining sites assembled during the final years of the boom by developer Garrett Kelleher and nothing had been done with it. Kelleher had bought Apollo House in 2006 for €42 million from Damien Tansey, a solicitor from Sligo. He bought it to demolish it and use the site and he also bought a nearby car park owned by the late Kerry developer John Byrne for €11 million, and then in March 2008 the Long Stone pub on Townsend Street for €5 million. He opened negotiations with the Office of Public Works about incorporating Hawkins House, the ugly home of the Department of Health. It would not be until 2020 that building work finally started after NAMA did a deal to sell all of the land to Pat Crean and Marlet for more than €100 million. Its College Square project – at a building cost of over €200 million – spans the demolished Apollo House site and the adjoining and cleared College House and Screen Cinema sites. Marlet raised €270 million in development finance facilities from a consortium of funders led by Apollo Global Management and Pimco and city planners and An Bord Pleanála (ABP) agreed that Marlet could add a ten-storey tower, comprising 54 build-to-rent apartments, to the top of the office scheme. It is most unlikely that anyone temporarily accommodated at Apollo will ever live in one of them.

Some of those campaigning against homelessness wanted a right to housing to be inserted into the Constitution. As with the bedsit ban, the aspirations seemed worthy but not necessarily achievable or practicable. If everyone who wanted a home was entitled to one, then it implied that people would not have to provide it for themselves but would be given one by the State. Would everyone take that option, then? Who would pay for their construction? What standard of accommodation would be offered? Would recipients of supplied accommodation get to choose what they wanted and where they wanted? Would the State be responsible for the upkeep and maintenance of all its accommodation? What incentive would there be, then, for tenants to keep it to standard if they could always call on the State to fix things for them? Would it be possible to cope with the demand, to provide enough housing given the previous problems in building quickly enough and the cost to the State if it was paying for all of the construction?

Experience with social housing in recent decades has shown that some applicants rejected offers of housing because it was not near enough to where they had grown up or because there weren't enough bedrooms or a big enough garden. The councils have also had enormous problems with collecting unpaid rent; while some of those who didn't pay may have had genuine reasons, others gamed the system, knowing that the council would evict only as a last resort. The councils have also been slow and cumbersome in arranging tenancies and inept when it comes to building, offering all sorts of excuses about a lack of funding but rarely taking responsibility for a lack of initiative.

It was true that in early 2023 the controversy over the lifting by the government of its temporary eviction ban was caused by the realisation that some people would lose their homes because they could not afford the rent. The central issue remained a shortage of supply of new units, and at affordable prices, to meet the needs of a growing population. However, homelessness is not always just an economic issue. It can often be caused by alcohol and drug addiction, sometimes arising from mental health issues, rather than an inability to afford a fair rent. Many of those who sleep rough on the streets suffer from these substance addictions and other mental health afflictions. The loss of a family member, a marriage break-up, being subjected to physical or sexual assault or the loss of a job can all be reasons for homelessness. For some, their circumstances triggered an emotional reaction that overpowered them. They can't cope and try to self-medicate with alcohol and drugs. They become detached from their networks, especially if they have left the area in which they grew up. They run out of money or do not have the means or opportunity to earn it. They misspend what money they have in paying for their addictions. There are also people who have serious psychiatric illnesses, who in previous generations would probably have been locked up in the mental asylums that used to proliferate the country, shamefully larger in number per head of population than any other country in Europe.

The care these people need includes the provision of a roof over their heads but also includes further support, especially medical and remedial. There are wonderful charities, like the Simon Community, Focus Ireland, the Alice Leahy Trust, or the Peter McVerry Trust, that provide emergency accommodation and also provide more permanent, or sheltered, facilities in the hope of putting a person back on their feet, allowing them to go to their own home again, be it back to their family or a one-bedroom apartment somewhere. The emergency accommodation is often basic, but it is clean and warm, there are medics available and there is a degree of security. It is not always safe, however. If there are people disposed to violence, or suffering from mental health issues, there can be trouble if there is not strict supervision, especially if people are bringing in and using drink and drugs despite efforts to stop them. Some of those who sleep on park benches or in alleyways, open to the depredations of strangers or other homeless people, have felt it safer to take those chances.

Some people, however, do become homeless for economic reasons, simply because they cannot afford the rents demanded of them or there is no accommodation to be had. Even if rent pressure zones have been in place since 2016, providing some protection to tenants, some landlords have sought to evict tenants on the basis of needing the home for a family member, to allow for a substantial renovation that affects the subsequent rent, or simply to sell. An eviction ban was put in place for Covid, removed, and then reinstated in late 2022. It was controversially removed again at the end of March 2023 and homelessness numbers in April soared to their highest-ever: 12,225, of whom 3,500 were children. They stayed in emergency accommodation, including hotel rooms, the silent casualties of government policy.

PART 6

OWNING THE CHANGE

Where the State exercises control over the use of land is in the operation of a planning system, taking the constitution and various pieces of legislation into account in making decisions in favour of or against applicants and taking the opinions of others into account. This requires good faith on the part of all actors, something that is not always forthcoming, and agreement as to what constitutes the common good, something that is also not always present, especially when there is money at stake or when people and companies put their own interests ahead of those of others.

TWENTY-FOUR

FAIL TO PLAN, PLAN TO FAIL: ZONING AND POPULATION TRENDS

Ireland's population was at its lowest in 1961, at just 2.82 million people. The latest census, in 2022, put the State's population at a record 5.12 million, up 361,000 in the six years from 2016. Between 2016 and 2022 the natural population growth – births minus deaths – was 171,338. At 190,333, net inward migration – the number arriving to live in the State minus the number leaving – was more than three times the level projected for that period of the national plan to 2040. Employment reached a record 2.57 million people by the end of 2022, a level the plans hadn't anticipated reaching until 2040.

However, the State's official housing needs projections are based on the 2016 figures and an anticipated growth in population of one million people by 2040. If trends at the time of writing are maintained, the State's population may grow by 1.5 million people by 2040. We're going to need way more houses and infrastructure: the targets of 33,000 extra housing units per year may need another 15,000–20,000 added to them.

The government's €116 billion national plan for 2040 is based on the assumption that the capital city's population growth by 2040 could be limited to 250,000; with further growth of 250,000 combined in the expansion of Cork, Limerick, Galway and Waterford; and the remaining

500,000 population growth occurring in regional centres, towns, villages and rural areas. Dublin's population grew by more than 75,000 after 2016; the other cities grew by just 29,000 in aggregate. This means the provincial cities will have to grow at more than three times the rate of Dublin between now and 2040. There is nothing to suggest that can or will happen.

These things can change: our history shows that a lack of jobs and housing brings about emigration. We've had an influx of immigrants previously that didn't last, but we are currently in a second wave. If the economy turns we may lose people again, easing the demand for housing. The lack of housing itself may be a driving force in that, and in making Ireland less attractive as a location for jobs. In that case, we could overbuild. But the greater likelihood is that we are not planning for and not building enough housing units.

In 2014, the Department of Housing surveyed how much land was potentially available for building houses and apartments, in a country that is the least densely populated country in Europe and has just 2 per cent of its total land area dedicated to settlement, a number unchanged since 1995. The Residential Land Availability Survey of 2014 estimated up to 27,300 hectares were available, with the potential for 611,000 new homes. Of this, 123,000 homes could be in Dublin city and county, with another 125,000 homes in the neighbouring commuter counties of Kildare, Louth, Meath and Wicklow. However, from 2013 to 2022, only 121,404 houses and apartments were built nationally, despite 220,253 planning permissions being granted.

Before there are planning permissions, the land on which these are granted will have been zoned for specific purposes. Zoning increases the value of land without the owner having to do anything other than own it. The designation of zoning does not require the landowner to make an application for planning permission. The granting of planning permission does not carry with it a requirement to build. Zoned land needs to be serviced with water, sewerage, electricity and other essential services to allow housing. The planning process can now take up to five years to complete, a period of time in which the financial basis of plans can change dramatically. The government introduced a zoned land tax of 3 per cent of market value in the 2022 Budget but delayed its implementation to 2024. The National Economic and Social Council (NESC) has pointed out that public decisions on zoning 'often confer disproportionately large benefits on the owners of land ... Planning, of the kind found in Ireland and Britain, can prevent undesired development, but lacks the ability to ensure that development takes place,' it said. 'Land can be zoned for housing, and even serviced, but there is no guarantee that it will be used within a reasonable period.' It noted there has been limited housing development on land sold by NAMA.

Developers claim that the local and national authorities have underestimated entirely the demographic changes in the country. Michael McEliggott of Tetrarch and chair of IPI has alleged that most councils had failed to address an 'increasingly scarce supply of zoned, serviced and suitably located land that will actually be developed in a development plan cycle to deliver the affordable homes we need.' He focused on how local development plans from councils were guided by population growth targets in the National Planning Framework (NPF) and a Housing Need and Demand Assessment prepared with guidance from the Department of Housing. 'The NPF is the flawed bible on which our entire planning system and population growth targets are based,' he said. He claimed local authorities were treating population and housing targets in the NPF as maximums rather than minimums and that historical data analysis showed that no more than 50 per cent of zoned land was ever developed during the six-year cycle of a plan. That implied that double the current quantities of zoned land was needed to achieve the already too-low targets. He claimed significant parcels of zoned land were in the wrong places, not serviced by the necessary utilities, removed from public transport, local schools and other public amenities or owned by people who don't want to or can't develop them. 'When deciding to retain the zoned status of lands, councils don't consider the probability of those lands being developed,' he claimed.

The NPF promotes what's called 'compact development' in urban areas and aims to prevent urban sprawl by limiting the amount of available residential land in the Dublin commuter belt. That provided the Kildare and Meath councils, in particular, with the excuse to reduce the amount of zoned land for housing, citing fears about population spillover from Dublin.

Kildare County Council decided on a reduced dwelling house target of 80 per cent in parts of the greater Dublin commuter belt, previously identified as being required to help meet housing needs. Major builders like O'Flynn, Cairn, Glenveagh and Ballymore – who together built more than 3,000 units in the county between 2017 and 2021 – sponsored a joint submission by property consultants Turley. 'Our clients are facing the very real prospect of having to close existing house construction sites and mothball the opening of new "shovel ready" sites because they might exceed artificially derived "housing target numbers" dictated by the [Department of Housing],' it argued.

The developers got the support of NAMA, which said Kildare's reduced housing target for 2023–9 would lead to the de-zoning of residential sites and to serviced land becoming unavailable for development, something that was not in the public interest 'particularly at a time of surging demand and chronic undersupply of housing'. NAMA worried that significant, 'well-located' and mainly residential land assets in Celbridge, Leixlip and Newbridge could be de-zoned under the plan. It noted how the six-year housing target for Kildare was a 50 per cent reduction on its last development plan. 'De-zoning serviced land to meet precision in housing targets is wasteful of costly infrastructure and is counterintuitive in times of a housing crisis, particularly where sites are appropriate for development by virtue of proximity to established development and services ... It would also undermine parallel objectives of government to dampen land prices.'

Glenveagh and Cairn challenged the council's county development plan in the High Court via a judicial review. They claimed that the proposed plan would allow for just 9,144 homes to be built in the area in the six-year period to 2029, less than half of the 22,272 homes allowed under the previous plan. They claimed the number of new homes materially underestimated Kildare's population growth and its current and future housing needs.

Local councillors are supposed to make decisions consistent with proper planning and sustainable development. The reality is that they bow to local pressure to minimise change and to limit anything that is new. TDs are no different. The Ceann Comhairle of Dáil Éireann, Seán Ó Fearghail, who is automatically re-elected by virtue of his position, did not forget his local constituency when he made a submission to the Kildare development plan. He said it would lead to 'excessive' housing density in large county towns and villages and push people away from rural areas. 'Indeed, the projected housing breakdown taken together with massively increased densities will inevitably give rise to a lack of social cohesion, cause difficulties with community integration and will create an urban environment that is entirely alien to the Ireland and Kildare we have known,' Ó Fearghail said. He alleged the plans would force 'applicants who meet the rural housing policy criteria to abandon those areas and available lands in favour of relocating to [homes] within towns and villages.'

Ó Fearghail's views were widespread but not always supported. 'It's hypocritical for politicians to criticise the government and developers for shortage of supply and high rental costs and house prices and then to go and contribute to those costs and shortages by objecting to developments or by advocating changes to draft plans that will, in turn, reduce supply and increase costs,' argued Hooke & MacDonald, a firm of estate agents, in one published review. It was a vested interest, no doubt, but one that had a point of view worth considering, especially given what was happening throughout Leinster, in particular.

Glenveagh and Cairn also campaigned against the Wicklow County Development Plan, which they said would impose limits on the number of homes 45 per cent lower than the housing target contained in the council's previous development plan and would mean 7,000 fewer homes than the previous plan had anticipated. Cairn's Michael Stanley said it 'makes no sense' to reduce the capacity for building houses in Wicklow while the population was increasing and the need for new homes was growing. In Meath, Sean Reilly, executive chairman of construction group McGarrell Reilly, complained to the *Business Post* about a site in Kilcock that he said has been zoned for residential use for about 20 years. The land has capacity for 800–900 homes, but in 2013 Meath County Council set a limit on how many homes could be built in its county development plan, which covered the next six years. McGarrell Reilly was told it could build the first phase of 350 homes on its Kilcock site, which it did, and could deliver the rest after 2019. It carried out flooding prevention works and serviced the site with the necessary utilities to allow the building of a further 500 units. Then the new Meath development plan removed the zoning of the lands for residential development. Further de-zoning removed land throughout the county on which 9,500 homes could have been built. There are still more than 600 hectares of land in the county zoned for residential development, but these have become more expensive to buy, which is logical when a shortage is created deliberately.

It happened in Dublin, too. Bizarrely, Fingal County Council (FCC) suggested delaying the development of lands at Dunsink that had the potential for 7,000 homes. Instead, FCC's 2023–9 draft development plan suggested putting them in a 'long term strategic property reserve'. NAMA was furious, arguing that the land needed to be developed quickly to tackle the immediate housing crisis, and that delay was at odds with sustainable development.

Ballymore, Ronan Group, Kennedy Wilson, Hines, Cairn and other developers all objected to the development plan for Dún

Laoghaire–Rathdown, again saying the local authority had underestimated housing demand. However, the independent planning regulator told the council to scale back zoning because it believed the draft plan allowed for 6,800 more homes than needed.

Ballymore, owner of lands at Shankill that straddle the M11 motorway, said it was 'disappointing' that the draft targeted the delivery of 'only 20,669' housing units, and suggested 35,000 'would be an appropriate target'. Cairn said the section of the Stillorgan Road corridor from Donnybrook to Stillorgan town centre had a number of large sites with 'substantial' redevelopment potential, particularly for tall landmark buildings. Jackson Way Properties, whose directors are James Kennedy (who died in August 2023) and Antoinette Kennedy of Regent's Park in London, owned 35.57 hectares at Carrickmines that straddle the M50. The land was the subject of one of the most controversial sections of the Mahon tribunal. It sought rezoning of 26.77 hectares southwest of the M50 for a mixed-use development comprising a hospital campus, a hotel and non-retail employment. Most of the land was zoned for agriculture and rural amenity. Marlet called on the authority to reconsider the 50 per cent dual aspect requirement for apartments and the minimum separation distances between buildings, saying this should be decided on a case-by-case basis.

In Dublin city, Ballymore had different issues. It said DCC's 'core strategy' was to deliver up to 35,550 units by 2028 in 17 strategic development and regeneration areas (SDRAs). 'We are concerned that the densities proposed within the SDRAs … are unrealistically high, that the quantum of lands capable of being developed within six years has been overestimated and that the complexity of developing the sites has been underestimated, which together will lead to a very significant shortfall in the delivery of housing within the plan period.' Glenveagh said DCC's view that building would be carried out on 80 per cent of all zoned residential lands in the plan period 'is not consistent with how development has been delivered previously and given the timeframe for securing permission, is unlikely to be achieved'. Castlethorn Construction said it was impossible to impose a minimum 40 per cent build-to-sell requirement for all apartment schemes in excess of 100 units, saying the threshold 'is way too low to start prescribing percentage mixes of tenure and it would completely undermine the investment and operational model on which [build-to-rent] developments are based'.

It is not as if councils have a monopoly on wisdom – or that they have learnt from the mistakes of the past in the way developers might not have. In early 2023, Galway City Council (GCC) was prepared to allow homes to be built on a floodplain that was previously designated for recreation and water-based activity. Minister for Housing Peter Burke had to write to the local authority in January 2023, instructing it to change 26 separate elements of the newly ratified Galway City Development Plan 2023–9, including the rezoning of a 1.3-hectare site on the Headford Road, land that is situated below sea level and is designated as a flood zone A area by the Office of Public Works (OPW). Despite objections from the Office of the Planning Regulator (OPR), councillors voted to ignore the recommendation of their own chief executive, Brendan McGrath, and to rezone the Headford Road site for residential use. The OPR had to contact the Department of Housing and request that it intervene to force GCC to change its development plan. Fortunately, the government had introduced Specific Planning Policy Requirements (SPPRs), which take precedence over any conflicting policies and objectives that are created by local authorities in their development plans.

TWENTY-FIVE

THE PROBLEMS WITH PLANNING

Ireland has an unfortunate history of corrupt planning decisions – especially in relation to the original zoning of land by elected councillors that gave the owners of that land an asset that became far more valuable. As the Planning Tribunal of 1998–2011 demonstrated in its public hearings and eventual reports: large sums of money were paid to have land redesignated, to the benefit of its owners. Few allegations against An Bord Pleanála (ABP) itself stuck, the problems usually being with developers and their agents, who sometimes turned out to be prominent politicians, abusing their positions.

ABP, which adjudicates applications to develop on zoned land, has a quasi-judicial function and is expected to fulfil its public service duties according to an ethos of integrity and impartiality, based on clearly stated considerations and reasons. A High Court judgment in 2013, in the case of *Craig* v *ABP*, noted that 'sad and sobering experience has shown that the planning process attracts egregious forms of corruption and dishonesty' and that 'constant vigilance is undoubtedly required to combat this plague'. In 2022, ABP got caught up in a highly embarrassing series of revelations that undermined many of the decisions it had made over a number of years.

The problems were caused by the interpretation by some ABP officials of the Strategic Housing Development (SHD) system announced by Fine Gael's Minister for Housing Simon Coveney in 2016 as part of the government's Rebuilding Ireland plan. The SHD was introduced in

2017 to allow developers to bypass local authorities when making applications for developments of more than 100 units. Instead, they could go directly to ABP for approval. More than that, SHDs were permitted to materially contravene the existing local authority set development plans for an area, except for zoning, provided they met certain conditions. Developers were allowed to use a 'material contravention' mechanism to avoid details such as adherence to mandated building height limits.

There was no secret as to the government's aim: to speed up the delivery of newly constructed units. It didn't matter if it was seen as a response to lobbying from developers or their financial backers who claimed the time-consuming nature of the planning system was a major obstacle to the speedy delivery of new homes because the government agreed.

The creation of SHDs as a main plank of Rebuilding Ireland was largely attributed to Dave Walsh, assistant secretary-general of the then Department of Housing, Planning and Local Government and head of its planning division. In October 2018, he was appointed chairman of ABP by Coveney's successor, Eoghan Murphy. Operation of the SHD applications within ABP was largely under the control of Paul Hyde, a qualified architect and planner who was appointed to the board in 2014 by former Minister for the Environment Phil Hogan. Hyde previously co-owned a racing yacht in Cork with Coveney. Walsh recommended Hyde's promotion to the position of deputy chairman. Murphy agreed. Unlike other State bodies, board members of ABP work in a full-time capacity and cannot hold any other employment.

The SHD did not work as efficiently as expected. Planning permissions were granted quickly in the bulk of more than 350 applications, but in a large number of cases, it was noted that ABP overruled the recommendations of its own inspectors, almost always to get the bulk of things done as developers sought. This meant a flurry of applications to the courts by protestors – in more than a quarter of permissions – and the successful overturning of many ABP decisions, sometimes on technicalities, sometimes on more substantive issues. The court cases led to exactly the type of delays the SHD was meant to eliminate and in some cases made them longer. In those cases, the system worked in the opposite way to what was intended; nor did it guarantee the construction of the units for which permission was granted.

Murphy may have confused things when he introduced the Urban Development and Building Heights guidelines for planning authorities in 2018. These guidelines caused friction between the central government and the existing city and county development plans, particularly in Dublin. They also opened the door to many of the judicial review applications made by opponents of SHDs.

AN SHD-LOAD OF PROBLEMS

Not all applications to the SHD were successful. In 2020, ABP ruled on 126 SHD applications, granted permission with conditions in 98 cases and refused permission in the remaining 28 cases. However, the successes attracted legal objections: 83 legal cases were lodged against ABP in 2020, up from 48 in 2016 and 55 in 2019. Many judicial reviews of SHD decisions were decided on breach of building height and density requirements, non-compliance with development plans, lack of public transport capacity and protection of green spaces. Three of every four completed judicial review challenges to the board's SHD permissions were successful, although some won on the basis of technicalities, such as clerical errors in documents. ABP won just two of the first 36 cases completed. Yet Minister of State Peter Burke bemoaned 'an industry' of judicial reviews as if ignorant of the reasons for the outcomes.

There were plenty of dark mutterings about what was going on at ABP. In May 2021, Walsh told the Public Accounts Committee of An Oireachtas that 'our existence and reputation are based on transparency and accountability. Indeed, I would challenge anybody to say there is anything other than proper consideration given to all applications and appeals that come before us.' However, from April 2022, Hyde became the centre of allegations of misconduct relating to decisions he had approved. The initial allegation, shown to be correct, was that he personally approved a planning appeal brought by his sister-in-law over works she undertook at a Dublin 4 investment property she co-owned with Hyde's brother, Stefan. Hyde claimed that he hadn't declared a conflict because he hadn't known who was taking the appeal or that it involved his brother's property.

Three senior executives at ABP were tasked with producing a preliminary report and spent several months examining hundreds of cases involving Hyde. They found that the issues raised in the media were justified but the publication of the internal report was suppressed because of fears of it provoking legal action or compromising disciplinary processes. They were careful not to make any definitive conclusions or findings against named individuals.

They did disclose, however, a case where an unnamed ABP figure retained a legal interest in lands situated close to another site where he had participated in a planning decision. There were also about 40 cases involving proposed alterations to SHD permissions and these were handled by two-person boards where the statutory framework required at least three people to do that work. They found ABP had departed from the inspector's recommendations in a quarter of 111 examined cases, a much higher ratio than was the norm. While ABP is entitled to depart from an inspector's recommendation, the trio said its examination of files and associated records indicated examples of information suggestions and requests, or even what could be perceived as directions, to inspectors to change their reports in substantive and material ways, including requests to reverse the main recommendation to grant or refuse permission. They also decided that files subsequently presented to the public as representing a full and transparent record were not. They also raised questions about the timing of the withdrawal of unnamed applications.

Hyde denied any wrongdoing and temporarily stepped aside from his role 'without prejudice' while a specially appointed senior counsel,

Remy Farrell, was tasked with a fuller review. Hyde resigned in July 2022 and by November 2022 the Office of the Director of Public Prosecutions confirmed that he faced legal proceedings. He was charged at a District Court in west Cork in early 2023, near his Baltimore home, away from the public glare. Hyde pleaded guilty to two offences contrary to Section 147 of the Planning and Development Act 2000, with Judge James McNulty hearing that one small parcel of land in Cork City – known as a 'ransom strip' – had not been declared by Hyde in 2015 and that in 2018 he had failed to declare properties which he still owned but to which receivers had been appointed. He received two jail sentences of two months each for breaches of planning laws, with the sentencing judge stating that 'ethical standards in public life matter'. McNulty described the 'mid-range' sentences as 'appropriate and proportionate', adding: 'If those in authority are lax and careless and non-compliant, what will those in the ranks do? They will be careless and lax, almost as if non-compliance is an option.' Hyde was released on bail, pending an appeal. Meanwhile, Walsh took early retirement citing 'personal and family grounds'.

As controversy raged, it became clear that ABP was not doing its job as it should because it had only five members on its board instead of the standard ten. It issued a public apology for 'not meeting' statutory timeframes for rulings on 'a large number' of planning files. Stephen Garvey pointed out that ABP had a staff of just 70 whereas the Central Bank had over 1,100 people dealing with financial regulation in the wake of the crash. Minister for Housing Darragh O'Brien appointed former Department of Justice official Oonagh Buckley as the board's interim chairperson. Buckley landed herself in trouble when she made comments at a conference that were critical of the actions of solicitor Fred Logue, who was involved in a very large number of judicial reviews and other planning cases, for which she apologised subsequently. Plans were announced to increase the board membership to 15, for a new ethics and corporate unit to be established and for directors of legal affairs and corporate governance to be appointed. Up to 30 additional staff were to be recruited but nowhere near enough. However, critics brought up issues as to the likely qualifications of the new recruits, future transparency, potential biases, whether ABP saw itself as a body to implement government policy, the extent of the discretion it should be allowed and whether or not it could cope with its workload even with new staff. There were also concerns about its adherence to environmental issues and its willingness to engage productively and fairly with the public. The entire controversy did not encourage confidence that the many issues would be addressed and that ABP would assist in faster and better decisions on planning applications.

ABP's job is not to solve the housing crisis but to grant planning permission based on the principles of proper planning and sustainable development and to ensure environmental protection.

The Irish Planning Institute was among those who felt the developers were being given too much power. 'It is the institute's view that these SPPRs fundamentally alter the plan-led ethos and have brought about, since their adoption, a developer-led process that is inimical to the "common good" principles that should underpin the planning system,' it said. 'The institute considers that, in general, all planning consents should be made at the lowest practicable level, which is that of the planning authority (City or County Council).' It said any overhaul of planning laws needed to include a 'meaningful' role for the public in planning decisions. 'There has been a regrettable over-centralisation of the planning system, with weakened powers and functions at a local level, and little power at the regional level. This has served to undermine public confidence in the operation of, and the impartiality of, the current planning system.'

A review of large-scale housing projects between 2018 to the end of August 2022 shows 91,860 houses and apartments – in large residential developments of at least 100 units – were granted planning permission. Of these, plans for 7,311 were quashed in the courts, with the fate of a further 15,760 houses and apartments awaiting the outcome of legal hearings. But this meant that plans for almost 70,000 of the units were unaffected by judicial reviews. Many of them were not built, despite getting through the process.

There often were good reasons why granted planning permissions were not exercised – and it was not always true that the price of land continued to go up, making it worthwhile in the absence of specific taxes to wait before developing. The financial rationale for developments often changed in the period between lodging an application and approval being granted. Builders said that two years could pass between an application being lodged and work commencing on site, but in that time cost inflation could change the projections upon which the initial application was made. Many of the permissions were for apartment blocks and – as noted earlier – the developers weren't willing or able to begin construction unless they had buyers guaranteed. Many wouldn't build if the institutions hadn't put contracts in place to buy once completed and the banks wouldn't provide finance for the required work. Few were confident that the apartments would be bought by the general public. But the delays in the planning process only made the whole set-up worse. And many of those delays resulted from objections, some made for selfish reasons, because people or companies thought developments would impact adversely on them, and others made because complainants said they were thinking of others – and not just of people either.

FOR THE BIRDS

Objections to applications for planning permission were sometimes for the birds. The inadequacy of surveys of migratory birds under the Habitats Directive, zoning issues, the impact on traffic and the overshadowing of existing homes because of excessive height featured prominently.

Some people simply didn't like the idea of many new neighbours. Micheál Martin as Taoiseach said only the impact of the Covid-19 pandemic outdid Nimbyism (Not In My Back Yard) in preventing the construction of new houses. 'Young people don't have time to wait,' he said. 'We're trying to shorten the delivery time in getting houses built.'

Marlet – run by Pat Crean with financial backing from M&G Investments, a major UK investment fund – has more development sites than most in Dublin, which may explain why it has experienced a greater variety of reasons for rejection than many other developers. Its plans for a 17-storey, 428-unit rental apartment block on Carmanhall Road, at the Sandyford Industrial Estate, were stymied by allegedly substandard bicycle parking plans in the 752 spaces it had proposed. Perhaps more pertinently, the planners decided the scheme was higher than the eight-storey limit under the County Development Plan.

There was a less often cited reason for the refusal of plans for 14 mostly four-bedroom houses on the site of the former Highfield nursery in Rathgar. ABP overturned DCC's grant of planning because of the proposed density of 22 housing units per hectare and the preponderance of four-bedroom houses; these would not provide an efficient use of serviceable land. It cited ministerial guidelines that generally recommend permission should only be granted for projects in excess of 30 units per hectare in urban areas.

On the northside of the city, Marlet purchased a 16.5-acre site that was formerly part of St Paul's College, next to St Anne's Park in Raheny. From 2018 it engaged in constant battles with local lobby groups, the city council and ABP in an effort to get permission for a variety of different plans. The site was the subject of four decisions by ABP and 10 sets of legal proceedings and then a de-zoning by city councillors that led to further legal actions. In those, Crean argued that the DCC vote in November 2022 to strip the site of zoning for large-scale housing amounted to an 'unjust and disproportionate attack' on constitutionally protected property rights. The new DCC zoning allowed only for recreational and open-space developments, and a limited degree of residential or commercial building that must meet criteria that Marlet said 'will not be possible to satisfy'. Marlet argued the decision was unlawful, irrational, unreasonable and beyond the powers of DCC councillors. It noted that planning officials and its chief executive had told the members they were not legally entitled to de-zone serviced land that is available for housing, but the councillors said they wanted the land for playing pitches.

The de-zoning came after Marlet had already been denied planning permission for a 580-unit apartment development, 100-bed nursing home, crèche and six playing pitches scheme because of concerns for the welfare of the Light-bellied Brent Goose, which migrates from Canada for the winter months. Although the city council received more than 230 objections, that was the one that did for the development, at least at the time of writing.

Arguments against developments are made more readily in high-income areas like Dublin 4. In December 2022, DCC granted planning permission to Cairn Homes for its eight-acre site that it had bought from RTÉ for €107.5 million, conditional on Cairn paying close to €10 million to the local authority 'in respect of the public infrastructure and facilities benefiting' the development in the area. Cairn can build 688 apartments made up of 416 build-to-rent apartments and 272 build-to-sell units, a 192-bedroom hotel, 17 'age-friendly living' units and a crèche facility, among other amenities across ten blocks. To achieve this Cairn would have to demolish the former RTÉ sports and social club and structures attached to the former Fair City set used for production of the TV soap.

This followed a lengthy to-and-fro in which ABP had previously granted permission for a scheme and then consented to quash its own position following legal action by three local residents, including Pat Desmond, wife of Dermot Desmond. The residents objected that the original nine-block scheme was of a scale and density far greater than allowed under the Dublin City Development Plan, that it would overlook and overshadow their homes and be 'totally out of keeping' with an area consisting of low-rise Victorian- or Edwardian-type houses, some of which are among the most expensive in the country. Dermot Desmond wrote to then Minister for Housing Eoghan Murphy arguing that the Cairn plan would be 'higher than the density of Ballymun Towers North Dublin, built in the 1960s to accommodate a housing crisis and subsequently demolished and replaced by low-rise homes'.

He added: 'We are replacing urban sprawl with vertical sprawl. Instead of considering the long-term social implications of high-rise, high-density housing, current planning policy is promoting vertical greed.' He claimed the proposed height of the Montrose development, ranging from four to ten storeys, was 'totally unsuitable to the area'. Among his complaints were that 'it is a complete over-densification of the site and it will significantly overlook and overshadow properties along the boundary (many of which are listed buildings) and will add to the already significant traffic congestion in the area and along the Stillorgan Road.'

Large-scale apartment blocks are not uncommon in the area, however. Under construction at Donnybrook, across the road from the rugby stadium, was a 15-storey build-to-let apartment block owned and developed by Irish company, Richmond Homes. The 148 apartments were sold to UK investment fund M&G for €99.5 million.[8]

The right to object is an important one because otherwise local residents would feel disengaged by what happens in their local communities and could find themselves living unhappily in the shadow of what may or may not be unsuitable developments that impact on the quality of their lives. Under Article 29 of the Planning and Development Regulations 2001–23, any individual can make a submission objecting to or supporting a planning application. In 2023 reports emerged of some activists, encouraged by a solicitor in a prominent Dublin practice, demanding money from developers to drop legal objections that would delay or stop the granting of permissions.

---

8   In July 2023, ABP refused permission for the 16-storey tower with the
     192-bedroom hotel and 80 apartments. It allowed the rest of the development
     to proceed.

Finding the balance is the difficult part, which is why an effective and fair planning system is considered so important. But just as Micheál Martin identified NIMBYs as interfering with progress, there was also a cohort who were described as BANANAs (Build Absolutely Nothing Anywhere Near Anything).

TWENTY-SIX

A CHANGE OF PURPOSE

The future for shopping centres might not be in what's implied by their name – shopping – but in offices and particularly in housing, if politicians and planners agree. A lot of money is at stake for the owners of the centres, who otherwise are seeing the value of their investments shrink. Other than housing, few things have exercised the planning system in recent decades as much as shopping centres have: the coming disputes are likely to involve the use of much of the land at those centres in the future for housing.

Shopping centres became the cathedrals of secular Ireland's twenty-first-century devotion to consumerism. The trend began during the end decades of the last century with the construction of centres in suburban or out-of-town locations all over Ireland. It was seen as a sign of modernising Ireland and increased prosperity, an Americanisation of the landscape as largely indoor malls became as popular as the Dallas-style houses around the countryside. Greenfield land could be acquired relatively cheaply and the building costs of new units at scale were potentially more attractive to developers than rebuilding on expensive land in established locations. The availability of copious car-parking spaces was an attraction too.

The proliferation of out-of-town and edge-of-town supermarkets, retail parks and shopping centres, all approved by councils looking for the money from planning levies, came despite the objections of small shopkeepers represented by RGDATA (Retail Grocery Dairy and Allied

Trades Association). It warned of the damage that might be done to trade in existing centres, operating from smaller premises and with a lack of car parking and yet still paying high rents and rates. Bigger stores in urban areas were revamped to fend off competition, but many smaller stores struggled and the quality of life in many towns and villages declined.

The shopping centres tended to be dominated by large supermarkets and clothes and footwear shops, the retail parks by DIY products, homeware and furniture and white goods such as electrical items. Both have enjoyed mixed fortunes over the years. As with all property, the prices paid at the time of purchase and sale can vary wildly. Some investors have been able to sell for big profits, while others have made big losses. There was a surge in development and purchase in the Celtic Tiger years as spending money seemed no object either for developers or consumers as both traded in debt. Many of the prices paid in those years to take ownership proved to be wildly excessive and the banks and NAMA were left with enormous problems. There has been huge trade in assets (and liabilities) since, with an estimated €7 billion spent on acquiring shopping and retail centres in almost every county over the last decade, with foreign money most active in that.

Some of the buyers in that time have made major capital gains, especially if they cashed out, but a peak in valuations may have been hit between 2016 and 2018. Some of those who bought later in the new cycle appear to be facing major losses as the nature of shopping has changed and footfall and spending at many centres have declined. The losers include major international private equity firms who it was assumed had timed their moves correctly.

Even before consumer prices rose during 2022 and 2023, and the costs of running units increased for retailers, the number of empty premises in shopping centres went up significantly. Research, conducted by Ernst & Young and released in March 2022, found an average vacancy rate of 15.6 per cent across 68 shopping centres surveyed at the end of 2021. Vacancy rates were most acute in the west of Ireland, where nearly a third of units are empty, whereas in 2016 one in five shops was empty in the region. In Dublin, the vacancy rate increased from 12.3 per cent at the end of 2016 to 15.2 per cent in 2021. Things got worse as 2022 and 2023 progressed; while spending went up, the increase did not match the rate of inflation. The shift to online shopping that took place during Covid intensified, although online customers apparently collect 50 per cent of their purchases and deposit 80 per cent of their returns at physical stores. A further issue for Irish shopping centres has been the exit of many British retail brands who, when they had to cut costs, saw Ireland post-Brexit as an early venue for retrenchment. The demise of the major department store Debenhams left gaping holes in some Irish retail centres or on main streets, for example.[9]

The change in shopping behaviours – and the difficult trading environment of Covid lockdowns added to the crisis – created major issues for tenants. This, in turn, means problems for landlords in collecting the rent. The Great Recession saw many tenants go out of business because they were not taking enough revenue to cover the rent. Many landlords were hammered at the time for not agreeing to rent reductions and for insisting on enforcing upward-only revisions as per the terms of contracts. Stephen Vernon of Green Property, owner of the Blanchardstown Centre until 2016, told me in an interview at the time of the sale of the centre that good landlords adjusted rent according to an assessment of the tenant's ability to pay. 'Rent is demand driven,' he said. 'It is a common fallacy that landlords set rents. Tenants do by competing against each other for space and what they offer to pay is dictated by what they think they can afford.'

'We did what any major landlord should,' he said in reference to dealing with the Great Recession. 'We knew our tenants and what they

9   The Limerick venue on O'Connell Street, that city's main thoroughfare, was bought by a Galway company, Dalespell, owned by Michael MacDonagh, which applied to turn it into an aparthotel.

brought to the centre and what we needed to keep. It was our objective to keep the centre largely occupied. It wasn't altruism, it was self-interest because there are still costs and charges to be borne if you have empty units or voids.'

In 2023, Brian Moran of Hines believed a combination of good retailers and locations would protect both tenant and landlord. 'From a landlord's perspective, the key is curating the right mix of retailers in your shopping centre. If you have old-school retailers, get rid of them,' he said. 'I think you'll see an evolution into partnership with retailers and landlords where rents will be linked to turnover.'

That may be a hard sell in an era where an increasing number of people – and not just young – do much of their shopping online and simply send back goods if they change their mind about how they look or if they are the wrong size. Retail analysts have suggested many shops will become more like showrooms than fully stocked stores, attracting customers with in-store activity, technology, customer service and entertainment. It'll be about 'experience' and building 'brand awareness', although how that converts into revenue remains to be seen – and raises questions as to how landlords will be paid if the consumer purchases online later after testing the goods in-store. Meanwhile, if some people regard shopping as something of a chore – although the home delivery of groceries has never grown to the extent often predicted – the visit to a shopping centre is now marketed as a day or half-day out, with a visit to the cinema and/or a restaurant now part of that 'experience'. This is how the owners of the centres will make money, but it is not the only way.

THE POWER TO OBJECT

A little more than half a century ago, Dundrum was Dublin's countryside. Urban sprawl meant the construction of many bungalows from Milltown outwards as well as two-storey homes. The village got a shopping centre that dated badly over the years – and is something of an eyesore from the adjacent bypass – but then in 2005, a new centre opened, the biggest in Europe at the time and an imposing and vast physical structure, a perfect symbol of the Celtic Tiger consumer frenzy.

The Dundrum Shopping Centre was built by Castlethorn Construction – owned by Joe O'Reilly and the late Larry Maye who went bankrupt before he died – but since 2016 has been operated by UK firm Hammerson when it co-purchased the giant building and its environs – all 27 acres – in partnership with Allianz. While the centre remains highly profitable, its owners have had to deal with trading issues caused by the loss of major tenants and falling revenue. Its efforts to squeeze the asset for more money also have been frustrated.

Part of the overall purchase was the six-acre site that hosted the original shopping centre, just north of the new complex. Hammerson saw the opportunity to use the land for a new purpose: housing. It got permission for 15 apartments within the Town Centre itself and for another 107 in a new building called the Ironworks at the Sandyford Road entrance. Work started on it in late 2022, with a completion date of 2025 announced. This permission gave Hammerson encouragement to go bigger on other parts of its land. The presence nearby of the 50 metre-tall pylon of the William Dargan Luas bridge gave the developers confidence, somewhat naively perhaps, that large apartment blocks could be built in the hollow coming down the hill from the centre, that height would not be an issue with local residents.

Hammerson proposed a €475 million apartment scheme with 881 units: 335 one-bedroom, 464 two-bedrooms, and 82 three-bedrooms. The scheme would be made up of 11 blocks across four zones, to range in height from 3–5 storeys on Main Street to 10–13 storeys on the lower level along Dundrum bypass. It would include a landmark 16-storey tower at the north-western end of the existing village car park, overlooking the pedestrian crossing that links the village to the library. The apartments were designed to higher build-to-sell standards even though they more likely would be offered as rental units. Parking would be provided for 318 residential cars, 1,750 cycle spaces and 55 public car spaces, with residents being encouraged to use the adjacent Luas. It was proposed that the new buildings would take up only about a third of the site, with the remainder being given to the landscaped public and private garden spaces for residents alongside a series of connected and landscaped courtyard developments. There would be a landscaped pedestrian route running parallel to and almost the length of the village's main street. This would also connect a new square, Church Square, to three mini parks that would have extensive landscaping in a section currently covered by buildings and car parking.

Immediately the objections were loud and many. Words like 'appalling', 'destructive', 'a visual catastrophe', an 'eyesore', a 'concrete jungle' and 'monstrous' dominated the submissions. Support came from Dún Laoghaire–Rathdown County Council, which told ABP that the proposed development would 'significantly detract' from the 'character' of the area and should be refused. It complained that the demolition of a number of buildings on Main Street would impact the town's Architectural Conservation Area and had not been adequately justified. It argued this even though they were not protected structures. At the time of writing, the APB website said the case required 'further consideration/amendment' but the expectation was that legal appeals would take place no matter what verdict was offered. Financial analysts also wondered if, with the changing interest rate environment, Hammerson was still interested in the risk involved in proceeding with the investment.

There has also been considerable local objection to the idea of 971 apartments over seven blocks at Blanchardstown Shopping Centre, proposed by its latest owners Goldman Sachs in a €450 million plan. It was American private equity giant Blackstone – not Goldman Sachs – that bought Blanchardstown Shopping Centre from Green Property in 2016. The centre attracted about 16 million shoppers each year and gathered rent annually of close to €50 million. Since its initial construction in the 1990s it had been expanded to cover 85 acres and 1.25 million square feet of retail space, had 176 shops, including 20 restaurants and food outlets, and Dunnes Stores, Debenhams (once Roches Stores), Marks & Spencer and Penney's as anchor tenants. There was a multiplex cinema and two retail parks, as well as commercial space and a hotel. There was space to park 6,000 cars and 600 buses that visited daily. There was a so-called 'master plan' that set out the capacity to develop another 1.6 million square feet of retail, office and leisure facilities, as well as 600 apartments. Planning consent for a 272,000 square foot extension to the main centre and underground car parking had been granted. But its owners, led by Stephen Vernon who held a 60 per cent share personally, were nearing retirement age and, instead of putting more money in, decided it was time to sell.

Interest in Blanchardstown at a suggested price of €1 billion was limited, but somehow the Irish sellers persuaded Blackstone to pay €945 million. Instead of being able to extract more rent from tenants Blackstone found many unable to pay even existing charges and then Debenhams, an anchor tenant, left. Still, Blackstone committed to the expansion of an additional 55,000 square feet of new retail space in 2019 at a cost of another €32 million. Soon Blackstone was in talks with the lenders to the 2016 deal about restructuring the loans backing the takeover. The lenders in the deal included AIB and Goldman Sachs; the latter ended up taking ownership in a restructuring that wiped out Blackstone's equity. It was calculated that Blackstone lost about €250 million on the deal.

In early 2023 Goldman Sachs found itself in conflict with some of its tenants, many of whom were among the objectors to the plans for apartments in one of the car parks, alongside local residents' groups. The proposed development over 6.6 acres comprised 971 apartments in seven blocks up to 16 storeys in height, as well as a shop, office, gym, restaurant/café, crèche, mobility hub, community facility and place of worship. ABP decided the project 'would also constitute an acceptable quantum of development in the brownfield town centre location that would be served by an appropriate level of transport and social and community infrastructure' and that 'it would not seriously injure the residential or visual amenities of the area or other properties in the vicinity and was acceptable in terms of urban design, height and scale'.

The outcome was of interest to the owners of the nearby Liffey Valley shopping centre. The land on which it was built – at Quarryvale on the west side of Dublin, just outside of the M50 – was central to the controversies of the planning tribunal that captured political attention for more than a decade. Liffey Valley was opened in 1998 just as the tribunal began its work. It proved however to be a valuable asset for its developers, Owen O'Callaghan from Cork and the Grosvenor Group from London, Britain's richest landowner; having started with 22,000 square metres of retail and leisure space it grew to include more than 71,000 square metres and more than 100 shops, with plans for even more. Ownership changed hands twice after the Great Recession. Hines, along with Hong Kong-headquartered bank HSBC, purchased a 73 per cent stake in Liffey Valley for €250 million in 2014, but then the entire property – and over 17 acres of adjacent development land with the potential for 1,400 new homes – was sold to Germany's largest public pension fund owner, Bayerische Versorgungskammer (BVK), in 2016 for more than €630 million. Hines got a contract to act as manager and developer because there were ambitions for further expansion.

By 2021, even in the middle of Covid, Hines was proposing a €135 million expansion, to the horror of rival The Square in Tallaght, which claimed it was 'wholly unsustainable' and 'a continuation of an outdated car-based 1980s-style mall template'. However, Hines received permission from planners for a mixed leisure, entertainment and retail extension to the shopping centre to be centred on a large public plaza, creating a new east–west street at the centre, anchored by two large retail units on either side of the plaza. In return for permission, Hines was told to pay €4.2 million for public infrastructure. Previous plans from 2017 – that had included an ice rink – had been rejected because of the likely impact on the road network in the area. The new plan had

855 additional car-parking spaces instead of 1,820 and 590 bike spaces instead of just 180. It also included a new €20 million bus interchange as a large hub in the National Transport Authority's new Bus Connects network.

It is a big gamble on the future profitability of retail but for Hines and BVK there might be opportunities to profit in the provision of housing on the adjacent development land, allowing people to live very close to a whole range of services.

Hines has suggested it could build 1,200–1,400 homes on the site within five to eight years. 'It is a 27-acre site, fully serviced and the utilities are all there,' said Moran. The residential blocks would be linked to the new Bus Connects transport hub by a high line-style walkway. 'We have long-term funding to deliver the project,' said Moran. 'Funding with pension funds is a much more sustainable way than funding with highly leveraged private investors.' But local politicians, led by Sinn Féin, campaigned against planning and the opportunity to build much-needed homes in the area has been missed so far.

ARNOTTS DEPARTMENT STORE

In the early years of this century, barrister Richard Nesbitt paid €267 million to take control of Arnotts and then bought the vast Independent Newspapers site – which included the old printing works when the newspaper titles were printed there and a listed façade facing onto Middle Abbey Street – and dozens of other buildings, to form a gigantic site around Henry Street, O'Connell Street, Abbey Street and Liffey Street. He planned the Northern Quarter, to include apartment blocks, hotels and entertainment facilities along with shopping, a 16-storey tower block as its centrepiece, at a planned cost of €750 million, using borrowed money from Anglo Irish Bank and Ulster Bank. It never happened.

IBRC, as Anglo was known now, sold its Arnotts debt to Apollo Global Management. Ulster Bank sold its debts to Fitzwilliam, a company owned by Noel Smyth, a solicitor who had long dabbled in property speculation. Apollo lined up Bluegem Capital, owner of the upmarket Liberty store in London, to take full control of Arnotts if Smyth would sell his share to them, but instead, Smyth teamed up with Wittington Properties, a Canadian company owned by Hilary Weston's husband, Galen. The Westons already owned Ireland's most expensive retail department store, Brown Thomas on Grafton Street, and along with Smyth paid €107 million to purchase the remaining debt held by Apollo and Ulster Bank. The Westons then provided Arnotts with over €100 million for a revamp of the 250,000 square feet of retail space at what remained Ireland's largest department store.[10]

Smyth didn't want anything to do with Arnotts as an ongoing business, nor the retailers with him. He wanted its property for development, albeit on a far more modest scale than Nesbitt had intended a decade earlier. The Westons took full control of the department store and Smyth took the bulk of the remaining property assets in the area, including the Boyers department store on North Earl Street, on the other side of O'Connell Street. He closed it and sold it to the UK billionaire Mike Ashley's Sports Direct retail chain for €12 million. He took part of the Arnotts store at 7, 8 and 9 Henry Street and converted it into a separate building of approximately 40,000 square feet in size. Next, the UK clothes retailer, took the bottom floor but the upper three floors remained vacant. Two car parks on Upper Dominick Street were sold to Ziggurat, a British student accommodation specialist, and developed into 800 student bed spaces. Smyth also built an eight-storey,

10   In 2021 the ownership of Arnotts and Brown Thomas on Grafton Street changed again. Both were sold as part of the Selfridges group owned by the Weston family, in a €4.7 billion deal to Central Group, a Thai/Austrian consortium, owned by the Chirathivats, one of Asia's wealthiest families, and Signa Holding of Austria. The Chirathivat family had the twentieth largest fortune in Asia, worth $12.9 billion (€11.4 billion), according to a November 2020 calculation by Bloomberg. Signa was founded by retail and real estate entrepreneur René Benko, who owns or has stakes in some of the world's most famous properties including the Chrysler building in New York.

365-bedroom hotel at the corner of Middle Abbey Street and Liffey Street, which Motel One was due to operate from 2020, but then, after Covid delays, from 2023.

His most ambitious, and complicated, idea involved Arnott's car park. Smyth wanted to put another nine-storey hotel on Middle Abbey Street, at the site of the Arnott's car park that opens onto the street. Having received the necessary permission for that in 2018, he had not started construction work before Covid hit in early 2020. Smyth changed his plan and asked DCC for permission to develop a 12-storey build-to-rent apartment scheme of 160 units, 60 being studios, 85 one-bedroom and just 14 two-bedrooms in size. His idea was that the top three open-air levels of the existing car park would be removed and replaced with five storeys of apartments. Another two-storey block would be located on the roof of the department store itself, with a new 12-storey element facing William's Lane, a narrow path off Middle Abbey Street beside Independent House. The most novel part of his plan – with the usual promise of 'communal residential amenities' – was a 'dog-washing room', which at least suggested that he, unlike many other landlords, would allow tenants to keep pets. DCC said his build-to-rent scheme was contrary to the city development plan policy aimed at encouraging sustainable residential communities with a wide variety of housing and apartment types. It also said the proposed development would, due to its excessive scale and height, appear visually incongruous on the skyline.

Then in late 2022 Smyth changed his mind again and went back to the hotel idea, involving the demolition and decommissioning of the top three open-air levels of Arnotts' multi-storey car park, resulting in the removal of 145 car spaces. Planning documents stated that his company owned the department store's 'air rights', allowing the firm to lodge the application for the above-Arnotts portion of the scheme. The DCC granted him permission for a nine-storey, 245-bedroom 'lean luxury' hotel on the basis that it would 'contribute to the regeneration and will have a positive impact on the surrounding area'.

SNAPSHOT: CENTRES AND OWNERS NATIONWIDE

The Whitewater Shopping Centre in Newbridge is Ireland's largest regional shopping centre, developed in 2006 with almost 30,000 square metres of floor space. There are also 1,700 car-parking spaces and 84 apartments. It was owned by property developer Sean Mulryan and the balance by the estate of the late Liam Maye, who was also involved in Dundrum Town Centre. It was bought by Deka Immobilien for €180 million. The German investor had previously built the €230 million Mahon Point shopping centre in Cork in 2005 in partnership with developer O'Callaghan Properties.

Iput owns The Park in Carrickmines and co-owns Airside Retail Park in Swords and Mahon Point Retail Park in Cork. Friends First bought Carlow Retail Park for €16.75 million, Kilkenny Retail Park, The Globe in Naas and Citypoint in Galway. Irish Life bought Childers Road Retail Park in Limerick for €44 million from NAMA. Deutsche Bank owns the Westend Retail Park in Dublin. Davidson Kempner paid €170 million to Bank of Ireland for five retail parks that included Nutgrove Retail Park in Rathfarnham, County Dublin, and Sligo Retail Park, but sold Nutgrove for €65 million to Bavarian investor AM Alpha. Oaktree assembled a €500 million portfolio of assets that includes eight retail parks and shopping centres in Waterford, Drogheda, Navan, Galway, Sligo and Limerick. Oaktree bought The Square shopping centre in Tallaght in early 2018, paying €250 million to NAMA.

Marathon Asset Management from New York sold Galway's Eyre Square Shopping Centre to Davy Real Estate for just under €9.6 million in early 2022 – for about a third less than it had sought and after major investment in refurbishment – and then sold its City Square Shopping Centre in Waterford to the Wexford-based construction company William Neville & Sons, again at a loss. It sold the Manor West Shopping Park in Tralee, County Kerry, to Marlet, for €56 million. Marlet also bought The Parks Collection portfolio from Marathon, which was made up of Belgard Retail Park in Tallaght, the M1 Retail Park near Drogheda, County Louth, and Poppyfield Retail Park in Clonmel, County Tipperary.

PART 7

OWNING THE FOUNDATIONS

The foundations of the State were rooted in the adherence to the mores of the most powerful social entity in the country: the Catholic Church. While it was not politically active directly, it had great political power arising from the deference of many politicians and the acquiescence of the public. But it also had enormous economic clout, arising from its ownership of land and property, either directly or through its religious orders. As its social and political power ebbed, its uses of the land and properties and their value changed too.

TWENTY-SEVEN

THE BIGGEST LANDOWNER IN IRELAND: THE CATHOLIC CHURCH

Much of the best land in Ireland, especially in Dublin, for delivering new housing and apartment blocks, is in the hands of the Catholic Church and its various orders, of whom there are over 180 in Ireland. The Catholic Church is the biggest landowner in the country, but it is a willing seller in many locations. At its height, the Catholic Church in Ireland owned or occupied more than 10,700 properties and controlled nearly 6,700 religious and educational sites. A 1978 survey by Dublin Corporation found that 363.4 acres of Dublin city were owned by priests, 443.8 acres were owned by Brothers and 704.6 acres were owned by nuns – a total of 1,511.8 acres in 187 sites. It amounted then to 5.4 per cent of the entire area of the city.

Much of the land owned by the Church that could be put to different use in the twenty-first century, especially in our cities and towns for new housing, was assembled during the nineteenth century. The multitude of churches built across the country was simultaneously an expression of defiance against the British State and a celebration of Catholic emancipation and a repeal of the Penal Laws – we'll build what we want for ourselves with what we have. It also implied subservience to Rome rule instead. The Catholic Church, with money provided from the shallow reserves of local congregations of the faithful, built not just churches but schools, hospitals, playing pitches and care homes of a sort. It established a form of Church control that became embedded in the early decades of the new twentieth-century State.

It wasn't just in towns and cities but in rural locations too, with over 1,800 Catholic churches constructed between 1800 and 1863, including the famine years. The building continued throughout the rest of the century and into the twentieth century, an expression of rising prosperity, albeit invested in the Church while many remained in poverty. In the first half of the twentieth century, the construction continued into the inner and outer suburbs of the cities to cater for new populations who were expected to display their piety by attendance at services.

As the twentieth century closed, the numbers in the churches thinned out as Mass-going declined in popularity. Many other buildings continued to be used as hospitals, schools and homes for the infirm and elderly. Some were developed with the aid of grants from the State, which must be repaid if the buildings change use. But much of the land alongside those buildings had plenty of potential other uses. However, the ownership structure of the land and the properties sitting on it is often complicated. Church congregations and their trusts and incorporated bodies are almost invariably charities with specified objectives. This means their property and other assets can only be used for the purposes set out in their charitable mission statements.

Religious congregations are separate independent entities in civil and canon law from the Church itself and, generally, are responsible directly to superiors in Ireland, who themselves answer to superiors in Rome. Properties and land with a value of over €3 million which any Church body wishes to dispose of must be approved by the Vatican.

If the assets are held in a trust, then the use is frequently dictated by the aims of that trust, which are often limited to educational or health-care purposes. Every parish is a separate legal entity in civil and canon law, as is each school in civil law. All 26 Catholic dioceses are also separate legal entities. A bishop has limited and defined authority when it comes to disposing of assets in his own diocese.

The biggest diocese, population-wise, is in Dublin. A 2021 document on the Dublin archdiocese's website stated that there were 197 parishes in the diocese and 241 church buildings, 127 of which were listed structures 'and more expensive to maintain'. There were also 142 pastoral centres and halls and 468 houses for serving, retired and sick priests. 'As in previous years, houses surplus to requirements are being sold in parishes as a result of the declining number of priests,' the filing stated. The number of residences owned by parishes exceeded the number of priests. In several places, parishes made unoccupied houses available to refugees from Ukraine.

Land is carried at fair value on the accounts and no land or buildings were held for investment. The accounting policies were based on the €231.4 million insurance value, but with a depreciation of over €100 million, the net book value amount comes to €130.8 million. Crucially, most of the land was not income-producing.

The calculation did not include school buildings and playing fields, the latter of which could also be useful for housing. The primary school land and buildings are vested in the St Laurence O'Toole Trust. The ownership of the school properties is in the form of custodianship and no values are applied in the financial statements. There are 449 primary schools under the patronage of the Archbishop of Dublin. He is not the patron of secondary schools, although there are 111 post-primary schools deemed Catholic in the diocese. He is represented on the board of management of 45 other secondary schools.

At the start of this decade, Catholic schools still accounted for 89 per cent of primary schools, while only about 5 per cent have a multidenominational ethos. The plan for the remainder of the decade was to deliver hundreds of multidenominational primary schools by 2030 by transferring the patronage of religious-run schools to others and building new schools. This so-called 'reconfiguration' approach involves the multidenominational patron 'becoming a tenant' in the religious patron's school. In other words, the Catholic patron would retain ownership and be paid rent that would be decided on a case-by-case basis given the level of State investment in the actual building. In the past, similar rental arrangements had been in the order of 10 per cent of local market rents. Trustees – typically religious bodies – own 87 per cent of publicly funded schools in Ireland while 9 per cent are owned by the Minister for Education, as representative of the department. The remaining 4 per cent are owned by education and training boards.

The archdiocese sold its most valuable piece of land, its old Holy Cross seminary at Clonliffe College where seminarians were instructed. It closed in 2000 because of the collapse in the number of vocations. All that it kept was ownership of the Archbishop's House and the former Mater Dei College building, which is being leased to Dublin City Council at a nominal rent as a hub for 50 homeless families. The seminary land is adjacent to Croke Park in Drumcondra and within walking distance of the IFSC and Dublin city centre. The archdiocese sold the land to the GAA, which wanted some of it for new playing pitches but also for a new 200-bedroom hotel which, if and when built, is to be operated by Dalata. But the GAA, which paid €95 million to the Church, in turn, sold most of the land to Hines, on which it has plans for the country's largest ever build-to-let apartment complex, with finance from a Dutch pension fund, APG, the largest in the Netherlands and one of the largest in Europe, and which owned build-to-rent apartment blocks all over the continent.

Hines put forward plans for building 1,592 apartments on the land – a €600 million-plus build-to-rent scheme comprising 540 studios, 603 one-beds, 418 two-beds and 53 three-beds across 12 apartment blocks, ranging in height from two to eighteen storeys. Local politicians, led by Mary Lou McDonald, were at the forefront of objections. The Sinn Féin leader, who had been given a personal tour of the site by Brian Moran of Hines, came to the conclusion that this additional supply of housing would only exacerbate the housing crisis.

'Stop tenements of the twenty-first century,' academic and former unsuccessful People Before Profit election candidate Rory Hearne tweeted in relation to Clonliffe, ignoring that the apartments would be built to mandated standards far superior to much of the existing accommodation in the area.

The stoutest of the objections came from a Catholic devotee who was outraged by the actions of her bishops. Fionnuala Sherwin from Foxrock brought a series of actions to challenge DCC first, and then ABP after it granted permission for development in November 2021. She was particularly upset by the removal of religious artefacts from a (deconsecrated) chapel, which she claimed constituted a 'sacking of this sanctuary' such that it could be turned into an 'amenity' or an 'amusement facility'.

'I also strongly object to the surreptitious and secret surrender and handover of Church properties and lands to the largest investment or vulture fund in the world, for their profits,' she said, adding that the lands were donated to the Catholic Church in 1859 and that such property can only be transferred, in exceptional circumstances, to entities with the same ethos. 'They cannot be gifted, sold off privately, to any entities, or Hines developers or any other financial or private international company for profit,' she claimed. The archbishops, 'especially' former Catholic Archbishop of Dublin Diarmuid Martin, had 'no moral authority or moral right to do what they are doing today'. She also said that if the bishops were teaching the faith as was their duty, 'we would have full seminaries with students studying for the priesthood and thousands of souls would be saved from eternal damnation'.

Having failed in that action, Sherwin took a judicial review action against ABP over its fast-track permission for the venture. As the case was heard in November 2022, lawyers asked her to stop praying decades of the rosary loudly from the back of the courtroom. Her prayers were to be answered, however, because one of her submissions – that ABP erred in law by permitting the demolition of a protected structure on the site – would succeed. In his judgment in early 2023, overturning the previously granted permission, Mr Justice Richard Humphreys decided that ABP had failed to follow the required approach to assessing the impact of the loss of 'striking brick arches' that lay 'within the curtilage of protected structures'. He also decided that ABP did not 'sufficiently engage' with DCC's 'serious concerns' about how mature trees and the 'historic landscaping' would be affected by a significant basement development. Humphreys noted that DCC's conservation officer had said the height, scale and massing of the 18-storey block were 'excessive in this context, and will entirely dominate and seriously injure the architectural setting of the protected structures': the former seminary and the eighteenth-century Fortick's Alms House, known as the Red House. It was also suggested that the tower would 'injure' the surrounding environs of Drumcondra and would be 'clearly visible in long-range views from other parts of the historic city'.

ABP's inspector differed and believed the removal of the 18-storey block unnecessary as it could sit side by side with existing protected structures without detriment. The judge said the board's inspector did not make any reference to concerns regarding the radically diminished curtilage of the Red House, which currently sits vacant but is being maintained by Hines at its expense to prevent dereliction. 'There is simply no way that such massively larger and bulkier buildings within the curtilages and attendant grounds could be said to respect the mass and scale of the protected structures,' the judge opined. The judge appeared to be making a decision that was influenced almost as much by his aesthetic judgements as by a legal one. He found further flaws in the board's 'extremely vague' approach to balancing the need for development and compliance with national policy on the one hand, and preserving the character and setting of the site and historic structures on the other.

Hines sought leave to appeal the judge's decision but he refused, leaving Hines to consider further legal options or starting from scratch again with a new planning application that would not be processed until 2024 at the earliest. It also meant that the economics of the entire development changed and almost certainly would not make any units of housing, if and whenever built, any cheaper for any eventual occupants.

DEVELOPMENT PLANS - AND OBSTACLES

This was not the only setback to the Church's plans to offload land for housing. In July 2022 the Archbishop of Dublin, Dermot Farrell, announced that he was looking for a full-time property expert to work on the portfolio. The problem facing a new appointment was that the Church wanted the Dublin councils to zone church lands for the building of homes at some point in the future. But Dublin City Council, in particular, has been reluctant to agree, not wanting to leave the Church with too much control.

The Church authorities found this irritating, especially as Darragh O'Brien, the Minister for Housing in early 2022, let it be known publicly that he had written the previous year to the Primate of All Ireland, Archbishop of Armagh Eamon Martin, seeking Church land and vacant properties that could be used as part of the government's new action plan on housing. O'Brien may have picked up on a suggestion from Glenveagh of 30 sites owned by religious orders that could be used for 6,500 homes, and that this land would be worth more than €500 million. The Church – and its orders – had lots in the size that big builders wanted for economies of scale.

O'Brien's request came as a surprise to the Church, as in Dublin alone local authorities and NAMA are said to control half the zoned housing land in the city, enough to deliver 70,000 homes. But it was willing to work with the State. The archdiocese had started its own programme of demolishing larger churches and seeking to put land to new uses. The 3,500-capacity Church of Annunciation in Finglas West, which opened in October 1967 to cater for a rapidly growing suburb, was demolished in September 2021. It was to be replaced by a smaller church building, capacity of 300, with freed-up space to be used for social housing and accommodation for senior citizens. This was done in agreement with DCC, which bought the land and oversaw the redevelopment.

The diocese announced a plan to potentially demolish 33 churches in areas such as Artane, Ballymun, Beaumont, Cabra, Drimnagh, Griffith Avenue, Navan Road, Raheny, Terenure and Walkinstown. Some of those church buildings, however, and those at three city parishes at Harrington Street, Church Street and St James's Street, were most likely to be regarded by the authorities as protected structures. It was a sign of the decline of the Catholic Church that many of the buildings high-lighted for demolition opened in Dublin during the long and politically dominant episcopacy of Archbishop John Charles McQuaid, from 1940 to 1971.

But that wasn't the main issue to hold the Church (or indeed some of its religious congregations) back from doing as they pleased. In early 2022 DCC, in common with counterparts all over the country, invited submissions on the local development plan for the six years to 2028. The archdiocese was worried that it would be prevented from using its land for housing redevelopment, even though it had been working with approved housing bodies and local councils to provide social housing. In its submission to the plan, it called for the retention of the existing 'permitted' and 'open for consideration' uses on Z15 zoned sites, the designation for Church lands. 'We suggested this be done by rezoning Z15 lands to Z12 – where residential is permitted – to more robustly support our stated objective regarding the delivery of much-needed housing,' the archdiocese stated.

However, retaining the flexibility of those zoning rules was not rec-ommended to councillors by Owen Keegan, the DCC chief executive. He claimed that Z15 zoning had resulted in many institutional sites being 'comprehensively redeveloped for housing', its wording not suf-ficiently robust 'to prevent the ongoing erosion and loss of these lands'. He decided to amend Z15 zoning to restrict development to 'highly exceptional circumstances' only. He said there was already sufficient zoned land within the city to cater for anticipated housing demand over the next six years. '[The Church lands] are not viewed as development opportunity lands,' he said. Keegan said most of the rezoning applications were 'premature' because the diocese had put forward no specific proposals for future development.

Keegan had read the mood of some of the elected councillors. They stood in the chambers and made speeches attacking Catholic institutions for selling land to boost their pension funds and as an investment commodity to promote build-to-rent. Labour councillor Alison Gilliland, Lord Mayor of Dublin for a year from June 2021, said that instead of selling land to developers, 'I think the good Christian thing to do would be for the Church to work with Dublin City Council on any land it does want to see used for housing to house those in most need with social housing and affordable housing.'

The Archdiocese of Dublin was furious, claiming this was exactly what it was being stopped from doing. It said that 'many of the subject sites are located in disadvantaged areas where the delivery of housing is taking priority over additional institutional land uses'. By late 2022, Keegan recommended that DCC look to effectively pick and choose what lands it wanted from the archdiocese and implied that these should be made available cheaply or even for free. But what was clear was that he wanted DCC to take control of how the land was to be used, not to allow that power to reside with the Church. The implication also was that if the Church decided to sell to other developers, the new owners would not get permission to develop.

The new owners of land sold by the Jesuit order at Milltown in Ranelagh, Dublin 6, had discovered that already. The Jesuits sold a 10.5-acre site at Milltown Park, on Sandford Road, beside the boys-only fee-paying private secondary school Gonzaga College, which it had owned for more than 160 years, to Ardstone Capital for €66 million. The new owners sought permission for a €300 million development of more than 600 build-to-rent apartments in blocks up to 10 storeys tall, at 32 metres double the height of the city's existing development plan, with only 67 more offered for sale.

Local resident groups and individuals contributed to 165 objections. Among their complaints was that the proposed scheme would be too tall and excessively dense, would destroy nearly 300 trees and would lead to 'major extra pressure' on traffic and school places (although it was most unlikely that anyone renting in the new apartments would be able to afford the fees Gonzaga would charge their sons if they gained admittance). They said the development seemed to be geared towards students or a 'transient population' and 'will change the character of the whole area, and not just the area but the whole city'.

Permission was granted in late 2021, even though the new DCC draft development plan made the site Z15, effectively blocking the project, as this bans anyone other than an institution from building in areas with this designation. The developers, Ardstone Capital, said the land should be redesignated as Z12, defined as 'institutional land with future development potential'. DCC argued that ABP gave Sandford permission to build the apartments while public consultations on its draft development plan were underway, implying the decision had been premature. The planners decided that the scheme would 'constitute an acceptable quantum and density of development in this accessible urban location, would not seriously injure the residential or visual amenities of the area and would be acceptable in terms of height and urban design'. It had allowed the height because it had the potential to meet government objectives to increase delivery of housing from its current under-supply. But that victory for the developers was overturned.

A few miles to the west of Milltown, the Irish province of the Order of Carmelites sought residential zoning on a 2.6-hectare site at Terenure College that was not needed for education, suggesting a €32 million valuation for the land, if sold. The order partnered with Lioncor, a joint venture company set up in 2018 by major international funds Oaktree and Alanis to manage construction on the land they had acquired in Ireland since the crash and to buy more for development. They produced a plan that included 21 houses for sale but was mainly build-to-rent: four apartment blocks rising to seven storeys in height, made up of 15 studios, 166 one-bed apartments, 174 two-bed apartments and nine three-bed units. The Carmelites argued that the transaction would allow older members of the community to downsize their homes. In common with all of the orders, it was not attracting new vocations as older members died or became infirm. The capital from the sale, reinvested, would provide retirement income for those who remained alive.

More than 210 objections were lodged. It was the usual list: 'overde-velopment' and 'completely out of character with the area', which 'will result in permanent and profound negative impacts on the residen-tial and visual amenity of existing residents and their properties'. One prominent objection said the largely build-to-rent nature of the devel-opment was 'not appropriate or ethical' and would provide only for a 'transient population that goes entirely against the sense of community in Terenure'. DCC refused planning permission for myriad reasons, including endangerment of 'public safety by reason of traffic hazard due to the creation of vehicular/pedestrian conflict'. However, the council's planner said that 'the principle of a residential development is acceptable on this site and notwithstanding some outstanding issues is broadly in accordance with the zoning objective for the site.' The planner listed the 'wide range of services and facilities' available, including its proximity to bus services and cycle lanes. Furthermore, the planner stated that a high-quality residential development on this site has the potential to contribute to the provision of housing in the area.

On the northside of Dublin, planning consultants acting for the Vincentian religious order made an application to Fingal County Council in 2022 for two plots of land at Castleknock College to be rezoned for housing. The order has educated boys at the site since the 1830s but said it had lands 'surplus to the requirements for the efficient running of the school'. It identified plots on the north-western and north-eastern peripheries of the 28.65-hectare campus as having potential for housing 'without upsetting' school activities. The worth of the land in the affluent west Dublin suburb was estimated at €8–10 million per hectare with planning permission. It also asked for residential zoning on seven hectares of land at a retreat centre near Swords in north County Dublin.

THE NEED TO REALISE THE VALUE OF ASSETS

One of the main reasons behind the twenty-first-century disposals of Church land and property was the need for the Church and its congregations of priests, brothers and sisters to pay compensation, or redress, for the sins of its members. The abusive treatment of former residents of religious-run institutions, such as orphanages, reformatories and industrial schools, by those in whose care they were placed required cash compensation.

The bill to the State was estimated at €1.5 billion in 2017 by the Comptroller and Auditor General, the public spending watchdog.[11] However, Catholic institutions entered a binding agreement with the government in 2002 to pay just €128 million to the State for redress. This was a highly controversial measure, agreed secretly with the government, in undue haste and for an amount many believed was scandalously low. That amount was revisited in 2009 as more details of serious wrongdoing emerged at 18 residential institutions specifically investigated by a commission run by Mr Justice Sean Ryan. The target payment from those 18 was increased to €353 million and that then, in turn, was revised down to €226 million, to widespread outrage. Much of the delivery of the promised amounts, either in cash, property or counselling services, came in

11   By the end of 2015, awards totalling €970 million had been made to 15,579 claimants – an average award of €62,250. Of these, 85 per cent were at or below a level of €100,000 per person. Legal cost payments of €192.9 million were made to 991 legal firms in respect of 15,345 applications, with 17 paid between €1 million and €5 million each and seven firms paid amounts between €5 million and €19 million.

below target and late, although Sister Liz Murphy, Secretary-General of the Association of Leaders of Missionaries and Religious of Ireland, an umbrella group of 180 congregations, claimed many congregations also quietly gifted property for social housing.

As part of governmental engagement with the congregations, a three-person panel, chaired by Frank Daly before he became chairman of NAMA, was set up to assess the resources held by the 18 groups. The report from this panel stated that the assets declared by the 18 congregations had a total value of €3.743 billion (based mostly on valuations made for insurance reasons). The property declared did not include all assets held by those congregations.

The Ryan Report, published in 2009, found that molestation and rape were 'endemic' in boys' institutions, chiefly run by the Christian Brothers, the largest provider of residential care for boys in the State at that time. The report devoted eight chapters to an organisation that began in Waterford city in 1802 when its founder, Edmund Ignatius Rice, opened a school for poor children. In 1831, there were only 45 Christian Brothers, but by 1960 that had increased to 4,000. Now there are fewer than 200 left.

The Brothers transferred school property with a value of €430 million to a new entity called the Edmund Rice Schools Trust between 2008 and 2009. It had no State involvement in its ownership and management and was given a remit to continue providing Catholic education in Ireland. It operates nearly 100 Christian Brothers schools in the State: 59 at second-level and 37 primary schools. About 35,000 pupils attend and are taught by more than 2,700 teachers.

The Brothers still had land and buildings, valued at €262.2 million, and financial assets amounting to €63.2 million. This would become relevant later when, as part of an offer of compensation for all the wrongdoing revealed in the Ryan Report, the order offered to set up a joint trust between the Edmund Rice Schools Trust and the government for 49 school playing fields and associated lands. These were valued at

€127 million in 2009. It might have been assumed that these lands would be retained for recreation. However, this offer was subsequently withdrawn by the congregation, according to the report of the Comptroller and Auditor General in 2016, and the order said it would transfer these lands to the Edmund Rice Schools Trust. Instead, the Department of Education told an investigation by *TheJournal.ie*'s Noteworthy unit in 2022 that the congregation offered 'a mechanism under which the State would receive 50 per cent of the proceeds of the disposal of 49 specified playing fields' and it is 'the department's understanding that, to date, none of the 49 playing fields have been disposed of'.

In a submission to the DCC development plan in February 2022, the Brothers complained that 'residential use is no longer open for consideration' except for 'highly exceptional circumstances' and that these changes imposed restrictions 'on delivering residential development and surplus and underutilised' lands. In other words, it limited the ability to sell the land at the price wanted.

The order has been an eager seller of land, raising €18 million in one deal alone when it sold land beside Clonkeen College in Deansgrange, County Dublin, to pay for redress. It was sold to builder Patrick Durkan, but only after the settlement of a High Court action taken against the Brothers by members of the school's board of management over the loss of sports pitches caused by the amount of land proposed to be sold. Under the original proposed deal, the school was to receive €1.3 million and be allowed to keep one area for use as a playing pitch. The board of management claimed that the sale breached a 2006 agreement with the congregation whose terms included that the playing fields would remain available for the school.

The board sought an order restraining the disposal of the playing fields that were the subject of a five-year licence for sporting use. However, the Brothers argued they had a binding contract to sell the lands to Durkan and would make significant charitable donations from the proceeds of the sale. In the end, the Brothers conceded a donation of four acres to the trust running the school, allowing it to put in the sports facilities the board wanted, including a full-size all-weather GAA pitch.

During 2022 the Christian Brothers were active in challenging planning local development plans from councils. Its submission to Fingal County Council about land at Swords was almost identical to that of adjacent landowner Bovale, which was not a surprise as both employed the same firm of consultants, BMA Planning. Bovale claimed that about 7,000 dwellings could be built on its 142-acre site at Lissenhall over ten years. Bovale's land surrounds 10.7 acres owned by the Christian Brothers which the order was 'actively looking to a more suitable long-term use' for property previously used as a retreat centre. It sought a 'suitable zoning objective to facilitate the development of the Emmaus centre lands for primarily residential use'.

In late 2022, former pupils of Blackrock College, a Spiritan (formerly Holy Ghost) fee-paying and partly boarding school in south Dublin, disclosed a litany of appalling sexual abuse perpetrated against them as boys and young teenagers. The public bravery of the men, now entering their sixties, prompted others to belatedly expose the machinations of the priests in whose care their parents had trusted their education. The school, sometimes criticised for its elitism, still educates over 1,000 boys annually. It is hosted on an enormous campus with its own swimming pool and a large number of rugby pitches and other sports facilities. The land has value for the construction of new housing, something the order recognised in 2019 when it put a portion three acres in size – and with two large boarding houses for its retired members, bordering Cross Avenue and close to the junction with Mount Merrion Avenue, about six miles south of the city centre – on sale with an asking price of €20 million. It got €16 million from Lioncor, which purchased on the basis of a site feasibility study that suggested the potential for either 121 units in build-to-sell or 154 units in build-to-rent options. There was the potential for build-to-sell to people in the area who might be looking to trade down.

The order said funds raised from the sale would be used to support its charitable work and to reduce debt within the province. However, it has become clear since that the order secretly was fighting off disclosure of the crimes of many of its members, most now deceased. This secrecy may have been motivated as much by the desire to avoid large compensation payments as embarrassment and shame at the actions of its members. The order may need further asset sales to cover the cost of compensation claims.

There are many other sales that could be listed in this chapter, but worth mentioning are the €105 million realised by the Oblate Fathers from the 2004 sale of Belcamp College and surrounding farmlands at Balgriffin in north County Dublin on which extensive building has finally taken place this decade. In 2015 the Redemptorist order received €42 million from Cairn for the Marianella seminary, church and grounds in Rathgar, Dublin 6.

Overall, it is reckoned that religious orders have raised at least €1 billion in property sales this century. They could make more if buyers were confident that any land purchased would be allowed planning permission for development.

TWENTY-EIGHT

A HABIT OF MAKING MONEY

The plan was to have a new National Maternity Hospital (NMH) open by 2022. The government's willingness to fund the project was announced in 2013, one of the first major capital commitments made by it despite being still under the control of the Troika. But rows between the State and the owners of the land designated for the hospital, at the St Vincent's campus at Elm Park in Dublin 4, meant that the final sign-off on the project did not come until 2022. It will likely take many more years before a hospital is there in which babies will be born.

While there are many maternity hospitals in the State – and three major ones in Dublin that take both public and private patients – the designated National Maternity Hospital at Holles Street has not been fit for purpose for decades, even though 9,500 babies a year are being born in a dilapidated and overly crowded building. There were suggestions that the replacement should be co-located with a new National Children's Hospital. But the decision was taken to co-locate the new maternity hospital with an adult hospital and St Vincent's was chosen. The owners of the St Vincent's campus had a controversial history and the future ownership of land on which the new hospital was to be built was to become highly contentious because of the implications for how it could be used and who would have the final say: the landowner or the State.

The land was held and the hospital was operated by the Religious Sisters of Charity (RSC), an organisation formed in 1815 by Mary

Aikenhead, a Cork Protestant who converted to Catholicism as a teenager, 'to give to the poor what the rich could buy with money'. The Religious Sisters of Charity was one of the most significant of all the religious orders, expanding to host almost 150 communities in Ireland, England and Scotland, North and South America, Australia, Nigeria, and Zambia. It was highly regarded for its hospice work and helping the homeless, prisoners, immigrants and those with addictions. It was a significant presence in providing healthcare in Ireland, from hospitals to convalescent and nursing homes. Somewhat against the initial instincts of its founder, her successors offered private healthcare facilities in luxury surroundings at St Vincent's Private Hospital on its Elm Park campus.

Far less positively, the order ran five industrial schools that featured prominently in various reports on the abuse of children by religious orders during the twentieth century. It also took over the running of the adoption agency St Patrick's Guild in 1943. State agency Tusla established that at least 126 births were illegally registered by the agency between 1946 and 1969. It was one of four religious orders that ran ten Magdalene Laundries, so-called 'homes' where unmarried mothers effectively were incarcerated and forced to 'atone for their sins' by working in punitive industrial conditions without pay.

Along with its counterparts The Sisters of Mercy, The Sisters of Our Lady of Charity and the Good Shepherd Sisters, the Religious Sisters of Charity 'declined' to make a financial contribution to the Magdalen Restorative Justice Ex Gratia Scheme after the 2009 Ryan Commission Report revealed decades of abuse endured by children in their care. It wasn't as if the order was short of property assets, or cash from those it had already sold. In 2001 it received over €46 million when it sold a 14.5-acre site alongside St Vincent's Hospital and opposite the Merrion Gates to developers Bernard McNamara and Jerry O'Reilly. In the previous decade, it had sold its Magdalene laundry in Donnybrook, which was redeveloped into apartments, St Anne's National School in Milltown in south Dublin for €8 million and a retreat at Stella Maris in Howth for €2 million. The sales brought to about £100 million the total value of lands and buildings sold or given away in a ten-year period. Three acres at Merrion Road were given to Dublin Corporation to provide homes for older people, those with disabilities and 'empty nesters' who had been renting authority houses bigger than they needed after their families had left home.

Giving away management of facilities – while keeping ownership – did not always work out well. The order established St Mary's Telford at the St Vincent's Campus in 1868 as a school and 'asylum' for blind women and girls. It gave up management of the nursing home and supported living apartments facility in 1996 but retained ownership of the land and campus and appointed two sisters to sit on the board of management. In 2020, the facility was closed, despite the fact that it housed 19 female residents. These residents, ranging in age from their 30s to their 80s, had been living there, some for nearly 60 years. Health Information and Quality Authority (HIQA) inspectors found the residents had not been given information or been 'consulted … on what was happening to their homes' and that management had failed 'to prioritise the needs of residents or keep them informed about … the application to the courts for voluntary liquidation'.

But even after these giveaways the congregation's land and building assets were valued at €233 million in 2009. The remaining property portfolio included almost 60 per cent of the neighbouring 115-acre Elm Park golf course and a car park valued at more than €20 million on the hospital campus, from which it received annual rent of more than €1.2 million. The hospital operations were held in a separate charitable entity, although the order retained the ownership of the land underneath, which was to become the central issue in the delay in commissioning the new maternity hospital. This greatly worried some campaigners, led by former Holles Street master Peter Boylan, when the deputy chairwoman of the HSE board, Professor Deirdre Madden, and patient advocate Dr

Sarah McLoughlin raised serious concerns about governance and the influence of a Catholic ethos on the work of the maternity hospital.

Although patronage of Holles Street was in the hands of the Catholic Archbishop of Dublin, he absented himself from stewardship of the hospital. The expectation of the doctors at Holles Street was that they would be able to practise medicine according to the laws of the State rather than the doctrine of one particular Church at the new location. The fear was that the continued ownership of the land by the nuns would give them some form of superior rights and control.

The initial offer by the nuns was that they would continue to hold ownership of the land and lease it to the State for 99 years. The company that ran the hospital on behalf of the nuns – St Vincent's Healthcare Group (SVHG), a private limited company with charitable tax status and fixed assets of more than €531 million – said it did not want the nuns to relinquish ownership because that would somehow affect the continuing quality of care across the two hospitals. This was viewed with suspicion by campaigners, who pointed out that the HSE BreastCheck cancer-screening clinic on the campus was held by a separate entity. The charity said that the new hospital would be 'an entirely independent secular civic body controlled solely by Irish law'. A lengthy and damaging stand-off ensued and the application for planning permission for construction was delayed until the NMH agreed to submit to the governance at St Vincent's after relocation.

By early 2022 a new compromise was proposed. RSC announced it would transfer its 186-year-old ownership of SVHG from the congregation to a new charitable body called St Vincent's Holding CLG. It insisted that the new body would be independent of the Sisters and that RSC would have no role in what took place at the hospitals on the land, having already withdrawn from the boards of the various hospitals four years earlier.

The Sisters boasted of giving away 'valued healthcare facilities' valued at €204 million. The package included 29 acres of land at Merrion Road and a further 3.2 acres at St Michael's Hospital in Dún Laoghaire. It kept ownership of one building on the site, which it leased to the hospital 'to provide income for the continuing work of the Religious Sisters of Charity and the care of our elderly Sisters'. However, the gift was not to the Irish State. The State would not own the freehold. Instead, it has a 300-year lease, at a nominal rent of €10 per annum, which the government said was as good as owning the land underneath the hospital.

The Vatican granted the nuns 'permission to transfer the entire issued share capital of St Vincent's Healthcare Group to St Vincent's Holding for the nominal sum of €1'. St Vincent's Holding was to be the charity run without involvement by the nuns. Boylan wondered if the Vatican would really approve the transfer of Catholic assets to a healthcare organisation that would permit procedures such as elective sterilisation, abortion and in vitro fertilisation. Canon law forbade any procedures being performed on Church-owned property that contravened Church teaching. 'To proceed without full knowledge of the terms set by the Vatican would be a serious failure of due diligence,' Boylan argued. 'The minister must also explain why the government would consider spending up to €1 billion on a critical piece of State health infrastructure only to gift it to a private company on the record as committed to upholding the Catholic values of the Sisters of Charity.'

Nonetheless, the government decided to ratify the deal between the NMH and St Vincent's, being overseen by the HSE, encouraged by the support of all the national directors of midwifery across the country. The director of Holles Street, all the assistant directors of midwifery at the hospital and 52 clinicians working there wrote a letter to the government pleading for it to go ahead. Minister for Health Stephen Donnelly cited strong legal guarantees that the hospital would provide 'all legally permissible services', including abortion, 'gender-affirming surgery and assisted human reproduction'.

The order surrendered the land to the new charity, but it kept a sizeable portion of land at Merrion, amounting to over 16 acres. In early 2022, the Sisters applied to DCC for planning permission to allow 'high quality residential development and to address housing need' at Merrion Road. This land, with planning permission attached, could be worth more than €50 million to it.

THE MATER PRIVATE HOSPITAL

The Sisters of Mercy is another order to have sold a hospital. The nuns founded their hospital on Eccles Street in 1851 and while that remains open to the public, it opened the Mater Private to paying patients in 1986. It was sold to management, led by businessman Brian Joyce, in late 2000 for just €42 million net of debts that were cleared. Joyce said the ethics committee of the Mater public hospital would continue to oversee the activities of the Mater Private. 'This is a commitment we have given to the Sisters of Mercy so that a Catholic ethos will be maintained,' he said.

The Mater public hospital became a limited company owned by the Mercy Order. The money from the sale of the private hospital was to be paid to the nuns over 20 years, to give a consistent income flow. 'It is not a commercial transaction,' insisted Sister Helena O'Donoghue of the Sisters of Mercy. It didn't seem that the nuns timed the sale well. Just seven years later the new owners sold on to CapVest, an investment vehicle run by Irishman Seamus Fitzpatrick and supported by overseas investors, for €350 million. It sold the hospital group – which by now had operations outside of Dublin, too – a decade later to US fund Harbourvest as part of a bigger deal. It, in turn, sold the hospital to the French company Infravia, already an investor in nursing homes in Ireland, for €500 million. It can be assumed that Infravia runs the hospital according to State regulations.

The order may have done better with other property transactions. It is among the largest of the religious order landowners, reckoned to have over 240 properties and plots of land as part of a portfolio valued at over €1 billion. It has been an active seller, having 'contributed' property and cash 'in excess of €33 million' to the State by 2022 as part of the Indemnity Agreement of 20 years earlier. Yet, it is estimated to still owe the State close to €100 million, though a large part of this was due to be covered by the transfer of the National Rehabilitation Hospital to the HSE. It was also estimated to have raised about €170 million from 260 separate property sales, although some were nominal amounts, well beyond perceived market value. Many of the properties it has sold were former Convents of Mercy, many in rural Ireland with relatively low sales prices, in Cork, Limerick, Clare, Galway and Mayo. However, it continues to run private medical clinics in Dublin, Cork, Limerick, Drogheda, Mitchelstown, Mallow, Mullingar, Navan and Sligo. It still has four hospitals – the Mater, Temple Street and the National Orthopaedic Hospital, all in Dublin, and the Mercy University Hospital in Cork – which have been valued for insurance purposes at €645 million.

Many of the order's schools have been transferred to Ceist, a trustee body set up in 2007 for voluntary Catholic secondary schools in Ireland. These secondary school properties were valued at €412 million and there are also primary schools valued at €256 million.

BON SECOURS

Another order of nuns that plays a major part in the provision of private healthcare is the Bon Secours Sisters. Indeed, it runs the largest private hospital network in Ireland with 810 in-patient beds. The Bon Secours Health System, as it is known, is part of the Bon Secours Mercy Health Group, based in Ohio, and is run as a not-for-profit, but it is profitable. Its last accounts, for 2021, declared profits of €8.1 million on a turnover of €365.2 million. It employs about 3,700 people.

It has sizeable holdings of land and property on which five private hospitals are located in Dublin, Cork, Limerick, Tralee and Galway, and a care village in Cork. It has detailed a €300 million capital investment programme in recent years, extending cancer services in Cork, building a new cardiology centre in Galway and upgrading operating theatres at all of its hospitals. It bought Barrington's Hospital in Limerick in 2016 for €15 million and is due to open another 150-bed hospital in the city by 2025. The private hospital group as a tenant makes large annual payments to its landlord, the Bon Secours Trustees Unlimited Company. This company 'acts as a trustee whereby it holds properties in trust on behalf of Sisters of Bon Secours Ireland'. The 2019 and 2020 accounts report annual payments of €4.2 million.

The order has sold Bessborough, on the south side of Cork city and the location of another controversial Mother and Baby institution, on a piecemeal basis in recent years, raising tens of millions of euro. It also 'gifted' over six acres, including all the buildings and parking spaces occupied by Bessborough Services, to the HSE, which undertook to run existing services, employing more than 100 people, having already put about €30 million of State money into the facility in the previous decade. The order kept the convent and the lands surrounding it, including the graveyard area.

The possible locations of more graves impacted the construction of new homes on the extensive grounds. The sisters began the sale of land to various property developers some years prior to the publication of the Ryan report. One company, Estuary View Enterprises (EVE), connected to Tony Walsh and Aidan Harte, two local Cork businessmen who own the Freefoam Building Products company in Glanmire, put forward plans costing €105 million to construct 420 apartments plus a café and crèche. EVE is the largest landowner in the Bessborough Estate, with more than 40 acres. It has suggested that mapping indicated the children's burial ground may be located 50 metres to the south of the proposed development. 'It is fully recognised that the site has a history as a Mother and Baby home,' a submission by consultants on its behalf to Cork City Council said. 'Notwithstanding its past, the land can contribute positively to the future social fabric of the area, to the provision of much-needed new homes and public open space, including parkland amenity.' The consultants further argued that 'significant public good' can come out of the potential development of the lands in a manner 'which respects the past and also ensures the setting of Bessborough House is maintained and enhanced into the future'. Much of the land on the estate is zoned for landscape and preservation.

ABP was cautious and refused planning permission for two fast-track plans by a small Cork-owned developer MWB Two for 246 residential units at a site to the south of the proposed development site. The Cork Survivors and Supporters Alliance, which campaigned against the building of apartments over the children's burial site, said any plans for housing in the midst of a housing crisis are to be welcomed, but that it was just a question of finding the right places on the estate.

QUIETLY LUCRATIVE

Many of the sales conducted by orders of nuns have been carried out quietly, possibly to avoid complaints from neighbours as to what would happen to convents or land subsequently controlled by developers. In some cases, it should have been obvious as to what would have to happen.

The last of the Dominican nuns at Muckross Park House convent, off Marlborough Road in Dublin 4 and located beside its Muckross Park College secondary school for girls, left the building in 2019, acquired in 1900 for £4,000, leaving it potentially derelict. The sale of the building and nearly three acres of land only became known when the new owners – Reilly Lands – made an application to have it rezoned for housing, even though the site shares an entrance with the school. Property experts suggested the transfer of the land may have been for about €20 million, dependent on securing zoning and planning permission for the building of homes.

The property and land assets belonging to the Daughters of Charity were estimated to be worth €286.4 million in the 2009 Ryan Report. At that time, the congregation had 215 members in Ireland, over 60 per cent of whom were aged 70 or older. Since 2016 the Daughters of Charity have sold four south Dublin properties for about €40 million, including the sale of a site on Temple Road, Blackrock, in 2017 for €30 million to Paddy McKillen junior's Oakmount. The site was put up for sale for €45 million three years later and, having failed to sell, again in 2023 for about €10 million less. Again, there are many other examples that could fill page after page of this book.

Any efforts to confiscate land, even if to force various orders to provide more money for redress, would most likely be caught up in legal challenges for years and might not succeed either. The remaining nuns may no longer have the popularity and respect of old, and around the country there were many complaints throughout 2022 and 2023 about old convents and buildings owned by male orders not being offered for use to refugees. But any effort at compulsory purchase might provoke a powerful kick from those who still care more about adhering to the ways of the past than conforming to current-day norms or looking to the needs of the future.

PART 8

OWNING THE NEEDS

No matter what age people are, they need a home, but occasionally people have to move out of what they have come to know as home. Young people often leave the family home, temporarily or permanently, when they finish school and begin college or university, as more than half do, rather than going straight to work as previous generations did. Older people, who are living longer in general, often need assisted living or a residence that might be more suitable to changed needs. Some investors see these requirements as commercial opportunities to be exploited.

TWENTY-NINE

STUDENT ACCOMMODATION CRISIS

There has been an enormous expansion in the numbers attending third-level education in recent decades. There are 80,000 full-time third-level students in Dublin and 26,000 in Cork. This has put extra demands on housing in the main cities, pitching an ever-increasing number of students in competition with workers and families for places. Many students now simply remain at home and sometimes choose courses according to location instead of content and personal suitability. Some have entered into long daily commutes or have been reduced to couch-surfing a number of nights each week. There is a student accommodation crisis in Ireland.

'Ultimately, I would hate it to be a situation that the Dublin universities are only for Dublin people. And Cork universities are for Cork people, and Galway universities are for Galway people,' said Linda Doyle, Provost of Trinity College Dublin (TCD). 'There's the international mix in as well. You just really want people from around the world to be able to come here and not be turned off by how hard it is to find somewhere to live.' The universities are also very dependent on the fees those foreign students pay, a multiple of what is charged to Irish citizens.

Trinity offers 1,600 rooms, mainly on its city-centre campus, but all are fully booked with long waiting lists. The university also has access to another 489 rooms through a third party. 'We are robbing this generation of a proper college experience,' Professor Doyle said. She said that college is much more than grades for modules, it's about personal development, friendships and new experiences and that this was being denied to many students. 'We need to solve the housing crisis in Ireland to solve the student accommodation crisis. We need to do it at speed.'

Trinity's efforts to expand its accommodation have met with financially well-resourced opposition. Residents in the prosperous Dartry area of Dublin 6 – including residents of Temple Road, where some of the country's most expensive detached houses can be found – launched a sustained campaign against a planned expansion by TCD of its Trinity Hall complex beside Palmerstown Park. It was a virtual rerun of the opposition from 20 years earlier to the original development when residents had decried the potential unruliness of students and damage to the value of their existing properties (all of which have soared in price since).

Trinity succeeded in getting permission for new buildings that would add 358 new beds to the existing 995, despite claims of anti-social, drunken and disorderly and other unsavoury behaviour from students. One local resident claimed Trinity Hall residents and their visitors 'regularly depart late at night in a loud, mostly drunken state on their way down to the Milltown Luas station', with further allegations made about urinating, vomiting, screaming and shouting. No consideration seemingly was made as to whether it might be the many teenagers and young adults living in the area who might equally be responsible for any such behaviour that actually happened. In granting the permission, ABP decided that claims about reductions in property values were 'not supported by any evidence' and said the location was desirable because of the public transport access, via Luas and bus, to TCD itself.

Many of the third-level institutions pulled back from the solution of building themselves. In 2019 Dublin City University (DCU) announced it would build 'affordable' accommodation for 1,240 students at its Glasnevin campus and had full planning permission and finance in place. It has stalled the build for now because the costs of construction were estimated at about €150,000 per student bed, meaning charges of more than double the existing rate of €5,500 per annum to customers. DCU wasn't the only university to either pull back or scale back, even though DCU got at least four applications for every bed space available for on-campus accommodation. The previous year UCD abandoned a €590 million plan to add to its existing 4,100 beds on campus, despite having already spent €29 million on the project, saying that an increase in construction costs made the plan unviable. However, in March 2023 DCU did announce a government grant of €40 million to supply just 405 beds.

International students are worth about €380 million a year to the Republic's colleges and universities. About 17,000, almost equal to the entire student body of TCD, attend third-level institutions in Ireland each year. Accounts for the seven universities represented by the Irish Universities Association showed they earned about €70 million a year renting out rooms to students. It wasn't regarded as commercial income, but as revenue to cover the cost of providing the accommodation and then refurbishment and replacement. And yet they didn't want to get more involved.

In late 2022, the Minister for Further and Higher Education, Simon Harris, announced a new policy to provide State assistance 'to stimulate the development of new and additional student accommodation for public higher education institutions … This new policy will unlock the construction of up to 700 beds with further engagement on an additional supply. This will involve the State for the first time assisting with the cost of building student accommodation in return for affordability commitments on rent.'

The plan was to activate a new supply where planning permission already existed. He also said that Technological Universities in the regions would be allowed to prepare for the construction of student accommodation. But the numbers involved – as against the need – were tiny. The role of privately-owned purpose-built student accommodation (PBSAs) would continue to grow as official policy.

Guidelines had been put into the Dublin City Development Plan in 2016 that allowed for a form of student co-living with small private bedrooms but shared kitchens and other amenities, including mini-cinemas, pool tables and even bowling alleys. The planning officers at DCC readily agreed to entreaties from the Higher Education Authority (HEA) and the third-level institutions, believing it would ease the pressure on the private rental sector. It was also regarded as a potential good use of brownfield land in the Dublin inner city, the Liberties area of Dublin 8 and around Summerhill in Dublin 7, near the proposed new location for the Technological University of Dublin close to Grangegorman, which hadn't been built on during the Celtic Tiger era.

Some critics argued that the PBSAs became over-concentrated in some areas of the city and displaced other types of needed development. The developers were happy to buy land in the selected areas as the accommodation was more financially attractive than standard apartments to build: the small units allowed for greater numbers who would pay rent. The buildings benefited from fast-track planning rules for housing, allowing developers to bypass councils and go straight to ABP for permission. The critics suggested that this drove up land values in those areas and excluded building houses or apartments for sale or rent because developers of those can't afford to pay the higher prices that the site owners were getting from student accommodation developers.

The Union of Students in Ireland (USI) was quick to complain that it was all too much, that most students didn't want luxury purpose-built student accommodation, just somewhere adequate and functional with a bed and a bit of space where they could study – at a price they could afford. An Ernst & Young (EY) report compiled for DCC in 2019 found that 79 per cent of the residents of PBSAs were international students; most Irish students couldn't afford rents that in 2019 averaged €250 per week in Dublin as opposed to the €197 per week paid by the average student at that time. Yet the same EY report anticipated a need for 13,000–14,000 PBSA beds by 2024, with an eventual need for 50,000.

Purpose-built student accommodation had also been exempt from legislation capping increases in designated pressure zones to 4 per cent per annum. When it was announced they were to be included, many operators hiked their rents by double-digit percentages, some by as much as a quarter, knowing they would be restricted in future. The most expensive on-campus student accommodation for the academic year was in Dublin, where top prices ranged from €8,000 at TCD to €11,000 at UCD, which was below what the private operators charged.

BUILDING FOR STUDENTS

The interest in student accommodation goes back to the turn of the century when property developers first were allowed to build student properties in return for generous tax reliefs over a ten-year period.

Cork has gone for particularly large-scale developments, mainly on the sites of old manufacturing plants or dilapidated warehouse-style buildings in need of renovation. The Bottleworks, a ten-storey 623-bedroom development, is opening in September 2023 on Carrigrohane Road, at the site of the old Coca-Cola bottling plant and in the shadow of what was once Ireland's tallest building, the Cork County Hall. The Bottleworks project is being led by Northern Ireland firm Farrans Construction, on behalf of US client CA Ventures. It is significantly bigger than the nearby UCC/Sisk Crow's Nest 255-bed development at Victoria Cross, which was built on the site of a demolished pub. Bellmount Developments has planning permission for a c. €30 million 243-bed student accommodation complex at Victoria Cross too. North Main Street in the city centre has become rundown in recent decades but is likely to benefit from a project by Bmor Developments, which is due to deliver 280 beds for the 2023/4 academic year. There is a new €35 million 280-bed development, Bróga House, on Washington Street, which is on the site of the former Lee Boot Manufacturing Company.

The development that attracted the most opposition was the 554-bed Ashlin House on Bandon Road, which opened in autumn 2022 and cost

€53 million to build. Locals were furious with the Cork diocese of the Catholic Church for making much of the land available on the site of what's known locally as the Lough Church, the apartments going into a very old and settled area of mainly small two-storey houses and cottages. Locals complained that they had paid for the upkeep of the church and grounds and didn't deserve then to see the Church profit from the sale of the lands and inconvenience them with such a large influx of additional students. They have complained also about anti-social behaviour in the area during times such as 'rag week' although this had been going on for years and when the majority of students in the area had been renting shared accommodation in older houses.

Provision became lucrative for many developers. Michael O'Flynn, CEO of the O'Flynn Group, had been early to the student apartment business, building, owning and managing 450 rooms across two blocks in Cork. The company built a 900-bed unit at the Point Campus complex in Dublin's East Point with the backing of New York-based private-equity firm BlackRock, which it sold then to German investor DWS for €172 million but continued to manage. US group Hines spent more than €140 million in Dublin through its Aparto student accommodation business. Its five buildings hold almost 1,800 beds.

But some of the most interesting money came from the Middle East. Multinational Round Hill Capital had as its partner NBK Capital Funds, the National Bank of Kuwait. They paid €85 million for a development in Dublin's Liberties on the former Brewery Block site close to Newmarket Square. It was still under construction in the spring of 2023 but is due to contain almost 370 student bedrooms when finished. Round Hill Capital also bought a 145-bed development on Farranlea Road in Cork in December 2018 and invested in a 216-unit apartment development called Bridgefield in Santry, Dublin 9. Meanwhile, Dubai-based Global Student Accommodation (GSA), operating under the Uninest brand, rented purpose-built apartments to students in 33 cities across eight countries around the world and came to Dublin when it bought a 500-bed complex on Gardiner Street from Carrowmore, run by developer Pat Cox junior, son of the former president of the European Parliament. It added five blocks in Dublin in a €400 million deal with Harrison Street for 1,900 rooms.

These may all have been short-term accommodation for those renting them, but the investors clearly saw long-term profits available. There is the added benefit of revenue during the summer months when the universities are on holiday: the State used some of the venues for emergency refugee accommodation in 2022 and 2023, although this created its own problems when these people had to be moved out to allow for the return of students, particularly in Sligo.

The future for further new construction remains uncertain, however, as the rise in interest rates has made the cost of financing the developments more expensive. There is only so much additional revenue that can be demanded of students, many of whom may need jobs to cover the rent or depend on financing from wealthy relatives. And by not building too much additional capacity, the value of what has been provided is protected.

THIRTY

A SMALL IDEA: CO-LIVING

How much space does a person need to live comfortably? Multi-millionaire Richard Barrett of Bartra believed an IKEA show apartment provided the answer. In a 2018 interview Barrett said, 'If you go to IKEA, for instance, it has two show apartments: one is 25 square metres and one is 35 square metres. You can walk into them and they're perfectly acceptable living spaces. It's a realisation that living spaces are a factor of how well they're designed, not some arbitrary size.'

He drew another comparison to defend his enthusiasm for so-called co-living, shared accommodation aimed at young professionals, similar to student accommodation and based on models in London and Berlin. 'In the communal living one, you have these storage spaces to store your suitcase, your case of wine, your bike,' said Barrett in a *Business Post* interview. 'You don't clog up your living space with all that stuff. You see on yachts and ships, the marine architects are able to fit in tiny spaces and make them perfectly liveable. Non-marine designers can do the same.'

Critics saw what might be acceptable for a week on a cruise ship as unsuitable for longer-term living, but suddenly glorified student accommodation for working people in their twenties and thirties, expected to sleep in small en-suite units fitted with fold-up beds, measuring approximately 18 square metres, was a housing solution. Critics said it was an attempt to normalise cramped living conditions and erode public housing standards, to take advantage of the desperation of tenants caused by undersupply.

Former Minister for Housing Eoghan Murphy will likely be long remembered for his support for this idea of high-rise developments catering for hundreds of people, with shared services offered to tenants. In July 2019 he was asked by a radio interviewer if co-living spaces resembled prison cells. 'No, not at all, it's more like a very trendy, kind of boutique hotel-type place,' Murphy said. 'It's something I'd seen abroad in other cities, where you have your own private room, en-suite, but you also have shared community spaces, a gym, a movie room, a games room potentially, a kitchen, a living room. I can see people coming to Ireland who can't sign a 12-month lease because they're not going to be here for 12 months maybe, who don't want to share a place with three strangers, and who want a bit of privacy, but also a bit of that communal or social aspect to living.'

The outcry provoked another statement from Murphy, in which he conceded: 'My analogy in response [to the prison cell comparison] wasn't a good one. But co-living elicits outrage in some because they wrongly assume it's what we propose as a response to families in crisis. It is not.'

Among those who saw Ireland as a mark for co-living was a British outfit called The Collective, which marketed itself along the lines of high-profile commercial property behemoth WeWork. It even had its own version of WeWork's messianic leader Adam Neumann, a young man called Reza Merchant. He raised private equity funds in Britain and Singapore and money from Jonathan Teklu, a German investor who previously helped bankroll Airbnb. Further finance came from Deutsche Bank and the Bermuda-based Catalina Re.

Before the pandemic hit, The Collective had 7,000 units of accommodation with a target of 100,000 by 2025. London, New York and Berlin were its main locations, with micro-apartments averaging 12 square metres per person in space with an additional 6 square metres per person in the communal spaces. Contrast this with Ireland, where the smallest allowed apartment for a new building was 37 square metres for a studio. Co-living essentially allowed three little rooms in that space.

Dublin was one of many other cities in its sights. In 2019, The Collective became involved in the purchase of a largely cleared half-acre site on Fumbally Lane in Dublin 8, which hosted a large cut-stone former distillery building, a protected structure that remains in situ. It announced plans to apply for 200–250 co-living units. The price it paid of €10.5 million was reportedly more than two-and-a-half times the price paid just two years earlier by the owners, Oakmount. It teamed up with Mm Capital, an Irish property investment and development company founded in 2014 by Peter Leonard and Derek Poppinga. Reditum, a London-based boutique financier, and Cardinal Capital funded the purchase of the site.

The willingness to pay so much extra for the site was regarded as a signal that land between Dublin's canals was worth more than many had thought, at least if applied to this type of development. The worry was that the land – as with student accommodation – would not be sold for other residential uses. There was too much money to be made in providing multiple units for high rents. There was no requirement either to make spaces available for social housing, as with apartment blocks. This was emphasised when Mm also sought to redevelop the ugly 1960s Phibsborough shopping centre – which it had bought in 2016 – as a 321 single-room co-living scheme, instead of as the student accommodation for which it had received planning permission as part of a €50 million redevelopment.

By 2022, however, The Collective had been laid low by the pandemic and the landowners had cooled on the idea of co-living. They wanted a 235-room hotel on the site instead. Ironically, Aloft, a hotel chain owned by Marriott International that operates just yards away on Mill Street, complained that the changes would result in 'the loss of much-needed residential units' and 'is unsustainable and goes against the interests of proper planning and sustainable development … the proposal will contribute to the over-concentration of hotels in the area which will jeopardise their vitality and viability.'

BARTRA'S CO-LIVING ETHOS

It was Richard Barrett's company Bartra, through its Niche Living brand, that became one of the most enthusiastic promotors of co-living blocks. It promised to spend €130 million on four sites in Dublin, at Ballsbridge, Castleknock, Dún Laoghaire and Rathmines.

'We need to embrace the more global and transient lifestyle lived particularly by younger people and respond to their needs. They want a more urban lifestyle, they want experiences rather than ownership. At the same time they want quality of accommodation, safety and security,' the company argued. Barrett gave an interview in 2019 in which he cited Murphy's approval of the idea. He claimed this 'more dense form of living' relieved pressure on 'ordinary accommodation' and 'that means you can make the rent less because you're getting more value from the site'.

Bartra sought permission – successfully – in 2019 for a 208-unit scheme on the site of the former CBS Christian Brother's school at Eblana Avenue in Dún Laoghaire, with financial backing coming from the Irish Strategic Investment Fund (ISIF). In its planning application, it stated that bedrooms would cost between €1,083 and €1,300 a month to rent, including bills and amenities. It contrasted these charges with build-to-rent apartments, which it said would cost between €1,200 and €1,850 a month. Tellingly, it contended that 'the shared accommodation would be affordable by persons at or just above the average earnings in Dublin, but the apartments would not be affordable for most earners.' By the time the co-living was available to book in January 2023, Bartra was advertising places starting at €1,880 a month each.

The online brochure for the February 2023 launch of the Eblana location boasted: 'From curling up with a book in the lounge or hanging out in the games room to hitting the gym with your workout buddy or cooking up a storm in the MasterChef-style kitchens – however you like to spend your downtime, there's a place for you at Niche Living.'

The rooms, described as private suites, include a double bed (which is a pull-out that doubles as a sofa) and a smart TV. The kitchenette, directly facing the bed, comes with utensils, a hob and a fridge. There is a full en-suite with shower, a 'work from home' desk, what's described as ample storage and a valuables safe. Utilities such as electricity, water and heat are included in the monthly fee and there is wifi throughout the building. Residents are allowed access to 'purpose designed co-working spaces with private meeting rooms, video conferencing and printing'. The room is cleaned fortnightly, with linen and towels provided and laundered fortnightly. The communal areas are cleaned daily and what's called a 24/7 'concierge service' for 'safety and peace of mind' is provided. Also included are a small communal cinema, games room, living rooms and co-working spaces. 'In Dún Laoghaire, every floor has two communal areas – there's a dining and cooking area, and the other is a lounge relaxation area. There are 40 rooms per floor, but there isn't [just] a single kitchen [in the traditional sense]. There's a single large kitchen area, with multiple hobs, sinks, food preparation areas. So, five or six people could be cooking at one time.'

Everyone pays the same monthly fee and it is emphasised the rooms are designed for singles, not couples. Bartra has described its target market as people aged 20–34 who would choose this over a similarly priced one-bedroom apartment because they don't want to live alone. The advert stated that there would be 'no hidden costs or nasty surprises'.

Bartra also started work on a 102-room development in Rathmines in Dublin after it received permission, but it wasn't always successful in its efforts. In September 2019 it submitted a fast-track planning application to ABP for a €40 million, five-storey 210-bed space shared living accommodation scheme on the site of the to-be-demolished Brady's public house on the Old Navan Road in Dublin. It's about 800 metres from Blanchardstown Main Street but, more pertinently, just 300 metres from Connolly Hospital. Its manager, Margaret Boland, supplied a letter to the planners arguing in favour of the development on the basis that there was a severe scarcity of accommodation in the area for potential employees. 'Many of our staff are key workers who come to Ireland on short to medium contracts and their accommodation needs are focused on affordability and proximity to the workplace,' she wrote. 'This allows them to save and maximise the amount of income they can send home to their home countries. There is a severe scarcity of such accommodation currently.' However, Bartra's plans were stopped by the High Court in mid-2020 when ABP conceded it had granted the permission against the recommendations of its own inspector. Leo Varadkar, as a local TD, had been one of the objectors.

When Bartra proposed a co-living development for an area that hosts some of the most expensive home properties in the country – Merrion Road in Ballsbridge, Dublin 4 – the protests didn't focus on the quality of life of those who would be resident in the new block. Instead, they focused on those living in bigger homes nearby. One couple complained the proposed building would mean that 'we would be observed like animals in a zoo'. Claims were made that it would be a security risk to the British Embassy on the opposite side of the road – as if terrorists would not be able to book rooms in the existing guesthouse.

ABP had approved the €25 million development despite its own planning inspector concluding it would be a 'substandard' development because of insufficient communal living and kitchen/dining facilities, which measured just 4.3 square metres. Bartra replied that international employers such as Facebook – which was planning to move into newly built blocks on the same road – would provide meals in the workplace and therefore there would be less demand for communal cooking/dining space. The implication was that only Facebook employees or similar would be able to afford the rent demanded and would be happy with what was on offer.

Most controversially, Bartra also contended in 2019 that residents in its developments have no protection under tenancy laws. It sent a legal memo to DCC and ABP claiming its shared living developments cannot be regulated under tenancy and housing laws. It argued that the protections of the Residential Tenancies Act do not apply to shared living residents. Bartra's legal opinion stated that rental and tenancy regulations are not applicable to communal living because occupants' bed spaces are not self-contained residential units. The concept of 'club membership' was argued. The legal opinion was that 'if a property is not let for rent but is held under some other basis, it does not come within the definition of a dwelling for the purposes of the [Residential Tenancies Act 2004].'

Bartra said the properties would be run on a 'hotel-like basis' and the 'spirit of the approach' would be similar to house-sharing where 'behaviour of all is regulated by a set of written or unwritten house rules that are to the benefit of all … Co-living is not suitable for couples, families or long-stay residents. It is also not suitable for singles who do not enjoy socialising with others.'

It also said it didn't expect security of tenure for the residents to arise as its research apparently showed people would typically stay for periods between two and 12 months, with very few staying a full year. But what would happen if they couldn't find anywhere else?

As the new Minister for Housing in 2020, Darragh O'Brien quickly banned new co-living developments, although those that had planning before his new laws were introduced were allowed to build. His predecessor Eoghan Murphy – who surprised his party by resigning his seat in April 2019, quitting politics – said O'Brien had been 'right to act' and that co-living was 'only ever intended to play a limited and niche role in the housing market. It was never intended as an alternative to conventional apartment or housing developments.'

But if there hadn't been a public backlash, would co-living have become an accepted alternative?

THIRTY-ONE

HOUSING AN AGEING POPULATION

Dermot Bannon, the architect who has become famous in Ireland for his television show *Room to Improve*, has not been afraid to offer unpopular opinions that might offend some members of his large fanbase. One is that too many older people continue to live in houses that are too big for them after their families have grown and moved out. These may be older couples or widows or widowers who continue to live in three-, four- or even five-bed homes long after their children have left them. He suggests that they should sell and move somewhere smaller, freeing up their homes for use by growing families who need the space more. He says there are many housing estates where children should be playing in the empty communal green spaces that are often quiet instead.

His suggestion has been taken up by others occasionally as having merit. However, no government is ever likely to take up the cudgels, even if it was to design measures, such as tax breaks, to help facilitate so-called trading down. Nor is it likely to build much senior housing in case it is seen as looking to transfer people out of their homes forcibly, even if it would make sense. No politician wants to alienate older people who are, after all, more likely to vote than younger people. The arguments against Bannon's idea – which is commonplace in Europe – are easy to list: the areas where people already live are communities where people want to stay because they know their neighbours and have facilities they have become used to frequenting daily; older people have become comfortable in their homes and, having paid for them, don't feel they should be moved on; they have nowhere else to go in the area, smaller properties being unavailable to buy (and they don't want to rent).

However, some of these people rent housing from councils and other voluntary bodies so the right to single tenancy of a three-bed or larger house when families are on waiting lists then becomes harder to justify. In addition, many of the same people who argue the point about there being nowhere else to go are those who also argue against the construction of new apartment blocks or houses that could be of use in their home areas.

It is an issue that the country is going to have to address more in the future because the population is growing older and is living longer. The ESRI has estimated that by 2030 one in five people living in the State will be aged 65 or over and that the population aged over 85 will have doubled from 2022. Indeed, over the next 20 years, the number of people aged 85 and over is projected to increase on average by around 6,000 each year, bringing the number from just under 90,000 to over 220,000. The HSE's annual report for 2021 noted that over the previous decade, the number of people in Ireland aged 65 years and over had increased by over one-third, twice that of the European average. Everyone concentrates on the likely impact on the health service, particularly demands at the acute hospitals, but the issue is also going to be a housing one.

That suggests that at least some people will consider following the Bannon recommendation, at least if they can find somewhere else suitable to live. Some may even see an opportunity to release capital from the ownership of their homes, to fund their retirements as a form of quasi-pension. Others, however, are reluctant to sell and spend what they may see as an inheritance for their family. The key is that there must be viable, attractive and reliable alternative homes available to them – but the housing crisis makes this much more difficult to achieve.

For those who are tempted to downsize, some Irish developers have sought to carve out a new niche market. Tetrarch, better known for its hotel operations and for providing refugee accommodation, has plans to build 1,500 homes over five years for up to €500 million, with a declared emphasis on schemes in the greater Dublin area for 'senior living accommodation' for the over-65s. Set up as Tetrarch Homes in 2018, its CEO Michael McElligott was listed as a near-quarter owner of the business. He got private equity backing from Revcap, a London-based private equity firm set up in 2004 by the former Lehman Brothers executives Andrew Pettit and Will Killick (before Lehman went bust in 2008, the first major casualty of the Great Recession).

Tetrarch's biggest acquisition to facilitate this idea is at Howth Castle and Demesne, just outside the village of Howth, 17 kilometres from Dublin city centre. The estate, which had previously been owned by the Gaisford-St Lawrence family for more than 840 years, was bought in 2019. It included a golf course (seen in the Apple TV hit *Bad Sisters*) and the Deer Park Hotel and covered more than 470 acres of walled gardens, woodland, heathland and rhododendron gardens, with great views over Dublin Bay and Howth Harbour. When Tetrarch sought to secure approval for the rezoning of the large demesne to allow for redevelopment, it made promises of extensive reforestation, 'forever green spaces' of about 120 acres, a public park, a sports campus and other amenities. However, in its bid to win over local public and political opinion, as well as the planners, it suggested a significant portion of the new housing would be made available for senior living.

'To address those concerns we will be proposing to [Fingal County] Council that any zoning of the lands to allow for the proposed uses will specifically condition the lands for the delivery of affordable housing only ... and for retirement use,' it stated in a document made available to the public. The proposal suggested the provision of a retirement community on one portion of the former golf course, as well as a 6.5-acre site on the Sutton side of the estate for 150 affordable two- and three-bed houses, at prices of less than €300,000 for proven local residents only.

Tetrarch's brochure to local residents pointed out that, according to the 2016 Census, 26 per cent of the Howth and Sutton population was over the age of 60, and that this number would increase. 'Like affordable housing delivery locally, there are currently no solutions at all being provided for older homeowners,' it said. However, Social Democrats TD Cian O'Callaghan argued that Tetrarch's 'formulation of words doesn't carry any weight … there is no zoning just for accommodation for older people or affordable [homes] only.' He also pointed out that the rules allowed for zoned land to be resold and 'outlines or projects that have been promised are not necessarily tied into that land'.

Tetrarch has had mixed success in getting approval for its senior living ideas. In early January 2021, it was allowed an estimated €50 million residential development of 224 apartments at Garters Lane, Saggart, 'with a focus on affordable housing and independent and senior living in Dublin's fastest-growing residential area'. However, in January 2023 Tetrarch was refused permission by DCC for a 78-unit 'over-65s' scheme on lands around the eighteenth-century protected structure, Sybil Hill House in Raheny. It had proposed three blocks, one rising to five storeys tall, on the Vincentian order-owned land located about 150 metres from an entrance to St Anne's Park and beside St Paul's College secondary school. It was told they had not been sensitively sited and designed. In May 2021 it bought less than an acre of land from Blackrock Rugby Club at Stradbrook Road with the intention of building 108 units in an apartment block for rent to 'senior residents'. It said the €50 million proposed scheme would 'provide a real alternative for older people who wish to move into accommodation suitable for their needs as they grow older'. Its 'integrated retirement community' application included indoor amenities such as a 'multi-purpose social space, a games room, breakout spaces and a TV/cinema room'. Local residents complained about a loss of car-parking spaces in the Blackrock grounds, among other things, and the proposal has become bogged down in the planning process.

Bartra was another developer to pitch in this sector. In May 2022, it sought planning for a five-storey, 39-unit (35 one-bed, four two-bed), build-to-rent apartment scheme for Woodlands Park at Blackrock, County Dublin, aimed at older people, complete with two roof-top hot tubs and a Trackman golf simulator room. It also proposed a cinema, meeting room/family dining room, library/reading area, gym, kitchen, hydrotherapy room, hairdressing room, massage facilities and private members club room with espresso bar.

A planning consultant on Bartra's behalf said the concept was 'to provide high-quality, specialist, age-appropriate housing for older people close to their existing communities, promoting vibrant retirement communities where people can enjoy a healthier and more active retirement'. Planning consultant Kevin Hughes of Hughes Planning and Development Consultants said 'social interaction is important' and that 'the goal is to create a close-knit community through shared spaces, lounges and amenity areas and to fundamentally change the way retirement housing is understood and delivered'. He also claimed that 'additionally, … providing people with the opportunity to downsize – or right-size – to appropriate accommodation … has the effect of freeing up under-occupied housing stock.'

The objections came quickly, and Dún Laoghaire–Rathdown County Council sought revised plans to reduce the number of overall units by increasing the number of two-bed units. Retired judge Paddy McMahon complained that the plan would 'create chaos in the area' and would 'wreck the place', the height of the building being 'outrageous'. The council also rejected plans for another Bartra 'age-friendly' build-to-rent scheme at Mount Auburn on Killiney Hill Road, saying the proposed 29-unit development would 'set an undesirable precedent for similar development'.

It remains to be seen as to how many more similar developments are proposed and if they become popular outside of Dublin, too. One of the problems, at least for the current generation of older people, may be the concept of renting instead of ownership. What happens to people if the money raised by selling their house runs out and they cannot afford to continue to pay the rent? Where do they go then? The facilities proposed by both Tetrarch and Bartra would imply high rents and additional charges and would only be affordable by those with considerable capital to draw upon, money that these people might otherwise prefer to leave in an inheritance when they die.

It wasn't just at the expensive end of the market that objections were raised to the construction of such facilities. In late 2022, DCC refused planning permission for a seven-storey, senior-living 'build-to-rent' scheme for Ringsend in Dublin 4 that would have included 30 units built and operated by an approved housing body. The proposal attracted over 65 objections, including one from the principal of St Patrick's Girls National School, who raised child-protection concerns because the apartments would overlook the school playground. Glencarra Ringsend argued that the scheme 'will provide much-needed independent elderly living units within the Ringsend area' and it 'is an ideal location for such a scheme'. Home Instead – which provides support packages to older people who qualify for HSE funding – maintained that 'this model of senior living with assistance provided by the private sector and funded by the HSE is the only way that large numbers of assisted-living facilities can be delivered quickly and efficiently'. It offered these as 'an alternative to a nursing home placement for older people who qualify for a full homecare package'. DCC said no, that the proposal constituted overdevelopment of the site. An appeal was made.

NURSING HOMES

If retirement complexes are one thing we may need for the future, then more nursing homes will be a definite requirement. At present about 3 per cent of our over-65s need care but the proportion increases to one-third for the over-85s. We are living longer and healthier, which is a good thing, but it also means more people will need some form of care in their later life, which is expensive and labour-intensive. Someone who enters a nursing home may spend two years there and the majority of those do not return home before death. Their capacity to make decisions may also be limited.

We will need more nursing home beds. As of early 2023, it was estimated that there were about 31,000 nursing home beds in the country, with less than one-fifth (5,500) supplied and operated by the State. However, a report for the Department of Health has estimated demand for residential long-term care is projected to increase by between 40 and 54 per cent over the analysed period of 2015 to 2030 and for between 40,700 and 44,600 units. That poses obvious challenges for providers, for the regulatory authorities and for the Exchequer. Who is going to pay for adding what could be about 12,000 new beds? And what about beyond 2030?

The answer might be foreign capital. By early 2023 almost two-fifths of all nursing homes were in the ownership of some 15 global nursing groups and international firms, alongside a few large-scale Irish operators, many of whom also were using foreign money. The rest tended to be small operators, although many had looked to sell to the expanding bigger players, especially if premises needed capital for upgrading and they struggled to raise finance.

A report produced by KPMG in 2022 for the National Treatment Purchase Fund (NTPF) and Health and Information Quality Authority (HIQA), found that bigger operators with more than 100 beds increased sharply between 2016 and 2021, while the number of smaller homes with fewer than 20 beds decreased. Early 2023 emphasised the problems for those who didn't have scale as they struggled to cope with inflation (particularly with energy bills) and staff shortages. Some of those who couldn't sell looked to close operations. Where would the people living there move? If existing small operators were struggling, then the chances of others, particularly in rural Ireland, entering the business were reduced because the return on investment was perceived as low and getting bank finance was difficult. The farmer or shopkeeper with a bit of land outside the town who decided to build a small facility was fast becoming a thing of the past. Yet, as an ESRI study noted, 'the optimum size of a nursing home [cannot] be defined by economies of scale. Some local communities simply do not have a population size that will support a large nursing home.'

A trend has developed where nursing homes are run by big corporations that can afford the necessary investment. It's reckoned that Orpea Group, a French nursing-home operator with almost 90,000 beds across the globe and more than €2 billion in international revenue, is the largest operator in Ireland, with nearly 2,000 beds. It has expanded by acquisition, buying the FirstCare group of six homes from businessman Mervyn Smith in a deal believed to be worth more than €100 million. It acquired TLC Group from Michael Fetherston for around €150 million, giving him the money to buy the K Club. It bought Brindley Healthcare, a chain of ten homes founded by Donegal businesswoman Amanda Torres and backed by Business Growth Fund Ireland (BGFI), a private equity group. It purchased Belmont Nursing Home, a modern 161-bed nursing home on Galloping Green in Stillorgan and appointed former Tánaiste, Minister for Health and Progressive Democrat leader Mary Harney and John O'Dwyer, the former group chief executive of the VHI, as part-time directors to its Irish board. It has been controversial in its homeland though and became a subject of some contention during the 2022 presidential election because of revelations of poor care in a book called *Les Fossoyeurs* (The Gravediggers).

Mowlam Healthcare owns or operates 27 care homes and at the latest published count had 1,592 beds. Founded in 2000, it funded much of its early growth through tax-incentivised investment schemes. It was majority-controlled by Limerick businessman Pat Shanahan until 2020 when Cardinal Capital Group's private equity fund took majority control in a deal believed to be worth over €50 million. The business is a specialist in aiding people with dementia and also provides so-called step-down care for patients recovering from acute hospital treatment but who will return home in time. The HSE has been criticised often for not having enough of these facilities.

CareChoice – which has over 1,300 beds in 14 facilities – was founded as an Irish business in 2006 before being bought by UK firm Emerald Investment Partners in 2014. In turn, it was bought in 2017 by Paris-based private equity firm InfraVia Capital Partners who went on to buy a further eight Irish nursing homes. There was a further change in ownership in 2020 when French firm Emera Group – a business that has 80 care homes across seven countries in Europe – acquired the majority shareholding in the company.

With more than 850 beds across ten nursing homes, Virtue Integrated Elder Care started as a privately owned family business, founded by former Leinster rugby player Cillian Willis and his brother, Ronan. It bought some of the most sought-after nursing homes in south Dublin, including the luxurious Fern Dean in Blackrock and Four Ferns in Foxrock, before spending about €35 million on purchasing SignaCare, a 233-bed nursing home group at four locations in Waterford and Wexford run by Margaret-Anne and John Dargan. It also expanded into County Louth. The brothers raised finance by selling a 70 per cent share to Emera. Virtue has since opened a new facility in Balbriggan in north County Dublin.

The Silver Stream nursing home group, owned by Dutch private equity company Waterland, announced ambitions to operate more than 1,000 beds. Trinity Care, with 683 beds across nine nursing homes, was founded as a private Irish business in the 1980s but was bought in 2021 by another French care home operator called DomusVi. Sonas Nursing Homes, which owns 12 nursing homes with 642 beds, sold some of its business to the French property investment fund, Pierval Sante. The French fund also bought four of five nursing homes owned by Brookhaven Healthcare and leased them back to the Irish company to operate.

When the Belgian REIT Aedifica bought its first nursing home in Cork, it said Ireland provided 'an attractive investment opportunity … since the care market is still very fragmented and the rapidly ageing population will lead to increased demand for healthcare real estate'. The investment in Ireland to date is estimated at over €450 million at 21 sites across eight counties, to give nearly 2,400 rooms. The scale is not surprising given it has 600 'senior housing' sites across eight European countries, which are valued at more than €5.3 billion. It bought three nursing homes owned by Mowlam Healthcare in Kilkenny and Waterford, but they will still be run by the original Irish operators.

One of Aedifica's other most notable deals was a €161 million purchase from Bartra of two nursing homes, at Loughshinny in Skerries and Santry in North Dublin – Ireland's largest step-down unit for patients leaving hospital at Beaumont Lodge in Artane – and another nursing home under development at Clondalkin in west Dublin. The deal allowed Bartra to continue to run the homes under long-term leases and it also allowed Barrett's firm to recoup much of the money it had already invested in the sector and still remain an active major player in it.

Bartra previously had announced plans to own and operate more than 1,000 beds across ten nursing homes in the greater Dublin area. Bartra has said that it isn't possible to make money out of operating a nursing home unless it has more than 100 beds. It also prefers to construct new, purpose-built facilities instead of buying existing properties. But it struggled to gain planning permission for some of its planned units.

Most famously, it bid to construct a five-storey, 104-bedroom nursing home on lands adjacent to broadcaster Pat Kenny's home in Dalkey, County Dublin, having been refused permission originally for 150 build-to-rent apartment units and 222 shared co-living units. It won permission from ABP in July 2023, two years after the local council had rejected the plan. 'Kathy [Kenny's wife] and I are flabbergasted by the decision, which is bizarre on so many fronts,' Kenny said in response to the decision. 'An Bord Pleanála's decision is wrong on so many levels and we can only conclude that the board is so overworked that they can't look properly at plans and analyse them because this makes no sense whatsoever … I don't believe that the board has a mandate to ride roughshod over local people. All we wanted the board and the council to do was to follow the rules and those rules involve protecting the badger.' Kenny continued, 'This is the badgers' Alamo – they have nowhere else to go. The board with this decision has effectively killed the badgers.'

Bartra was refused permission for another five-storey nursing home and step-down scheme, with 131 beds, at Cookstown Industrial Estate in Tallaght.

Barrett's source of financing has created a lot of interest. He has tapped his Chinese sources as a form of cheap debt financing, meaning the Chinese do not get eventual ownership. He has been an eager advocate for making it easier for potential Immigrant Investor Programme (IIP) investors to gain their visas, and to use the money for investment in social housing and nursing homes. Bartra claimed that if there was a reduction in the investment threshold to €500,000, then the State could draw €2 billion in annual investment to Ireland.

Bartra's arguments are self-serving, but it also appears that much of the foreign money of recent years has been devoted to buying existing trading assets rather than constructing new ones. The development costs of new units are so large that very little Irish money has been invested.

By early 2023, fresh problems emerged. In the low interest rate era, many foreign investors had been prepared to accept returns of 4–5 per cent per annum on their investments in this sector. As interest rates went up the risks involved in nursing homes – and the low profit margins – influenced a slowdown in international investment. This became a major problem for operators who wanted to expand to get economies of scale but who couldn't get the capital for new projects because they couldn't offer investors sufficient returns.

The State's 'Fair Deal' system of funding nursing home care also became a bone of contention and a threat to continued further investment by the private sector. Nursing Homes Ireland took a complaint to the European Commission in late 2022 alleging that the Nursing Home Support Scheme (known as Fair Deal) discriminated against its members in favour of State-run facilities through higher payments and that the public nursing homes also received other general HSE funds not available to the private and voluntary sectors.

Public and private/voluntary nursing homes are subject to the same laws and regulations, but the public sector gets more money from the State. In 2022, the average price paid in respect of a public nursing home resident was €1,674 per week, but for the private/voluntary nursing homes, the amount was €1,047 per week. The National Treatment Purchase Fund (NTPF) makes arrangements with private/voluntary nursing homes on the prices at which long-term residential care services are provided, but it doesn't do so with public homes. Instead, the HSE determines the cost of care for each public nursing home but offers no transparent explanations as to how it reaches its decisions. Nursing Homes Ireland has claimed that public nursing homes get about 30 per cent of the overall budget for Fair Deal but provide care to less than 20 per cent of all residents. This allows the public homes to provide more favourable working terms and conditions to their staff, such as higher pay rates, sick pay and pension schemes, than private and voluntary nursing homes. Private and voluntary nursing homes also invest their own capital, but public nursing homes get what they need from the HSE. Private nursing homes pay commercial rates, but public nursing homes are exempt. It has been calculated that 45 small nursing homes – with less than 40 beds each – closed between 2018 and 2022.

The government has pointed out that payments to the private sector amount to more than €450 million, the type of figure likely to give rise to public outrage. Yet the reality is that the State regularly goes to the private operators and buys temporary space as a way of getting patients out of acute hospitals. Nor is the State likely to have the financial capacity to build and operate all of the new beds that the demographics predict are going to be necessary. Its efforts to add its own new stock are paltry compared to what is needed.

The State has been accused of neglect and of allowing 'wholescale privatisation of the sector without debate or consideration of how this affects care provision' by Professor Des O'Neill, consultant geriatrician at Tallaght Hospital. 'The minimum space for a resident's room under the national nursing homes standards is smaller than the minimum size of a parking space mandated by Dublin City Council,' he said. 'How can we expect to fit an armchair and some beloved furniture and belongings into such a small space?'

An investigation by the Health Information and Quality Authority (HIQA) has made very disturbing finds as to what happens in some privately run homes. There were cases where patients were given monthly charges for activities in which they weren't capable of taking part; extra fees imposed for the use of basic equipment such as hoists, chairs and exercise bikes; fees for social visits during the pandemic when visiting was banned; even charges for attending Mass.

O'Neill disagreed with having large units of more than 200 beds sited distant from neighbourhoods. 'We need to look at relatively small units embedded in localities near people's homes, designed in the form of small sub-units with a domestic scale and feel, including kitchen, sitting rooms and private spaces,' he said. 'It is clear that there needs to be a radical increase in HSE and voluntary provision of nursing home care to achieve this type of more sophisticated care setting, the sort that we would wish to be in.'

The State made limited efforts. In late 2022 the Department of Health made much of the first-ever public–private partnership for community nursing, announcing the construction of seven new units in Louth, Westmeath, Tipperary, Kerry, Kilkenny and Cork. The European Investment Bank (as an EU-owned institution), Bank of Ireland and

Nord LB, a German state bank, came together to provide €250 million to fund 530 new nursing home beds across the country on land already owned by the HSE. The project was to be built, financed and maintained by a joint venture between UK-based investment manager Equitix and Irish builders John Sisk and Son, called Equisisk. The HSE agreed to pay €24 million rent a year for 25 years, although the sites would remain in State ownership for the entire period and all patient care services would be provided by the HSE. After 25 years, the facilities will be handed back to the HSE.

The largest home, a 130-bed unit, will be built in Killarney, County Kerry. There will be two in Cork, a 50-bed unit in Midleton and a 105-bed unit in St Finbarr's in Cork City. A 95-bed unit will also be built in Thomastown, County Kilkenny, and 50-bed units will be built in Clonmel, County Tipperary; Ardee, County Louth; and Athlone, County Westmeath. Many of the units had dedicated space for those with dementia. Again, many more will be needed. The prevalence of chronic disease increases with age and a dramatically increased number of people living with dementia threatens to become a major issue for society and the State. There are projections that the number of people in Ireland living with dementia could rise to over 150,000 by 2046.

Amid all the fanfare about the new State investment, the reality was that each project was effectively a replacement for existing outdated facilities. In other words, the net additional bed numbers were small. The HSE needs not just to add additional capacity but to replace existing outdated properties. That is going to cost billions of euro. It's why foreign capital has been arriving, quietly, without attracting the flak that foreign funds building or buying apartment blocks have received. The questions are: how much more is needed, are we prepared to accept it if the foreigners are prepared to provide it, and if they will build new additional facilities instead of simply buying existing stock?

PART 9

OWNING THE SOLUTIONS

If we are going to build the new towns and suburbs that the growing population requires, or redevelop the so-called 'brownfield' sites in our towns and city centres, then it is the private sector that is well placed to deliver both the capital and the labour. The question for the State is whether it works with that sector to provide a sufficient quantity of new housing and amenities with acceptable standards, or stands in its way, a desire for perfection being the enemy of progress.

THIRTY-TWO

AN IDA FOR LAND

The State decided that it was not going to fund the building of new houses and apartments in any significant number via its many local authorities. That put it under pressure to either finance or build by other means, including investment in third-party outfits or the establishment of State bodies that the government would finance.

The Irish Strategic Investment Fund (ISIF) – as the successor to the National Pension Fund – was not set up to invest in housing exclusively, but it committed to investing €950 million in housing to deliver 16,000 new homes by an unspecified date. It invested €500 million in Activate Capital, a company that financed the construction but not the purchase of residential developments, some of which were ultimately sold to international funds. ISIF put €25 million into Irish led-fund Avestus Capital Partners and €140 million into the Irish Life Residential Property Fund, which assembled a portfolio of hundreds of suburban apartments in Dublin. Avestus had been buying homes to rent since 2014, but in 2018 set up a €290 million fund with Nordic and German institutional investors, as well as the ISIF as another partner. The ISIF also promised to invest €500 million in five regional cities – Cork, Galway, Limerick, Waterford and Kilkenny – to create new places to work and live while regenerating the city centres.

The State also established Home Building Finance Ireland as a state agency to make cheap loans available to developers who couldn't get money from the banks. The Housing Agency set up the Croí Cónaithe fund of €1.25 billion to give payments to developers if they would complete apartment schemes for owner-occupiers who said they would otherwise be unable to complete developments. It was to be used in the major cities to ensure that existing planning permissions for apartments would be used by the end of 2025. It included a subsidy for the construction of high-density developments and encouraged height.

Money wasn't just aimed at developers but at non-institutional buyers, too. One State initiative to help people purchase a new unit was the First Home shared equity scheme for affordable housing. It was run by the department of housing in association with the main lenders and was designed to help first-time buyers bridge the gap between the available deposits and mortgage eligibility and the price of a new home in a private development. Oddly, the First Home Scheme was not regulated by the CBI. Michael Stanley of Cairn applauded shared equity as a necessary countermeasure for house buyers disadvantaged by the CBI's mortgage rules but said it would have a marginal impact: he believed only thousands of people would get it when the need was for hundreds of thousands. Garvey said that while it and the Help-to-Buy scheme would provide 'much-needed support for home-buyers, they won't be enough to solve Ireland's accommodation crisis if planning policy and the planning system do not get the reform they need so urgently'.

Developers said that the scheme – which could provide 30 per cent of the purchase price, allowing the buyer to pay a mortgage on just 70 per cent for the first five years, before then paying a low interest on the 30 per cent thereafter – was slow to catch on with Irish people but was very popular with the new Irish looking to settle permanently. At the time of writing, some were also hopeful that the government would introduce rules to waive development fees, VAT and other charges levied by the State that make up about 30–40 per cent of the final price of an apartment, making them affordable to individual and family buyers. The quid pro quo is that the apartments would not be sold to institutions.

The programme for government agreed between Fine Gael, Fianna Fáil and the Green Party in 2020 to secure a coalition government included a provision for cost-rental schemes, where tenants would be charged rates that were above council rates but below market ones. The rent would be based on the cost of building, managing and maintaining the homes, rather than on market rates, and tenants would be offered long-term leases. The issue – given expensive building costs – was how much cheaper this would make the units compared to those rented on the open market. However, rental price increases would only be in line with increased costs of maintaining the housing, not the market increases. The cost-rental model was aimed at people whose income is too high to qualify for social housing but who struggle to pay market rents or get a mortgage to buy. It was to compete with the private rental market, not to be an expanded version of social housing.

And then there was Project Tosaigh, which was given a €1.25 billion budget to buy land with planning permission with the potential for more than 150 homes, or projects where development had stalled largely due to a lack of finance. There were objections to 'rewarding' private developers by buying from them or guaranteeing their future profits through a 'forward purchase agreement' to acquire homes with payment on completion, as long as they could then be provided to tenants or buyers at affordable prices. Critics were promised that there would be no room for very expensive, higher-end properties and no big profits for developers who would be happy to be able to finish developments and cover the costs they had incurred. Project Tosaigh aimed to secure 5,000 homes in a series of bids over five years. In just three months it received offers of more than 100 large sites, giving it the potential for 15,000 homes, if it were to agree to all of the submissions. While this was welcomed it raised concerns as to why so many builders were willing to divest assets in which they have made considerable investment already, either by securing planning or, in some cases, laying foundations and more. It raised suspicions that the scheme was acting as a 'bailout' for financially overextended developers.

Project Tosaigh was run by the Land Development Agency (LDA), which was nominated also as the State's main developer of cost-rental homes (as well as being central to activating dormant planning permissions). The LDA was promised initially in 2016 as part of the government's Rebuilding Ireland campaign but it wasn't established until two years later, in September 2018. Its remit was to deliver more than 25,000 cost-rental and affordable housing units by 2026 and it was also given a longer-term target of building 150,000 homes over 20 years, using mainly State land but with a mandate of 'strategic land assembly' of private sites, if necessary. It was first suggested that up to 60 per cent of the houses it would build could be for the private market, with 30 per cent assigned to affordable housing and 10 per cent to social housing. This was quickly changed following opposition to the idea of State land being used for private house acquisition, being condemned as the privatisation of public land.

There was hyperbolic talk of the LDA having as big an impact on housing as IDA Ireland had on foreign direct investment by business. John Moran returned to public service when he agreed to become the LDA's first part-time board chairman. He saw this as his chance to implement some of his big visions for the future of housing in Ireland. His proposed pilot project was for Colbert Station in Limerick city centre, the terminus for trains arriving in the city and home to its bus station. The project was to become a big disappointment to him: by the time plans for the Colbert Station Quarter were finally announced in 2022, Moran was long gone from the LDA, frustrated by its lack of ambition and speed of implementation, something he blamed on complacency and insufficient care on the part of public servants.

The Colbert plans announced in 2022 were to provide up to 2,800 affordable homes, parklands, commercial spaces and pedestrian and cycling infrastructure on over 50 hectares of State-owned lands along the rail network, over the following 20 years. Announcing it, Minister for Housing Darragh O'Brien boasted of 'the largest ever transfer of State land for housing'. But as far as Moran was concerned, the scale of the project was nowhere as ambitious as he had formulated. 'Colbert should be closer to the 10,000 people than 5,000 – or even 15,000 – because you want a dynamic neighbourhood rather than a suburban neighbourhood downtown. To grow the city by 50,000 people you actually need ten Colbert stations. According to the population projections for Limerick, all of those areas have to be delivered in 15 years.'

Moran was also despairing of the time-wasting that has taken place. 'The lack of development at Colbert Station is an example of inertia. We can rebuild the city around the old railway lines that have been left to go into disrepair and therefore have a really sustainable city,' he argued. 'The vision I would've had at the time would've been 20,000 people, all living two minutes away from the main train station, which connects them to Dublin and Cork and the five minutes-walk from what is considered to be the city centre.'

Moran believed the LDA was underfunded as well as insufficiently ambitious. The government's Housing for All strategy allocated €2.5 billion in capital funding for the LDA, with a provision for a €1 billion top-up in 2025. That was nowhere near enough. It was also slow to get going, despite the enthusiasm of its CEO, the former NAMA executive John Coleman. In September 2021, Coleman promised the LDA would become the State's biggest builder within five years, far surpassing the output of Cairn, Glenveagh and Quintain, producing about 2,000 homes per year.

While he wanted local authorities to 'use us to provide social and affordable housing', and said the LDA would 'create an affordable homes sector, especially a cost rental sector that's sustainable and capable of covering its cost', he experienced a distinct lack of support from other elements of the State who were either indifferent or deliberately obstructive. Some showed a reluctance to hand over 'their' land or to cede responsibilities for development that they had demonstrated themselves unable to implement previously.

His was a lofty ambition because it was 2022 before the LDA started construction on its first scheme of 597 social and affordable homes at Shanganagh, in south Dublin, the first homes due in 2024. The LDA lodged applications for more than 2,300 homes on State lands on sites in Dundrum, Balbriggan, Skerries and Naas. 'We can build a home in 16 to 20 weeks but some sites are taking four to five years to get through planning,' lamented Coleman.

He was running into the same planning headaches as private developers. One of the big test cases was to be the speed with which the LDA would deliver a major project on the site of the former Central Mental Hospital at Dundrum in Dublin 14, less than 500 metres from the Windy Arbour Luas stop and 800 metres north of Dundrum Town Centre in a near €400 million scheme. It was a perfect location for new housing and a potential good use of now-redundant land, but it ran into the usual sustained campaign of opposition from locals who argued about the impact on already heavy road traffic in the area. The LDA responded by promoting access to the Luas and cycling opportunities as an alternative. It wanted initially to build over 1,000 units but agreed, after consultation, to scale that back. Eventually, in May 2023, permission was granted for 852 homes over nine blocks ranging from two to seven storeys in height. Its immediate fear was that development would be delayed further by more legal challenges. It will be 2025 at the earliest before anyone will live there.

The LDA ran into more trouble when it wanted to build a 22-storey tower as part of the construction of 700 homes on the site of St Teresa's Gardens, the 1950s DCC flat complex that had become known for drug use and criminality. The site is beside the former Player Wills cigarette factory and Bailey Gibson packaging plant on the South Circular Road, very close to the new National Children's Hospital where Hines has been delayed in its plans by objections from local residents. The LDA took on the redevelopment on behalf of DCC, which retained ownership of the site. The plan was for 30 per cent of the homes to be retained for social housing, and 70 per cent used for a cost-rental scheme aimed at middle-income people who couldn't get mortgages. The Donore Project includes four buildings, ranging in height from two to 22 storeys to 'ensure an efficient use of the council's lands in this established residential neighbourhood in a highly sustainable location'.

St Teresa's Gardens was earmarked for regeneration in 2005, but the plan was scrapped in 2009 because of the collapse of the property market. In 2013, the council announced plans to demolish ten of the 12 blocks of flats and refurbish two blocks to create 52 modern apartments, and to build 54 more houses and apartments. Demolition began in February 2015. Construction of the houses eventually began in December 2018. Sinn Féin led local protests about the LDA 'taking over' the site, saying it preferred DCC to do the building because 'the LDA hasn't proved itself'. Well, DCC had proven itself incapable.

The LDA ran into objections wherever it turned. Opposition politicians were furious that the government planned to allow the sale of local authority sites to the LDA without requiring approval from elected councillors. Sinn Féin's Eoin O'Broin argued that local authorities should be directly funded instead to build large volumes of 'good quality social and affordable homes' on such land rather than allow the potential for private developers to make large profits. 'There is a misconception that the LDA is going to end up privatising State land, and develop non-affordable market housing on State land,' said Coleman. 'I want to stress the LDA is squarely focused on social and affordable housing. The idea that we will be engaging in flipping sites on to make a profit is simply not the case.'

The core idea behind the LDA seemed a good one: let it assemble as much State-owned land as possible and either build on that land itself or hire contractors to do the job for it. It was easier said than done, though; it was slow to assemble that land and even slower to build upon it. In 2022, the limited progress made included ground being broken at the former HSE site, St Kevin's Hospital in Cork, with the first of 265 homes to be delivered in 2024, six years after the LDA came into existence. There is planning permission for 817 homes at a site at Castlelands in Balbriggan, 345 homes in Hacketstown in Skerries, and 219 homes at Devoy Barracks in Naas, County Kildare.

In mid-2023, to speed things up, it decided to buy privately owned large sites with planning in place for over 200 units near the five main cities. It had to do something because an early 2023 report on the use of public land was loaded with so many caveats that it suggested a timeframe of more than ten years to achieve its objectives. The Report on Relevant Public Land identified 83 State-owned land sites and assesses them as having the development potential for up to 67,000 homes in the medium- to long-term. But the LDA offered only up to 9,760 of the potential homes as deliverable over the following five to ten years, subject to the land involved being made available, due diligence and the planning process. These were classified as Class 1 public lands because they should be the easiest to deliver. A further 17,440 homes were proposed on Class 2 sites, considered to have medium- to long-term potential, and a further 39,710 on long-term, Class 3 sites.

Much of the land suggested was 'brownfield' and located in existing urban centres with strong public transport links, suitable infrastructure, and other facilities nearby. All were state-owned and either under the control of local authorities, other State bodies or commercial semi-state companies. However, it was clear that many of those State owners would fight tooth and nail to keep them for their own uses, or to be sold for the highest price possible so the money could be used for other things.

The LDA report admitted that much of the land was fully or in part in operational use and that some might require rezoning. By including sites in the report, the LDA didn't state that they should be developed, but rather invited the government to consider their potential use for affordable and social housing delivery. In certain cases, the government can require public bodies to sell certain land sites to the LDA if a decision is made that it's in the public interest, but the likelihood of anything that might involve confrontation seemed slim. The LDA has no power to compel landowning bodies to provide access to land for the purposes of carrying out development. It was also conceded that even on the most straightforward sites it might take six years before housing could be delivered. Coleman said that the LDA is 'committed to working closely with the public bodies involved to find common ground for the release of land for affordable housing purposes and for the common good'. The reaction from many State entities to the report was anger: the LDA fielded written complaints from the HSE, complaining about the inclusion of ten sites that it said 'did not appropriately reflect their utilisation by the HSE and its funded agencies or our future plans to develop these sites'. An Post and ESB also complained that they regarded lands included in the LDA report as essential to their future plans. The most strongly-worded objection was from Shannon Foynes Port Company, complaining about the inclusion of lands it owned in the Limerick docks area.

Almost bizarrely, there were also arguments that the LDA's mandate was too narrow. Approved housing bodies (AHBs), which were charities and associations that provided social housing with donations and State funds, suggested that the LDA should acquire privately-owned sites adjoining State lands, something which has been too expensive for the AHBs to do. 'For the LDA to be a true land-management agency its ability to acquire private land should be on an equal or comparable footing to its ability to acquire public land,' the National Economic and Social Council (NESC), an official agency relied upon by the government for advice, suggested. It said the LDA should have the capacity to pursue CPOs for land in the private market, 'especially given the reluctance or incapacity of local authorities to do so'. But that would have meant a change of status for the LDA from a commercial agency to a non-commercial public agency if it were to comply with EU state aid rules.

There are also limitations to the finance available to the LDA. One way for it to raise additional finance would be for it to set up and manage funds in which outside institutions could commit investments. Coleman said this would probably require a portfolio of about 10,000 homes to be put together to attract such an outside investor, with any sum paid by a pension or investment fund being used to fund the delivery of other housing. Any effort to do that, however, would almost certainly be derailed by political objections to allowing quasi-private ownership of publicly owned or supplied housing. Because no matter how big the need is, perfection in policy is required.

THIRTY-THREE

EMPTY EYESORES: VACANCY AND DERELICTION

It is one of the great shames of modern Ireland that we have as many as 180,000 properties unoccupied at a time when we have a housing shortage and when rents and the asking prices for new and second-hand properties are beyond the reach of many. Dereliction is often an eyesore too, an aesthetic blight on how cities, towns and countryside should look.

Vacancy and dereliction are easily observed but not so easily quantified. Local property tax returns, census results and GeoDirectory all offer different vacancy results. There's little or no data on land use or available floor space either, or the monitoring of the condition of buildings. Identifying the ownership of vacant buildings can be hard too. Revenue Commissioners data shows that people paying the LPT own a total of 57,000 vacant homes, but it is estimated that the number of vacant properties is about 180,000, especially if vacant units over retail units and offices, both in use and not, are taken into account.

We talk about creating new supply to meet the demand – building about 35,000–50,000 new units of houses and apartments each year – because that would stop seemingly ever-rising prices. But what about revitalising and rejuvenating properties that exist but are unused at present as part of the solution? Some of the vacant properties may look as if they are in a desperate state, fit only for demolition. However, experts say that many could be restored and repaired, providing solid accommodation. It could be done at a reasonable cost in many cases because water, sewerage and electricity connections could be re-established with relative ease. Finding builders to do the work can be a problem, and it may be a financially better use of construction workers to put them to work on estates or apartment blocks where a larger number of new units can be built more quickly. Some people might think there is better value to be had by putting money into something new rather than restored.

In Europe, a vacancy rate in urban and town settings of below 5 per cent is considered acceptable. Once it touches 11 per cent remedial measures are activated. Research in Ireland has estimated the vacancy rate in Tipperary town's centre at 31 per cent, 25 per cent in Tralee and 24 per cent in Dundalk. Sligo Town, Letterkenny and Ballyshannon in County Donegal and Ennis in County Clare all have rates approaching 20 per cent, and Monaghan Town and Donegal Town near 15 per cent. The rates vary from year to year, but Ballina in County Mayo, Mohill in County Leitrim and Drumshanbo in County Cavan have all varied at around 20 per cent. In many places, empty premises have been commonplace and taken for granted. It might not be unusual for a building to be lying empty for 15 to 20 years.

Jude Sherry and Frank O'Connor are designers who returned to Cork in 2018 after years of living out of the country. They set up a sustainable development research consultancy called Anois, but in their own time began blogging on social media about the dereliction and vacancy they observed on walking tours of Cork – a project that spread nationally and brought them to the attention of the Oireachtas Housing Committee. Invited to present to the committee, O'Connor described how 'dereliction is a pollutant that visually reflects the inequalities in Irish society' and 'a social crime'. He and Sherry argued that 'the most sustainable building is the existing one … Every building that can be saved is a building that doesn't need to be demolished and rebuilt.'

They have promoted the concept of 'meanwhile use'. This involves the use of vacant sites and buildings for outdoor gyms, art galleries, restaurants, shops, libraries and allotments while they await future development. They pointed to the successful prior use of the concept in the development of Temple Bar in the last century when DCC acquired buildings intended to be part of a large transport development that never materialised. The units were let on short-term leases for low rent. 'This flexibility and affordability attracted and facilitated many creative uses, and informally created a hotbed for a new cultural district which emerged and is still being celebrated as a tourist destination today,' Sherry and O'Connor said.

They have also worked with Alison Harvey, a regeneration specialist at the Heritage Council who has devised the Collaborative Town Centre Health Check (CTCHC) programme. This involves providing business groups in towns with methods to help identify and quantify issues affecting their town centres. Harvey's work is based on collecting information, such as footfall data, consumer sentiment, property uses, building ownership and environmental metrics like noise levels.

One measure that could be used is that of CPOs, forcing private owners to sell to an arm of the State, but these are regarded as difficult to enforce and expensive. Instead, Harvey and Anois have advocated compulsory sale orders (CSOs), which would allow private interests to buy properties owners have left vacant. A report by the Scottish Land Commission in 2018 decided that one of the reasons why some sites remain vacant for extended periods is that the owner has unrealistic expectations about the value of the site. 'This mismatch between the price the market would be willing to pay and the price that the owner may be willing to accept can lead to sites remaining unused indefinitely as the owner waits for the market to improve in the expectation that prices will improve,' it said. It suggested an auction process 'which would give all interested parties the opportunity to submit a bid reflecting their independent valuation of the site, CSOs would provide a mechanism for revealing the true market price of any given parcel of land, directly addressing this market failure.'

However, while some owners of vacant properties allow them to sit and spend no money on maintenance or improvement because they believe that in the future the property could be sold for a higher price than it could be sold for now, the reasons can be more complicated than that. There are examples of where that can happen, but only if land values are rising in an area by more than the income that could be raised from renting the building. A property loses value over time if it is going to become more expensive for new owners to repair and restore, even if overall values in an area are still rising. The latter may be unusual. Dereliction tends to happen in clusters, with one-off examples more the exception than the rule.

Sometimes buildings can be left because the owner has died and probate has proven difficult to process; there are plenty of examples of family disputes where pig-headedness means some would rather let a property rot than see other members of the family profit from its use or sale. Some owners have been in dispute with lenders. Some have no need for income and just let it sit there, useless. Others don't have the money or the wherewithal to hire an architect, make a planning application or raise the required finance.

In addition, barely a quarter of vacant or derelict properties in the Republic may be financially viable for renovation, even when State aid is available. A study by the Society of Chartered Surveyors Ireland (SCSI) published in early 2023 assessed 20 possible renovation projects, 13 residential/owner-occupier type properties and seven investor types. It found just five – three in Dublin, one in Galway and one in Cork – were financially viable to renovate, meaning the market value of the renovated property must be greater than the starting market value plus the cost of renovation.

The report found that while the costs of renovating a property depended on its type, size, condition and location, properties in more affluent areas were more financially viable to renovate as they commanded bigger market values. What were described as 'hard costs', the bricks-and-mortar element of construction, typically made up 87 per cent of the total costs, with 'soft costs', such as land, professional fees and VAT, making up the balance. The SCSI argued that it can be more difficult for borrowers to access funding for a renovation project when compared with new or second-hand homes; lenders are worried about things being more expensive than anticipated. It also suggested that building regulations, particularly those relating to fire safety and access and use, were too restrictive when it came to restoring older property units. It proposed that the State provide feasibility grants to help prospective purchasers assess the viability of projects.

There can be planning issues too, as many residential units above retail units may not have the required fire escapes and other safety requirements – and these may be too expensive or difficult to install.

In 2022 the Housing Agency hired consultants to advise local authorities whether commercial properties, large homes and hospitality buildings, such as hotels and B&Bs, can be repurposed for social housing. The focus was on acquiring large homes to house families, and on buildings that could be renovated and repurposed as homes. But such a process might also involve a waiving or simplifying of planning procedures that prevent or inhibit retail premises from being turned into homes.

The government's Our Rural Future report, launched at the end of March 2021, was a five-year plan designed apparently to make it easier for people to move from cities to live and work in Ireland's network of towns. It was to encourage remote working, revitalising rural towns and villages, jobs for rural Ireland, rural living, rural tourism and supporting existing communities. One of its remits was to put empty buildings back to use as both new homes and commercial premises, with 400 new shared offices proposed for civil servants. It specifically mentioned the conversion of pubs into new community spaces and co-working hubs, along with former bank premises.

The threat of tax may be one way of incentivising the owners of vacant properties and land to use them. Taxes aren't just about raising money for the government. They can be a signal that the government desires its citizens, or foreign owners of Irish assets, to behave in certain ways, to force actions for the common good. Taxing an unproductive asset forces a decision. Owners could still hold onto their properties – maintaining their constitutional rights – but they face a tangible financial cost for doing so.

Officials in the tax policy division of the Department of Finance claim there are actually very few vacant properties in the country, having conducted sample studies, and therefore little to tax, although a vacant property tax comes into effect from 2024 at a rate of 3 per cent. It remains to be seen if it is enforced more stringently than the separate derelict site tax. Local authorities can collect a 7 per cent levy from owners of properties listed on derelict site registers. On 31 December 2020, there were 1,456 derelict sites tracked by local authorities, with more than €5.4 million levied in fines during the year. However, records held by the Department of Housing show that only €378,763 worth of fines were collected. Cork County Council, for example, collected €10,000 of the €1 million in fines levied on landowners who control €20 million worth of derelict property. 'Local authorities aren't applying levies, they aren't collecting levies and they aren't resolving dereliction. That is the reality. Leaving houses to rot in the middle of a housing crisis is akin to hoarding food in a famine. It is wrong and it must be stopped,' Thomas Gould, Sinn Féin TD for Cork North Central charged.

But there are multiple problems when it comes to the operation of the planning process in solving all of that.

THIRTY-FOUR

NEW SUBURBS

As our population grows quickly, new suburbs in our major cities are emerging slowly. Despite the obvious need for new houses and apartments, particularly to accommodate the immigrants we need to fill jobs, there has been a tardiness in the approval by officialdom of the ideas offered by developers. Serviced land is available, but rows about how many units should be built and to what standard, how many social and affordable houses would be part of the mix and what prices would be charged for any units provided to local councils, means delivery of needed units has been far behind requirements.

THE POOLBEG SAGA

The saga at Poolbeg in the Dublin docklands, where Irish Glass Bottle once operated a large manufacturing plant, is one of the most shocking delays in the use of land, out of many examples. Its 25 acres of land were purchased in 2006 for €412 million by a company called Becbay, which was owned by McNamara, Derek Quinlan and a State agency, the Dublin Docklands Development Authority (DDDA), with loans provided by Anglo Irish Bank. It was one of the landmark overpriced follies of the Celtic Tiger era. NAMA appointed receivers and took control of the land in 2011 and 2012 – land that had been identified as highly vulnerable to flooding in coming decades because of rising sea levels caused by global warming. Nonetheless, the State identified it as a good location for major housing development; presumably, proper water defences will be put in place.

In May 2017, Minister for Housing Simon Coveney ordered the provision of State funding for 650 affordable homes, hoping this would win
over DCC councillors to approve the overall plans of 3,500 homes for the
area. To the government's frustration, however, DCC and NAMA – two
parts of the State apparatus – could not agree to terms on a 'commercial
agreement' for funding the purchase of the new units by DCC once
constructed. Instead, NAMA offered 80 per cent of the site for sale, seeking bids in excess of €125 million. To general incredulity, it was Johnny
Ronan, with backing from US investment firm Colony Capital, who
won the auction, and with a bid of nearly double the advertised amount
sought. Despite their previously toxic relationship, NAMA could not
deny Ronan the legal contract once he showed proof of funds. While
the near €250 million price was a financial 'win' for NAMA, it had
consequences: it immediately increased the price of all of the housing
units that would be built eventually on the site. It gave the new private
partners control over the process, too.

Ronan didn't win the contract on his own. He formed a consortium
involving Lioncor, a property development company jointly owned by
Oaktree and Dublin-based Alanis Capital. When it came to making
payment, however – which happened months later than the contracted
deadline – Ronan had a new partner replacing Colony: Oaktree itself.
The US investor was certainly enthusiastic. Charles Blackburn, its managing director and co-head of Europe for Oaktree Global Opportunities,
wrote to the government to say 'There is no other site in Europe like this,
based on a combination of proximity to the city, location on the bay,
connections to nature, etc.' He omitted to mention that views of the bay
will be restricted by the sight of hundreds of acres of containers used
at Dublin Port, the Dublin regional wastewater treatment facility and a
giant incinerator, much of which borders the site for the new housing.

Ronan and Lioncor offered to develop 3,800 homes on the strategic
development zone (SDZ) but over many years. The first phase was to

be of 1,448 homes and the second of 2,293 homes. The developers were required to deliver 25 per cent of the units as either social or affordable to comply with the SDZ conditions and statutory requirements. However, Ronan and Lioncor submitted indicative costs for social units that were about 50 per cent more than government-set unit-cost ceilings for two- and three-bed apartments. Then Ronan suggested the density of the site could be increased, to allow for between 5,000 and 6,000 housing units, through changes to unit mix (presumably increasing the number of smaller units) and building design. But that would require approval by the council's elected representatives and a new submission to An Bord Pleanála, delaying things further. It was rumoured that Lioncor was interested in reducing the number of housing units and using a chunk of the available space to build a private hospital for elective surgeries.

Even though long-term leasing by councils is due to be phased out, this is exactly what Ronan's consortium offered: the leasing of units for at least 40 years at rents more than 20 per cent below market value, with an option for DCC to then acquire the properties for a nominal price. It also contacted the Land Development Agency to see if it would agree to 'forward-purchase' homes that were yet to be built. Sinn Féin's housing spokesperson Eoin Ó Broin suggested that NAMA should be made to transfer its remaining 20 per cent holding to DCC. Just how that would have helped anyone remains highly debatable.

There was to be all sorts of toing-and-froing in the coming years, with offers and counter-offers as to how many houses would be made available for social and affordable housing and at what price. Even though Ronan's consortium received approval in early 2023 for 324 units as the first phase of the development, in May 2023 DCC refused planning permission for the second phase of the development, for 516 apartments made up of 143 build-to-rent apartments, 52 social housing units, 77 afford- able housing units and 244 apartments, over two blocks of four and 10 storeys in height on a five-acre part of the site. DCC refused permission after concluding that the scheme would, by itself and by the precedent it would set for other development, 'seriously injure the residential amenities' of future residents of the development. The 100-page council planner's report had issues with 'unacceptably poor levels of residential amenity', both in terms of the 'daylight/sunlight availability internally within the apartments and also within the courtyard spaces, providing a poor outlook for the courtyard facing apartments'. While it admitted the need for housing, it stated, 'This does not warrant poor levels of compliance with standards which have been put in place for the protection of the residential amenities of future occupants.' Concern was also expressed about the impact dogs being walked by residents would have on wildlife in the area; if that is the case, then it would seem that almost every possible development is at risk.

In June 2023, there was yet another twist. NAMA sold its remaining 20 per cent shareholding to Ronan, Lioncor and Oaktree, to the fury of locals and opposition TDs. 'This is a commercial asset of NAMA and we have got our own commercial objectives,' Brendan McDonagh, NAMA's chief executive said. 'We are legally obliged to act in the best interest of the taxpayer.' At last though, construction started.

CLONGRIFFIN-BELMAYNE

Clongriffin, about 10 kilometres northeast of Dublin city centre, was one of the first major casualties of the Great Recession as most of its main developers got into deep financial trouble and stopped building. There seemed no point anyway. Of the thousands of houses and apartments built, only about one-third were occupied in 2009 and many of the shopping and business units were vacant. Even the local DART station was not in use.

The original master plan for the 143-acre site in 2003, driven by Gerry Gannon, provided for 3,600 residential units. About half of that was achieved before the crash but the bulk of its infrastructure was put in place, including roads, a rail station, water and drainage, as well as social and community facilities at the 54-acre Father Collins Park. The

DART station was opened in 2011 and since then building has resumed.

Cairn Homes was one of the first back in and was joined by Twinlite, a company founded by Eugene Larkin in the late 1980s and where his sons, Rick and Michael, are now directors. Twinlite has invested about €650 million in its various developments around Dublin and has built almost 3,000 homes. At Clongriffin it acquired a major site with full planning permission from UK developer Hollybrook and financed it with money from the State-supported Activate Capital. UK firm Tristan Capital Partners came in as a joint venture partner and they developed two build-to-rent apartment schemes with more than 650 units.

Gerry Gannon wanted to fulfil his original vision. However, in July 2022 DCC recommended to ABP that it refuse planning permission for his €1.15 billion plan under an SHD, made up of 2,527 residential units for Belcamp Hall, Malahide Road. The scheme was to comprise 1,780 apartments, 473 houses and 274 duplex units. Gannon offered to sell 532 homes for social and affordable housing to Dublin and Fingal county councils at a price of €243 million, keeping 558 apartments himself to rent. However, DCC said deficiencies in the existing road network would render it unsuitable to carry the increased traffic likely to result from the development. The National Transport Authority said the proposed development wasn't served directly by public transport and the nearest bus stops, on the Malahide Road, were too far away for people to walk, leading to the potential for too much car dependency – as if new bus services would not be introduced. It said a new town with an anticipated population of almost 8,000 people couldn't be built without prior agreements for supporting infrastructure and services. It was chicken-and-egg stuff.

Sean Mulryan's Ballymore looked to become involved. It took an option to spend €40 million on a 27-acre site with planning permission for more than 1,800 homes, a 209-bedroom hotel and nearly 23,000 square feet of commercial space. But Ballymore withdrew from the deal in late 2022 when it became concerned about infrastructure provision in the area – a planning decision on the Clongriffin–Dublin city-centre BusConnects project, which was due in October 2022, was put off for nine months at least, denying residents a more efficient bus service – and the changing financial environment as interest rates rose.

In July 2023, the LDA moved to pay more than €40 million for Gannon's 24.7 acres, the first time it was to buy private land anywhere, albeit via NAMA. The plan was to spend about €1.2 billion building 2,500 'affordable' homes on this and neighbouring land it was also purchasing from a company called Barina, a family business owned by the Langan brothers, but also in the control of NAMA. The existing planning permission expires at the end of 2024 so the rush will be on to contract a builder and to get working before that.

ADAMSTOWN

Adamstown was one of the country's big pre-Great Recession plans. Located on the western outskirts of Dublin, on the train line to Cork and in close proximity to Lucan and to Celbridge and Leixlip in County Kildare, the plans were to build a town centre roughly the size of Drogheda with a population of 30,000, at a cost of €1.2 billion, one of the largest mixed-use planning applications in the history of the State. But less than 20 per cent of the 7,000–9,000 dwellings envisaged for Adamstown were built before the crash, even though a sizeable portion of the required infrastructure was in place, including a railway station, primary and secondary schools and a neighbourhood shopping centre.

Adamstown was allocated €20 million by the State to assist in providing key access roads and two parks, including a new road linking Adamstown to Celbridge Road and the N4–Leixlip Interchange. However, it was left to the private sector to fund the bulk of the infrastructure. Joe O'Reilly's Castlethorn said it had spent over €90 million, which took the burden off the taxpayer but meant a higher charge to buyers of its houses and apartments. O'Reilly tried to keep going and sold about 1,150 units in Adamstown. Castlethorn introduced a rent-to-buy scheme to entice occupiers and buyers, but even that petered out and work halted in 2014. There were rows with the local council when the latter reduced the number of houses that could be built in each tranche of the development from 800 to 600.

O'Reilly's loans connected to Adamstown land became part of the Project Clear portfolio of Ulster Bank loans. Some were bought by Cairn, who became a builder of three- and four-bed homes in the area, but the majority of these were acquired by John Grayken's Lone Star, which is how Quintain took things over.

Quintain (the construction offshoot of Lone Star) has been driving development in recent years, building premises for two major super-market chains, five restaurant outlets, additional retail units and a multi-storey car park as well as new housing at The Crossings, in a €500 million project. It owns 220 acres in the Adamstown/Lucan area, where it plans to develop over 4,000 new homes and about 23,225 square metres of commercial space. It has built over 1,000 homes so far, with over 85 per cent occupied by first-time buyers. However, it has begun selling to investors: the Dutch investor Orange Capital Partners teamed up with GIC, the sovereign wealth of Singapore, to spend €110 million for 279 apartments at The Crossings.

CLONBURRIS

Clonburris sits between Adamstown and Clondalkin, on about 750 acres of former farmland, 10 kilometres from Dublin city centre, on either side of the railway line that carries trains southwest of the capital. In 2001, the government earmarked it as a strategic corridor in the to-be-abandoned national spatial plan. In 2008 it was designated as an SDZ, the first one. The financial crash meant nothing happened and it was not until 2015 that the ideas were revisited.

The Clonburris project is being promoted now by South Dublin County Council (SDCC). Its website reads like a sales brochure from an estate agent in the Celtic Tiger years: 'Imagine a new Dublin neighbourhood with the perfect balance of urban living and open nature. Connected to the city by train and cycleway or greenway, and to the rest of Ireland by motorway and train – this is Clonburris: a community sustainably built on 280 hectares of canal-side parkland. Featuring exceptional homes that are designed to the highest quality, catering to every individual's lifestyle, and allowing neighbourhoods and communities to thrive – Clonburris is well designed for living well. Vibrant and multi-serviced urban centres with crèches, schools, healthcare, retail, and sports and leisure facilities are matched with numerous and vast open spaces like playgrounds, pitches and parks where the biodiversity of the area can be seen to flourish. These excellent amenities, unrivalled transport links and considered infrastructure will make Clonburris the place for everyone to be, to relax and to enjoy the best of modern Ireland in a brand-new town that's built to last.'

The Minister for Housing Darragh O'Brien spoke at its launch: 'Clonburris will be a well-designed town with over 8,700 homes, good transport links and vital amenities and services. Up to 2,600 of these homes will be social and affordable homes delivered by my department and South Dublin County Council.' Planning permission for the construction of four kilometres of roads, bus corridors, cycle lands and pedestrian routes is in place and the planned public transport infrastructure investment includes an electrification of the Dublin–Kildare railway line as part of the Dart Expansion Plan, as well as a high-speed bus to Tallaght to meet the Luas line. SDCC said the town's ultimate population will be between 20,000 and 25,000, similar to that of Naas, Navan, Wexford and Kilkenny City.

The reality is that it will be delivered by the private sector. Cairn is going to be the major developer in the area. Already owning 174 acres, it bought a further 97 acres from NAMA and O'Callaghan Properties in 2019 for €21.7 million.

CHERRYWOOD

Dún Laoghaire–Rathdown Council has not been as proactive in assisting with building at Cherrywood to the southeast of the city, at the
interchange of the M50 and the N11. Bordering the established areas of
Cabinteely, Loughlinstown and Rathmichael, southeast of Carrickmines
and northwest of Shankill, it was identified as Dublin's newest suburb
in 2010 and designated as an SDZ. By that stage, much of the land was
under the control of NAMA.

Cherrywood's history as a potential location for significant amounts
of new housing goes back to the late 1980s when Phil Monahan's
Monarch Properties bought 280 acres of what is now the site for
IR£10 million. Dunloe Ewart, a Dublin-listed property firm led by solicitor Noel Smyth, took over Monarch in 1998 and brought in British Land
as a partner, increasing the site to 412 acres. At one stage the land had an
assumed value of €1.2 billion, a sign of the madness of the time. Dunloe
and other developers with property in south Dublin, such as Johnny
Ronan's Treasury Holdings and Michael Cotter's Park Development,
contributed €15 million towards the €90 million cost of extending the
Luas line out to Cherrywood because of its potential.

Smyth lost control of Dunloe to Liam Carroll in the early 2000s,
after a *Bonfire of the Vanities*-style battle that also involved Dermot
Desmond and Paschal Taggart, an accountant from Northern Ireland
who became a major investor in property deals over a number of
decades. The planning process delayed things, and then the financial
crisis intervened and Carroll's empire collapsed in 2009 with debts of
over €1.2 billion. It left Cherrywood with nothing but an industrial
estate and the Luas stop.

The 2010 plans for Cherrywood as an SDZ were to build a new town
comprising more than 7,700 new homes, six schools, shops, cafés, three
parks and sports and leisure facilities, all to be serviced by four stops on
the Luas green line. Cherrywood is both close to the sea, visible from
various elevations, and at the foothills of the Dublin mountains, offering

a wide variety of social amenities. Cherrywood is 15 kilometres away from Dublin city centre but easily accessed by public transport. By car, it should take just over 30 minutes to reach both Dublin Airport and the Port Tunnel via the M50. It is eventually expected to have a population of 25,000 people, according to its promoters, led by Hines as the main developer.

Hines bought Cherrywood in 2014, from receivers working for NAMA and a number of banks, for about €280 million, working in conjunction with King Street Capital to secure about 60 per cent of the available building land. It recouped part of its money in January 2018 when it sold eight office blocks at the business park on the site to San Francisco-based Spear Street Capital for €145 million, and it also sold two lots in Cherrywood to Cairn Homes and 118 acres to Quintain, for which the Lone Star offshoot paid €120 million in 2019. Quintain plans to deliver 3,000 new homes in total and have 1,300 built by 2025. Of those it intends that 60 per cent will be available to buy at prices below the €500,000 threshold first-time buyers require to qualify for the government's Help-to-Buy scheme.

Hines also entered a joint venture with Dutch investor APG Asset Management in early 2018 to develop the second phase of Cherrywood: a €1 billion, 2.1 million square foot town centre development over 15 blocks, including 1,269 build-to-rent apartments, retail and office space and leisure facilities and all associated roads, streets and public spaces and services. The village is being built on a 65-acre site and is set to include 27 acres of green space and over 4,300 square metres of retail and civic amenities. The apartments in the blocks have been designed without internal corridors, which used to be standard for fire protection within units. Hines proved to the relevant authorities that the installation of a sprinkler system made them safer and that saved internal space. Just over half of the Hines residential units are two-bedroom in size and have been built to the most modern environmental specifications.

By early 2018, Hines already had done much of what was necessary to enact the master plan, providing the necessary infrastructure and services. It had set down 5.4 kilometres of roadways, installed water and electricity supply networks, constructed three brand-new flagship parks, Tully Park (similar in size to St Stephen's Green), Ticknick Park and Beckett Park (similar in size to Merrion Square), a state-of-the-art all-weather multipurpose pitch, six new tennis courts and a sports pavilion, four grass sports pitches, pedestrian footpaths, cycle paths, greenways and over 3,000 trees. It had gifted four new school sites to the Department of Education and started work on the town centre. And then the council came looking for money: €31.5 million for public infrastructure contributions.

After some debate between the parties, Hines brought the council to court – reluctantly given the need for an ongoing working relationship, but essential given the sum of money involved. Hines claimed Dún Laoghaire–Rathdown County Council had no lawful basis for the demand because Hines had received an express understanding and had a legitimate expectation it could offset the approximate €57 million costs of works completely against whatever development contributions would be claimed. It said the works were completed in accordance with the council's requirements and subject to its oversight. Hines claimed the council had said that if payment was not made, the ongoing development being constructed by Hines under the 2018 permission would be rendered unauthorised.

On the day the case was due to be heard, the council settled and Hines resumed its work. At the end of May 2023, the council finally took possession of, and opened to the public, the three major parks that had been built for it by Hines and all the things within them. It boasted how the 'facilities will be for the use of residents and clubs of the emerging communities in the Cherrywood area. The pupils of the six schools in the area will have full access to these facilities to support their sports programmes.'

But the press release from the council – full of quotes from local politicians, officials and the Minister for Housing – didn't tell the full story. Not only did it fail to mention how more than 90 per cent of the work had been done by Hines but it didn't tell how the majority of these facilities had been completed years earlier – before Covid – and that the council had refused to take them in charge. The public who could have been using these facilities had been made to wait until officialdom was ready.

THIRTY-FIVE

THE REGENERATION OF DUBLIN'S LIBERTIES

Many people loudly criticised the choice of location for the new National Children's Hospital, arguing that the land adjacent to St James's Hospital in Dublin 8 was inappropriate for a venture of such scale and ambition – inappropriate for many of the same reasons that a previously chosen site at the Mater Hospital had been abandoned.

Proponents of the Dublin 8 location, on the other hand, trumpeted the nearness to Heuston Station for people coming by train from the south and west of the country and of the Luas line running through the campus, and the benefits of being beside an adult hospital for ease of access to doctors there. Critics asked if people would really use public transport to get to a hospital and lamented the limited car parking for both staff and families of patients and the potential for lengthy traffic jams. They argued that a new site, preferably outside the M50, would allow for the construction of a more easily accessed hospital for people from all over the country, not just Dublin, and would be cheaper to build.

But there was less spoken about the reason for the government's decision: it would help with the rejuvenation of an ageing part of the city, encouraging people to live there. St James's Hospital is in the Liberties, an area that's home to about 25,000 people and which, since medieval times, has hosted traditional trades and industries, such as brewing, distilling, tanning and weaving, many now largely redundant. Many of the privately-owned houses are old and badly in need of renovation, especially with climate change considerations in mind, and much of the public housing has fallen into states of disrepair and contributed to serious issues of social deprivation. What the area surely needs is more modern housing, even if some locals complained about the 'gentrification' of the area when apartment blocks were built close to the Coombe Hospital prior to the crash.

GUINNESS IS GOOD FOR YOU

The Liberties is an area most readily associated with Guinness, and not just because of the vast brewery complex that draws its water from the River Liffey for the making of its famous stout. Guinness got a deserved reputation as a good employer and the family that owned it originally set up the Iveagh Trust to assist in the provision of housing and social services in the nineteenth and twentieth centuries. What it built is everywhere in the area.

In recent decades, the number of employees required to brew dropped enormously because of new technologies. The company received permission to invest €200 million in Ireland's first purpose-built carbon-neutral brewery for all of its beers and lagers at a greenfield site in Newbridge, County Kildare. Periodically there have been fears that production of Guinness might be discontinued on the site, that the board, now headquartered in London, would decide that the brand and not the product was the most important thing and that it could be brewed elsewhere. Fortunately, Guinness's sales increased internationally as volumes dropped domestically and the company committed to continuing at St James's Gate as it has since 1759. However, not all of the 50-acre site is needed for brewing.

The owner, now the multinational drinks company Diageo, has shown responsibility towards its heritage and use of the vast assembly of land. It established one of the country's most popular tourist attractions at the Guinness Brewhouse, including the Gravity Bar with some of the best views of the city. Diageo restored certain buildings, such as a former home of founder Arthur Guinness on Thomas Street, which had been built in the 1770s and is now offices. It also committed to the continued maintenance of the iconic St James's Gate at the entrance to the brewery, the picture of which has featured in so much advertising over the years. But Guinness had to find ways to reuse and repurpose vat houses, brew houses and cooperages that were centuries old while protecting the integrity of their structures.

Diageo applied to repurpose its Brewhouse 2 into a new Irish corporate headquarters. In 2017, it announced plans to redevelop 12 acres of its complex for housing, offices, shops and businesses, a genuine regeneration within walking distance of St James's Hospital and the new children's hospital. It awarded a contract to Ballymore to develop the Guinness Quarter as Dublin's first 'zero carbon district', reusing as many buildings as possible and installing renewable energy.

Ballymore had exited NAMA four days before Christmas 2016, having repaid €3.2 billion in debt. Ballymore was active in Dublin already, not just with Oxley in the docklands but with CIÉ on the development known as Connolly Quarter, to develop 741 new homes adjacent to Connolly Station in Dublin city centre. It demonstrated extensive relevant redevelopment experience in London.

It came up with a plan for 336 apartments, a hotel, a 300-seat performance space, a food hall and marketplace, commercial works spaces and more than two acres of landscaped public spaces. The homes would be available to buy or rent and social housing was included, possibly with the Iveagh Trust as a partner. Diageo said it consulted with more than 120 community groups, public representatives, local businesses and other parties. The Guinness Quarter may take up to 15 years to build, but it is an imaginative regeneration and badly needed. Planning permission was granted in July 2023.

Most of what is happening in the area is driven by private-sector interests. Harry Crosbie developed the Vicar Street venue as a smaller alternative to the Point Depot and brought many outstanding music and comedy acts there. He has planning permission for a hotel of 185 bedrooms and a rooftop bar and restaurant on a site next to Vicar Street but is willing to sell it for about €10 million. Others have built hotels in the area, including Denis O'Brien. There is a digital hub in the Thomas Street area, a cluster of small and innovative tech firms, particularly in digital and media, in a hub of rented shared space at reasonable prices and with State support. This has encouraged the return of independent retailers, small enterprises and tourism and hospitality operators. DCC upgraded the streetscapes of High Street, Thomas Street and James's Street. A new public park was added at Weaver Park on Cork Street and St Audeon's Park on High Street was refurbished.

NEW USES FOR OLD SITES

Guinness is bordered on one side by the River Liffey and on another by the Grand Canal. There's a site at Grand Canal Harbour previously owned by the UK construction group Laing O'Rourke, next to the Guinness Storehouse, on the site of the original Grand Canal terminus. It dates from the mid-1780s and was used up to 1960 when the last barge left the harbour with a cargo of Guinness. The original curved harbour warehouse and walls remain, along with three large water features celebrating the industrial history of the area. But it has to be put to use.

Marlet bought the site for €32.5 million in 2017. Its original plans were for student accommodation, an aparthotel and a hotel, but DCC blocked that after opposition from locals and the Irish Tourism Industry Federation (ITIF), which worried that a 13-storey tower would affect the views from the Gravity Bar at the Guinness Storehouse. In a move that showed there were alternatives to hotels and student accommodation, Marlet returned with plans for nearly 600 apartments, albeit build-to-rent, across five blocks ranging in height from three to 13 storeys. The plan included shops, restaurants, medical facilities, co-working spaces and a crèche. It received permission. It has been designed as a fully pedestrianised environment, with over half of its site given over to public spaces, including a large public plaza to be made available for open-air markets and events. Marlet announced in early 2023 that it had organised funding for the development with AIG and Activate Capital, the latter meaning that the State was actively involving itself, albeit indirectly, in a build-to-rent project. Activate was established in 2015 in partnership with Ireland's Sovereign Investment Fund (ISIF) and global investment firm KKR. It has stated that since being established it has lent more than €1.75 billion to its customers, 'supporting development projects with capacity for 19,500 new homes'.

Not far away, the Players Square development site consists of two former factories – the Player Wills cigarette factory and the Bailey Gibson packaging plant – on the South Circular Road over nearly 11 acres. The site was assembled originally by developer Ciarán Larkin, but his loans of nearly €100 million went into NAMA and he lost control of the site to Hines and Dutch pension fund APG in 2018.

Hines ran into a campaign of objections, legal actions and goalposts moved by the local authority that delayed building and pushed costs up, although they were settled in Hines's favour following a finding by the Court of Justice of the European Union (CJEU) in early 2023. A case had been brought by two local residents – who complained about the height of the development, its density and traffic implications – and the High Court's Mr Justice Richard Humphreys sent it to Europe in November 2021.

The first plan from Hines was to develop 416 homes, including a 16-storey apartment block, on the Bailey Gibson site. Hines was also granted permission for 732 apartments on the Player Wills site, retaining and incorporating the factory building, as well as building a 19-storey tower as the biggest of four apartment blocks. The size of the tower, even though 150 metres away from the nearest housing, and the intention to offer co-living in the refurbished factory caused controversy.

The three-storey factory, fronting onto the South Circular Road and built between 1924 and 1927 and significantly extended in 1935, is now a protected structure. DCC's conservation section described the building as a 'remarkable example of a purpose-built early twentieth-century factory building ... A modernist influence on the building's design can be seen in the flat roof and extensive glazing to all elevations while the render consoles and frieze to the 1920s storeys indicate an Art Deco influence on elements of the design.' The factory had an 'imposing presence on South Circular Road', creating a 'striking contrast to the predominantly domestic architecture of the street' but the use of brick 'allows harmonisation with the prevailing architectural composition of its surroundings'.

Hines said it originally had 'no intention' of developing a co-living scheme until the retention of the old factory was mooted. It wanted to retain only the front of the factory and complained that the council's own original plans for the site had not proposed its protection. 'The brickwork is not an artistic element. It is a building element and should be considered as a component of its architecture – not as art,' Hines said. It decided a co-living scheme was the only viable option, both economically and architecturally, because it meant it would not have to punch holes into the façade as it would have for offices or standard apartments or hotels.

The plans for the co-living scheme – one-third of the whole development – were approved by ABP; the application was made just days before Minister for Housing Darragh O'Brien signed his co-living ban into law. Brian Moran said he had considerable interest from the nearby hospitals where management thought that co-living, on a temporary basis, would be of great interest to junior doctors and nurses in training.

When it happens, if at all, remains in doubt. After the cases were won in Europe, Mr Justice Humphries rejected attempts by the initial applicants for a judicial review, but after an appeal against that, he decided in May 2023 to allow it. That meant a hearing at either the Appeals

Court or the Supreme Court and further delays and bills adding to the costs.

Beyond the Guinness factory, further up the Liffey, there is potential to transform the almost 180-year-old Heuston station and its 20 acres. CIÉ has spoken of 1,500 homes, as well as offices and retail space. It is part of the Heuston Gateway, which under the last Dublin City Development Plan was suggested as a western counterpoint to the city's docklands, with the potential for buildings of more than 50 metres (16 storeys) in height. However, Joe O'Reilly's plans for a 29-storey apartment block across the river on Parkgate Street, as part of that, seem unlikely to come to fruition for some time yet, if at all.

The early completion of the Heuston South Quarter, on the other side of the river from Heuston Station, also seems unlikely. The existing scheme comprises 266 apartments, offices and commercial space built by developer Padraic Rhatigan over four years, just before the 2008 crash. It has another 3.5 acres that attracted Henderson Park Capital, an English private equity company, which spent €222 million to buy it from Marathon Asset Management in 2018. However, Henderson Park looks to have overpaid so much for that and for Green REIT a year later that it will be reluctant to risk adding to its investment in Ireland for some time yet. Further encouragement for the potential of the area came when CK Hutchinson Holdings, controlled by Li Ka-shing, Hong Kong's richest man, paid €175 million to buy the former Eir headquarters from the US property group Northwood Investment. Eir subsequently decamped to cheaper accommodation in Citywest; it isn't known if CK Hutchinson knew of Eir's intention to move when it purchased the property and that it would need to seek a new tenant.

PROMISES AND BROKEN PROMISES

At Kevin Street, possibly the closest point in the Liberties to the city centre, about 300 metres away from St Stephen's Green, Shane Whelan's Westbridge Real Estate is looking to develop 571,671 square feet of office accommodation over two 11-storey blocks, alongside 299 apartments across three buildings of up to 14 storeys in height, a new public square and café, a crèche, a community space available to the public and a double-height extension to the existing Kevin Street Library. Consultants EY have estimated that his scheme will create a total of 7,645 full-time jobs and that the total economic impact of the redevelopment would be €1.9 billion.

Whelan bought the 3.5-acre site, the former Dublin Institute of Technology facility, for €140 million, the bulk of the money coming from New York-based high-net-worth family office investors (that is, privately owned companies entrusted to ensure generational wealth for already rich families). Debt finance for the deal was provided by Fairfield Real Estate Finance and a London-based lender called Greenoak, which was led by its Dublin-born vice-president Allen Crampton, a member of the famous building firm. GreenOak was also a major financier to Press Up Group. The site has been cleared but construction may be slow. Whelan's appetite for risk does not seem to have been diminished by the experience of his father, Pat, a former Irish rugby international player and manager and a member of the Munster team that famously beat New Zealand in 1978. As a former developer during the boom, he was the recipient of a Personal Insolvency Arrangement (PIA) that allowed him to write down almost all his debts, which at one stage topped €133 million.

But the most controversial building in the area, and the one that emphasises that private developers don't always deliver what they promise, is the Iveagh Markets building on Francis Street. It was built by Edward Cecil Guinness, the first Earl of Iveagh, who saw it as central to the Iveagh Trust's philanthropy for the 'labouring poor' and donated it as a gift to the people of Dublin. Designed by Fredrick G. Hicks, it was built to a very high standard, completed in 1906 and given to Dublin Corporation on a 99-year lease to be 'held and maintained' as a market. No change in use was to be allowed without the Trust's permission. It was made up of two linked halls, one a dry market where clothes and furniture could be sold, another a wet market for fruit, vegetables, meat and fish. There was a laundry complex for disinfecting clothes and places for people to wash in the time before the arrival of indoor plumbing. The building was constructed with red brick and granite and with its elegant pillars and fine detail was regarded as an outstanding example of Edwardian architecture and quality construction.

More than a century on and the building is in an advanced state of dereliction and unsafe. It is not in immediate danger of collapse but could get that way very soon if remedial works are not completed. When it closed in 1997 the market only needed minor work. But an assessment in 2018 put the essential repair bill at €13 million. Further deterioration since then, because of damage caused by wind and rain, and increased construction costs mean the bill now would be likely at least double. Nature has been reclaiming the Iveagh, a form of rewilding, as water penetrates, slates slip and vegetation grows. The hall's rusting pillars hold up an unstable balcony. Many panes of the glass roof are broken or missing as are the original white wall tiles. Much of the wood is visibly rotting. The laundry buildings and a tall brick chimney were demolished and have been replaced by a large, green, marshy pit instead of a hotel.

It is an enormous shame. In 1997, DCC closed the building but quickly came to a deal with Martin Keane, the owner of the Oliver St John Gogarty pub and Blooms Hotel in Temple Bar. He paid the council €1.4 million for the leasehold title on the condition that he pay a nominal rent, redevelop it and pay DCC a profit share of 6 per cent, rising to 10 per cent. The deal envisaged and allowed him to build a hotel. But he didn't build anything. He got planning permission twice but didn't act upon it, claiming problems with the property's title made it too difficult to raise the necessary finance.

Tired of the delay, DCC moved in 2017 to repossess the building. Keane refused and instead announced a new proposal to create an Iveagh Markets Quarter on the site, proposing a European-style food hall along with a public realm, flower market, distillery, cookery school, restaurants, music venue and studio space for artisan producers and craftspeople. The market building's adjoining sites would accommodate the construction of a four-star hotel, a three-star hotel and a youth hostel. Keane was already the owner of the large Mother Redcap's Tavern across the road from the back of the Iveagh, on Lamb's Alley, which had also been vacant for decades but which he now proposed incorporating into the hotel and retail complex. DCC rejected his final planning application in January 2020 as it didn't believe Keane had enough money to do as he suggested and that, crucially, his application was lodged 'without the council's consent as landowner'.

Enter Edward Guinness, the fourth Earl of Iveagh. Born in County Kildare, he grew up in Dublin but now lives in Suffolk, England, where he operates a 22,000-acre estate. He has always remained interested in the fate of the Iveagh Markets. 'The local community has been let down by the closure of a much-valued community resource,' he said. 'I am minded to uphold the wishes of my great-great-grandfather, as he created and gifted the facility to the people of Dublin. It is his tremendous generosity which led to the formation of the markets, which gave rise to many decades of the site's much-cherished civic purposefulness. So many people remember the operation of the markets with tremendous affection.'

Lord Iveagh took practical action. He went back to the original 1906 deed and invoked a so-called 'reverter' clause bringing ownership of the property back to him, as representative of the Guinness family, because it no longer fulfilled its stated use of being a market. It has been an expensive move for him because not only has he now had to pay for security at the site but he was sued by Keane, who claimed unlawful forcible entry. Keane also sought legal orders giving him possession. Lord Iveagh responded that the Iveagh Market is a protected structure and national monument that had been damaged and filled with waste while in Keane's care. Keane denied neglect and claimed he spent 'millions' in archaeological and legal fees. He also started legal actions against DCC for the planning refusal. A High Court judge urged the three parties to engage in mediation. They did for two years but failed to find a solution and ended up back in the courts. Meanwhile, early in 2023, DCC went to the government for funds to begin the necessary preservation of the roof. But much more money and compromise would be required to ensure this great building of Dublin's past can contribute to its future.

THIRTY-SIX

THE REGENERATION OF CORK CITY

My late father worked in the Marina Bakery in Cork, in the shadow of the R&H Hall mills and adjacent to the Dunlop tyre factory and Ford car manufacturer. The bakery, Dunlop and Ford all closed in the early 1980s (and R&H later), doing enormous damage to employment in Cork. In 1983, one of my teachers at the North Mon conducted a quick survey of the 37 pupils in my Leaving Cert class. There were 21 of us where nobody in our homes worked. The prospects for employment for many of us seemed dim.

Over the past decade, Cork has been transformed. The number of people working for foreign-owned companies in Cork county has doubled to almost 45,000. Apple has been in the city for over 40 years, Dell EMC has been there for more than 30 and other major employers include IBM, VMWare, Boston Scientific and a cluster of more than 70 international technology companies spanning cybersecurity, integrated circuit design, manufacturing and software development.

The Marina is still one of Cork's untapped assets, even if some of the land was used for smaller employers over the 40 years since those closures. Early in 2023, I walked from the GAA stadium Páirc Uí Chaoimh, at the far end of the Marina, up to the city centre. Nearly a decade earlier Michael O'Flynn had stood with me at the top of the Elysian, Ireland's tallest apartment block (which he later surrendered to Blackstone as part of reducing his debts) and pointed out the vast expanse of land that he believed could become a major new hub for the city, all within walking distance of the city centre.

O'Flynn is now helping the Cork County Board deal with the massive debts that accumulated in the partial rebuilding of the GAA stadium when two new stands and a new pitch somehow cost about €100 million. Those debts are forcing the GAA to use the stadium for conferences, events and concerts, such as Ed Sheeran's in 2022 and the first-ever rugby match when Munster played South Africa. Beside the ground is the venue for the smaller Marquee concerts that have become a staple of summer in Cork. Further up the river, towards the city, property company Urban Green operated by Tom Coughlan, runs the Marina Markets on the Ford site. Between those locations, the starting work has begun on the Monahan Road extension to allow for over 1,000 residential units on the former Ford distribution centre, to be built by Glenveagh in its first major venture outside of Leinster. Marina Park is also to include woodland, marshland, meadows and water features 'to provide a high-quality realm, [that will] help deliver the vision for the city docklands'. It will be five times the size of the city's Fitzgerald's Park on the Mardyke.

Cork City Council and the LDA are cooperating on a plan for the Marina that could lead to 6,500 new jobs and, more importantly, a multiple of that number living in the area. The Cork City Docklands Delivery Office is to use almost 146 hectares of land along the north and south quays, and down as far as Tivoli on the northern side of the River Lee, in a plan aimed at creating 29,000 jobs and homes for 25,000 people, a 'town within a city'. The population of Cork City is targeted to grow by 50 per cent, to more than 300,000, by 2040 and much of it should be in the city centre area instead of continuing the expansion into the suburbs. The government committed to investing €353.4 million in the scheme, under the Urban Regeneration and Development Fund. It is envisaged that Cork Docklands will attract further private sector investment topping €5 billion over the next 20 years.

Much will depend on the private sector, though.

O'CALLAGHAN PROPERTIES

O'Callaghan Properties (OCP) – now run by Brian following the death of his father, Owen – has been one of the most active developers in Cork for nearly half a century. In the city centre, O'Callaghan senior developed the Merchant's Quay shopping centre that fronts onto Patrick Street, the Opera Lane shopping precinct that also connects to Patrick Street, the nearby Paul Street shopping complex, the Half Moon Street and Lavitt's Quay office developments, Lancaster Gate, a high-end apartment development near University College Cork, and in the suburbs the vast Mahon Point shopping centre. Although in NAMA, OCP completed the Navigation Square development of four separate buildings with 360,000 square feet of office space near the City Hall. In 2018, Deutsche Bank bought OCP's NAMA loans, appropriately named Project Lee, for €300 million.

OCP has plenty of land in the Marina area, having bought 32 acres from Origin Enterprises, for €47 million, to take control of a complex of grain and flour mills and warehouses, and also the former Goulding's fertiliser factory. It has applied to demolish the 90-year-old R&H Hall silos, two buildings over 33 metres in height that dominate the skyline after they were found to be suffering from structural issues that apparently made a viable repurposing of them impossible.

It is expected the project will involve ten buildings, ranging in height from two to 14 storeys, to provide more than 92,000 square metres of development space, including 25,000 square metres of public space, as well as 1,325 apartments, offices, retail space, a cinema and a 130-bed private hospital run by French group Orpea. This will involve the restoration and repurposing of the derelict Odlums mills on Kennedy Quay, which has not been in operation since 2009. It was designed along traditional nineteenth-century lines but is in a good position to be restored while retaining all of the fabric at the front, rear and side façades of the original building. It's estimated the entire development will cost over €350 million although it will be delivered in phases, construction of the first 300 apartments due to begin in 2024 to be completed two years later.

The economics of apartment building in Cork are not favourable, however. They cost as much to build as in Dublin but the number of people commanding the salaries in Cork who could afford to buy new apartments is limited, as is the number who could afford the rents that would be necessary to cover developer's costs. This may explain why one of the bigger plans for adding accommodation in the Marina, courtesy of developer John Cleary, was shelved. He proposed building 201 build-to-rent apartments on the site of the old Carey Tools building, almost across the road from the Goulding's site, on Albert Quay. This would have involved building two residential blocks of nine and 12 storeys and a landmark tower of 25 storeys. He also proposed restoring a railway house and terminus building from a long-gone train line. Initially, he pointed out that there had been no major apartment development since O'Flynn's nearby Elysian of 2008, but then he changed his mind and opted to apply for a 16-storey commercial office block instead, building work on which has not started. Controversially, he demolished the Sextant pub near the Marina complex in 2020 as part of his bigger plan. The Sextant was a landmark building that some people loved looking at from the outside even if they didn't frequent the inside.

JOHN CLEARY DEVELOPMENTS

Cleary has been one of the more dynamic figures in the reinvigoration of Cork this century. He set up John Cleary Developments in 1996 and completed retail, commercial, industrial park and data centres worth more than €600 million in Cork, with another €320 million in value under construction at the time of writing. He kept at it during the Great Recession: his €70 million project at City Gate Park in Mahon is one of the country's largest open-plan office developments and, at 280,000 square feet, the biggest built in Ireland during the recession.

He sold two of the blocks to Irish Life in 2013 for €40 million. Cleary now has 35 multinational tenants across his buildings, where over 5,500 people work, and arguably has done more to regenerate the city centre than anyone else. The One Albert Quay scheme overlooking the River Lee near the City Hall was sold to Green REIT and this encouraged Cleary to build another office project at Penrose Dock incorporating two-century-old buildings, over 24,000 square metres.

He doesn't just deal in new buildings. The South Mall and Grand Parade are full of beautiful old buildings on the outside, some of which have fallen into disrepair and disuse inside. Eventbrite, the global ticketing and event company, is now Cleary's tenant at 97 South Mall, a landmark Italianate building that has hosted AIB and the *Irish Examiner* over the years. Built in 1865, it was extensively renovated and re-let in 2020 after a decade of vacancy. JCD installed lifts, cables, telecom systems and server rooms into a period building with protected features, and in just six weeks turned an old-fashioned if beautiful building into a modern office for a twenty-first-century digital company.

One of the most successful post-recession developments was the construction of The Capitol, a development of retail and office space on the site of an old cinema, with frontage onto both St Patrick's Street and Grand Parade. It takes in space beside the English Market, the scene of one of the memorable parts of Queen Elizabeth's visit to Ireland in 2011. The 100,000 square foot scheme has three retail storeys and two floors of office space overhead and included the refurbishment and reopening of one of Cork's favourite pubs, the Oyster Tavern, renovating a protected structure. Cleary gambled about €6 million on buying the site in 2015. Two years later, redeveloped and four-fifths let, with Facebook subsidiary Oculus taking the top floor, he sold it to Real I.S., a German property company, for €45.6 million.

It was a start for Patrick Street. It may be Cork's prime retail street, but despite the widening of the footpaths to provide a much more pleasant pedestrian shopping experience the numbers coming into the city centre have disappointed retailers for decades. Some traders have complained about the reduced access for cars, but that is not necessarily the issue. The vacancy rates on the street are commonly at 20 per cent with some shops, particularly on the western end of the street, too small for many retailers. Worse, the very large landmark Roches Stores department store, which then became Debenhams, has been closed for years, although Elvery's, the Mayo-headquartered sportswear company owned by the Staunton family, agreed to purchase the building for about €20 million in May 2023. However, things have improved for the area since the city council put considerable investment into the adjacent Cornmarket Street and the Coal Quay, which was made possible by reworking existing buildings for modern purposes. The decision to allow pubs, cafés and restaurants to offer outdoor facilities during Covid-19 also brought people back into the city.

PLANS AND OBSTACLES

Cork city centre is a curious mix. In February 2023 I took an early morning run through the city centre I knew so well as a child, teenager and young adult, observing the dereliction in many parts and yet the tremendous refurbishment and refreshment in other parts. There are many clearly dangerous buildings, structural supports visibly in place to prevent them from falling as too many have in recent years, particularly around the North Main Street and Washington Street area, but there has also been work done to rebuild some buildings. There are far too many vacant shop units, but would they be used if refurbished because of their size and because the custom simply might not be there?

It's not that the City Council lacks ambition. It wants to put a public plaza in front of the former Beamish and Crawford brewery and has multi-million euro plans for the entire area of French's Quay, Keyser's Lane, Proby's Quay, Crosse's Green, Clarke Bridge and Hanover Place, all in the shadow of the centuries-old Elizabeth Fort and St Fin Barre's Cathedral, with improved pedestrian and cycle access. But 12 years after planning permission was first granted there's still a hole in the ground on South Main Street in Cork, at the old Beamish and Crawford brewery with its beautiful street frontage, where a major events centre should be built. The question is when. Opposite the legendary former Sir Henry's music venue, sadly long closed, the plan is for an indoor stadium with a capacity of 6,000 and, importantly from a business point of view, the ability to host conferences of a larger size for which the function rooms in the city's many fine hotels cannot cater.

The delays in getting it built have become epic. Planning permission for the original decision was granted in 2011, but not enough government funding was provided. The economic recovery meant it was 2016 before the sod was turned, with the goal of having everything done and the facility open by late 2018. The plans were then changed in August 2018 for a redesigned €80 million project, with about half of the money coming from the State and the rest from global concert group Live Nation and building contractor BAM Property.

A woman called Eleanor Hunter delayed proceedings with objections; she wanted the inclusion of a Viking heritage centre together with a replica longboat moored alongside the River Lee. She worried that the centre would cover the foundations of 19 wooden Viking homes from the eleventh and twelfth centuries, discovered only between 2016 and 2018 when excavation work was being done on the site for the new centre. All that has been built to date on South Main Street by BAM is a major new student accommodation facility. At Sullivan's Quay, BAM got permission for a 12-storey cylindrical tower hotel plus a six-storey office block on the former premises of the Revenue Commissioners that was sold to it by the OPW. A 200-bed hotel on 22,000 square metres of riverbank was planned to stand in view of BAM's event centre on South Main Street, but while work was due to commence in 2020, it remained an undeveloped site in early 2023.

There are legitimate worries as to what will be done and when. For the past number of years, promises of a Cork city light rail system – a

Luas line – have been underway. The proposed locations for many of the 25 stops have already been outlined, with a route running for 17 kilometres from Ballincollig on the western suburbs of the city, through Bishopstown and Munster Technological University, moving onto UCC on the Western Road, going into the city centre, briefly going north of the river to Kent station before returning south to the docklands and onto Blackrock and then Mahon. It's estimated that the project would cost €1 billion but it'll almost certainly be higher if it happens. Already there is a sense of drift, of announcements and promises being made but delay after delay in implementation, with the suggested deadline of 2030 for completion looking ambitious despite the obvious need.

TOWER HOLDINGS

Two of the most ambitious suggestions for Cork's development have come from a Kerryman who made his fortune in New York. The first is a proposed 15-storey office building on a narrow, 3,000 square foot site next to the city's bus station at Clontarf Street. Positioned on a triangular-shaped, brownfield derelict site it is to be called the Prism, inspired by the landmark 22-storey Flatiron building in New York.

The second, for which permission has been granted, will be Ireland's tallest building, a 34-storey tower on the site of the former Port of Cork building on Custom House Quay on a site formerly owned by the Cork Harbour Commissioners. It is to include a five-star 240-bedroom hotel as well as food and beverage outlets along with a distillery in the accompanying listed bonded warehouse. At about 140 metres the centrepiece tower would eclipse the 79-metre Capital Dock in Dublin as Ireland's tallest building, as well as Obel Tower in Belfast, which at 85 metres is the tallest on the island of Ireland. It would be about twice the height of the nearby Elysian, which had become KW's only asset outside of Dublin when it paid Blackstone €87.5 million for the tower in April 2018.

The Kerryman behind the project is Kevin O'Sullivan from Ballinskelligs in south Kerry, owner of Tower Holdings. The basis of his wealth was Navillus Contracting, one of New York's biggest construction companies, which he founded more than 30 years ago with his brothers, Donal and Leonard. It was involved in the construction of the magnificent 9/11 Memorial and Museum in New York City and had multimillion-dollar contracts on several other major skyscraper projects in New York. However, his brother Donal and sister Helen were convicted in 2021 in a federal court in Brooklyn of charges of wire fraud, mail fraud, embezzlement from employee benefits funds, submission of false remittance reports to union benefits funds, and conspiracy to commit those crimes. They appealed to have the verdict overturned, but it may have contributed to a delay in building work in Cork.

The Irish Georgian Society, An Taisce and a local artist had all objected to the proposal, worried there would be inadequate protection to the fabric of the Custom House and Bonded Warehouses, which were built between 1814 and 1849. ABP acknowledged that the development, entailing modern design interventions and a tall building, will have a significant impact on the urban and visual character of the area, with the 34-storey hotel introducing 'a major new element visible in key views'. But it said it would retain the maximum amount possible of surviving historic fabric in situ and noted that without redevelopment, the risk of dereliction increases. 'It will be prominent and will attain primacy in an emerging cluster of high buildings at this transitional location between the city centre and docklands,' ABP conceded. 'The juxtaposition of the new and the old provide for visual interest which would add to its visual attractiveness.'

Cork City Council Chief Executive Ann Doherty supported the plan and said it was working 'to create a city of sustainable urban growth and a true counterbalance to Dublin – a city that can strike a sensitive balance, that reflects the past while embracing the future'. She also said she was 'heartened to see an opening up of the bonded warehouses to the public and a visitor centre that celebrates our unique maritime heritage'.

If the Tower Holdings hotel does not happen, there is also concern for Tetrarch's plans for a 165-bedroom budget hotel over seven storeys at 7, 8 and 9 Parnell Place, Deane Street, and Oliver Plunkett Street with a protected frontage of nineteenth-century warehouses adjacent to the bus station and alongside the Prism office tower site. Preparatory work started on the site but quickly stalled. Tetrarch has done little with a site at Parnell Place, beside the city's main bus station, that it bought from Cork City Council (CCC) in December 2017 despite announcing plans to develop 'a hip new urban budget hotel concept aimed at the millennial traveller'. The property comprises two warehouse buildings and a vacant adjacent site, but all appear untouched.

BAM has developed a six-acre site at Horgan's Quay, near the Kent railway station, a site that had been the source of a major controversy involving Minister Michael Lowry in the mid-1990s. For years it contained little more than disused railway lines, but BAM and Clarendon Partners spent €160 million on building three office blocks and 237 apartments as well as bars, restaurants and shops, as part of an income-sharing arrangement with the landowner, CIÉ. It has created a new economic district and an eastern entrance to the city centre. Apple is among the companies to have taken space there.

UNIVERSITY COLLEGE CORK (UCC)

As UCC grew beyond the capacity of its beautiful Western Road/College Road campus – there were about 6,000 students there during my time between 1983 and 1987, there are now 21,000 full-time students – its Cork University Business School (CUBS) has decided to move into the city centre, just a 15-minute walk away. First, in 2018, it opened a Centre for Executive Education at the refurbished Savings Bank on Lapp's Quay, at the eastern corner of Parnell Place. It had been built in 1842 and, like several other buildings that distinguish the South Mall, has a classical façade and a banking hall with stucco decorations and fittings of Spanish walnut. The premises were bought by CCC for €850,000 in

2014 and then sold to UCC two years later for €1.4 million, one arm of the State selling to another.

Thia Hennessey, the Dean of CUBS, had bigger ideas for the old Brooks Haughton builders-providers site at Copley Street in the city centre, which had been bought by the Dairygold co-op in 2008 for €15 million and for which it had gained planning permission for an office development. It is directly across the river from the College of Commerce and close to the School of Music and Hennessey wanted a six-storey building to dominate the riverscape at the city end of South Terrace, extending to 15,675 square metres and catering for 4,500 students and 225 staff daily. It is to include a 350-seat lecture theatre, teaching and research spaces and a restaurant. UCC provided Dairygold with a €2.25 million profit in 2019 when it bought the site. Planning permission was granted in May 2023.

Cork, where I still visit regularly, is a city centre that divides opinion dramatically: some see it as growing and thriving and others see it as contracting and failing. It clearly needs investment and delivery upon promises once made is a major issue; it is a city that is often let down. But if the country is to be more than just Dublin, and if we are to have regional cities as the centres for balance, as official plans desire, then investment in cities like Cork must be made.

PART 10

OWNING THE FUTURE

There are basic things the country needs to function properly and that, to ensure that they are provided, must be in State ownership: water, roads, public transport, electricity, broadband, seaports, airports and even banks, are among the things that come readily to mind. But the list of what the State needs to own, and what it can finance, is debatable and is often compiled on ideological rather than pragmatic assessments. Some State assets get to be regarded as the family silver, ownership of which should never be surrendered. But silver gets tarnished if it isn't treated properly, and there is no point in having silver on display in a glass cabinet if there's an emergency; there may be times when it is necessary to smash the glass, remove the contents and sell them, even if the best price possible isn't attainable. Even in good times the rapidly growing population of the State and its changing demographics may require more spending on essential infrastructure than the State can afford, and may mean the involvement of the private sector in the financing of assets for the public benefit.

THIRTY-SEVEN

SELLING THE FAMILY SILVER

The Convention Centre Dublin, overlooking the River Liffey on the North Docks and possibly the most distinctive piece of architecture in the area, is sometimes mistakenly referred to as the National Convention Centre. Built on behalf of the Office of Public Works (OPW) by Treasury Holdings during the boom years – at a cost of over €400 million – it is widely assumed to be a fully State-owned building, particularly as it was used during Covid restrictions as a temporary home for Dáil Éireann, its vast concert hall allowing for social distancing between TDs. It was where Micheál Martin was sworn in as Taoiseach and was the venue for one of the main events in honour of Queen Elizabeth of the United Kingdom when she came on a State visit in 2011. But essentially it is owned by the giant American private equity firm KKR.

Or at least it is owned by the UK firm John Laing Group, which in turn is owned by KKR. John Laing describes itself as a leading international investor and active manager of core infrastructure assets. In 2023, it completed the purchase of a 25-year contract to operate the Convention Centre Dublin. This was one of three major Irish infrastructure assets it purchased from the Irish Infrastructure Fund. Included in the deal was Towercom, described as Ireland's largest independent telecommunications tower company, with a nationwide portfolio of 409 towers used by all the major mobile network operators to provide their signals. Also included was Valley Healthcare, Ireland's largest primary care centre operator and developer, which leased its 20 centres to the

HSE. The price was not disclosed but the assets were valued at around €1 billion apparently.

Despite its name, the Irish Infrastructure Fund (IIF) is not owned by the State. It was established by Irish Life Investment Managers (in turn owned by Canada Life since 2013) in 2011, to seek out opportunities from a planned fire sale by the government of up to €3 billion of assets. In an effort to hedge its bets, the State itself became an investor in the IIF, putting about €250 million into the fund as the largest of about 30 investors. The money came from the remnants of the National Pension Fund, now known as the Irish Strategic Investment Fund (ISIF).

John Laing boasted that the acquisition was the largest single investment in its history, all underpinned by long-term contracts with the State. 'We are also excited by the chance to invest in Ireland, the fastest-growing economy in the eurozone and a country where we expect to see a pipeline of further investment opportunities,' it said.

FIRE SALE

Many other State assets were sold in the aftermath of the boom. The government put the National Lottery up for sale in 2012 and promised the proceeds would pay for the construction of the National Children's Hospital. Only about half of the €405 million raised from the sale to the Ontario Teachers' Pension Plan was transferred for that purpose and the cost of the hospital soared beyond €2 billion. In 2023, the Canadians sold the business to the French gaming company Française des Jeux for a reported €350 million, despite only ten years of the twenty-year licence being left.

The gas and electricity supply business of Bord Gáis, including the Whitegate power station, was sold to the British public company Centrica for €1.1 billion, although the network itself remained in State ownership. It was a case of needs must, because the sale in 1999 of Eircom, the State-owned telecommunications company, was regarded universally as a disaster. It hadn't just lost money for many small shareholders, it also provided incredibly easy riches for big investors who traded ownership of it, including the likes of George Soros and Tony O'Reilly, and also the staff who got to own a big chunk of the business. Eircom then went bust at a time when it was not making adequate investment in expanding telecoms infrastructure, such as broadband.

The once proud national asset, renamed as Eir, passed into new ownership in April 2018, with French billionaire Xavier Niel taking 64 per cent of the company and hedge funds Anchorage and Davidson Kempner the balance. Together they paid about €650 million to take control of Eir and over the next four years, the shareholders received nearly €1.75 billion in dividend payments. Niel's share was €858 million because part of the remainder of the money was used to repay the debt the funds had provided to finance the acquisition. Meanwhile, controversy continued to dog the slowness of the nationwide rollout of broadband by the new company – National Broadband Ireland – given the contract to provide to rural Ireland what Eir and other private service providers wouldn't.

One way that Eir raised money for shareholders was by selling part of its fibre network to infrastructure funds. The unwillingness or inability of Eir to expand broadband throughout the country as quickly or widely as wanted prompted the government to seek others to do so. Its National Broadband Plan was a response to enormous rural pressure politically to deliver high-speed broadband to every premises in the country, the biggest-ever telecommunications project undertaken by the State. NBI said it would design, build and operate the network using a combination of State subsidy and commercial investment. As it happened, almost all of the money was risked by the State but those who set up the company made substantial profits out of doing so – once they had won a competition for the contract that became mired in controversy and cost Minister for Communications Denis Naughton his job when his secret meetings with lead bidder, Boston businessman David McCourt, were disclosed.

The plan was to provide high-speed broadband to nearly a quarter of the population in about 570,000 homes, farms, schools and businesses, mainly in rural Ireland, who were doing without. It was a plan that was to fall well behind schedule; while NBI blamed Covid difficulties for the delay, the Department of Communications felt that told only part of the story. But if the rollout of services was slower than expected, the speed with which the investors exited was much faster.

When NBI signed its contract with the State in 2018 it was owned by: Oak Hill Advisors, a US hedge fund; Granahan McCourt (GMC), an investment vehicle run by David McCourt; Tetrad, controlled by the family of the late US billionaire Walter Scott who had been a close friend of McCourt's; and Twin Point Capital, a specialist telecom private equity firm. Oak Hill had 49 per cent, while the others shared the balance. The State guaranteed the provision of up to €2.7 billion if needed, but the investors agreed to contribute €223 million, mainly through loans with very little in equity, a common practice in so-called private equity deals. It wasn't revealed until late 2020, and then by a report in the *Business Post*, that McCourt had invested just €116,000 in equity personally. Ownership was structured and held in Luxembourg, apparently largely for tax reasons.

It came as a surprise in 2022 when Oak Hill and Twin Point sold to Asterion, an experienced Spanish infrastructure investor, giving it 80 per cent of the company. The Spaniards paid €425 million, although the State received €43 million of that money as part of a contractual provision that should give it three more payments over the next 20 years based on the performance of the company. Granahan McCourt remained on board, presumably to take its profits at a later date. The hope is that Asterion, as the lead operator, will speed up delivery.

WATER WORKS

There was a determination that our water infrastructure would not fall into private ownership. The government decided in 2015 that the gas, electricity and water networks must remain in national ownership. This was a response to the public campaign – organised under an anti-austerity guise by political parties of the left – against the government's plans to raise revenue by charging the general public for home supplies.

Irish Water (renamed Uisce Éireann in 2023) came into being in April 2013, to centralise the water services under the control of local councils. The government limited Irish Water's income to fund necessary future investment on behalf of all of us, making it dependent on State funding by not charging homes. Decades of underinvestment in the national power grid and public water infrastructure by successive governments was causing very serious problems and those fed into our housing issues. The underinvestment can be blamed partly on a lack of ambition or understanding of the needs emerging, but it was largely down to money – and also to complaints by people who didn't want to do what was necessary for overall good because of local concerns.

The River Shannon is a national asset, not a regional one. There is an opportunity to use part of its flow to provide much-needed water to Dublin and the Leinster region to cope with population growth. At 224 miles in length, the Shannon is not just Ireland's longest river, it is longer than any in Britain. It drains the Shannon River Basin, which has an area of 6,512 square miles, approximately one-fifth of the island. It flows generally southwards from the Shannon Pot in County Cavan before turning west and emptying into the Atlantic Ocean at the Shannon Estuary, with Limerick standing at the point where the river water meets the seawater. The river represents a major physical barrier between east and west, with fewer than 35 crossing points.

The first suggestion of diverting part of the flow came in 2011 when Dublin City Council (DCC) published a plan to supply up to 350 million litres of water a day from Lough Derg to Dublin city and region. Nothing came of it. In 2016, the Parteen Basin in Tipperary, to the south of the lough, was chosen by Irish Water as the proposed site of extraction. Water would be pumped to a break pressure tank at Knockanacree, near

Cloughjordan in Tipperary, to be gravity fed from there by a 170-kilo-metre pipeline to Dublin. It was projected originally to cost €1.3 billion and posited as the best way to ensure a sustainable water source for both Dublin and major towns in the midlands, providing an additional 330 million litres of water a day that Irish Water said will be needed by 2050 when the region's population will likely be 2.1 million.

Irish Water engaged with the public before making a formal plan-ning application but received hundreds of objections from groups like the River Shannon Protection Alliance and the Fight the Pipe campaign, representing 500 landowners along the route. Emma Kennedy, a former corporate lawyer at London firm Clifford Chance, was one of the most formidable protestors, motivated by the proposed pipeline crossing her husband's family farm in County Tipperary. She argued that the pipe would simply pump water into the city's leaking mains. Irish Water said the future needs of the eastern and the midland regions 'cannot be met by fixing leaks alone', even if leakage in Dublin is 'unacceptably high'. It admitted 207 million litres of water were lost daily in the greater Dublin region, a leakage rate of around 36 per cent. While investment was made in replacing damaged pipes, new leaks sprung across 9,000 kilometres of waterpipes, many of them dating to Victorian times. The age and condition of pipes, poor performance of certain pipe materials, soil conditions, length of the network and 'lack of investment in water infrastructure over the past 150 years' created something of a crisis. It estimated existing raw water sources for the Greater Dublin Area would be at capacity by 2025, and worried that extreme weather events, such as drought in summer or multiple bursts and water shortages following storms or snowfalls, would crash the system.

Irish Water is spending billions of euro every year to bring the water and wastewater network up to a basic European standard after decades of underinvestment by local councils before its establishment as a national body. It completed a major upgrading of the wastewater treat-ment facility at its Dublin docklands location but is awaiting permission for another major plant at Clonshaugh, in north Dublin, which would get rid of wastewater many miles out to sea.

Developers claimed Irish Water was struggling to connect new houses and was responsible for the delay in some building work. The Construction Industry Federation (CIF) claimed 'chronic delays' in connecting new housing developments to freshwater mains and wastewater systems added €6,000 to the price of new homes. Galway was cited as the worst area for delays in water connections, but areas on the outskirts of county Dublin, such as north Wicklow and east Meath, were also badly affected. The developers received support from the Housing Supply Coordination Task Force for Dublin, established in 2014 to track residential development and identify supply-related issues. Its 2021 report stated that 19,980 homes in Fingal County Council's jurisdiction were held up because they were 'dependent on Irish Water investment'. It also noted 4,400 homes were held up due to the need for Irish Water investment on sites in the Dún Laoghaire–Rathdown area.

WASTE DISPOSAL

There are just three landfills still in operation in Ireland where waste is disposed of underground. Bord na Móna operates the largest landfill in the country, at Drehid in County Kildare. However, Ireland outsources much of how we deal with our waste. We produce about 1.7 million tonnes of municipal waste every year but export about a fifth of it to incinerators in Germany and the Netherlands for processing. We could have a major 240,000-ton waste-to-energy incineration facility at Ringaskiddy in Cork, but Indaver has sought permission unsuccessfully for the past 20 years for an investment that could cost it over €175 million. In September 2022, the Supreme Court refused an application by local activists to appeal a High Court order of the previous June to allow ABP to review planning again.

The Belgian company had an incinerator at Duleek, County Meath, and Dublin had a large plant at Poolbeg in the Dublin docklands opened by US-based Covanta. Together, they produce over 90 mega-watts of electricity but could do so much more. As home heating bills soared from early 2022 because of the impact of the Russian invasion of Ukraine, a great opportunity to reduce bills was lost because of the failure of the State to put district heating schemes in place, particularly from the Covanta plant: it was producing enough waste heat to fuel 50,000 homes in the nearby area. Instead heated water was pumped into Dublin Bay.

AER LINGUS

Aviation – and the provision of access onto and from the island – is always a sensitive issue for Ireland because of our lack of a land con-nection to either Britain or continental Europe. For generations of Irish people, the presence of Aer Lingus was regarded with some pride. Established in April 1936, here was an airline owned by the Irish State on behalf of its citizens, a flag carrier going around (part of) the world, with its distinctive livery highlighting our presence. There were better, more tangible reasons too: it brought much-needed international connectivity to the rest of the world, especially to the USA in the post-Second World War era. It encouraged and facilitated foreign direct investment and brought in much-needed tourism revenue. That the vast majority of those Irish people could not afford the fares charged – or flew only on the most special of occasions – was conveniently ignored, at least until Ryanair came along, a privately-owned company that made getting on and off the island more affordable.

Every time Aer Lingus got into financial trouble it went to the gov-ernment for large sums of money. When it needed money to expand for commercial reasons, the government was reluctant to provide it. Its early twenty-first-century CEO Willie Walsh – whose cost-cutting actions were credited with saving the company from extinction in the wake of the aviation crisis caused by panic after 9/11 – offered to buy the company from the State in 2004, but was rewarded by unsubstantiated and unwarranted claims from Taoiseach Bertie Ahern that he was trying to 'steal' the company and 'shaft' the workers.

Eventually, in 2006, Ahern's government sold a majority of shares by way of a stock market flotation, deciding it was preferable to sell a State asset to faceless international institutional investors instead of identifiable Irish individuals who might be seen to profit. The sale put a value on the airline of over €1.1 billion. To widespread horror, Ryanair immediately swept in to buy 16 per cent of the newly available shares and offered to buy the rest, putting a value on the airline of nearly €1.5 billion. Both the company and the government rejected O'Leary's approach on competition grounds, but also as undervaluing Aer Lingus. This immediately led to accusations that the government had sold too cheaply.

The sale of the remaining shares in Aer Lingus came relatively late as part of the government's post-crash, Troika-enforced drive to raise cash through asset sales. In 2015 the State sold its remaining 25 per cent shareholding in the airline for €350 million – which put a valuation on Aer Lingus of €1.4 billion, a little less than Ryanair had offered in 2006. The buyer was IAG, a company that included British Airways and Iberia among the airlines it owned and had Qatar as a 10 per cent owner, a figure it has since increased to 25 per cent. IAG's boss was Willie Walsh. The government justified the sale by saying it had secured 'important guarantees in respect of Ireland's future connectivity, particularly to London Heathrow, and on the maintenance of Aer Lingus' iconic brand and of its head office in Ireland'. The future of the 23 Heathrow take-off and landing slots controlled by Aer Lingus was regarded as essential to national interests. Even as a minority shareholder, the government had kept a veto over the use of the slots, valued at the time at €900 million. The sale of the remaining shares to IAG involved a legal right to veto a subsequent sale by IAG of any of the slots. It also guaranteed their use to service routes only to Ireland, but only for at least seven years.

Covid, and its impact on aviation globally, threatened to change things for Aer Lingus. In 2021, Lynn Embleton, the company's CEO, said: 'The centre of gravity of Aer Lingus, I want it to be Dublin.' This may have been the first time many people thought it was in doubt. The business lost over €700 million in 2020 and 2021 and IAG had to provide €900 million in additional capital, something the State would have been hard-pressed to do at the time had it remained as the airline's owner. Aer Lingus also took a €150 million loan from a state agency, the Irish Strategic Investment Fund (ISIF), on terms that were not disclosed.

But questions arose as to whether too much had been given away in selling Aer Lingus to international interests. Aer Lingus now operates to the US and Barbados out of Manchester – flying over Ireland. Ryanair of course flies hundreds of routes daily that do not involve Ireland, but it does emphasise that Aer Lingus is not ours any more in the way Irish people liked to think of it. It is the eighth biggest operator of transatlantic routes, however.

Some assets remain in State control but the issue of land in private ownership that could be useful to the State is one that affects Dublin Airport.

It remains one of the enduring images of the crash. In 2010, on the day before the Troika arrived at Dublin Airport to take control of the nation's finances, then Taoiseach Brian Cowen went to the brand-new Terminal 2 to attend its official opening. He discovered that Ryanair boss Michael O'Leary had gone there first and stolen the attention of the waiting media.

In advance of the cavalcade of chauffeur-driven state cars, a hearse pulled up at the entrance to the new terminal. Out stepped O'Leary, dressed in an undertaker's garb of black tails, white shirt and black tie, and sporting a small moustache (in support of the Movember campaign for the Irish Cancer Society). A coffin, draped in the national tricolour, was produced and ushered inside, to the mirth of some and the horror of others. 'It's a statement of modern Ireland. A big bankrupt property development. It's a new place to welcome IMF executives,' the cosplaying O'Leary gloated to the waiting media.

The cost of the terminal was the subject of considerable dispute: was it really a symbol of excess and waste or was it a necessary investment by the State with future benefit in mind? A few years later the Commission for Aviation Regulation produced an official estimate that the total cost of Terminal 2 and its associated projects had come to €923 million, 20 per cent more than the €771 million allowed by the Commission when the project was approved in 2007.

The DAA rejected that, claiming what the regulator described as 'associated projects' were actually 'a collection of developments not part of Terminal 2'. It said the overshoot was just €28 million. However, it then added 'project and planning fees', which it said brought the overall spend to €745 million. That was a pretty significant 'add-on' and it was hard to believe that it somehow was not noted in the original budget.

O'Leary's problem wasn't with having a second terminal, per se; he had campaigned for one to cope with the growing traffic at the airport. His issue was with the State-owned DAA constructing and operating it, believing it would be a gold-plated effort that, after an expensive overbuild, would result in excessive charges to airline customers. In fact, he had offered for Ryanair to build and operate Terminal 2 itself at one stage – an offer the government did not take up because it did not want what it regarded as a key national asset in private commercial ownership. Ryanair has never operated out of Terminal 2 since it opened, but while Terminal 2 struggled to attract the number of customers promised in its early years it turned out to be a necessary piece of State-owned infrastructure. It even included an underground Metro station ready for completion in the basement, should the train line ever be built (as promised, yet again, by the government in 2023 for what seemed like the umpteenth time).

More than most sectors of business, aviation suffered enormous financial losses because of Covid as the numbers travelling by air were restricted by lockdown policies. However, the rebound after reopening exceeded expectations and by 2023 the DAA expected over 30 million passengers to pass through Dublin Airport in the year. There were projections of 40 million people per annum by the end of the decade, then rising to 50 million, as airlines used the extra capacity provided by the investment in a new second main runway of more than three kilometres in length, at a cost to the State of €320 million.

That created its own problems. The existing planning permission at the airport only allowed the two terminals to cater for a maximum of 32 million passengers a year. O'Leary campaigned in 2023 to extend the number of gates operating at Terminal 1. But even after such an extension, capacity at the terminals could quickly reach their maximum. O'Leary has indicated Ryanair would support a Terminal 3 as long as it is not run by the DAA.

All of this was predicated on the assumption that near-exponential growth in passenger traffic at Dublin Airport would continue. That made a few assumptions for the coming decades: continued national economic growth (more than likely, even if there will be blips along the way); a continued lift in inward tourism numbers (assuming hotel beds being used for emergency immigrants get back to normal use); more outward journeys (a safe assumption given the growing population and the desire of Irish people to travel); use of the airport as a hub for onward connecting long-haul flights (an ambition of the DAA and airline owners such as IAG); and the introduction of sustainable aviation fuel (which is a more controversial assumption). Little consideration seemed to be given to the likelihood of restrictions on international air travel as a way to combat the emissions that aviation contributes to global warming. It also assumed that the regional airports will not grow as a counterbalance to Dublin and that they will not suck business away from the capital.

All of this made a parcel of land adjacent to Dublin Airport, its ownership and its value, very pertinent. Ulick and Des McEvaddy have owned 123 acres of land adjacent to the airport since 1996. The brothers were considered multi-millionaires because of the success of their in-air refuelling business, Omega Air, which serviced the US military for great profits. Ulick loudly demanded, on many occasions, the right to build a privately-owned terminal to link with the airport runways. He was always denied, despite friendships with many leading politicians.

By 2023, and in his retirement years, he gave up his ambitions as a developer – and combined his land with that of neighbouring landowners Seán Fox, and Brendan and Orla O'Donoghue, to offer 260 acres for sale. Their three adjoining lots are located between the north and south runways and near the control tower. The land has obvious potential for airport use at some future point and is zoned by Fingal County Council for that purpose. But what is the land worth without planning permission for a terminal or other uses? Is it something that the State needs to own, or to control who else owns it?

The McEvaddys couldn't make any promises to potential buyers that the land could be used to build a terminal. The vendors said the lands were 'essential' to the airport's development, but that was a sales pitch. The DAA said the priority should be on new transport links with existing terminals rather than 'speculative projects' on the other side of the campus 'that aren't required in the medium term and are devoid of transport links and other necessary airport services'. That was a pitch to bring the price down.

Apparently, the DAA had made an offer in 2017 of about €20 million to take control of the McEvaddy portion of the land for 'secondary' airport activities – but the brothers had looked for an extra €100 million on top of that. The McEvaddys noted how a car-park site near the airport – but not within the campus itself – had reportedly sold for about €1.6 million per acre when the DAA bought it for €70 million. This showed the value of land for car parking, but there was no way car parking would be allowed on this site for access reasons, and no use other than a terminal would justify a high transfer price.

However, by offering the land for public sale, the McEvaddys have forced the DAA and/or the government towards doing something.

Somebody else might buy it – possibly even a foreign sovereign fund – but will the State want to spend a small fortune on something that might remain as farmland for decades? Or will it take a longer-term view and have the land in reserve for use at a future date without then having to impose a compulsory purchase order?[12]

12   The State doesn't want to go through the embarrassment again of what happened when it bought a farm, at Kilsallaghan in north Dublin in 2005, for almost €30 million, or €200,000 an acre. The land was to house a brand new 1,400-capacity prison called Thornton Hall but, instead, ended up being rented to a farmer for grazing rights for just €200 per month. On top of land costs, another €30 million-plus was spent on additional land purchases, road access development costs and the provision of water, telecommunications and sewerage services, as well as legal and 'consultancy' fees for a prison that was never built.

THIRTY-EIGHT

GREENING OUR ENERGY

A nation's independence and prosperity depend on the supply of energy and the cost of it. The electrification of Ireland in the 1920s was possibly the most transformative practical element of our new-found independence. The establishment of the ESB as a State-owned producer of energy – harnessing the power of the River Shannon and new technology to make electricity at the dam built at Ardnacrusha and distributing it to the entire country – was one of the new State's greatest achievements. But as the country developed, the population grew. The demands for power supplies increased the need to import fossil fuels and created dependencies. Events like the oil crisis of the 1970s brought economic carnage to Ireland as we struggled for supplies and to afford what we could get. A new generation discovered this in 2022 when Russia invaded Ukraine and supplies of gas from Russia to the EU dropped dramatically, increasing the price of natural gas sourced elsewhere.

Many European countries responded by quickly building terminals to store and distribute a different form of gas, liquified natural gas (LNG), which came from other geographic locations frozen and then liquified before being restored to its original condition at the point of use. LNG is cleaner than other fossil fuels, but it is not clean enough for environmentalists, especially if imported from fields where the controversial process of fracking – effectively drilling by way of explosion and upsetting the existing land formation – was used to extract the gas.

Ireland didn't have existing LNG capacity and decided wilfully not to put it in place. An American company, New Fortress Energy, was willing to spend €650 million to install an LNG plant on a 128-acre site in Kerry, where the imported gas would be fed onto the Shannon–Foynes gas pipeline. The location itself was uncontroversial: on the southern side of the Shannon estuary between Tarbert and Ballylongford in County Kerry, near Tarbert's ESB oil-fired station, closure of which has been deferred, and the huge Moneypoint coal-burning generator just three kilometres across the Shannon, which is due to be kept open beyond 2025 despite its massive carbon output, it being as bad a fossil-fuel contributor to carbon emissions as imaginable. Even so, the government refused to implement an approval.

The irony of the government's deliberate inaction was that it was Micheál Martin who had made the first announcement of the proposed terminal in 2006 when he was Minister for Enterprise. Oil company Hess Corporation was granted the original permission by ABP in 2008 but abandoned the project after a long delay over regulatory issues. Hess spent €67 million but never got to construction before its permission expired. It sold the land to brothers Paddy and John Power and their Sambolo Resources who, in turn, sold it to New Fortress Energy in a deal that could be worth over €20 million to them if the project goes ahead. New Fortress fared little better despite loud support from locals throughout the Shannon Estuary and nearly all political parties. There were a series of legal disputes which went first to the High Court and then to the European Court of Justice because of complaints brought by the Friends of the Irish Environment.

The New Fortress CEO Wesley R. Edens wrote to Martin, by that stage An Taoiseach, in 2022 to claim the LNG terminal was 'necessary' to support 'intermittent' renewable energy sources in Ireland. He said the facility would 'not increase' Ireland's gas use or 'lock-in' natural gas: 'As the State or EU is not investing in the LNG terminal, no taxpayer funding is at risk irrespective of usage. Hence, no State funding is diverted away from investment in renewable generation. The reality is that our flexible 600-megawatt power plant and LNG terminal are necessary to support intermittent renewables in Ireland.' Edens said New Fortress was in discussions with renewable companies to develop the site for hydrogen – a clean environmental ambition – and to connect offshore renewables to the electricity grid. He said the project was 'shovel ready' and could be constructed in a year, once it had permission. Right-of-way agreements had been 'executed with all landowners along the pipeline route' and future developments over a further 500 acres 'could include other energy projects such as strategic gas storage, offshore renewable development and green hydrogen production'.

ENERGY POLICY

The need for alternatives to fossil fuel to deal with our contribution to man-made global warming has influenced energy policy in recent decades and now, finally, drives it. It is an expensive process that requires enormous capital investment. Whereas in the early decades of the State we created our own national companies, such as ESB, Bord na Móna (to burn turf, a process now outlawed) and what was to become Bord Gáis, the capital requirements were such that we had to open up to private enterprise creating power and selling into a regulated market, sometimes with mixed results. An extraordinary array of foreign capital has taken control of much of our future production of energy on this island, getting involved particularly in building gas-fired generation plants, installing wind turbines on land and investing in their likely construction in our seas, examining the possibility for biomass electricity generation and even generating power from the light of the sun.

For decades, solar power was seen as unviable because of our lack of strong sunshine for sufficient hours. The technology has advanced and dropped in price. Installing solar is now considered much more straightforward than building a wind farm, but the big problems for developers can be securing a connection to the power grid and negotiating the planning system in a timely manner.

Norwegian utility company Statkraft plans a €1.5 billion investment in solar energy in Ireland. It already develops, owns and operates renewable energy projects across the technologies of onshore wind and offshore wind, battery storage – building the country's first grid-scale battery in Kerry – and grid services (distributing power) in Ireland. It arrived in 2018 and started construction on Ireland's largest solar farm, which will create enough energy to power over 40,000 homes. It is located in Ballymacarney, County Meath, on about 650 acres of land across four different sites, leased from four local farmers who will be able to keep sheep grazing between the rows of solar panels. Cattle and other livestock are too big, and would potentially damage the panels. The solar farm will supply Microsoft and Statkraft has partnered with Copenhagen Infrastructure Partners to develop a major supply of offshore wind in Ireland.

Engie, the Paris-based multinational with roots in the Suez Canal and France's former state-owned gas monopoly, operates from an office in Kilkenny. Irish solar developer BNRG secured backing from another French company, Neoen, to invest €220 million in over 20 Irish solar farms. Neoen also paid nearly €26 million for eight wind farms that formed the Republic's section of an all-Ireland wind portfolio initiated by Energia, with support from the State-backed Irish Infrastructure Fund.

Energia claims to provide about 20 per cent of the total energy capacity for the island of Ireland. It has invested about €1 billion in Ireland to date and plans to commit another €3 billion. Energia is owned by US investment firm I Squared Capital. It has a gas-fired power plant at Huntstown in north Dublin where it is building a €50 million bioenergy plant to take 70,000 tonnes of organic waste annually from Beauparc's Panda brown bin collections, which will be digested into biogas to fire a power plant. It also owns and operates 15 wind farms across the island

and plans four solar PV projects on the east coast of Ireland and two offshore wind farms off the east coast.

WIND ENERGY

Almost any drive around rural Ireland is likely to reveal the presence of one of the many wind farms that have emerged over the last 30 years, dotted all over the country on hills or wide open flat spaces. The power produced by these wind farms has allowed the country to reduce its reliance on imported fossil fuels and mitigate somewhat the rise in carbon emissions caused by burning fossils to create electricity, albeit not enough yet. They have not always been popular, though, even when located in remote areas.

The issue of how close wind farms should be to people's homes has been contentious since the very first was built at Bellacorick, County Mayo, in 1992. New regulations were agreed upon at Taoiseach Enda Kenny's last cabinet meeting in 2017 that retained the mandatory minimum 500 metres set-back distance for the construction of turbines near homes. What changed was that in residential areas turbines would also have to be built a distance away equal to four times the height of the turbine. Breaches of noise restrictions could lead to turbines being turned off and a zero-tolerance policy on shadow flicker (the effect of the sun, low on the horizon, shining through the rotating blades of a wind turbine) casting a moving shadow was also introduced. Operators were also required to pay a 'community dividend' to areas affected by construction.

Wind farm developments have provided private investors with an opportunity to profit, especially as ESB, the State-owned main generator of electricity, was slow initially to be among the main investors in the sector, other than building a five-megawatt wind farm in Crockahenny, County Donegal, in 1998. The problem in the early years, as ESB executives told me in 2008, was one of storage: water could be stored behind dams and released to produce power as and when required, but wind could not be stored to provide power when demand went up. It was not until recent years that the ESB invested more heavily to have 19 onshore wind farms on the island.

The ESB's involvement has not been without controversy. In 2022, the ESB confirmed that the Derrybrien wind farm of 70 turbines in the Slieve Aughty Mountains in County Galway – which produced about 1 per cent of the State's installed wind capacity – was to be decommissioned, after a near 20-year controversy caused by a peat slide in 2003. The farm was built without an Environmental Impact Assessment (EIA) as Irish planning law at that time did not require that EU standards apply. A landslide during excavation work caused extensive damage, resulting in the European Commission (EC) taking Ireland to court in 2008; it ordered a retrospective EIA, but this was not carried out. The landslide disturbed 450,000 tonnes of peat over more than 60 acres and sent 250,000 tonnes of material downslope. About 50,000 fish died in an 18-kilometre stretch of river down to Lough Cutra. The State was fined €17 million by the EC for an ongoing failure to ensure proper standards.

It was not the only controversy of this kind. Michael Murnane, a private investor from Macroom in County Cork, has been one of the largest developers in building wind farms, amassing a portfolio of power plants to rival many large international players and utilities. His company Invis is responsible for the 19-turbine project at the Meenbog wind farm, County Donegal, on behalf of Amazon. It came to national attention when it had a spectacular landslide in November 2022. Thousands of tonnes of peat washed into an internationally protected salmon river and residents witnessed pieces of bog carrying standing trees floating down a hill. The bog slide led to concerns about pollution in a number of rivers in the Foyle catchment. In a previous EIA produced by Invis, the risk of peat slippage was 'designated trivial and tolerable following some mitigation/control measures being implemented'. However, the developer and the planning authorities were warned in 2018 by experts in peat bog stability that the development might trigger a slippage. There had been significant opposition locally, including from Mick Hucknall, the Simply Red lead singer, who co-owns the Glenmore Rivers Estate on the River Finn in east Donegal. Invis was fined €1,500 and had to pay for restoration works.

This incident has not stopped Murnane's overall success, however. His main development company, Craydel, retained profits of €25 million before it became an unlimited company in 2011, reducing its disclosure requirements. That year it teamed up with Asper, a London investment firm previously part of Hg Capital, to form Invis Energy. In July 2017, Invis Energy sold a 60 per cent stake in five of its wind farms – across Cork, Kerry and Galway – to a Japanese consortium comprising Sojitz Corporation, Kansai Electric Power Company (Kepco) and a financial subsidiary of the Mitsubishi group. The deal was said to be worth up to €330 million and has the capacity to power 150,000 homes. In recent years, Invis became Amazon's partner as the multinational developed its own renewable energy sources to power its data centres.

Other State bodies got involved in wind energy in the early years but sold when the State needed cash after the Troika's arrival. When Bord Gáis was sold to Centrica, the operator of British Gas, its wind farm portfolio was sold separately to Canadian asset manager Brookfield. Its Cork office now manages 17 wind farms with over 360-megawatt capacity and is apparently looking to double that.

State-owned forestry company Coillte sold its stake in its four wind farm joint ventures with ESB, SSE and Bord na Móna for €136.1 million to Greencoat Renewables. Greencoat was set up in 2017 and raised €270 million through the stock markets in Dublin and London. It is managed by the UK-based Schroders Greencoat, which describes itself as an experienced investment manager in the listed renewable energy infrastructure sector and has over stg£9 billion of assets under management. Greencoat owns 75 per cent of the Cloosh Valley wind farm in Galway which was developed by SSE and Coillte and is the biggest and most productive in the country. It bought two farms from BlackRock and the Dromadda wind farm in County Kerry from Impax in May 2018. Greencoat Renewables' investors included the State's ISIF and other Irish-based institutions, such as AIB, Irish Life, Investec, Tilman Brewin Dolphin and Irish Life. But there is also international money, mostly British from the likes of Fidelity, M&G Investment Managers, Aberdeen Standard Life and Baillie Gifford.

FuturEnergy Ireland is a joint venture established by the ESB and State forestry company Coillte to invest €1 billion in onshore wind farms. It is not having things all its own way, though. It received permission from ABP for a €175 million 21-turbine wind farm on a 1,434-hectare site at Castlebanny, mainly owned by Coillte, to the east of Ballyhale in southeast Kilkenny, in partnership with ART Generation. It was expected to generate enough clean, green electricity to power the equivalent of around 70,000 homes annually. However, the Save the South Leinster Way group took a High Court judicial review of the ABP permission and nearby resident Henry Shefflin, one of the greatest hurlers of all time, was among those who led the objections. FuturEnergy paired with SSE Renewables, a Scottish firm, to offer to build a 21-turbine wind farm at Sheskin, County Mayo, at a cost of more than €100 million, which the developers claim will produce enough electricity for 83,000 homes.

There has been a great reliance on overseas bankers to provide finance. In 2022 *The Currency* website analysed the loan charges provided at 70 wind farms and found that 25 of them had borrowed from German bank Nord/LB and nine from another German bank, HSH Nordbank. Dutch, French, Norwegian, Spanish and Japanese banks have all provided credit.

Wall Street giant BlackRock partnered with NTR plc in 2011 when the latter moved from operating toll roads throughout the country to become an investment manager in renewables. NTR's main assets now are outside of Ireland.

RWE Renewables, known as Innogy when it first came to Ireland, is the renewables division of Germany's second-largest electricity utility,

RWE. In early 2023, it submitted an application to Clare County Council for the Fahy Beg wind farm, which could power about 20,000 homes a year, as part of a plan to spend €1.5 billion on green energy projects in the Republic before 2030. It already owns a wind farm in Kerry and battery storage facilities at Balbriggan, County Dublin, and Lisdrumdoagh, County Monaghan, the latter an investment of €25 million that can store up to 60 megawatts of electricity. Battery storage is used to balance highs in renewable electricity generation with actual demand by holding unneeded power for a period until the national grid seeks it. RWE was involved in controversy in Germany in early 2023 as the owner of the controversial Garzweiler coal mine in Lützerath where climate activist Greta Thurnberg was arrested for her part in a protest against an expansion of production at the open cast mine, thereby demolishing a village.

Amazon was not the only company to take action for its own future energy needs. Ikea, the giant furniture store with premises in north Dublin the size of Croke Park, acquired its own 7.65-megawatt wind farm in Carrickeeny, County Leitrim, in 2013 to power its Dublin and Belfast stores. The Ikea farm was one of three built and operated by Mainstream, the company started by Eddie O'Connor, who was boss at Bord na Móna when it built its own first wind farm.

BORD NA MÓNA

Bord na Móna is a commercial semi-state body more than 90 years old, set up to harvest peat from the bogs of Ireland to sell as fuel to homes and to fire power stations in the midlands – and to provide employment. The damage these activities did to the environment meant this couldn't continue; harvesting stopped and the power plants were closed in 2019.

Now, Bord na Móna appears to have a major future as the main State-owned company engaged in climate solutions and renewable power. It produces power using a mixture of wind, biogas and biomass facilities across its 200,000-acre landholding, to which it intends to add solar plants. It is committed to actions that bring no return on investment in a conventional sense but aid large-scale carbon storage and biodiversity gains: in 2022, for example, it rehabilitated 8,000 acres of peatlands.

Its new purpose is to help Ireland become carbon neutral by 2050. It has a ten-year plan – the Brown to Green strategy – to invest more than €1.6 billion in clean energy, carbon storage and resource recovery. It aims to double its renewable generation capacity by 2030. In May 2022, it committed to a solar farm with a €270 million investment and construction commenced on two of Ireland's largest wind farms, generating sufficient electricity to power 120,000 homes. It also has major offshore ambitions (see Chapter 39). And that, for a variety of reasons is where Ireland's gold rush may take place.

THIRTY-NINE

FROM LAND TO SEA

For decades some speculated that the real wealth for Ireland was to be found not in our land but in our seas. Our sovereign rights in the Atlantic Ocean and the Irish Sea are seven times the land mass of the Republic. Under maritime law, the legal continental shelf extends out to a distance of 200 nautical miles from the coastline, or further if the shelf naturally extends beyond that limit (as it does in Ireland's case). In this vast area, full of very deep water, oil was sought as the prize to be exploited. It would have provided energy security, meaning we would need to import less. Oil, all imported, comprised about 45 per cent of our energy use in 2020. A find big enough might allow us to be self-sufficient but also to sell to overseas markets and give us wealth like Norway or Scotland, providing money that could be put to other uses.

Who would benefit became a big political and ideological issue. Exploration took place, in the years before concerns about the impact on the environment of burning fossil fuels took hold, carried out by corporate entities in receipt of licences from the State, not by the State itself.

There were political rows on the rare occasions that commercial finds were made of gas, which is less lucrative than oil. These came to a head when a gas field was exploited off the coast of Mayo, the Corrib field deep in the Atlantic, in the early 2000s. The resource had been discovered in 1996, the first reported commercial natural gas discovery in Ireland since the Kinsale Head gas field in 1971. The benefits went to foreign private sector interests, not to the Irish State, or so left-leaning politicians claimed angrily. The State replied that the investors had taken the risk, we were getting gas at a good price, a share of the revenues and that jobs were created, both onshore and offshore, in facilitating its distribution, and that taxes were paid to the State too. All of this took place against the background of a bizarre campaign against the construction of the refining terminal at Bellanaboy Beach and, more specifically, the 83-kilometre pipeline from sea to shore in which the raw gas would be transported. Local activists became convinced that they would be all killed by allegedly inevitable explosions when the gas in the pipelines under their land combusted.

The ownership of the Corrib field has changed a number of times in recent decades and was shared by various partners. Enterprise Oil, a UK company, was bought by Royal Dutch Shell in 2002 and it took on the management of the project: hence the Shell to Sea campaign, which wanted the processing of the gas to be carried out offshore. Shell, in turn, sold its 45 per cent share of Corrib to the Canada Pension Plan Investment Board in 2018. The Canadian investors hired Vermilion Energy as the project's operator and it bought a 20 per cent share itself from the Norwegian company Statoil, now called Equinor. In 2021, Equinor sold the balance of its shares in Corrib to Vermilion for €382 million. It seems that the Canadians have gambled on finding ways to extract extra value once the gas runs out, as is expected by 2025. Europa Oil and Gas had licences to explore for gas close to the existing Corrib field but required ministerial approval to proceed with drilling. If there were to be a find, extracted gases could be linked to the existing Corrib infrastructure. Supporters of the idea argued that the gas would be 'greener' than gas imported either by pipeline or by LNG. It was also argued that a boost to Ireland's gas reserves would reduce our reliance on imports.

For decades private interests spent, or mostly wasted, hundreds of millions of euro in speculative drilling around the Irish coast. There were four gas discoveries in total – at Kinsale, Ballycotton and Seven

Heads off the Cork coast and at the Corrib field– out of a total of 160 wells drilled. Would the critics have preferred the State to waste its own money gambling on making an oil or gas find instead through the actions of a State-owned exploration company? Imagine the reports from the comptroller and auditor general, the rows at the Public Accounts Committee about speculative waste. Was it not better to set terms that gave the State a cut of any money coming from an exploited find and increased tax rates on any profits that might accrue from the successful exploitation of any finds and to ensure the security of supply? It worked well for us when the Kinsale gas field off the coast of Cork supplied gas for decades, at least until its reservoir was exhausted.

It's not clear what irritated the critics more: the potential for foreign multinationals to make a profit from our oil or that rich Irish individuals would form companies to do so. The most prominent of the Irish oil gamblers was Tony O'Reilly, for many years one of Ireland's wealthiest and most prominent businessmen, a controller of Independent News and Media (INM, the largest private sector media company) and chairman and CEO of the giant American food company, Heinz. He was the driving force behind Atlantic Resources, one of the most speculative stock market-quoted Irish entities ever, where fortunes were made but mostly lost on wild movements in the company's share price as it raised and spent more than €250 million for little or no return. It morphed into Providence Resources and then, late in 2022, after once billionaire but now bankrupt O'Reilly had departed the share register, it became Barryroe Offshore Energy, the name reflecting the one asset it had kept.

That asset is the licence rights to what may be the one new lucrative oil and gas reserve offshore for Ireland to exploit. In the first decade of this century, preliminary drilling took place at Barryroe, an oil and gas field about 50 kilometres off the coast of Cork. It was found to contain high-quality light crude of an amount undetermined but, according to initial estimates, possibly between 80 and 300 million barrels of oil. However, Providence couldn't get financial support for further drilling, the reckoning being that oil prices at the time did not justify the investment required to get any oil out of the rock beneath the Atlantic. On three occasions Providence thought it had found new partners – including Chinese companies – with expertise and money to bring the venture to the next stage, but each time was disappointed when the deals could not be consummated.

Things became even more complicated as the understanding of the damage caused to the atmosphere by the burning of oil improved. The government wished to act against further carbon emissions. Laws were passed in September 2019 to prevent further exploration but conceded that the government had to honour existing licences issued prior to 2019. Few expected there would be any moves in that regard.

Within three years things had changed. Oil prices soared and the value of the estimated reserves at Barryroe more than doubled, to €6.5 billion. Additionally, it was believed further reserves of gas would be discovered once oil was extracted. Barryroe needed to drill an appraisal well to test the geology at the site, get a better sense of the extent of the reserves and assess the difficulty of its extraction. It needed permission from Eamon Ryan as the relevant minister. In autumn 2022, Ryan denied Barryroe a licence to resume drilling, claiming it did not have the financial resources for an endeavour that would cost about €65 million. It seemed a cute feint but was followed by the surprise emergence of Larry Goodman, already a shareholder in Barryroe, who committed to providing loans that could be converted to equity once approval was granted by Ryan to move the project to the next stage. Ryan faced a dilemma. If he continued his refusal, Goodman could sue to get permission or for damages over a failure to allow the fulfilment of the licence.

In May 2023, the Department of Energy confirmed that it did not believe Barryroe's finances were sufficient to allow it to take the risk. Goodman initially reserved his position but a 20 per cent minority partner in the project, Lansdowne Oil and Gas, a UK-registered company, immediately indicated legal action and that it would be seeking damages of about €100 million for being denied the right to exploit what it claimed would be a highly valuable field. Then in June, Barryroe's shareholders decided to close the business before Goodman persuaded a court to allow the appointment of an examiner to keep it in business. But it was an example, perhaps rare, of where the State had exercised its muscle against the potential exploitation of property or land, this time at sea, by a private owner and prevailed.

Exploiting any oil found at Barryroe would potentially result in hundreds of millions of barrels of oil being drilled out of the rock, burned into the air and added to the globe's existing carbon problems. But it would give Ireland considerable energy security and, in any case, we're likely to be burning hundreds of millions of barrels of imported oil over the coming decades notwithstanding our clean energy ambitions. There's an argument that we may as well use our own oil instead of importing it. Instead, we have opted to feel better about ourselves by not adding to the amount of oil extracted globally and will use our seas for a potentially far more lucrative and environmentally friendly pursuit: wind energy.

HARNESSING AN OPPORTUNITY

There is an enormous opportunity for using the wind that blows in the Atlantic and the Irish Sea to power wind turbines that would create 'clean' electricity, not just for Ireland but for the rest of Europe. If that were to happen, there might be fewer rows about the location of data centres in Ireland. Prices to consumers in their homes and to businesses could be slashed. We would also have an income flow that would rival the take from the sale of vast oil reserves: Ireland has the potential to export seven to ten times more than our own energy requirements, according to some experts.

But again, who is the 'we' and what is the likelihood that we can avail of this opportunity? Many of the same arguments and practical problems that blighted the search for oil and gas might hinder and lose us our capacity to take advantage of our highly valuable marine territory. Added to that is a lack of imagination as to what is possible and an unwillingness to do what is necessary onshore to facilitate what can be done offshore.

Eddie O'Connor was central to bringing wind energy to Ireland, first on land and then in the sea. As CEO of Bord na Móna, he realised almost before anyone else that cutting and burning bog was bad for the environment and that his company was a major polluter. He set up an environmental products division at the company to prepare for change. O'Connor was both ahead of his time and too ambitious for the civil servants who controlled the company. When he gave a speech in which he declared, 'I hold the State, in all its manifestations, wholly responsible for the lack of flair, creativity and innovation in Irish business,' he made enemies who conspired to bring him down.

After he left the company in 1996, he borrowed money and persuaded friends to back him in establishing a wind energy company called Airtricity. In the early 2000s, it led the building of Ireland's first offshore wind farm, off the coast of Wicklow at the Arklow Bank. The Codling Wind Park was granted a 99-year foreshore lease, covering an area of about 55 square kilometres of sea, about 13 kilometres off the Wicklow coast. The area was to the east of a shallow sandbank, allowing for the construction of the wind turbines. Airtricity's partners in the deal included Johnny Ronan and Richard Barrett, who owned a half-share of the project. It was a groundbreaker for Europe, a generation ahead of what almost every other EU country was doing, but it was not capitalised upon.

Official State policy became to engage with issuing licences to build wind farms on land, but not at sea because the latter was deemed too expensive to provide with support. In 2007 plans for the second phase of Arklow Bank were cancelled. Onshore was less expensive and far easier and faster, both physically and administratively, despite complaints in local rural areas to the sight and sound of the wind turbines, to connect to the grid on land.

It was an opportunity missed.

'In this country, we have very little ability to see the future,' O'Connor said. He admitted it is more expensive to build offshore but maintained the returns on investment are almost double. 'Economists comparing the cost of onshore versus offshore ignored capacity factors or how much energy a turbine can generate on land or at sea,' he said. 'The beauty of offshore is that turbines can be bigger – and the wind blows more strongly, more regularly.'

Ireland now has enough installed wind energy capacity to supply up to 36 per cent of our electricity needs. But we should have much more. Further large-scale, on-land wind farm development in Ireland seems most unlikely.

'Firstly, Eirgrid hasn't developed the grid as it should have,' said O'Connor. 'But secondly, nimbyism has gone beyond all previous levels. People are not prepared to tolerate noise, shadow flicker, visual intrusion, all that stuff. But in any case, the capacity factors offshore are way higher, about 45 per cent compared to 28 per cent on land, because the higher the wind, the higher the capacity factor and the more return you can get on investment. Off the west coast, we can get 65 per cent capacity, by far the best in the whole EU. The problem is that Eirgrid hasn't planned to accommodate all that.'

He is not alone in being critical of Eirgrid, even if he is more outspoken and direct than others. The chair of the Commission for Regulation of Utilities (CRU), Aoife MacEvilly, has also warned about the delays in building new grid infrastructure and planning.[13] Yet despite its on-land

13   Eirgrid has been handicapped somewhat by objections in its desire to implement a significant and costly upgrading to the system. For example, in June 2022 the High Court gave permission for Frank Dunne – one of the shareholders in the family supermarket business Dunnes Stores – to pursue judicial review challenges over the access of workers to his Kildare stud farm, which had been identified for an electricity line upgrade. He and horse-breeder Ann Marshall, along with their company Hamwood Stud, took two separate but interrelated actions over ESB and Eirgrid plans to refurbish the 22-kilometre electricity line between Maynooth and Woodland in counties Kildare and Meath. Dunne and Marshall claimed the intended works would have a 'significant effect' on their

failings, Eirgrid retains the responsibility to develop a new offshore power grid to bring onshore the renewable energy generated at sea. The government has set targets to install the capacity for seven gigawatts (GW) of offshore wind capacity by 2030, with a further 30GW added by 2050. The EU Commission is pressing us to achieve these aims because of the benefit beyond Ireland.

'I think it is possible we could create an industry in Ireland more than twice the size of the entire farming, food, ingredients and fishing industry, just in terms of sales of electricity to Europe. And it's sustainable,' said O'Connor. 'But there is a lack of competence, a lack of planning. We don't do planning in Ireland very well. We don't have a civil service that actually understands that you have to spend small quantities of money and that the private sector will weigh in behind it then if it sees the government trying to do something and creating the right incentives. But there have never been any real incentives for offshore wind here. The dead hand of government works on the basis of trying to ensure that private interests don't make too much money out of its efforts.'

Much of the capital is likely to be from abroad – which will likely raise suspicion and hostility in some quarters. Ronan and Barrett sold their half share in Arklow Bank in 2020 to Électricité de France (EDF) in a deal that may have been worth about €100 million to them. The other half of that project is owned by Norwegian marine group Fred Olsen, part of the larger Bonheur stock market-listed group. Together the French and Norwegians have plans for Arklow Bank phase two, which would pitch over 220 turbines across 14 rows at an estimated cost of between €2–3 billion. It could generate 1.5GW of electricity annually,

prize bloodstock and breeding operations. They expressed fears there would be a 'real prospect' of foetal loss among their mares and cows. Eirgrid responded that the upgrades were necessary because of constraints on the transmission network and to secure additional capacity. Dunne died late in 2022 but his estate immediately moved to keep the case against the Kildare and Meath county councils, Eirgrid, the Attorney General and Ireland itself alive.

nearly one-third of what the government expects to get from offshore wind to meet 2030 climate targets.

Others worry about the viability of what's on offer to them as investors and as to how difficult the State makes things. In November 2021, Norwegian firm Equinor, which had been working with the ESB since 2019 to build a €5 billion, 1,400MW floating offshore wind farm off the Clare and Kerry coast, quit the project, citing frustration with the regulatory and planning process. Had a major multinational abandoned a planned onshore project of that scale, in any sector, there would have been a public uproar. This hardly caused a ripple.

Oil giant Shell withdrew from Ireland a year later. It was to partner with Simply Blue Energy, a Cork-based company, on two offshore projects off the coast of Clare as part of its transition to more environmentally friendly energy but withdrew even though it had planned to spend billions of euro on the 1,350MW Western Star Floating Wind project. Simply Blue also had the Emerald Floating Wind Project, a proposed turbine network floating 35–60 kilometres south of the Old Head of Kinsale in County Cork, but Shell pulled out of that late in 2022, despite almost two years' preparatory work having taken place.

Shell may have been spooked by the expenses and uncertainty of the auction system being used by the government to decide on licence-holders. Applicants are required to spend millions on feasibility studies in advance of planning permission that might never be awarded. The first step is to get a licence to survey seabed areas, but that can cost an applicant in Ireland €10 million before even applying for planning, ten times more than would be necessary in Poland, for example.

'THE WIND IS ALWAYS BLOWING SOMEWHERE'

It wasn't until early 2019 that the State-owned ESB made a major commitment to offshore wind energy in Ireland – despite having already bought into two major projects in other countries. The ESB bought up to 35 per cent of the Oriel project, a wind farm to be located 22 kilometres off the coast of Dundalk using 55 large turbines, at a projected cost of over €700 million. Once operational, it is expected to generate enough capacity to cover the energy needs of 280,000 households, equivalent to most of the population in Louth and Meath, and contribute to the reduction of Ireland's carbon emissions by 600,000 tonnes per annum. Oriel was set up by the since-deceased Brian Britton, a key executive previously at Larry Goodman's beef business, with financial support from billionaire Martin Naughton. But before the ESB became involved, Oriel secured support from the Belgian offshore wind developer Parkwind. The Belgians also bought up to 35 per cent of the nearby Clogherhead project, which the ESB said would be progressed under a separate planning application.

In early 2023, the ESB looked to invest in two multibillion-euro offshore wind projects off the coast of Scotland with Canada's Northland Power, adding to the capacity it already owned off Scotland in partnership with France's EDF Renewables. The ESB wants to develop 5GW of wind energy projects off the coast of Ireland and in June 2023 it announced that the Danish wind farm operator Orsted, which said it had spent €700 million on Irish wind farms onshore in the previous two years, would be its new partner in a planned offshore energy expansion. It also signed a memorandum of understanding with the Port of Cork to support the development of Ireland's offshore wind and green hydrogen sector.

Green hydrogen is hydrogen generated by renewable energy or from low-carbon power, through the electrolysis of water, so it generates no polluting emissions into the atmosphere. Green hydrogen has significantly lower carbon emissions than grey hydrogen, which is primarily produced by steam reforming of natural gas. As of 2021, green hydrogen accounted for less than 0.04 per cent of total hydrogen production.

Echelon and SSE are interested in Arklow Bank phase 2, which is currently in the pre-planning public consultation phase. This would see 76 turbines installed in shallow waters off the Wicklow coast at an estimated cost of €1–€2 billion. Their 520MW capacity would dwarf any existing wind farm in Ireland.

The German RWE Renewables has also taken a 50 per cent share in County Kerry-based Saorgus Energy's Dublin Array, a proposed 600MW wind farm stretching off the coast from Bray to Dalkey. RWE bought East Celtic wind farm off the Wexford coast from Irish company Western Power Offshore Holdings. Located in the Celtic Sea between nine and 36 kilometres off the Wexford and Waterford coasts, East Celtic's first phase will deliver 900MW of electricity, roughly similar to two power plants, by 2030.

As mentioned earlier, Bord na Móna is planning two offshore wind projects in a joint venture with Ocean Winds. These are likely to cost more than €6 billion, by far the biggest investment in Bord na Móna's 90-year-plus history. Headquartered in Madrid, Ocean Winds was formed as a joint venture between EDP Renewables, the Spanish energy company, and Engie, the French multinational. The first project is Réalt na Mara, 12 kilometres off the coast of south Dublin and north Wicklow, the second is the Celtic Horizon development, almost 14 kilometres off the Wexford and Waterford coastline. If completed, these projects will deliver one-third of the country's entire power demand or enough to power up to 2.1 million homes.

Adequate preparations have been slow in coming, however. The regulatory and planning process for offshore developments was based on the outdated 1933 Foreshore Act. There were long delays in passing a new Maritime Area Planning (MAP) bill and establishing a new Maritime Area Regulatory Authority (MARA). This meant the postponement of the first Offshore Renewable Energy Support Scheme (RESS) auction for offshore wind projects. Six offshore wind projects, known as Phase 1 projects, with an estimated combined potential to deliver 3.9GW of renewable power, were delayed for years. A rare bit of positive news was the creation by ABP of a dedicated marine and climate unit to handle renewable infrastructure projects – good news if you believed the unit would prove itself more capable than its onshore counterparts have been.

The Planning Commission is likely to be busy with applications for onshore enabling facilities to support construction, installation and maintenance, particularly at our ports, assuming the capital to construct them is forthcoming. Otherwise, the largest offshore wind projects may have to be built at ports outside of Ireland. The State will have to invest in infrastructure at our ports – possibly at a cost of billions of euro – or turn facilities over to the private sector. In early 2023, only one port on the island of Ireland, Belfast Harbour, was ready to be used to construct offshore wind farms. Industry experts estimated that capital of up to €1 billion will be needed at Bremore Port in County Louth to develop a purpose-built facility to handle offshore wind infrastructure, and at least €100 million in new investment will be needed at the Port of Cork (Ringaskiddy), Galway, Moneypoint, Rosslare, Shannon Foynes and Foynes Island. Smaller amounts of less than €50 million will be needed at Killybegs in Donegal and Ros an Mhíl in Galway. Irish Rail, which operates Rosslare Port, announced ambitious plans to establish an offshore renewable energy (ORE) hub in the region, with the potential to create up to 2,000 jobs. It will require investment of around €200 million, with an ambition to complete by 2026. It is potentially a risky and expensive investment for these ports if they cannot be guaranteed the arrival of the off-shore wind projects and the payments that would be made to them. Equally, these investments have the potential to be transformative for rural and coastal Ireland.

O'Connor is now 75 and has created and sold €2 billion-plus companies, first Airtricity and then Mainstream Renewable Energy, making himself a half-billionaire in the process. He is active again in partnership with Norwegian green investment group Aker Horizons, looking to provide the infrastructure for the future of offshore wind. The latest company is called SuperNode, to which he has committed €30 million personally to date: to build a pan-national underwater grid. The business is being developed at the UCD campus. 'If you want a Super Grid in Europe, you have to move from a native nationwide electricity supply to a continent-wide electricity supply,' O'Connor argued. SuperNode aims to build a meshed super grid that O'Connor believes could supply up to 900,000MW of offshore renewable wind energy to over 500 million people in Europe, giving it power by way of superconducting transmission technology that could be the key enabling solution to powering the world with 100 per cent renewable electricity. He believes it could halve the price of transmitting electricity. 'If we can get it done quickly enough, before the Chinese come into it, this will be the new Microsoft,' he said.

He sees huge potential and growth for Ireland in this, as well as major environmental benefits: 'The wind is always blowing somewhere. Research has come from the International Energy Agency which shows if you blend wind from Northern Europe with solar from around the Mediterranean basin, where it's really shining strongly, you get an almost perfect anticorrelation. If you have a grid to share it all you have constant supply.'

'This government has said that we would be building 30,000MW offshore. We could do that [times] ten if we wanted to,' he said. He believes Ireland can create a new industry, sales of electricity, jobs from the construction and maintenance of wind farms, and the financial services that flow from the greening of our economy. 'To decarbonise Europe fully, we need to build 750GW of offshore energy. Ireland can be the main player in that.'

The foreign money appears ready to support us, but concerns about the imagination or drive, or even the basic competence at an administrative level to deliver it, persist.

FORTY

THE CARBON CAPTURERS: TREES AND LAND-UNDER-FOREST

Dealing with global warming is a necessity that is going to have an enormous influence on our use of land in Ireland in the future. Climate action legislation, backing up the carbon budgets announced by the government, is binding and requires many uses of land that already are highly controversial, especially in rural areas. By 2030, Ireland is bound by law to have reduced its carbon emissions by 51 per cent from the level they were at in 2018. The chances of that being done seem slim, and they are non-existent if lobby groups who want to protect the status quo or limit change get their way, aided by populist politicians who want to deny the science of global warming and its already visible impacts, many about to get much worse.

If wind is going to be crucial in our transition from the use of fossil fuels, then trees are going to be essential to our efforts to capture carbon and store it. Forests absorb carbon dioxide from the atmosphere and store it in repositories, called carbon pools, which include trees (both living and dead), root systems, undergrowth, the forest floor and soils. Live trees have the highest carbon density, followed by soils and the forest floor. Our problem is that we don't have nearly enough forests. We can blame pre-independence occupation for cutting down our old forests, but the truth is our farmers don't like them much either, preferring grasslands for dairy and beef production or for tillage.

The country had a forestry cover of just 1.6 per cent when it achieved independence 100 years ago. The amount of forestry we have in Ireland now is disputed. The EU is working off an official base level of 11 per cent, according to Eurostat, but the National Landcover Map[14], produced by Tailte Eireann (formerly known as Ordnance Survey Ireland) in March 2023 and using satellite imaging, produced new figures that estimated our base forestry cover is actually at 13.35 per cent. If scrub and hedgerow are added to that the number rises to 18.27 per cent. This is relevant to the demands being placed upon us by the EU to increase our forestry cover for carbon capture. But even at 18 per cent we don't have enough forestry cover … and even if we will never reach the EU average of 38 per cent, we're not doing enough to improve it.

The annual afforestation programme for the new forestry scheme (2023–7) is 8,000 hectares compared with 2,000 hectares planted per year at present. Previous experience suggests the targets will be missed. The previous forestry programme which ran from 2014 to 2020 (and was then extended to 2022) also had an 8,000 hectare per annum target. Of the targeted 72,000 hectares over the nine years of that plan, only marginally more than half was planted. This is even though Ireland can grow trees much faster than other European countries. At the current rate of less than 5,000 acres per year, it would take 224 years for

14   The National Landcover Map produced by Tailte Eireann in 2023 gave a fascinating breakdown into how our land is distributed. Buildings take up just 0.59 per cent of all the available space, with ways (roads and streets) taking up 1.66 per cent and 'other artificial surfaces' a further 1.55 per cent.

The breakdown of agricultural land is as follows: improved grassland (in other words, farmed land) 41.53 per cent, wet grassland 9.47 per cent, amenity grassland 1.82 per cent, dry grassland 1.13 per cent, raised bog 0.66 per cent, blanket bog 3.54 per cent, cutover bog 1.56 per cent, bare peat 0.75 per cent and fens 0.04 per cent. Bracken makes up 0.4 per cent, dry heath 2.82 per cent and wet heath 3.25 per cent.

The Tailte 2023 survey also noted that exposed rock and sediments make up 0.93 per cent of Ireland, coastal sediments 0.13 per cent, mudflats 0.46 per cent, bare soil and disturbed ground 0.33 per cent and burnt areas 0.03 per cent, sand dunes 0.15 per cent, saltmarsh 0.08 per cent and swamp 0.03 per cent.

the State to reach the government's target of 18 per cent forestry cover by 2050.

The government's Climate Action Plan required the State to add close to 1.25 million acres of new forest area by 2050. The State-owned forestry agency Coillte is central to this. It currently manages over a million acres of forest, about 7 per cent of the land in the State and about 70 per cent of all forested land in the country. Coillte plans to increase the size of its forest estate by more than a fifth by 2050. That would allow it to capture 28 million tonnes of CO_2 from the atmosphere by 2050, close to half of Ireland's annual carbon emissions. Of this total, Coillte said 18 million tonnes of CO_2 will be captured by the creation of new forests and 10 million tonnes by improving the management of its existing forests.

That will be an expensive process. In April 2022, Coillte CEO Imelda Hurley estimated the cost of acquiring land and planting new forests at €1.7 billion. She promised a further €200 million investment in re-designing 75,000 acres of its existing estate by rewetting or rewilding some locations for climate or ecological benefits. Of its 6,000-odd properties, it plans to have a quarter 'managed for nature' by 2025. It also plans a further €100 million investment in new visitor destinations, adventure centres and walking trails throughout its forests by working with private operators.

This was a big change from the State's aspirations for Coillte less than a decade earlier. Consideration was given to selling Coillte during the economic crisis, as a way of partially paying down the national debt. Economist Colm McCarthy first suggested this in 2009 and then modified the idea in 2011, suggesting selling the forests but keeping the land underneath them. An Australian bank, Macquarie, was commissioned to examine the idea of an €800 million sale. Economist Peter Bacon, central to the creation of NAMA, said a deal would need to be done for €1.2 billion to give the State a profit. That valuation did not include the intangible values of the recreation, biodiversity enhancement and nature conservation elements of the forests.

The State wasn't in the business of making a profit at the time but of raising cash, even if it meant selling at a discount. However, a sustained public campaign, Save Ireland's Forests, in which the likes of musicians Christy Moore and Paddy Casey and actors Jeremy Irons and Sinead Cusack featured prominently, alongside politicians, made plenty of noise. Another group, the Woodland League, argued that ownership of Ireland's natural resource base by a private monopoly could result in restricted access to forestry lands and rivers for recreation and fishing, a loss of revenue from commercial logging, and a further loss of biodiversity. Its online petition attracted almost 30,000 signatures. The campaigns dissuaded the Labour members of the coalition government from authorising the sale.

Keeping it, meant that Coillte had to be given its head to expand. Coillte set up a partnership with a private sector body called the Nature Trust to plant new native trees on a non-commercial basis. Money came from investors who wanted to meet environmental, social and governance (ESG) goals. But that was only a small part of its expansion plans.

In early 2023, Coillte disclosed a deal with a London-based pension fund, Gresham House, to buy and manage tens of thousands of acres of new forestry on its behalf. The fund was called the Irish Strategic Forestry Fund (ISFF), which started with an ambition to raise up to €200 million in private capital from Irish and international private investors. ISIF, which we've met many times on earlier pages, was first in, with a foundation investment of €25 million. The idea was to develop an initial forestry portfolio of 30,000 acres within the next five years, by buying the land, planting trees on it and managing the forests in return for a management fee. But the plans went further than that, with suggestions that private investors would provide €2 billion in funding to allow Coillte to meet its target of planting 250,000 acres of new trees by 2050. Potential investors were told that their returns would be generated from EU forestry grants and single farm payments to which they, but not Coillte, would be entitled; a 2003 EU decision had banned Coillte, as a

State-owned body, from claiming state forestry premiums for planting trees as it had for many years.

Coillte said it would ask other government bodies about using public land for some of the new planting. Less valuable land in the west and northwest of the country, at about €3,000 per hectare, was targeted. However, there were complaints from rural TDs. Marian Harkin, the independent Sligo–Leitrim TD, condemned a 'land grab' that would push land prices way beyond the reach of active local farmers. 'They'll have to stop this. It'll be all vulture funds that will own the land,' Michael Fitzmaurice, the independent TD for Galway–Roscommon complained. He also predicted that the buying power of the fund would drive up prices for agricultural and forestry land. Coillte insisted that it would buy land in 'a responsible and proportionate way' and that it wasn't in its interest to make its own further purchases more expensive.

The objections didn't seem to take into account the reluctance of farmers to invest in forestry. The average forestry plantation is little more than 15 acres. Many farmers lack interest in forestry because they do not see it as a sufficiently profitable use of productive land, which they want to keep for animal or tillage farming. Yet about four-fifths of the targeted increase in forestry between now and 2050 depends on private investment. Even now, the private forestry sector is greater in size than Coillte and is expected to outproduce it in log supply over the coming decade. However, it receives just 5 per cent of the Department of Agriculture's annual €1.86 billion budget. The Society of Irish Foresters has claimed that nearly 475,000 hectares of marginal land could be made available for afforestation without negatively impacting agricultural production. The government offers tax-free forestry premiums, which have been doubled in recent years. While this offers an income, it can be at least 30 years before the crop can be harvested. There is also a requirement that replantation to replace the crop must take place, the beginning of another expensive cycle. It means that once a farmer or owner commits a land to forestry, it is a near-permanent decision.

The State doesn't necessarily make it easy to do either. The Department of Agriculture issues licences to plant forests, a process that includes an extensive environmental assessment by the landowner. Applicants also need a licence to build a forest road to bring in tree-harvesting machinery, and a harvesting licence to fell the trees when they mature. Unfortunately, the department regularly failed to meet its own target of issuing 100 new forestry licences per week and a large backlog of applicants developed. The forestry industry lobbied the department to eliminate the licensing system, but Philip Lee Solicitors provided a legal opinion that the system was necessary to comply with EU environmental rules, and so it remained.

While carbon capture is the driving force of the government's plans for expanded forestry, there are other potential benefits. There is a target to build 80 per cent of Irish homes in future using timber frames, rather than cement and steel, as happens in Scotland. At present, just 25 per cent of Irish homes are built with timber frames. The idea is that this will create a bigger domestic market for Irish timber companies but, more importantly, will turn future homes into environmental assets that store carbon. It is a major plank of the drive to reduce emissions in the construction sector by 2030.

One of the problems that environmentalists have with these worthy aspirations is the dependence on the Sitka spruce, a conifer that accounts for around 80 per cent of all Irish forestry. Sitka spruce is blamed by them for reducing forest biodiversity. But landowners don't want to grow broadleaf trees because they can take 70 years to mature and even then can only be used for firewood. There's a lack of commercial viability unless compensation is paid by the government. As it happens, farmers are being paid to grow a broader range of trees, but foresters who plant Sitka spruce trees have to set aside 20 per cent of their plantations for broadleaf trees instead of the previous 15 per cent. A further 15 per cent of the sites have to be left as open space. Yet 60 per cent of the annual tree-planting target remains for spruce. It is difficult to see just how Ireland will come anywhere close to meeting its reforestation targets.

THE FUTURE USE OF THE LAND

By now you may have drawn the conclusion that there is little in this book about land used for agriculture, something that was central to the land arguments before the rebellion against British rule and independence. That's true. But there's a good reason. Agricultural land is no longer nearly as important to Ireland as it was once, at least not from an economic perspective. It provides just 1 per cent of the nation's jobs and 4 per cent of what's called gross value added (GVA) – a good measure of economic value. It's true that farming makes an additional indirect contribution to the economy as its products are used in food and drink manufacturing. However, that sector provides just 2 per cent of employment and 2 per cent of GVA.

The majority of Irish land is used for agriculture but not as much as had been thought. The often-quoted measurement of grassland in Ireland was '80 per cent of Ireland is farmland and 80 per cent of that is grass'. That implied that 64 per cent of Ireland is covered in grass but it's not. Considerably less than half of Ireland is actually covered in improved grassland. It is only when wet grassland (the many fields that are losing the battle to rushes) is added that the 50 per cent threshold is reached.

Farming is changing for demographic and environmental reasons. Traditionally, farming is a family affair, with farms passed down from generation to generation. However, the number of younger farmers is declining as the average age of farmers in Ireland increases. According to the CSO's Census of Agriculture (2020), the portion of farmers aged 65 and older increased from 26 per cent (36,600 farmers) in 2010 to 33 per cent (44,000 farmers) in 2020. The average age of an Irish farmer is 57. Family members who may replace potential retirees on the farm often now opt for different employment and there can be financial challenges in generational transfers that discourage younger people from doing what so many of their ancestors did. The *Irish Farmers Journal* produces an annual land sales report based on publicly offered land for sale through auctioneers and estate agents. It doesn't include inheritances or unadvertised private sales but suggests that Irish farmland very rarely comes on the open market for purchase. It has been estimated that an average of 32,728 acres of farmland change ownership each year. Between 2010 and 2020, the total number of farms decreased by approximately 4,800 (3.4 per cent). This was largely due to a decline (of about 3,500) in the number of beef farms, as some farmers took advantage of the removal of milk quotas in 2015 to transition and expand their holdings often through renting additional land rather than buying. Dairy cattle numbers in the Republic increased by 331,000 between 2015 and 2022, as farmers reacted rationally to the potential for additional sales of milk. They did so only to subsequently find an environmental tide moving against them.

The impact on our climate – and that of other countries – because of human-induced global warming is scientifically undeniable, although that won't stop some people from trying to engage in denial, often encouraged by those who have the most to lose because of necessary change. We have agreed – as part of the Climate Action Budgets passed by all parties in the Dáil with relatively small dissent – to cut the national emissions of carbon by 51 per cent come 2030, working off a baseline from 2018. The problem for agriculture is that it is responsible for 38 per cent of Ireland's total emissions, largely a factor of the number of cattle and sheep in the country approaching six million, greater than the human population. A combination of sentiment and fear of aggressive lobbying by the agricultural sector meant that the government set the smallest emission reduction target in the Carbon Action Plan 2022. In a KPMG/*Irish Farmers Journal* study in 2021, it was identified that a 21 per cent cut in emissions would cause a €1.1 billion hit to the rural economy and a loss of 10,000 jobs. When the decision was made, a

25 per cent cut in farming emissions by 2030 was set, while other sectors were required to achieve cuts ranging from 35 to 75 per cent.

Having a target is one thing, achieving it another. The Environmental Protection Agency (EPA) suggested farming will achieve only a 4 to 20 per cent reduction because it is also slow to switch to safer (more expensive) fertilisers and to change livestock feed additives, as well as reducing the size of herds. In June 2023, the EPA declared that Ireland was not on target to achieve its mandated reductions of emissions by 2030 as part of our EU climate change commitments. Even if every climate action measure committed to is acted upon fully, Ireland will still fall short of emissions reduction targets and achieve only 29 per cent. If the new actions promised are not taken – and if we continue doing only what has been implemented to date – then the fall will be just 11 per cent.

Methane, which comes from cows, is a deadly offender, which is why the idea of significantly reducing the number of cattle has been mooted, despite being desperately unfair to farmers who, when milk quotas were lifted in 2015, invested in increasing their herds and all the facilities needed to support that. The department of agriculture did calculations based on getting rid of 200,000 cattle between 2023 and 2025 by paying farmers not to restock. Not surprisingly, the document setting out the plan to do that was not published officially; when it emerged, it was condemned immediately and loudly. The pushback by dairy and beef farmers is understandable. They may be asked to give up their entire way of work and life, even if compensated for what would effectively be redundancy and even if they could use the land for other purposes. All agricultural policy in Ireland is now designed to remove land from productive livestock-based agriculture. Economists such as Lorcan Roche Kelly at the *Irish Farmers Journal* believe that 2022 may have seen the peak of Irish farm output as environmental demands dominate.

Yet given the way things are going in many other countries, with agricultural land being rendered unusable or less viable by the effects of global warming, and with the global demand for livestock-based proteins increasing as populations increase, the world might actually need more production of Irish food to make up for shortfalls from elsewhere. If Ireland produces less food it is likely to be done elsewhere instead, and with less regard to environmentally responsible measures, which might be somewhat self-defeating. But the process is underway and appears unlikely to be reversed.

It has been estimated also that about 100,000 hectares of land could be lost to intensive agriculture practices over the next decade, and half of that entirely to traditional agricultural practices. This is because Ireland has an estimated 330,000 hectares of drained, farmed peatland. The rewetting proposals could see 30 per cent of that restored by 2030, with half of that amount rewet. At the time of publication, the European Parliament had failed to agree on a new EU Nature Restoration Law that would have made such developments compulsory.

What cannot be ignored either is that the Dáil on an all-party basis – not just the Green Party as some of its detractors seem to think – declared climate and biodiversity emergencies in 2019, explicitly linking them. Ireland was the second country in the world to officially declare a national biodiversity emergency. Which is fine, but only if you do something about it. Both the climate and biodiversity situations can be mitigated by increased afforestation and better water-table management, including the rewetting of land, especially peatland.

We will also have to follow and enforce EU biodiversity-related laws and directives, all following the 1992 Habitats Directive that empowered governments to set aside land in order to conserve valuable fauna (wildlife) or flora (organic matter like flowers) as well as habitats that sustain them (such as turloughs). We have special areas of conservation (SACs) – 439 of them – but their supporters claim they are ignored often or that get-out clauses allow developers to ride roughshod over them.

The Citizens' Assembly on Biodiversity – a group of 100 concerned citizens who met over six weekends to learn, discuss and decide their position on the topic – produced a report that noted Ireland has a poor reputation for implementation of EU nature legislation and 'even habitats and species afforded the strictest protection under the directive are deteriorating; 85 per cent of the protected habitats are still in unfavourable conservation status.'

Its chair, UCD academic Aoibhinn Ní Shúilleabháin, has been a powerful advocate from outside the political system: 'Our bogs store more carbon than the Amazon rainforest ... twice, nearly three times as much. They are probably the most valuable asset in the EU, but over 70 per cent are in bad status ... we are really not looking after them at all. We need to look after our bogs like we look after the Book of Kells.' In interviews after the publication of the report, Ní Shúilleabháin said the evidence is that Irish hedgerows are disappearing, water quality is worsening and we're losing species at an accelerating rate: 'The State has comprehensively failed to adequately fund, implement, and enforce existing national legislation, national policies, EU biodiversity-related laws and directives. This must change.'

But is the will there? The State and its citizens, those born in this country and those who have chosen to make a life here, face a myriad of compelling and competing claims for the use of our land. The State, by law, must take regard of climate action. It, seemingly by popular demand, must support the habitat and biodiversity.

It also has to act upon the needs of those who seek affordable housing, support those who provide the jobs that bring about the tax revenues and be fair to those who enjoy property rights under the Constitution and to those who don't. And it must be aware of the power of money, its purchase and its purpose in an era where, if it ever didn't, capital reigns, no matter its initial source.

In reality, we are all tenants of this country, as we are of this planet, all passing through between birth and death, with ownership merely a temporary concept or conceit. But surely we should be minded to leave Ireland in a better place than we found it, to give back as much as we take for those who follow after us?

POSTSCRIPT

The bursting of the residential property bubble brought about the 2008 crash that took the banks with it. In mid-2023 – at a time of high consumer inflation and with interest rates at a decade high – the Central Bank of Ireland seems most worried about the potential impact of a fall in the value of commercial real estate on the Irish economy. Could history repeat itself, but this time the destruction being caused by a different part of the property market?

There is a simultaneous combination of oversupply of office and retail space and falling demand for it. While the Irish economy enjoys full employment and enormous corporation tax revenues, expansion has slowed sharply. Many companies are either more cautious about investing in further growth or have retrenched, especially in the tech sector which was responsible largely for the boom of the previous decade. Add in the impact of hybrid working and employers don't want or need as much office or retail space.

Commercial properties in Ireland – and in Dublin in particular – are overvalued. Even though they fell by nearly 10 per cent in the first quarter of 2023 they have the potential to fall further. In 2022–3 office vacancies rose more rapidly in Dublin than in almost any other major European location but, initially, at least, prices didn't fall accordingly. The European average first-quarter fall of commercial real estate values was 13 per cent, and in the US it was 14 per cent.

2022 was the most active year for Dublin office completions since the crash, with more than 200,000 square metres of new space delivered. A similar amount is anticipated for 2023. However, office and retail vacancy rates remain above pre-pandemic levels at 10.9 per cent and 8.2 per cent respectively, even before new supply becomes available. The overall figures don't tell the full story because while some companies are prepared to use the new accommodation, on suitable terms for which they can now bargain, lower quality office units in need of restoration looked redundant.

The CBI, in a risk assessment, worried about 'further downward pressure on both capital and rental values' that would 'give rise to losses for financial institutions and investors'. Pity about them perhaps, especially given the profits they have made over the last decade, but these things tend to have all sorts of adverse consequences as we've learnt previously. Few things happen in isolation.

The problem is also being caused by the rise in interest rates mandated by the European Central Bank as a means to deal with consumer price inflation. Higher interest rates mean that low-risk government bonds are paying 3 per cent per annum and investors require a higher rate of return from riskier commercial property investments; they want comfort against the possibility of tenants not paying the rent and the capital value of the acquired properties falling. The CBI is concerned because more than €50 billion is now invested in commercial property in Ireland. Foreign investors are reckoned to own about two-thirds of this. The CBI fears that their valuations of Irish assets will be marked down according to international trends. It fears that a sudden stop or reversal in foreign investor demand will increase the probability of further declines in Irish commercial real estate prices: a domino effect.

But at least the domestic exposure to falling property values is more limited than a generation previously; the purchase of Irish commercial property by international funds, rather than by Irish investors funded by the Irish banks, now becomes a form of protection. In 2008, over one-third of all Irish bank loans were to commercial property investors and that played its part in the crash. Now the proportion has fallen to under 10 per cent. Even better, it is less concentrated in riskier developments; the Irish banks have become more careful about what they back and have demanded higher equity input. It reduces the possibility of another domestic banking crisis. The CBI is confident that 'the knock-on effects for the banking system and wider economy appear at this stage to be relatively contained'. Admittedly, the CBI's confidence in the stability of Irish banking before the 2008 crash was wildly misplaced but this time the financial foundations look significantly more solid.

The CBI is concerned that banks or funds will simply stop financing future developments. It already sees how investments by the funds in the controversial residential build-to-let market are slowing – and how this will have adverse consequences unless the State moves to replace them, in as much as it can afford to do so. And if commercial property is potentially the main economic issue, then residential property is central to political debate.

In mid-2023, estate agents Hooke & MacDonald highlighted how the slowdown in private rental sector (PRS) investment was being offset by State purchases in the social and affordable sector. The PRS spend in 2022 was estimated at €1.154 billion in 16 main transactions, 91 per cent of which were new builds. It said about 25 domestic and international investors had established PRS portfolios in the wider Dublin market through direct investment. But now these oft-criticised institutions are slower to buy, their calculations of risk being influenced both by the interest rate movements and concerns about the ability of tenants to pay higher rents. Housing completions went up sharply in 2022 but fell in 2023 because developers were reluctant to build without guaranteed buyers in place. Increases in the cost of finance, as well as construction and building materials, along with shortages of skilled labour, have all left the volume of new housing supply well below what's needed, although there are hopes that the skills issue will be partly addressed by a transfer across from commercial building.

In normal economic circumstances, it might have been the case that residential property prices would fall too, especially with mortgage interest rates up significantly. As house prices and rents are now above pre-crash levels, questions arise naturally as to whether housing is overvalued again. But demographics and undersupply of new stock suggest a protection against a fall. In the US, the authorities dealt with the lack of affordable supply by subsidising higher-density apartment developments in urban areas. It was one of the measures investigated by the Housing Commission that met in private from late 2022 onwards – a combination of civil servants, trade unionists and developers – as well as the possibility of the State passing on VAT entitlements and other levies if the constructed units would be sold or rented on a social and affordable basis. However, it is a hard one to sell politically and publicly, the idea of guaranteed profits, at the expense of the State, to developers, no matter how much need it is designed to solve.

The politics of housing in 2023 is that it must become more affordable and available to those who need it, that it has become expensive after residential prices have risen by 130 per cent since 2013. But there are many people with a vested interest in keeping the prices of existing housing from falling, especially the nearly 680,000 households that exist without a mortgage, where the owners take comfort from the wealth provided to them by the value of their houses. There are another 530,000 households where mortgages exist but where the owners presumably look forward to the day when the loan is cleared and they'll own the asset without debt. Those who live in the 183,000 households currently provided by local authorities or approved housing bodies presumably don't care too much as long as they can afford their existing rent. That leaves the 330,000 who rent from a private landlord either wanting cheaper rents or the opportunity to buy at cheaper prices than exist. They are a minority and policies don't tend to be changed dramatically to suit minorities, especially when there is so much money involved. The hope perhaps for the disenfranchised is that those in more comfortable positions will be interested for the sake of their children, that they want them to have the same opportunities as have been afforded to them. But then again that cohort has often objected to any new developments in their areas if they perceive that they will reduce the existing value of their established properties.

It is also a case of what the State can afford. The spending possibilities from an expected €65 billion budget surplus from 2023 to 2025 are enormous, but so are the demands. They range from tax cuts to welfare and public sector pay increases on the current spending side and major infrastructural projects on the capital side, even before the housing construction budgets are set. Pragmatism demands that the State cannot do it all, that domestic savings will be risked only in small measure and that foreign money will be required even if that gives the new capital rights over what we might see as our land and our assets. Practicality also requires that we continue to facilitate foreign investment in every way possible to give us the jobs and tax revenues we need. In making those compromises, the danger is that Ireland becomes even more compromised, that the reality of limited control over our own identity, the reality of being tenants in our own land hits us even harder.

ACKNOWLEDGEMENTS

There are many people who were patient with me and forgiving of me over the two years I spent researching and writing this book and I would like to thank them greatly for that. There's my family: my children Andie, Aimee, Millie, Zach and Harry, and of course, their mother and my wife Aileen, who put up with me locking myself away and didn't complain about my absences. Or maybe they weren't too bothered!

There was also my production team at *The Last Word* on Today FM, Diarmuid Doyle, Liz O'Neill, Orla Carney and Aoibhín Meghen, to whom I'm indebted on a daily basis. Thank you also to my *Irish Daily Mail* editor Conor O'Donnell and *Business Post* editor Danny McConnell (and his predecessor Richie Oakley) for their patience and help in waiting for copy over the last couple of years as I laboured with this book.

As for the content of the book, there are countless people who gave interviews, both on and off the record, and sometimes for my *Magnified* podcast, who helped me flesh out the detail that I had gathered. To them I owe deep and sincere thanks. I'm not thanking other sources publicly, as not all of them are quoted, lest those who helped off-the-record are identifiable by a process of elimination.

Special thanks are reserved for my editor Rachel Pierce, who, for the fourth time we have worked together, continued to have wonderful ideas as to how to structure and sharpen the text, as well as a forensic eye for detail and accuracy. It was an absolute pleasure to work with her, as always. I must also thank my agent Niamh Tyndall of NKM and everyone at Gill with whom I have interacted on this book.